Medieval Material Culture

This publication was made possible by the Ruud van Beek foundation with a contribution from the Foundation Nederlands Museum voor Anthropologie en Praehistorie

Medieval Material Culture

Studies in honour of Jan Thijssen

Editor
Hemmy Clevis

Foundation for the Promotion of Archaeology

Colofon

© 2009 SPA Editors, Zwolle
I.C.W. Foundation for the Promotion of Archaeology

ISBN/EAN	978-90-8932-016-2
Editor	Hemmy Clevis
Production	Hemmy Clevis
Translation	Xandra Bardet, Susan Mellor, Sam Pasiencier
Photo Jan Thijssen	Rob Mols (Bureau for Archaeology and Monuments of the city of Nijmegen
Design	Hidde Heikamp
Druk	Upmeyer, Zwolle

All rights reserved. No part of this publication may be reproduced, stored in a retrieval system, or transmitted in any form or by any means electronic, mechanical. photocopying, recording or otherwise, without the prior permission of the Publisher.

The Goals of the Foundation for Promoting Archaeology (SPA) are to promote archaeology and archaeological research in its broadest sense.

www.spa-uitgevers.nl

Contents

Jan Thijssen. Vierlingsbeek revisited Peter Deurloo	9
16th-century sheaths for *kortjan* sailor's knives and *snellebek* marlinespikes Olaf Goubitz	13
Notes from medieval Brielle. A 15th-century leather case with inscribed waxed tablets from a cesspit near the Maarland harbour Arnold Carmiggelt	29
Toying with miniatures. Finds of 'doll's-house items' from Alkmaar Peter Bitter	47
Late medieval bling-bling. A collection of decorated leather and metalbase mounts in the National Museum of Antiquities in Leiden Annemarieke Willemsen	67
Early medieval glass linen smoothers from the *emporium* of Deventer (the Netherlands). A comparative study of the context and use of glass linen smoothers in Deventer, the Low Countries and northwestern Europe (AD 700-1200). Michiel Bartels	95
A peek into the kitchen cupboard. The grange of the Kranenburg in the 20th century Michael Klomp	115
Gothic book clasps and book furnishings from excavations in Eindhoven and their contexts Nico Arts	121
Potter or retailer? Sixteenth-century ceramic rejects from Zwolle, the Netherlands Hemmy Clevis	131
Oosterhout pottery II: industrial waste from the Leijsenhoek Piet Kleij	147
Fields, farmsteads and sherds. The spatial phasing of the medieval cultivation of the Looërenk near Zutphen Michel Groothedde	163
Columns in houses. Domestic architecture and the stone trade in late-medieval Flanders Marie-Christine Laleman	179

Frankforter Potten. De import, de namaak en de invloed op het Nederlandse assortiment 1760-1940 193
Adri van der Meulen en Paul Smeele

List of Authors 225

Jan Thijssen

Vierlingsbeek revisited

Peter Deurloo

Jan Thijssen has been peering at the ground for all of his life. "I am always finding things", he says, and produces a plastic carnival token from the pocket of his denim jacket. "I've been finding money ever since I was a kid. And old earrings; I've got a whole cigar box full of those. It's just a matter of looking." "I'll recognise a person I meet for the rest of my life. I never forget a face." A photographic memory is a useful asset for an archaeologist. Collecting, identifying, classifying – things that Jan Thijssen has been doing from an early age. Even now, he occasionally returns to the village where it all started, Vierlingsbeek. "One day, a classmate dropped by. His dad had found some pots on the Vliegenberg. Out we went, into the autumn storm and lashing rain. There were a mortar and a drinking cup of Gallo-Belgic ware. I was free to take them home there and then." These were Thijssen's first archaeological finds; and he was hooked for life. "I took these objects to Nijmegen, to Museum G.M. Kam. There I was met by Mr Van Buchem, then the curator. He told me that these objects were Roman and came from a 2nd-century grave. And he showed me round the collection compiled by Mr Kam, the founder of the museum, to look for comparable finds. Soon I was obsessed."

Geology, natural history, archaeology; classifying, determining, systematising: Thijssen's passion. "From the manual by Piet Stuart, '*Gewoon aardewerk uit de Nijmeegse castra*', I taught myself to identify Roman potsherds." At the same time, he was the youngest correspondent with the then ROB (Rijksdienst voor het Oudheidkundig Onderzoek, State Service for Archaeological Investigation). In 1964 he embarked on a degree course in biology, which he continued up to the batchelor level, in 1973, with geology as a secondary subject; meanwhile he was given the opportunity to work on the excavation of the *castellum* and *vicus* at Cuijk. This entailed his first encounter with Nijmegen professor Jules Bogaers and the Late Roman Period. "During this excavation I developed a huge fascination with that period."

This was the start of a university career lasting almost 25 years – right up to december of 1988 – as a perennial undergraduate. He read archaeology at the Albert Egges van Giffen Instituut voor Prae- en Protohistorie at the University of Amsterdam, stringing together a series of research assistantships. In four consecutive years (1968-1971) he spent several months as a site assistant at Mucking (Essex, England).

It is a long time, 24 years of being a part-time student. "There were no jobs going in archaeology. And all I wanted was to be the municipal archaeologist in Nijmegen. I considered myself to be the best suited for that post. In late 1987, while moving house from the Lower Town to the Hatertseweg, I wrote my master's thesis for the University of Amsterdam in three months. It was on the animal bones excavated at Nijmegen's *castra* and at the *castellum* at Woerden." This finally allowed him in 1989 to be employed as a graduated archaeologist in his beloved Nijmegen. Why Nijmegen? Among other things because of the city's Roman origins, and the *fossa* at the Lindenberg that he and Bogaers discovered in 1969.

4From June 15th, 1989, Jan Thijssen called the shots in the archaeology of Nijmegen. He was the city's first municipal archaeologist. What started as a one-man office grew into the country's largest municipal archaeological agency, Bureau Archeologie, employing sixty people, with Thijssen at the centre like a spider in its web.

On 1 July 2006, Thijssen took formal leave of the local authority of Nijmegen. In the preceding seventeen years (and a bit), Thijssen and his team excavated every building site with any archaeological potential. In some cases, old ROB sites were re-excavated. "In the old days, the ROB was the only agency to carry out excavations; later it was joined by Nijmegen university. In hindsight, the quality of these early excavations proved less than satisfactory. They had too little knowledge in the field. Sites were given up too lightly, while others, not under threat, did get excavated. Parts of the Hunerberg, the site of nursing home Margriet, the Kelfkensbos, the Kops Plateau, these could have been done better."

From 1989 on, excavation followed upon excavation. The

Roman city *Ulpia Noviomagus*; the Rivierstraat site, the temples on the Maasplein, the bathhouse at the Honig site near the Waalbandijk, the Weurtseweg with its houses, and graves on the Sperwerstraat and the Kraayenhoflaan. On the Hunerberg, excavations uncovered the successive Roman army camps, while at the Kruisweg and the Hengstdalseweg Roman cemeteries were brought to light. On the Mariënburg in the city centre, large parts of the Late Roman cemetery and medieval buildings; the medieval monasteries on the Hessenberg; the Roman ditches in the Kelfkensbos, excavated for the construction of Museum Het Valkhof. The Josephhof, the oldest town centre called *Oppidum Batavorum*, excavated in the jubilee year 2005, when Nijmegen celebrated the 2000th anniversary of its foundation. And not to forget, from 1995 on, the excavations in the Waalsprong, ranging from prehistoric to Roman sites, a hugely rich area.

"Together with my team at the Bureau, I put Nijmegen on the archaeological map. I expressly say 'with my team', as it was very much a team effort. "I have given hundreds of lectures, including one at the *Limes* Conference in Amman in 2000. There I promoted the city in the presence of Jordanian royalty."

Thijssen feels that he operated in the brief heyday of Dutch archaeology. In his seventeen years as a municipal archaeologist, archaeology enjoyed a growing interest from the press and the public. The quality of the excavations was high, and for the first twelve years in particular, archaeology received a great deal of support from local politicians. But precisely since the long-awaited implementation of the Malta Treaty in Dutch legislation in 2007, archaeology appears to be out of favour and paradoxically, the quality of research nationwide has been declining, Thijssen argues. These are national trends that are experienced in all cities. "Content is being pushed out while management and regulation are gaining ground, a trend not limited to archaeology. This means that we're losing sight of what archaeology actually is about: understanding the past." It leads to measures being adopted in Dutch archaeology that on the surface appear to be commendable but in fact are mere window-dressing. Archaeology in the Netherlands is going through hard times."

"I'm currently working on a book about the finds recovered from cesspits in the Lower Town by Stichting Stadsarcheologie Nijmegen. And I'm describing the finds that I collected as a boy in Vierlingsbeek. In the next few years I intend to reexamine and publish my flint collection. I'm working on several articles about Nijmegen and a book about Cuijk."

"*Ulpia Noviomagus* was a very important place in Roman-Period *Germania inferior*. In the hierarchy it was surpassed only by Cologne and Xanten. To us in the Netherlands, it is a rich findspot. But if in terms of material culture you compare it with Germany, France or Britain, the sites there may well be two or three times larger and richer. Nonetheless, Nijmegen is full of interest. With its successive army camps and complex urban evolution, it is quite unique. At our Bureau – and the team is full of top-quality people – we invested a tremendous amount of energy in studying those. This isn't tinkering in the margins; in fact we can easily stand comparison with foreign institutes. As Nijmegen's Bureau, we operate in the top echelons of Dutch archaeology.

The foundation Stichting Stadsarcheologie Nijmegen was initiated as a bit of a laugh. I had challenged Bogaers to undertake excavations in the Lower Town, but in vain. So with a few people we got together and decided to monitor the demolition and construction sites in the Lower Town. Whenever anything was happening, we'd call each other. Soon the foundation ceased to be a joke. We came to realise that this was our last chance to document the many stone-built medieval houses still present in the ground. Up to a hundred of them!"

How was Nijmegen structured? It brings Thijssen to the connecting theme running through his theory: the continuity of habitation from Roman-Period Nijmegen to medieval Nijmegen. Even now, many researchers respond to this proposition with skepticism. "Yet I'm not asserting that Nijmegen always remained a city, just that it continued to be inhabited and always retained a special attraction and status. At any rate there was a church from a very early date and contact was maintained with Rome. It was not for nothing that Charlemagne came to Nijmegen. He found the Late Roman *castellum* on the Valkhof still standing. The palatine system made use of the remnants and built onto them. Charlemagne came from a family who originally were major Roman landowners in the Rhine-Meuse region. They were shrewd managers, and would not have established a palace at any old location." To Thijssen's mind, such continuity of habitation is a fact.

A more extensive version of this interview can be found in Roman Material Culture. Studies in honour of Jan Thijssen. The Netherlands, Zwolle 2009.

16th-century sheaths for *kortjan* sailor's knives and *snellebek* marlinespikes

Olaf Goubitz

"I've got kids by ten wives
Me knife for some lives
Aye we sailors be scum
Yoho an' a bottle o' rum"

A fragment of an old shantey as remembered by Will Marsh, an acquaintance of the author's. An ex-mariner, born in Blackpool, seasoned at sea, brine in his veins.
The sound of waves, the flapping of canvas sails. The wind singing in the rigging, the rise and fall of the deck, the smell of tar and tan. The salty spray from the bows as the ship rides the waves. The anxious eye on the lookout for the treacherous shallows of Breeveertien, or the cliffs of Hellesund. The first seagulls heralding the approach of the yearned-for solid ground, which one will yet want to leave so soon again. Cogs, clippers, sailing barges, cutters... seafaring in the days of sail - this is the heaving backdrop to the sailor's knife (in Dutch known as *kortjan*) and the awl or marlinespike (*snellebek*) and their protective sheaths.
Most of the 16th-century sheaths discussed below, made of wood, and carved or decorated with pewter inlays, relate to life aboard the old-time sailing ships.
In 1989 a North Sea fisherman found in his net "a fish-like pipe with scratchings". It was through the good offices of ROB colleague A. van Duyn from the fishing village of Katwijk that the object came to the restoration department of the ROB. It turned out to be a wooden knife sheath with a carved inscription and with pewter binding around the throat (fig. 1).
It transpired that at an earlier date, in 1971, a similarly shaped wooden knife sheath, also with metal bindings but lacking an inscription, had turned up in an excavation by what was then the archaeological department of the state agency developing the newly reclaimed IJsselmeerpolders (now NISA: Netherlands Institute for Marine and Underwater Archaeology, at Lelystad); it was found inside the wreck of a 16th-century fishing vessel in the polder of Oostelijk Flevoland, once the Zuiderzee sea floor (fig. 2).
In 1991, Mr J.A.Th. Oosterhof found a wooden knife sheath washed up on the southern harbour pier of IJmuiden. It was of a type that differed from the two mentioned above, with a separate compartment for an awl (fig. 3).
A fourth wooden knife sheath, bound with pewter inlays, most of which had gone, was washed up on the beach of Terschelling in 2005 (fig. 4).
NISA preserves four wooden knife sheaths, recovered from a shipwreck in the Scheurrak channel in the Wadden Sea by divers from their department of Underwater Archaeology (figs 5-8). Two of these have an extra compartment for an awl (figs 5 and 7). Two of the four are bound with brass fittings and one has iron bindings. Figure 9 schematically shows the shapes of a 16th-century working knife, and three types of awl or marlinespike: a metal one with a grip, a wooden, bone, horn or antler awl made in one piece, and a metal spike made from a large nail. The other knife shown is a 16th- or 17th-century table knife, for which sheaths like those shown in figs 17, 18 and 19 were used.
Excavations in Amsterdam between 1974 and 2005 produced eight knife sheaths. Five of these have (or had) pewter bindings made up of horizontal strips with vertical connections (figs 10-14). The sixth has spiral bindings (fig. 15). Number seven is decorated with carved biblical scenes (fig. 16), just like two sheaths from the open-air museum at Arnhem, to be discussed below. The eighth sheath (not illustrated), one with pewter decorations, is still being examined by the archaeological department of Bureau Monumenten en Archeologie (BMA) in Amsterdam. These eight sheaths were found in or close to contemporary inner harbours and canals.
From a cesspit in Zwolle comes an elaborately decorated sheath which has a pewter lip with cord tunnels, a chape in the shape of an animal's (wolf's?) head and a centrally placed man's head that simultaneously faces left, right and forward (fig. 20). The binding around the mouth was cast in one piece with the lip, which afterwards was decorated in zigzag fashion with a narrow, chisel-like burin. The lip with its cord tunnels appears to have been bent backwards.
Checking out various Dutch museums with maritime depart-

ments or smaller collections of artefacts relating to marine fishing or seafaring has so far failed to produce any further specimens.

The Nederlands Openluchtmuseum at Arnhem has several dozen wooden knife sheaths. However, all are in the tradition of figures 17, 18 and 19. Almost without exception, they are carved with biblical scenes and edifying inscriptions down both sides, some also with a silver band around the mouth. The period in which these were made is the second half of the 16th century. Many of these sheaths come from the Wiegersma collection, a set of over 600 objects of an ethnographic nature acquired by the museum. Unfortunately the provenance of the sheaths is unknown, although most are thought to be from the provinces of Noord-Brabant and Limburg. Given their delicate ornamentation, it is unlikely that they were in everyday use by sailors. These sheaths most closely resemble a sheath, dated 1589, which was found at Lesja in the Gudbrands valley in Norway, and a sheath of unknown provenance dated 1550, also from Norway. These two originated in the Low Countries (figs 21a & b), whereas a sheath with biblical motifs from the Setes valley is Norwegian (Schia 1965). Another wooden knife sheath was found in the harbour quarter of Bergen in Norway (fig. 22a), two in the harbour of Oslo (fig. 22b&c), and one in Hamburg (fig. 22d; Grieg 1933). Beside the river Thames too, a 16th-century sheath was found (fig. 22e; Museum of London, A 6350).

The Dutch knife sheaths found in Norway may have ended up there through Hanseatic contacts, or were brought along by Dutchmen who for example worked in the local iron mines. Yet it seems more likely that Norwegian sailors signed up on Dutch ships and brought home Dutch knife sheaths, which is also what Erik Schia suggests (1969).

Edward de Groot (1989) when discussing the Dutch sailing ships in the 19th century says: "The crews of the large ships in

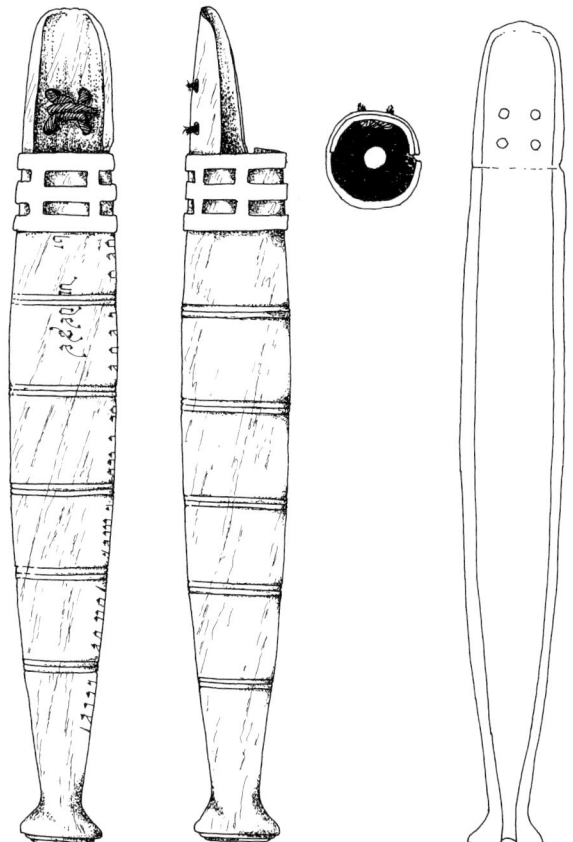

01

Knife sheath recovered from the North Sea in a fishing net, 1989 (through Mr A. van Duyn). Sheath without its knife. Lime wood. Length 22 cm. Lathe-turned, with a lip in one piece with the sheath. 16th century. Pewter binding around the mouth, consisting of horizontal and vertical strips. On the left-hand side of the mouth is a groove left by the knife's cutting edge. Four holes in the lip, with remnants of a suspension cord. Five evenly spaced sets of three encircling grooves, and an inscription incised at right angles to them:
al woude ee(n) mens nae sijn eigen / (w)ens lange leve(n) also hem de doot / daer uut stoot wat heeft hi dan / bedreve(n) ee(n) jaer met sonder dies / di deze (...) / b(...). [Even if a person would live as for as long as he desired, when death pushes him out, then what has he done a year without this, that this (...)]
Transcription kindly provided by Mr G. Boink.

Private collection.

those days consisted mainly of foreigners; crews were made up of Norwegians, Swedes, Prussians and sailors from the Baltic states. There were barely any Dutch sailors". Maybe things were not very different in the 16th and 17th centuries.

All these sheaths are called knife sheaths. The question is whether this is always correct. Published descriptions never mention the shape of the inner space of a sheath: thin and broad to accommodate a blade, or round and pointed, shaped like an awl. Knives have handles, as do many awls, so the top half of their sheaths will reserve spaces shaped accordingly (fig. 5, top view). We shall here consider only knife sheaths, with or without a separate compartment for an awl (fig. 23).

For an awl's spike, a round borehole right to the bottom and out through the tip of the sheath will suffice. Or a few borings close together to admit an awl with a curved point. To make a space for a blade, a close row of thin borings are required, with

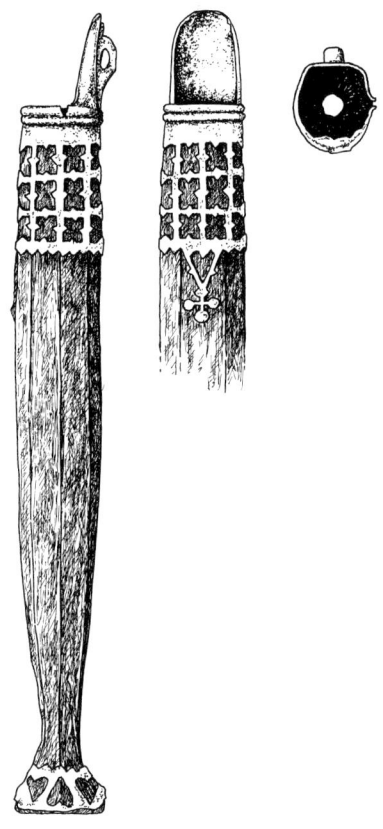

02
Knife sheath from the wreck of a fishing vessel, excavated in lot W 10, Oostelijk Flevoland, by the then Archaeological Department of the Dienst voor de IJsselmeerpolders at Ketelhaven (now Nederlands Instituut voor Scheeps- en Onderwaterarcheologie NISA at Lelystad), 1971.
Lathe-turned, octagonally faceted, oakwood. Length 21 cm. Second half of the 16th century. Ornamental pewter binding around the throat with a design of indented squares, and around the bottom end with heart-shaped motifs. Eye for a suspension cord cast in one piece with the lip. On the left-hand side of the mouth is a groove left by the knife's cutting edge.

Collection of NISA.

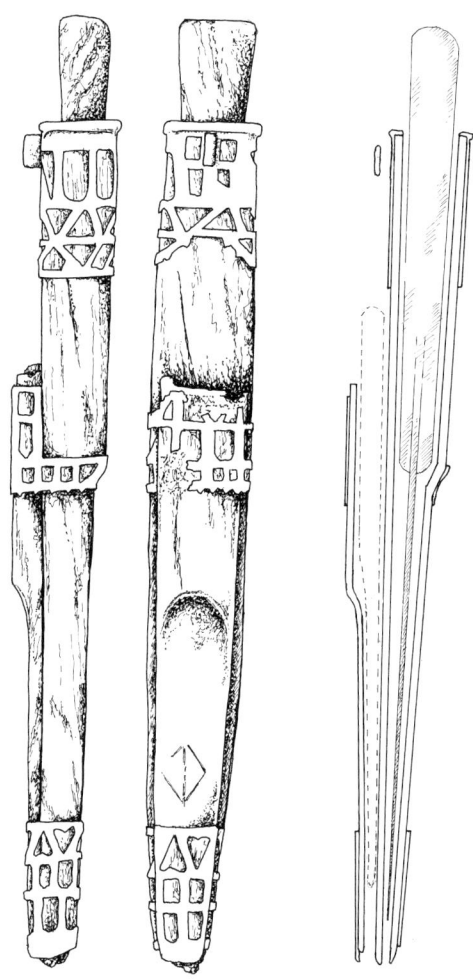

03
Knife sheath, washed up on the southern harbour pier of IJmuiden, 1991 (through Mr J.A.Th. Oosterhof). Knife sheath with an awl compartment. Knife handle still present; the blade and the iron awl have corroded away. The awl compartment was added on separately. Three zones of ornamental pewter binding, with oblong, triangular and heart-shaped motifs. Two suspension-cord tunnels on the upper zone of metal binding. A mark was scratched into the bottom half of the awl compartment. Oak wood. Length 22 cm. 16th century.

Private collection.

the middle one passing through the tip. The resulting ridges between the borings must afterwards be chiselled away so the blade will fit in.

All investigated sheaths have a hole through the bottom of the tip, to allow any rainwater or spray to drain away. The briny seawater especially is a good reason for using a wooden sheath. However well greased, the swelling and shrinking of leather through moisture makes a leather sheath for a knife or awl undependable and therefore dangerous when one is at work in the rigging. A slipping knife or awl may prove fatal to a man in the rigging or on the deck beneath. Which is not to say that every sailor carried a knife, or indeed a knife in a wooden sheath. Some leather sheaths will have been worn aboard ship, made of thick, beaten cowhide which after stitching was force-dried into a rigid cylinder. The *kortjan* knife and the *snellebek* awl or marlinespike both were indispensable tools for chores

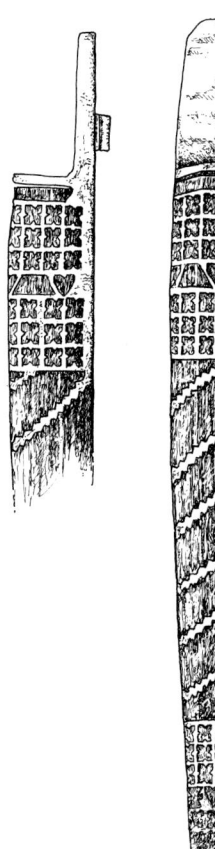

04 Knife sheath, washed up on the beach of the island of Terschelling, 2005.
Pewter ornamental binding around the throat, onto which is joined a pewter lip which has twin tunnels for a suspension cord. The pewter binding continues down the body of the sheath in spiral fashion. At the bottom, more horizontal binding. The horizontal bindings have indented squares and heart shapes. Much of the pewter binding now lost. Slightly faceted. Length 25 cm. 16th century.

Collection of Museum 't Behouden Huys, Terschelling.

05 Knife sheath, recovered by NISA divers from a shipwreck (Scheurrak Oost 1) in the Wadden Sea, 1996. Knife sheath with an awl compartment. Wooden lip in one piece with the sheath. Faceted. Bound with four encircling, inlaid, moulded brass strips. Three brass studs on the middle section. A (leather?) covering had surrounded the throat and the middle zone. The tip had been covered with a (metal?) chape. The once covered areas are depressed. The lip holds a brass eye for the suspension thong with a remnant of the latter. On the left-hand side is a groove left by the knife's cutting edge. Length 22 cm. Final quarter of the 16th century.

Collection of NISA, Lelystad, no. SO 1/14762.

on ships. The knife as a cutting tool, the awl to punch holes through canvas when sails needed reinforcing with rope sewn into their hemmed edges. The awl, like the smaller marlinespike, was also used for lifting and braiding the strands in the splicing of rope and cables. Even in World War 2, the marines' pocket knives besides two cutting blades still had an awl. But apart from these practical uses, the knife served other purposes as well, as hinted at by the words in the quoted shanty. A Dutch dictionary in 1941 describes the *kortjan* as "a sailor's knife, specifically when used as a weapon (formerly usually carried in a leather sheath); synonym: *krakeelijzer* [brawling iron]". Which is a vague description, since it fails to clarify what is meant by "formerly" and what the current situation might be. The term *brawling iron* is self-explanatory.

Among the sheaths used by sailors there are two principal types, each with their variants: the sheath for just a knife, and the sheath to hold both a knife and an awl. Variable elements are the presence or absence of a lip, the suspension method,

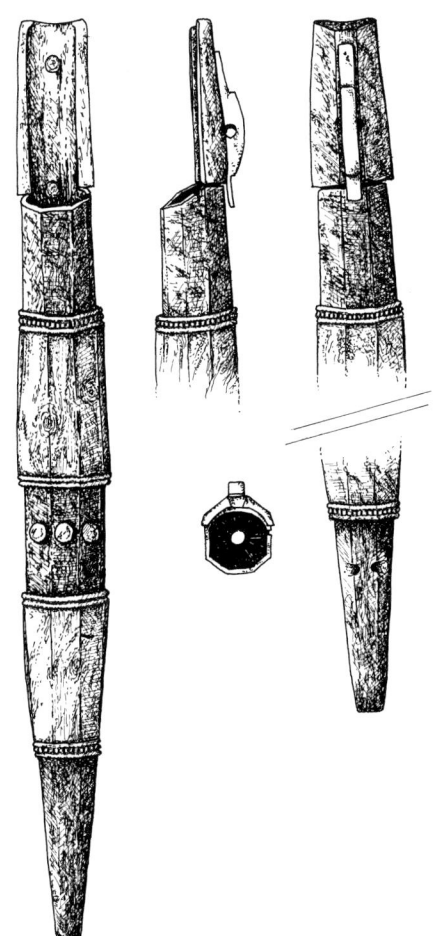

06
Knife sheath, recovered by NISA divers from a shipwreck (Scheurrak Oost 1) in the Wadden Sea, 1996. Octagonally faceted. Wooden lip in one piece with the sheath. Inlaid with four encircling, moulded strips of brass. Three brass studs on the central zone. A (leather?) covering had been present around the throat and the central zone. The tip had been covered with a (metal?) chape. The formerly covered zones are recessed. On the back of the lip is a brass eye for a suspension cord. On the left-hand side is a groove left by the knife's cutting edge. Pinewood. Length 24 cm. Final quarter of the 16th century.

Collection of NISA, Lelystad, no. SO 1/7473.

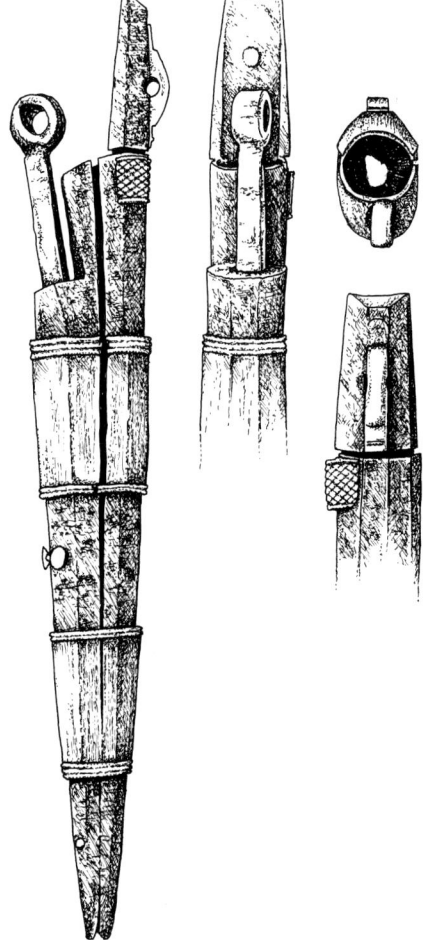

07
Knife sheath, recovered by NISA divers from a shipwreck (Scheurrak Oost 1) in the Wadden Sea, 1996. Knife sheath with an awl compartment. Octagonally faceted. An iron marlinespike (a long nail with an eye) corroded to the sheath. Wooden lip in one piece with the sheath, with an iron eye for a suspension cord on the back. Bound with four inlaid, encircling, moulded iron strips. Three iron studs on the central zone. A covering had been present around the throat and the central zone, probably leather (a remnant survives beside the suspension-cord eye). The tip had been covered with a (metal?) chape. The formerly covered zones are depressed. On the left-hand side is a groove left by the knife's cutting edge. Boxwood(?). Length 25 cm. Final quarter of the 16th century.

Collection of NISA, Lelystad, no. SO 1/8501.

the material used for ornamentation, and the method and style of ornamentation. Yet the similarities far outweigh the differences, which is why these sheaths are a quite distinct group. The most extreme variant is the sheath with a separately constructed compartment for the awl, joined to it with the metal bindings (fig. 3).
Of the twenty Dutch sheaths discussed here, eleven have a lip. The purpose of the lip, which projects above the mouth, is to guide the point of the knife safely into the opening. On ten sheaths it is clear that the cutting edge of the knife has scratched a groove into the metal rim around the mouth (fig. 2). This groove in all investigated sheaths is on the same side: the left-hand side when the sheath is viewed from above with the best side turned outwards. When the sheath is worn on the right-hand side of the body, the groove points forward, and if worn on the left it points backwards. This means that when a right-handed person draws the knife from the sheath, it will lie in the hand with the cutting edge up. Which is the opposite from how we usually handle a knife, that is with the cutting edge down. But a flick of the hand will turn the knife over. This is facilitated by the smooth grip with its rounded shape and no projecting quillons or pommel. When one places the knife

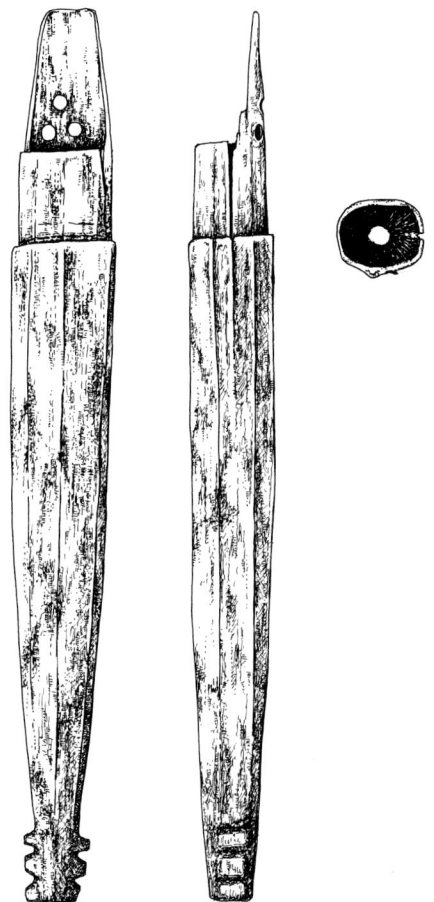

08 Knife sheath, recovered by a diver from a shipwreck (Scheurrak Oost 1) in the Wadden Sea, 1996. Wooden lip in one piece with the sheath. Three holes in the lip for a suspension cord or thong. Faceted. The throat had been covered (with a metal binding?). The tip has carved, serrated wings.
On the left-hand side is a groove left by the knife's cutting edge. Beechwood. Length 23.5 cm. Final quarter of the 16th century.

Collection of NISA, no. SO1/14763.

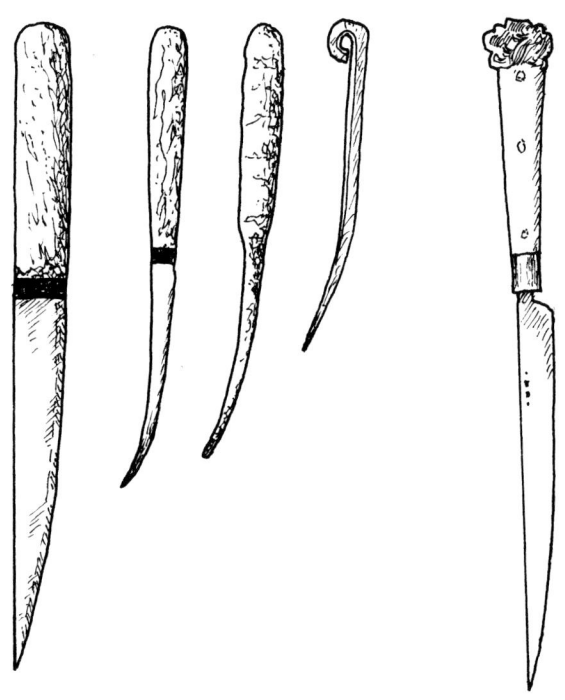

00 Schematic representations of knives and awls. Knife with a wooden grip; metal awl with a grip; awl entirely of wood, bone or antler; iron awl (marlinespike); 17th-century table knife, as carried in sheaths like those in figs. 16, 17 and 18.

into the sheath with the cutting edge to the left, the back of the blade will touch the right-hand side of the opening, often guided by a lip, or, as the case may be, unguided; thus one may feel that the knife is indeed entering the sheath. While at work, one cannot always see the sheath, so one must be able to do this by touch. This seems the most likely explanation of the groove cut into the left of the opening.

A few exceptions apart, all sheaths mentioned here have a rim of pewter or some other material around the opening and often around the throat. Apart from looking smart and sometimes providing an attachment for a lip and suspension device, the bindings serve to reinforce the thin wood against splitting and to protect the rim from the sharp knife.

It is only the sheaths from the wreck in lot W10 in Flevoland (fig. 2) and from Terschelling (fig. 4), Amsterdam (fig. 10) and Zwolle (fig. 20) that do not have a wooden lip but one of pewter, cast in one piece with the rim. These lips have holes, or metal eyes or tunnels attached to the back to hold suspension cords. The eyes on the lips of some sheaths are attached with metal rivets. The sheath in figure 5 still bears remains of a thong. Thus the sheath was suspended from the belt by a short or long thong or cord, as preferred, just like the leather sheath

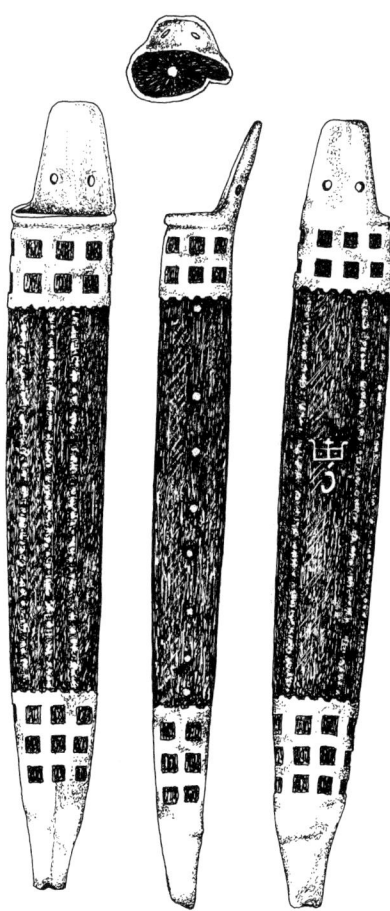

10 Knife sheath from Amsterdam, Rusland 17 (ditch fill), 1989. Top and bottom zones of pewter binding with cut-out squares. Down the front and back are illegible inscriptions and an owner's or maker's mark in pewter. Lip cast in one piece with the binding, with two holes for a suspension cord. The oval mouth is distorted. On the left-hand side is a groove left by the knife's cutting edge. Length 21 cm. Between 1525 and 1575.

Archaeological department, municipal Bureau Monumenten en Archeologie (BMA), Amsterdam, no. RUS-269.

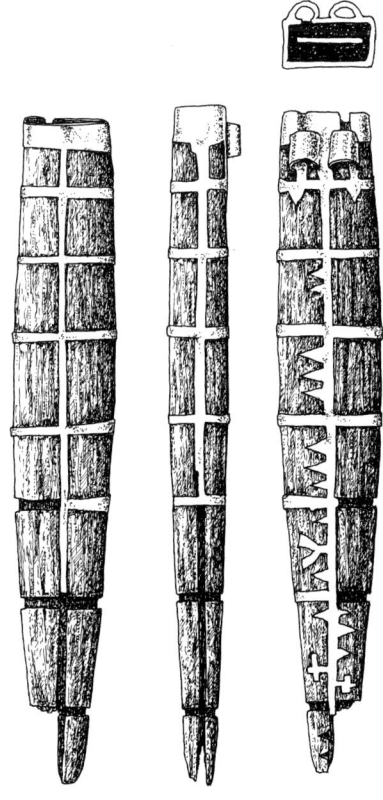

11 Knife sheath from Amsterdam, Prins Hendrikkade (Metro Oostlijn), 1977.
Pewter binding of horizontal and vertical strips. Two tunnels for a suspension cord. A strip of fancy decoration down the back. Rectangular mouth and section. Length 17.6 cm. Juniper wood. 16th century.

Archaeological department, municipal Bureau Monumenten en

for any blade weapon from the Early Middle Ages up to the present day. The sheaths in figures 1, 8, 16 and 21b simply have holes in the wooden lip, by way of suspension device. The sheath in figure 1 still has remains of a cord there. The sheaths in figures 3, 4, 11, 12 and 20 do not have a suspension eye but twin tunnels of pewter to hold a cord or thong. Of six of the sheaths discussed here (figs. 13, 14, 15, 17, 18 and 19) it is unclear how they were carried; maybe tucked into the waistband or belt.

Images of sailors, a category of people often despised, are rare and provide little evidence of how these men carried knives or awls in sheaths. The occasional print or painting may show an object dangling from a belt, which might be a sheath with a knife, and the same goes for the occasional sailor in an old photo who has something that might be a knife protruding from his waistband and held in place with his belt.

At this point, knitting sheaths decorated with intricate carving should be mentioned, because of their somewhat similar

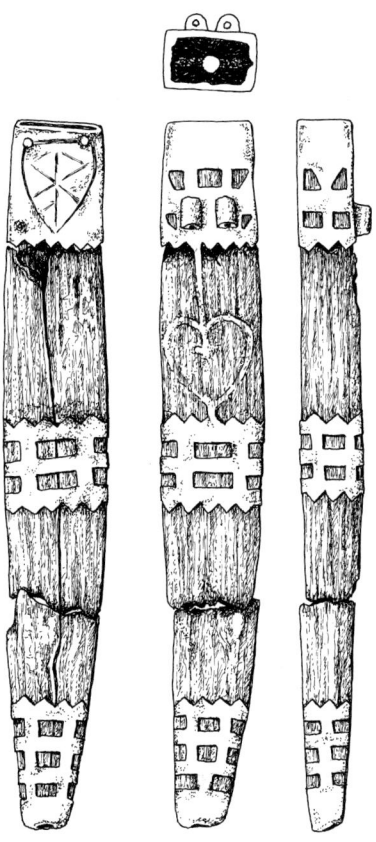

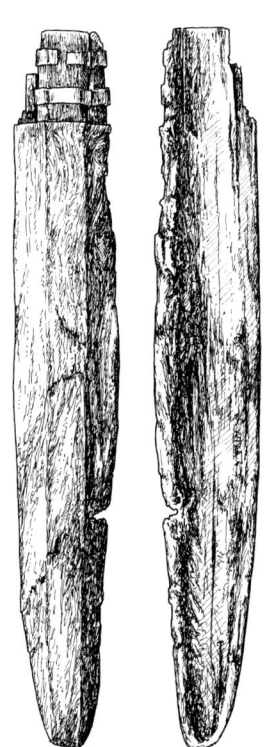

12 Knife sheath from Amsterdam, Nieuwe Amstelstraat 15-23 (Metro-Oostlijn), 1974. Three zones of pewter binding with a hearth shape connecting the upper two on the back. A coat of arms scratched into the front of the throat binding, with two nails to hold the binding in place. Two pewter tunnels for a suspension cord. Rectangular mouth and section. On the left-hand side is a groove left by the knife's cutting edge. The wood is broken in two places. Length 19 cm. Spindle-tree wood. 16th century.

Archaeological department, municipal Bureau Monumenten en Archeologie (BMA), Amsterdam, no. MH3-2.

13 Knife sheath from Amsterdam, Prins Hendrikkade (Metro-Oostlijn), 1977.
Pewter binding around the bottom end, of horizontal strips with vertical connections. The throat is damaged and its binding is missing. Three sets of horizontal grooves between the metal-bound zones. Lathe-turned, round in section. Length 18.2 cm. Boxwood. Second half of the 16th century.

Archaeological department, municipal Bureau Monumenten en Archeologie (BMA), Amsterdam, no. ML4-21.

14 Knife sheath from Amsterdam, Waterlooplein, 1981. One half of a knife sheath. The sheath had been decorated only around the throat with an ornamental binding of presumably pewter. Octagonally faceted. Length 19 cm. Boxwood. Between 1592 and 1597.

Archaeological department, municipal Bureau Monumenten en Archeologie (BMA), Amsterdam, no. WLO-155-77.

appearance. By some stretch of the imagination, one may consider the backdrop of undulating heathland as a parallel to the heaving sea. The shepherds while herding their flocks knitted their own clothes, and if they needed to free their hands for instance to fling a clod at a straying sheep with the scoop on their crook, they would stick their knitting into the knitting sheath that they carried tucked into their waistband. The Nederlands Openluchtmuseum at Arnhem owns some two hundred of such sheaths. These too are traditionally decorated and may be provided with a feature to keep the sheath in place, held by the girdle (fig. 23). In fact, not only shepherds used knitting sheaths. The find of a 16th-century knitting sheath in the centre of Amsterdam (fig. 24) points also to other users, such as fishermen or stall holders who wished to spend their time productively, knitting while waiting for customers. The decoration of a sheath clearly was an important element, and together with the sheath's material and shape, may have played a role in the wearer's status. Moreover, to a sailor, a fine, decorated sheath will have been a cherished personal possession. Maybe even his most important, valuable and irreplaceable possession on board. This is suggested by the the inscribed initials and dates on several sheaths.

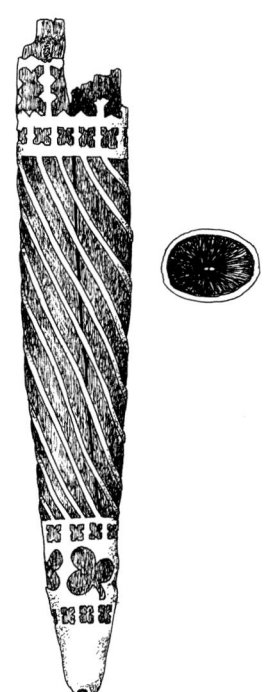

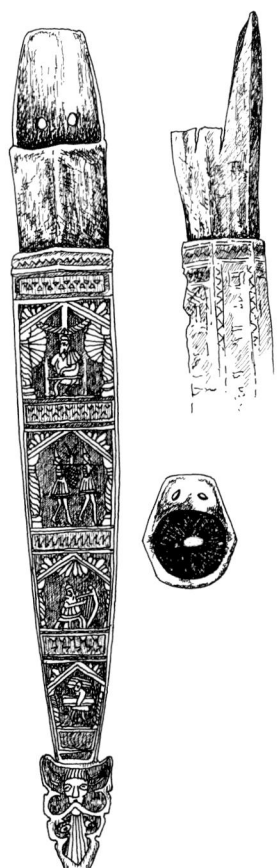

15 Knife sheath from Amsterdam, Prins Hendrikkade (Metro Oostlijn), 1977.
Decorative zones of pewter binding around the throat and the tip, and twelve spirally wound strips connecting them. The bindings have indented-square and leaf motifs. Mouth damaged. Oval section. Length 18 cm. 16th century.

Archaeological department, municipal Bureau Monumenten en Archeologie, Amsterdam, no. MC6-139.

16 Knife sheath from Amsterdam, Waterlooplein, 1985. Sheath decorated with four carved biblical scenes on the front. The throat has lost its covering. Carved, winged chape; wooden lip in one piece with the sheath, with two holes for a suspension cord. Illegible inscriptions on both lateral surfaces.
Rounded front, faceted back. Length 22.4 cm. Dated between 1592 and 1597.

Archaeological department, municipal Bureau Monumenten en Archeologie, Amsterdam, no. WLO-11-1.

Then there are the inscriptions. Apart from its pewter throat binding and the grooves, the inscription is the only ornamentation on the sheath in figure 1, and not necessarily intended as such.

al woude ee(n) mens nae sijn eigen (w)ens lange leve(en) also hem de doot daer uut stoot wat heeft hi dan bedreve(n) ee(n) jaer met sonder dies di deze b(...). [Even if a person would live as for as long as he desired, when death pushes him out, then what has he done, a year without this, that this (...)]

Such inscriptions were probably intended to offer comfort and moral support at stressful moments during battles with the elements. Or in the struggle against seductions which will beset people on long voyages.

Apart from the sheath from Lesja (fig. 21a) with the inscription *Der Menschen tyt verlopt sneluyt gelyck een glas / Vreest Godt altydt doet nyemant spyt doot komt ras 1589* ['Man's time runs out fast like an hourglass / Always fear God, spite no-one, death comes soon.'], there is another sheath from Norway, findspot unknown, which bears the carved words: *Dient god en wilt hem vresen en sprect voor wedwen en wesen* ['Serve God and fear him, and speak up for widows and orphans'] and *Wafr ghi sit u selven kent wat ghi dinckt of doet wacht op (en) spint*. [Wherever you are, know what you think and do, be vigilant and industrious.] Thus Norway has two knife sheaths originating in the Low Countries, decorated with biblical motifs and edifying inscriptions. A familiar line on a sheath in the Nederlands Openluchtmuseum in Arnhem reads: *Dient Godt wyet hem frsen ende spreckt fore wedwen en wesen anno 1552* (fig. 19). The sheath with biblical scenes from Amsterdam also has an inscription, but this has so far proved illegible (fig. 16).

The prominence of the decorations means that these possessions were worn visibly, so they could be shown off. This desire is not unique to seamen. On shore as well, and as long as people have openly been carrying knives and the like, these have been objects of display. Over 70 percent of leather knife sheaths are decorated or worked in some way or another. This applies to all peoples and periods. The knife or sword is a man's most valued possession, even more highly prized than for instance jewellery.

Ten of the twenty Dutch knife sheaths discussed here are decorated with pewter bindings. Four of them share the same decorative element: squares with notches, "indented squares" (figs 2, 4 and 15, as well as no 25, a knitting sheath). Such squares also occur on three sheaths that do not come from the Low Countries (fig. 22). The other pewter-ornamented sheaths display similar bindings with prominent horizontal and diagonal strips. Four sheaths also include heart shapes in the binding, and leaf motifs.

17 Table-knife sheath, presumably from the southern Netherlands. Decorated on the front and back with nine carved biblical scenes. At the top, a protruding jester's head with a vertical hole to hold a suspension cord. The tip has a round, carved knob and above it the inscription WGWH 1588. Boxwood. Length 21.5 cm.

Collection of the Nederlands Openluchtmuseum, Arnhem, no. NOM 27870.

18 Table-knife sheath, presumably from the southern Netherlands. Decorated on the front and back with eight carved biblical scenes and inscriptions referring to Lot and his daughter, Abraham's sacrifice, Batseba bathing, David playing his harp, and Samson. A broad silver band around the mouth. Carved, winged tip. Dated 1552 on one of the sides. Oakwood. Length 21.5 cm.

Collection of the Nederlands Openluchtmuseum, Arnhem, no. NOM 3417.

The frequent occurrence of the indented square as a decorative element is an interesting feature (fig. 2). The pewter on the recovered sheaths has a grey patina, which means that the cut-out shapes are more prominent than their pewter frames. On the Amsterdam knitting sheath no pewter was used (fig. 25), but still the squares are quite distinct. The frequent occurrence of the indented square may be indicative of a particular tradition, or simply reflect a preference for a motif that is easy to cut out with a knife or a sharp-angled gouge. At the Nederlands Openluchtmuseum, this element is found on all sorts of items with chip-carved decoration: household utensils, furniture, chests, racks, doors and wagon parts.

There are two principal forms of decoration: metal bindings and carving. This includes combinations of pewter ornamentation with fine carving or inscriptions.

All the pewter is inlaid. To this end, the outlines of the previously cast or sawn-out pewter inlay would be marked on the sheath and the area excised. The flat-cast or sawn-out pewter was then pressed into the the recessed area, starting from the centre front, and then folded round to fit into the cavity. To facilitate this, pewter with a higher than usual lead content was used. Where the two ends met at the back of the sheath, these would be welded together.

Although the sheaths with biblical carvings like the others have a lip (or indeed a carved jester's head) with holes for a suspension cord, it seems unlikely that these sheaths were worn aboard ships, and almost certainly not by Jack Tar. In Marquardt's catalogue of table cutlery (Marquardt 1997) these exquisitely worked *Köcher*, for a knife or for a knife and a two-pronged fork, are presented as holders for table cutlery,

19 Sheath for table cutlery: knife and fork. Presumably from the southern Netherlands. Decorated with biblical scenes on the front and back and edifying inscriptions on the sides. Carved tip with wings. On the right-hand side of the mouth, the knife's cutting edge has left a groove. Dated ca. 1600. Length 20.5 cm.

Collection of the Nederlands Openluchtmuseum, Arnhem, no. NOM 27088-56.

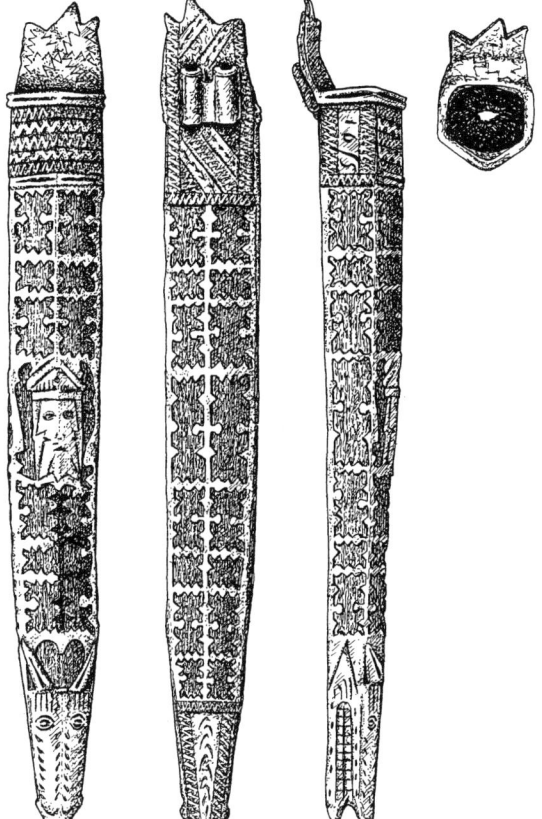

20 Knife sheath from a privy vault, Rode Torenplein, Zwolle, 2005. Inlaid all over with denticulated vertical and horizontal strips of pewter. Pewter binding around the throat marked with the date 1615. Lip with two suspension-cord tunnels, cast in one piece with the throat binding. Pewter chape in the shape of an animal's head. The centre front of the sheath shows a bearded man's face in pewter. Length 18.8 cm. On the left-hand side is a groove left by the knife's cutting edge.

Archeologische Dienst Zwolle. RTP 05-1-1-18

while also the term *Gürtelbesteck* ('girdle cutlery') is used. The catalogue shows 16th- and 17th-century sheaths made in the Low Countries and the Lower Rhine region. This prompts the question of who produced these sheaths. Most of them were too professionally crafted to suggest that they were made by the sailors. This certainly applies to the metal fittings of pewter, brass and iron. These involved casting procedures that are unlikely to have been carried out aboard because they required a forge (an unacceptable fire hazard), as well as specialist skills. In the case of the elaborately carved sheaths, one might consider the possibility that roughouts were bought off the ship's carpenter and that the owners did the fine carving on the easily worked wood. In their designs the men would have incorporated the traditions of ornamental work they knew at home

21a: Sheath for table cutlery, found near a farm at Lesja, Gudbrandsdalen, Norway. Produced in the Low Countries. Decorated on the front and back with eight carved biblical scenes. Carved, winged tip. Possibly owned by a farm worker from the Low Countries. Dated 1589. Dogwood.
On the sides are carved inscriptions, reading: Der Menschen tyt verlopt sneluyt   gelyck een glas / Vreest Godt altydt   doet nyemant spyt   doot komt ras. ['Man's time runs out fast like an hourglass / Always fear God, spite no-one, death comes soon.']

Private collection, Norway.

Lit.: E. Schia, 1969.

21b. Knife sheath from an unrecorded findspot in Norway. Produced in the Low Countries. Knife sheath with an extra compartment for an awl, second knife or fork. Decorated on four sides with numerous carved biblical scenes, some entitled: Paradis, David, Sam(son), Asverusi, Sameveli, Salamon, Susanna, Van Lot, Barse, Abram, Ivdick; and with inscriptions:

Dient god en wilt hem vresen en spreckt voor wedwen en wesen ['Serve God and fear him, and speak up for widows and orphans'], and Wafr ghi sit u selven kent   wat ghi dinckt of doet wacht op (en) spint. ['Wherever you are, know what you think and do, be vigilant and industrious']

Wooden lip in one piece with the sheath, with three holes for a suspension cord or thong. Below the two mouths, the sheath is bound with windings of silver wire. Carved, winged tip. Boxwood. Length ca 21 cm. Dated 1550 on one of the sides.

Historisk Museum Bergen.

Lit.: E. Schia, 1969.

and what they saw in foreign ports. This included ornamental carving and chip-carved decoration on wooden artifacts and ceramics. And the tradition of scrimshaw: the engraving or carving of sperm-whale teeth, ivory, and whalebone objects as the handicraft of a ship's crew while at sea.

In any case, adorning a sheath with inlaid pewter is no less labour-intensive than the carving of biblical scenes, as the author found out in the course of making a replica.

All four of the sheaths from the wreck *Scheurrak-Oost 1* have not only their metal bindings, or, as in fig. 8, a carved tip, but also recessed zones with a rough surface which suggests that these areas once had a covering. The question is: what were they covered with? The tip, also recessed, probably had a chape, a metal fitting to cover the point, as might also be found on many leather knife and dagger sheaths, and certainly on the sheaths of swords and other long blade weapons. In the first place as a practical and protective end for the sheath; but secondly the knob or chape would serve an ornamental pur-

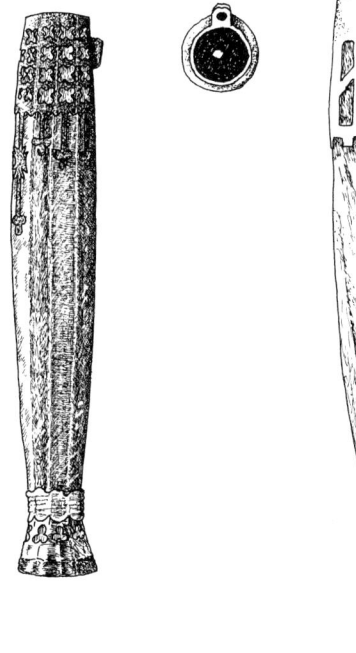
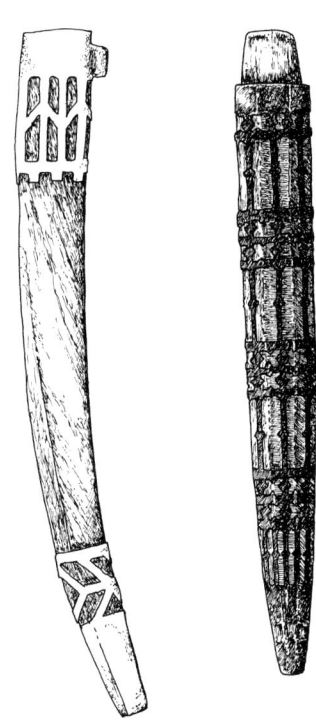

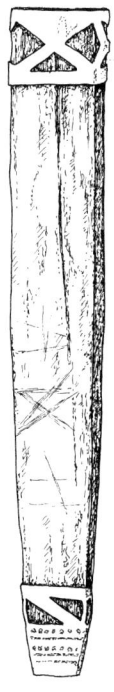

22 Five knife sheaths with ornamental pewter bindings, recovered in:
22a: Bergen, Tyskebruggen, 1909. Faceted. Binding with a pattern of indented squares or quatrefoils, and trefoils. Tunnel for a suspension cord. Length 19.9 cm. 16th century.

Historisk Museum Bergen, no. B.6385f.

22b: Oslo, harbour, 1863. Binding with horizontal, vertical and diagonal strips. Tunnel for a suspension cord. Length 19.7 cm. 16th century.

Lit.: S. Grieg, 1933.

22c: Oslo, harbour, 1863. Faceted. Binding with zones of indented squares connected by balusters. Lip cast in one piece with the binding; tunnel for a suspension cord. Length 17 cm. 16th century.

Lit.: S. Grieg, 1933.

22 22d: Hamburg. Binding with indented squares, heart and acorn motifs. Museum für Hamburgische Geschichte.

Lit.: S. Grieg, 1933.

22e: London, Whitecross Street. Binding of horizontal and diagonal strips. Length 16.3 cm. 16th century.

Museum of London, no. A6350

pose. A hole close to the tip on three sheaths from the wreck *Scheurrak-Oost 1* even more strongly points to the former presence of a chape: here a small rivet of some kind had kept the tapering chape in place.

The recessed zone halfway down and the zone around the throat presumably were covered with some perishable material. A small fragment survives on the sheath in fig. 7, which turned out to be leather impressed with a pattern of crisscross lines. The use of leather as a covering seems contradictory to the earlier remark about its unfavourable shrinking and stretching properties when exposed to moisture. As a surface covering, however, this plays no role. The leather may be sewn on around the sheath with some extra space to allow for shrinkage, and when the leather stretches, it will stay put because it surrounds a recessed zone. Alternatively, the leather may have been glued on, but three centuries of immersion in brackish water will have dissolved the glue and leather alike.

Another possible covering for these zones is a binding of metal wire. This is suggested by the faint horizontal impressions in the wood of the sheaths in figs 5 and 7. Silver wire wound around a sheath is found in the Historisk Museum Bergen (fig. 21b).

The three metal-bound sheaths from the *Scheurrak-Oost 1* wreck probably were all made by the same person, given the similar application of the ornamental metal bands and the three metal studs down the middle of each sheath. Also the

24
Knitting-needle sheath. Shepherd's sheath for holding knitting needles; the knitting would hang outside. Incised decoration, including lettering and the date 1817. A deep constriction halfway down to fit the sheath under a waist belt. Length 18.5 cm.

Collection of the Nederlands Openluchtmuseum, Arnhem, no. NOM 27316

23
Knife sheath with marlinespike from shipwreck Scheurrak Oost 1 (cf. fig. 7), with a remnant of its throat covering of line-impressed leather below the lip.

25
Knitting-needle sheath from Amsterdam, Nieuwe Herengracht 47-49 (Metro Oostlijn), 1975. Sheath for holding knitting and knitting needles. No constriction for a waist belt. Decorated all over with incised 'indented squares'. The (metal?) tip covering at the bottom end is missing. Length 15.8 cm.

Archaeological department, municipal Bureau Monumenten en Archeologie (BMA), Amsterdam, no. MH5-131.

attachment of the suspension eye to the back of the lip by means of rivets, points to a single maker. Still, the binding, studs and suspension eye slightly differ from sheath to sheath. The pewter decoration on the sheath from Zwolle (fig. 20) is unusual because of the three-faced head and the chape with an animal's head.

A curious fact is that, together with this curiously and elaborately decorated sheath from Zwolle, it is the three knife sheaths from the North Sea - the one fished up and those on the shores of IJmuiden and Terschelling - that are the most interesting. The first because of the inscription, the second because of its construction in two parts and the third because of its unusual spiral decoration. It was the fished-up knife sheath (fig. 1) that prompted the author to write the present article. In 1989 this find meant a restoration job with entirely novel conservation aspects. Therefore a number of preventative measures were taken to ensure its survival. The superficial and poorly legible inscription was regarded as the most significant aspect and at the same time the most at risk. Therefore the inscription was first drawn (fig. 1), photographed, and eventually also preserved as a cast: after the sheath had been desalinated through weeks of rinsing, a thin layer of silicon rubber was spread over the lettering. A piece of nylon stocking was pressed onto the rubber while still soft. After setting, the rubber easily let go from the wet wood and the nylon backing allowed the cast to be stretched out flat. This served as a rubber mould, onto which a thin layer of grey plaster was cast. After setting, the plaster was wetted and rubbed with white plaster so that the now positive inscription filled with white matter and again became legible (fig. 26).

Once the inscription was preserved in the form of a drawing, photos, and a plaster cast, the conservation of the wood could be undertaken. This was done by soaking it in polyethylene glycol, followed by freeze-drying and an after-treatment with paraloid.

Instead of a conclusion, here is an enigma

In J.H. Isings' famous Dutch school picture of Willem Barents' crew wintering in 1596 in their makeshift accommodation *Het Behouden Huys* on the island of Novaya Zemlya, the men are carrying wooden knife sheaths decorated with gleaming metal bindings, not unlike the sheaths in figures 10 and 12.

26 Knife sheath recovered from the North Sea (cf. fig. 1). Its nylon-backed, silicon-rubber cast is stretched on a board, next to the plaster cast of the inscription.

27 Detail of the school picture The wintering on Novaya Zemlya in 1596, by J.H. Isings (1950). © Wolters-Noordhof bv, Groningen/Houten. Romanticised image of Willem Barents' crew confronting a polar bear. They are shown carrying knife sheaths with metal bindings. Such sheaths were never identified among the finds from the site of the makeshift winter quarters known as Het Behouden Huys.

We can no longer find out how Isings obtained the various detailed data for his historical scenes, but the picture of the wintering, dating from 1950, not only presents the main theme and the atmosphere, but very realistically, and better than the contemporary illustrators of Gerrit de Veer's eye-witness account of the expedition (de Veer, 1598), shows how people dressed in those days and what kinds of implements and weapons they used (fig. 26). Various expeditions have recovered finds from the remains of *Het Behouden Huys,* starting with that of Carlsen in 1871, right up to 1995 (Arctisch Centrum, Groningen and the Arctic and Antarctic Research Institute, St. Petersburg), which have been exhibited in the Rijksmuseum in Amsterdam. However, no wooden knife sheaths were ever found there (Braat 1998). Considering the effort that it took the author to collect data about these far from numerous artefacts by studying the actual sheaths, the iconography and descriptions, it is quite baffling to imagine how Isings got hold of the evidence about these knife sheaths, and how he managed to depict them so accurately, as well as getting their chronological and socio-economic context just right.

Note: Drawings and photographs by the autor.

The autor wishes to express his gratitude to NISA (Lelystad), the Nederlands Openluchtmuseum (Arnhem), Museum 't Behouden Huys (Terschelling) and Bureau Monumenten en Archeologie (Amsterdam) for their cooperation in allowing him to examine, draw and photograph objects in their care.

References

Braat, J., J.H.G. Gawronski, J.B. Kist, A.E.D.M. van de Put and J.P. Sigmond (eds.), 1998. *Behouden uit het Behouden Huys. Catalogus van de voorwerpen van de Barentsexpeditie (1596), gevonden op Nova Zembla. Rijksmuseum collectie, aangevuld met Russische en Noorse vondsten.* Amsterdam.

Grieg, S., 1933. *Middelalderske Byfund fra Bergen og Oslo.* Det Norske Videnskaps-akademi i Oslo.

Groot, E.P. de, 1989. *De glorietijd van het zeilschip.* Alkmaar.

Marquardt, K., 1997. *Europaïsches Essbesteck aus acht Jahrhunderten.* Stuttgart.

Schia, E., 1969. En hollandsk knivslire fra Lesja. in: *Årbok 1965 – 1966 Universitetets Oldsaksamling.* Oslo.

Veer, G. de, 1598. *Waerachtighe Beschryvinghe van de Seylagien / ter Werelt noyt soo vreemt ghehoort.* Illustrated by C. Claesz and L. Hulsius. Printed by Cornelis Claesz, Amsterdam.

Vries, M. de, L.A. te Winkel *et al.*, 1864-1998 (1941). *Woordenboek der Nederlandsche Taal.* Amsterdam.

Notes from medieval Brielle

A 15th-century leather case with inscribed waxed tablets from a cesspit near the Maarland harbour

A. Carmiggelt

Introduction

Before the construction of a residential building on the Coppelstockstraat in Brielle (also known as Den Briel), the Archaeological Department of the city of Rotterdam (BOOR: Bureau Oudheidkundig Onderzoek Gemeentewerken Rotterdam) carried out an archaeological excavation, commissioned by the municipality of Brielle (Fig. 1).[1] The excavation took place between 6 May and 6 June 2002. The excavated area is located in the inner city of Brielle, between the Langestraat, Coppelstockstraat, Kerkstraat and Maarland-Zuidzijde. During the excavation, a leather case, a stylus and five (mostly inscribed) waxed tablets were found. This special find is the subject of the present paper.

This paper briefly reports on the excavation results, the history of the excavated area, and the contents of the cesspit in which the waxed tablets were found. The use of waxed tablets in the Netherlands will then be discussed, followed by a description of the leather case and the waxed tablets from Brielle. Next, the text that is inscribed on the tablets will be presented. A commentary on and interpretation of the text follows a brief outline of the herring trade in Brielle in the Late Middle Ages, which is necessary for understanding the text on the tablets. Finally, the meaning of the find for the interpretation of the excavation results will be discussed. Happy to contribute to the present publication, I dedicate this paper to Jan Thijssen. He too has studied waxed tablets: a confession book from Nijmegen. The text on the tablets described in this paper is of a more secular character (the herring trade), although it does seem to contain a religious component as well (*godspenning*). Anyhow, the modern distinction between the religious and the secular is an anachronism for the medieval period.

Brielle - Maarlandse Haven: excavation and historical background

The intention of the archaeological excavation was to document only those archaeological features that were likely to be destroyed by the digging of construction trenches for the new building. The excavation was limited to a trench parallel to the Langestraat (Trench 1) and a second one next to the Kerkstraat (Trench 2). A small trench was located next to the Coppelstockstraat (Trench 3), and some observations were made when in a later stage part of the area was excavated to a deeper level (Fig. 2).

The archaeological research has demonstrated that the excavated area was already inhabited in the Roman period. It has also been established that the area was raised in the late 14th or early 15th century. The redevelopment of the area is probably associated with a donation of land by Aelbrecht van Voorne to the city of Brielle in 1394.[2]

The deed of donation mentions a location where the water mill of the Seigniory of Voorne once discharged its water, and that would now be used to construct a spill basin and a sluice. Water would be stored temporarily in the spill basin, and could then be drained through the sluice with some force. In this way the harbour of Maarland could be flushed out to maintain its depth. The spill basin covered the rear part of the Maarland harbour (later also called Verloren-Kost), directly adjacent to the northern edge of the excavated area (Fig. 3).[3] The sluice that was built around 1394 was located in a dam between the new spill basin and the Maarland harbour, presumably close to the present Kerkstraat. The dam formed a connection between the two sides of the Maarland, and is shown on Van Deventer's city map of around 1560 (Fig. 4).

The changes to the Maarland harbour at the end of the 14th century seem to have had an impact on the development of this part of the town. The Kerkstraat (Maarlandse Kerkstraat), first mentioned in 1397, probably came into existence around this time. Habitation on and beside the dike on the northern side (*noordzijde*) of the Maarland, which was part of the Oosterland polder, also seems to have occurred from this time onward.[4]
In the 15th century, two important buildings were located on Maarland-Noordzijde: the Heilige Geesthuis (Hospital of the Holy Ghost) of Maarland, and to the east of this building, more or less across the dam, the Women's Hospital.[5] Some more background information on these two institutions is needed to clarify the excavation results.
The Women's Hospital was founded shortly after 1473, upon the death of foundress Geertruid Arent Beyensze.[6] It consisted of one large house and five smaller houses. Geertruid was the widow of Aernout Beyen, who must have died before 1443. In that year, Geertruid donated 13 beds and accessories to the Heilige Geesthuis, which was located next to her house on the Maarland, and promised this foundation half of 37 *gemet* (a unit of land measuring approximately 0.4 hectares) of land in the De Goote polder after her death. In return, the wardens of the Heilige Geesthuis would be obligated to hold a mass in the Maarland church twice a week in memory of Geertruid and her husband Arent Beyen. In 1467, Geertruid decided that her own house should upon her death become a women's hospital. One of the conditions was that the women living there should supply the inhabitants of the Heilige Geest hospital with beer (*dunnebier*) every morning and food (*potasie* or *potspyse*) every evening. In 1541, the women left their abode on the Maarland and moved into the Beguinage on the Vrouwenhoflaan. This signalled the end of the Women's Hospital on the Maarland. The former Heilige Geesthuis also ceased to exist around this time or even earlier, since there is no record of it in the archives after 1541.[7] The number of fire buckets that the Heilige Geesthuis and the Women's Hospital were obligated to have in 1523 suggests that the two buildings were of similar size.[8]
The archaeological excavation shows that the first (timber) houses on the Kerkstraat were built in the early 15th century (Fig. 5). Whether there were any wooden buildings on the Langestraat, Coppelstockstraat, and the Maarland-Zuidzijde

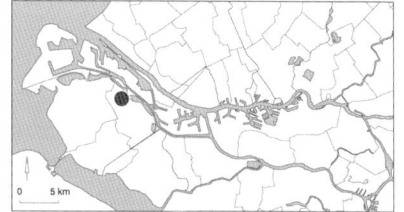

01 Brielle; the location of the research area. Scale 1:7500.

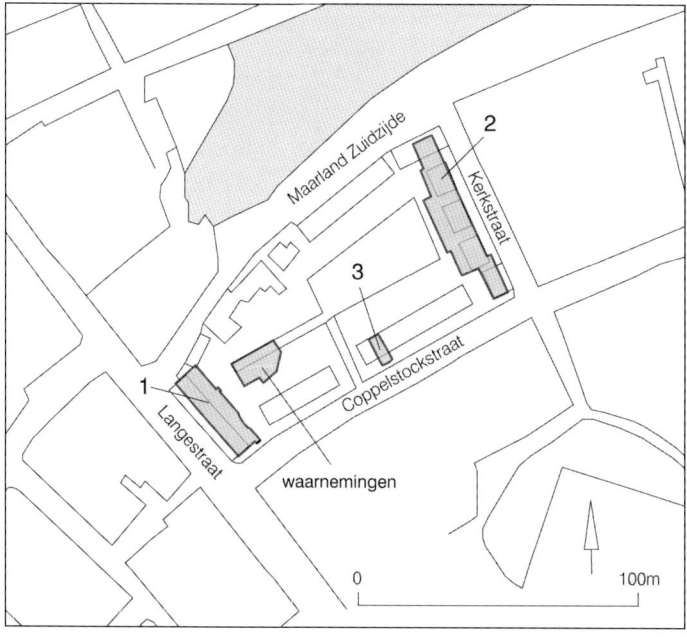

02 The location of the trenches within the research area.

03 Cadastral map of Brielle from 1824 with the location of the buildings and structures mentioned in this paper. 1=St. Catharijnekerk; 2=Maarlandse or St. Pieterkerk; 3=St. Catharina convent; 4=Clarissen convent; 5=Heilige Geesthuis and Women's Hospital; 6=Beguinage; 7=dam in the Maarland; 8=Verloren-Kost; 9=Zuideindse hospital; 10=Noordeindse hospital.

at this time is unknown. 15th-century structural remains and finds turned up both on the Langestraat (Trench 1) and the Coppelstockstraat (Trench 3), but no clear remains of dwellings were identified. This could be due to the small size of the trench on the Coppelstockstraat and the small area of the deeper level of the trench on the Langestraat. The houses on the Kerkstraat, four of which were (partly) excavated, measured 4.5-5 by 11 metres. The wooden walls were set in trenches. The houses had earthen floors and one hearth (or a succession of superimposed hearths) in the front part.
Wells (constructed from one or more barrels placed on top of each other), were found in the back yards of the houses on the Kerkstraat; when they were no longer used as wells, they served as rubbish pits. The finds from the wooden houses and the pits date mainly to the 15th and first half of the 16th century. After that period, the timber houses were replaced by brick-built ones. It is uncertain whether the replacement of wood by brick around the middle of the 16th century was related to the large town fire of 1548, but this seems very likely.

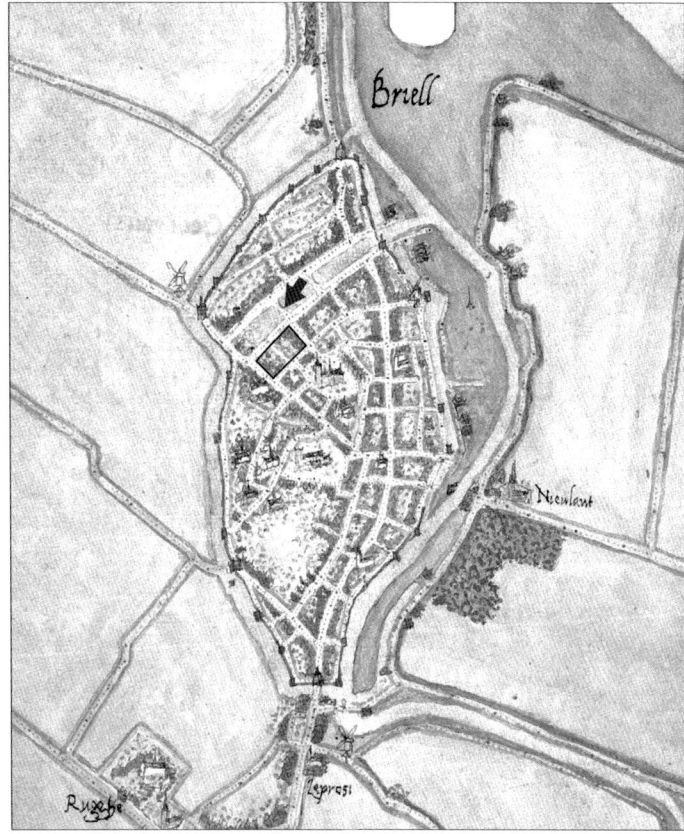

04 Detail of a map by Van Deventer from around 1558 with the location of the excavation site (frame). The arrow indicates the dam in the Maarland.

05 Trench 2 with the location of the cesspit (bp1) and the traces of wooden houses and barrel-lined wells/rubbish pits found on the Kerkstraat.

The earliest mention of houses on the *Maerlantsche Kerkstrate* dates to 3 November 1397.[9] The record in case mentions two houses with yards, situated on the Kerkstraat. We read: *Welke voirseyde huyse(n) ende erve gheleghen syn in die Maerlantsche Kerkstrate binnen dese lantmerken: dat Maerlantsche kerckhof an die zuytzide alrenaest ende meester Jans emonts erve an die noertzide alrenaest.* ("The houses and yards which were mentioned above are located in the Maarlandse Kerkstraat, adjacent to the Maarlandse cemetery on the southern side and Jan Emonts' yards on the northern side.")

A record from 1426 implies that the yards must have been located on the western side of the Kerkstraat.[10] In that year, Peter Bruustensz van Asperen and his wife Marie Willemsdochter donated an annuity to the regular clergy of Rugge. The annuity was to be covered by the house they lived in, which was located *gheleghen bi der Marlantsche Kerckstraet binnen desen lantmerken: die Maerlantsche Kerckstraet aen die ostzide, Arnt Gout aan die zuutzide, Kathelijn meyster Jan Emonts aen die noortzide.* ("near the Maarlandse Kerkstraat, with the Maarlandse Kerkstraat on the eastern side, Arnt Gout on the southern side and *kathelijn-meester* Jan Emonts on the northern side.")

Considering that the yard of Jan Emonts seems to have been on the western side of the Kerkstraat, we can assume that the record from 1397 also concerns yards on the western side of the Kerkstraat. The exact location of the yard of Jan Emonts is unknown. It may have been near the Maarland-Zuidzijde on the western part of the Kerkstraat, but it could also have been situated more to the south. *Kathelijn meester*, the term used to indicate Jan Emonts' position, can be read as 'Katherijn

06 Impression of the excavated brickwork in Trench 2 on the Kerkstraat, seen from the north. The upper part of the cesspit in which the case with the waxed tablets was found is seen in the foreground. In the background, the tower of the St. Catharijnekerk is visible.

meester'. This suggests that he may have been the church warden of the St. Catharijnekerk in Brielle.
In the 15th century, it seems that a brick building occupied the corner of the Kerkstraat and the Maarland-Zuidzijde, despite the other houses on the Kerkstraat being timber ones. Indications for this are a large brick cesspit and 15th-century brick masonry found in this part of the excavated area (Fig. 6). It was in this cesspit that the leather case containing the waxed tablets was found.

The cesspit

The cesspit in which the waxed tablets were found had a diameter of 260 cm. It was constructed from bricks measuring 21x10x4.5 cm. The upper limit of the cesspit was found at 111 cm + NAP (Normal Amsterdam Level); the lower limit was found at 166 cm - NAP. Four find-containing layers could be distinguished within the pit. The layers were numbered from top to bottom as layers 1, 2, 3 and 4. These layers were separated by deposits containing few finds. A layer of brick rubble was found between layers 3 and 4.

A large number of finds were collected from the cesspit, mainly from the bottom layer (layer 4). The case with the waxed tablets was also found in this layer. The finds from layer 4 date to around the middle of the 15th century (Fig. 7). Many finds turned up in the southeastern part of the pit, which suggests that the chute was located on this side or above it. Layer 3 contained few finds. Layers 1 and 2 date to the first (and possibly second) quarter of the 16th century. After the cesspit had been filled in, a barrel-lined well was dug into it. Relatively few finds from the 16th century were found in this feature, and these were possibly mixed with finds from the cesspit itself.
In layer 4, fragments from at least 81 ceramic artefacts were found. Most of the sherds were red ware. Fragments of tripod pipkins (n=34), chamber pots (n=16) and frying pans (n=12) were the most common. Fragments of bowls, a lid, a dripping pan and the knob-shaped foot of a *drinkuit* vessel were also found. A find from Zwolle of a *drinkuit* contained within a wicker basket has led to the assumption that this type of *drinkuit* was not a beaker used for drinking games, but as packaging material for some kind of liquid. Remarkably, many of the finds can be associated with a monastic context.[11]

07 Various ceramic artefacts, a vertebra from a sperm whale and a bronze candlestick from layer 4 of the cesspit on Maarland-Zuidzijde.

Grey-ware fragments of at least two unspecified artefacts were found, as well as at least ten stoneware objects: jugs and jars (n=9) and a drinking cup (n=1).

As far as glass is concerned, layer 4 yielded fragments of only two glass cups of forest glass (*maigeleins*) and several window panes. A toy top, a small lid, and an unidentified object (possibly a handle) were made of wood. A pair of hinged scissors, a lid and a (strongly corroded) pan were made of iron. Also part of a broom made out of twigs tied together was found. Another find was a bronze candlestick. A remarkable find was a vertebra of a sperm whale, with a diameter of circa 28 cm. The vertebra is probably from a whale that lost its way in the North Sea and became stranded.[12] The vertebra may have been suspended or used as a lid, since it was perforated by a nail. Finally, some mineralised fragments of a woven fabric were found in the cesspit, possibly the remains of sanitary towels. Hand-collected zoological remains from layer 4 were identified, as well as several small fish vertebrae from a botanical sample.[13] Remains of sprat or smelt, eel, herring, cod, ling and plaice were found. Two phalanges from cattle, a scapula, ulna and skull fragment from pig and several rib fragments can be seen as kitchen waste. The skull fragment is from a sucking pig; the remaining pig fragments are from subadult animals, probably younger than one year old. The cattle phalanges are from animals older than a year. However, most of the remains in layer 4 are bones from animals that were not consumed. Remains from at least two adult dogs were found, as well as a femur from a cat. The femur had been fractured, and the two parts had overlapped and fused together in this position, the result being that the cat's left leg was at least 1 cm shorter than its right leg.

The analysis of botanical macro remains showed a very limited range of food plants compared to other 15th-century samples from urban contexts in the Netherlands.[14] Oats, wheat, rye, apple, plum, cherry and mulberry were found. With the exception of grapes and figs, which were very common at that time, no exotic imports were identified. Therefore, the people whose excrement filled the cesspit do not seem to have had a high social status. On the other hand, the absence of buckwheat indicates that their status was not very low either. The occurrence of bran of oats in the waste is remarkable. These fragile remains are seldom found, and their presence indicates that the low botanical diversity is not a result of poor preservation. The remains from wild plants in the cesspit are almost all from arable weeds that grew among the wheat. Pollen analysis of the contents of the cesspit has demonstrated the presence of pea or broad bean and chervil, as well as the cereals oats, wheat, rye and barley. The pollen sample also contained eggs of the parasitic whipworm (*Trichuris*) and roundworm (*Ascaris*). These are common finds in medieval excrement and indicate hygienic circumstances which were normal for that period.

The botanical and zoological analysis of the contents of the cesspit, as well as the ceramics and the near absence of glassware indicate the low social status of the people who used the cesspit. Therefore the large, brick cesspit, although clearly contrasting with the wooden barrel-lined pits of the timber houses on the Kerkstraat, did not belong to a rich household. An alternative explanation for the occurrence of such a large cesspit is that it belonged to some kind of institution (a monastery, hospital, inn or the like). However, the records do not mention the existence of such an institution at this spot in Brielle in the 15th century.

Late medieval waxed tablets in the Netherlands

In Classical times, writing on waxed tablets was common. Many finds of styli and waxed tablets are known from the centuries before and around the turn of the Christian era, as well as numerous iconographic images of people writing on waxed tablets. In the Netherlands, several styli and waxed tablets are known from the Roman period.[15] Waxed tablets remained in use during the Middle Ages, at first mostly in monasteries, the ecclesiastical world and the royal courts. Several beautifully decorated ivory tablets have been preserved in museum collections across Europe, but wooden tablets would have been far more common. One Dutch example of the latter from the Carolingian period is an archaeological find from Dokkum. In the Late Middle Ages, the use of written texts increased. The waxed tablets from that period come in various dimensions, as can be seen in surveys by Elisabeth Lalou and Kristina Krüger, of European waxed tablets from archaeological and museum collections.[16] The large and medium-sized tablets have usually been preserved above ground in archives, having been used by ecclesiastical and secular administrations. The smaller tablets, sets of which were often combined into a kind of notebook, are mainly known from archaeological contexts. They were used by pupils and students and by merchants for making business notes. The use of waxed tablets declined during the 15th century, when they were replaced by paper. Locally, waxed tablets remained in use for a longer period. The table lists the various features of the late medieval wooden waxed tablets (forming part of notebooks) that are known to me. It is evident that woodworkers used various kinds of wood for the production of waxed tablets. Chemical analysis of the wax from foreign tablets has revealed that the main ingredient in the wax was beeswax, to which substances such as charcoal, clay, linseed oil or tallow were added. The additions were necessary to colour the wax so that the inscription in the wax contrasted with the background, and to give the wax the right consistency.[17]

The notebooks which were composed of several waxed tablets (*codices*) had a front and back cover, which were covered with wax only on the inside. The inner 'pages' were made from tablets that held wax on both sides. The number of waxed tablets in *codices* varies. The tablets could be held together by a piece of parchment, string or a leather band, but may also be found separately. Notebooks like this were usually kept in a leather case or container.

Location of find	Source	Date	Context	Number/sides	Type of wood	Dimensions (mm)	Text/language	Comments
Brielle		15b/c	cesspit	5/4x2; 1x1	sycamore	98x61x3	business/Dutch	fragment case and stylus present
Delft	De Vries 1894 (postscript, p. 6)	15	probably archaeological find from near Waterpoort	8/ 7x2; 1x1	beech	60x45x2a3	commerce	two holes per tablet for wire connection
Deventer	Clevis and Kottman 1989	14d-15a	cesspit	1/1x?	sycamore	80x50x?	commerce/Dutch	
Dordrecht	Sarfatij 1984	15?	child's grave			200x?x?		
Groningen	Helfrich et. al. 1995, cat. no. 7.2	16A	cesspit near school	9/?x?	box tree	90x55x5	text+sums/Latin	connected by two wires
Groningen	Helfrich et. al. 1995, cat. no. 7.1. Casparie and Schoneveld 1991	15d	cesspit of parsonage of the St. Walburgkerk	4/3x1;1x2	sycamore	90x55x3		
Hoorn	Van der Walle 2002	14A	rubbish pit	5/4x2; 1x1		75x45x1,5		case present. 65x60x17mm
Nijmegen	Thijssen 1996	16?	cesspit orphanage	5/3x2; 2x1		130x80x?	confession book/Dutch	outside covered with leather; connected by string or leather
Ooltgens-plaat	Olivier 1994	13B/14	drowned settlement	1/1x1		61x33x2		
Oud-Diemen	Pers. comm. W. Krook	15b/c	rubbish pit		alder (frangula alnus)			fragments only
Schelde (near Westkapelle)	Grol 1940, p. 61-69	15a	sea chest	6/??		110x70x?	commerce; sums	case with stylus; coin weights, coins and other finds were also found in the chest.
Veere	Goubitz 1996	15b-d	cesspit	6/4x2;2x1	apple/pear	75x50x3		holes for connection present; fragment of leather case found in pit contents
Zwolle	Klomp s.a.	14B-15a	rubbish pit	5/??		75x50x3		leather case present

Characteristics of rectangular wooden waxed tablets found in the Netherlands, that were part of notebooks (apart from the specimen from Dordrecht). An oak waxed tablet from 's-Hertogenbosch from the 14th century is not included in the table. This specimen is considerably larger (16 x 10 cm) than those in the table and provided with a handle; it was not part of a notebook.[18]

The case with a stylus and inscribed waxed tablets from Brielle

Case and stylus

In layer 4 of the cesspit on Maarland-Zuidzijde, five waxed tablets with two decorated leather fragments were found (Fig. 8). The leather fragments were held together by an iron stylus, which was inserted through both parts. The leather fragments, part of the front section of the case and the front and upper sections of its cap, together measure circa 6 x 9 cm and are decorated with two rows of stamped vine decoration. The stylus (length: 9 cm) is inserted through two holes in the leather. In this way, the stylus served to close the case containing the waxed tablets (Fig. 9).

The use of the case can be reconstructed as follows. The case with the waxed tablets from Brielle consisted of two parts: a container (holding the waxed tablets) and a cap that could be slid onto the container. The cap and container would have been connected by a cord (Fig. 9). With the stylus inserted at the front, through both the cap and the container, both parts of the case were secured and the case was held shut.

Unlike waxed tablets and leather cases, metal styli are frequently found in archaeological contexts from the 14th and 15th centuries. The flat end of the stylus can be used to erase the text inscribed in the wax by flattening the wax. Krüger rightly points out that a stylus of this type could be used as an eraser on the smaller tablets, but the larger tablets needed another type of implement.[19] The larger tablets would mostly have been used indoors, while the smaller ones were intended for outdoor use.

A similar, almost complete, case was found in a 15th-century context in Zwolle (Fig. 10:1).[20] The stylus is missing in the case from Zwolle, although the holes in the leather through which the stylus could be inserted, were present. The case from Zwolle also contained five waxed tablets, but no text was visible on these tablets. Yet another fragment of such a case is known from Veere (Fig. 10:2).[21] The fragment was found in a cesspit (dated 1425-1500) that also yielded six waxed tablets. This case also shows openings in the leather through which the stylus could be inserted.

08 Front of a leather case (decorated with vine leaves) and stylus from Brielle. Scale 1:1.

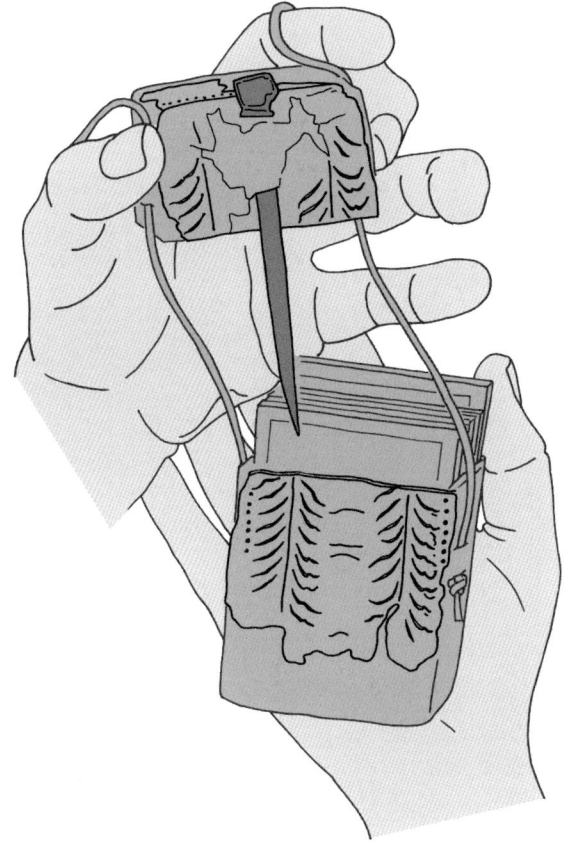

09 Reconstruction of the leather case.

Similar cases or containers of waxed tablets, but with different decorative patterns, are known from several other locations.[22] From Hoorn, five 14th-century waxed tablets are known, as well as part of a case with a stamped design of some kind of hunting dogs in medaillons (Fig. 10:3).[23] From abroad, various cases with sets of waxed tablets (bound together or unbound) are known.[24] However, the degree of similarity between the cases from Brielle, Veere and Zwolle with regard to their decoration and date (second/third quarter of the 15th century) is remarkable. This type of case with waxed tablets possibly stemmed from a particular production centre.

Waxed tablets

For the five waxed tablets from Brielle, only sycamore-type wood (*Acer pseudoplatanus* type) was used (Fig. 11).[25] This is a diffuse, porous type of wood with an extremely regular distribution of the veins. This results in a fine surface texture. Moreover, this type of wood has broad radial rays, which makes it suitable for cleaving. The waxed tablets were all extracted from the log in a radial direction.

The types of wood of waxed tablets have also been identified

A

B

C

D

E

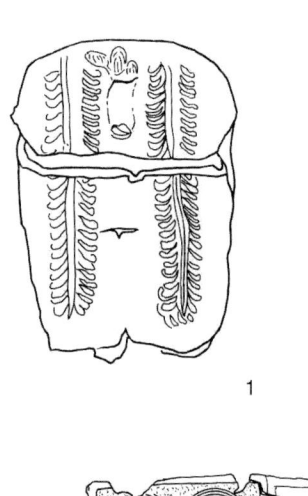

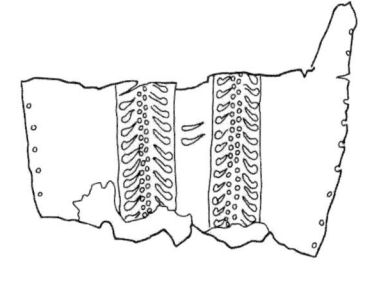

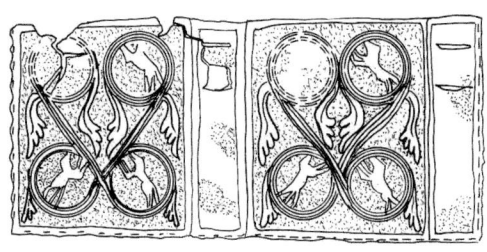

1   2

3

10 (Fragments of) leather cases for waxed tablets from Zwolle (1, after: Klomp s.a.), Veere (2, after: Goubitz 1996) and Hoorn (3, drawing: Archaeological Service Hoorn). Scale 1:2.

11 The front and back of the waxed tablets from Brielle (70 % of true size)

elsewhere in Europe. Sycamore appears to have been widely used, as was beech. Interestingly, beech is also a diffuse porous type of wood, be it with a greater density and a less regular distribution of the veins. Beech contains even broader radial rays than sycamore, so this type of wood is also easy to cleave straight.

What is special about the find from Brielle is that most of the wax on the tablets was preserved. The colour of the wax is black to grey. The black colour is probably a result of adding charcoal to the beeswax, the main ingredient of the wax on the tablets. As far as could be observed, no scratches or scoring had been made on the wood of the tablets from Brielle. Such roughening was sometimes done to make the wax adhere better to the wooden surface.

The waxed tablets from Brielle make up a 'notebook'. Such sets of waxed tablets were usually either connected by a piece of string or leather, or held together by parchment. On some of the Brielle tablets, several notches were observed on the lower edge of the tablets, indicating that these tablets had been tied together originally. How they were connected is impossible to reconstruct. Originally, the notebook from Brielle probably consisted of six tablets, of which four were waxed on both sides, and two (the front and back cover) on one side. One of the outer tablets, covered with wax on just one side, is missing.

The text

Four of the five waxed tablets from Brielle bear some text. The text, although applied to the wax in regular, experienced handwriting, is not easy to read. This is caused by the sometimes slight depth of the lines in the wax, as well as by the structure and relief of the layer of wax.

The waxed tablets will be referred to below by the letters A, B, C, D, and E. The text is written in the longitudinal direction of the tablets. In the transcription below, the lines are numbered. The line numbers are also used in the commentary (Chapter 8). Tablet A is the one that was only waxed on one side.

Waxec tablet a
(front or back cover; one-sided)

(1) dit is den heige gest

(2) cloten 1   toen herinc

(3) jacop arent z 1

(4) peter rosert   1

(5) jan lote 1

(6) mes huge

(7) villem villems z

Waxed tablet b

      ja   p
(1) (...) (..)co(.) (...)er z 1

(2) jan jacopz

(3) (.)n (...)

Waxed tablet c

(1) xiiii tonen herinc iiii soten
(2) (.)en gheven iiii p(.)stelae
         o
(3) (.) xvi gheven om xxxii pont
                              n?
(4) (.)viii ton xviii poent en iiii
            —
(5) .n noch i toe arnt monch
                    —
(6) iiii pe(.)
         —

Waxed tablet d

          pon
(1) (...) ote toe en (...)t
(2) (.........)

Waxed tablet e
(no inscription)

Since the text on the tablets is concerned with herring barrels and trade, a brief description of the 15th-century herring trade in Brielle will precede the commentary on and interpretation of the text.

Herring fishery and herring trade in Brielle[27]

Herring was an important food source in the Middle Ages for the rich and poor alike. On the many fasting days of the Roman Catholic Church, the consumption of meat, dairy products and eggs was prohibited. Partly for this reason, fish formed an important part of the diet. Sprinkled and packed with salt, the herring could be preserved for a relatively long period and was easy to trade.

Commercial herring fishery, which started off mainly as an inshore fishery, seems to have spread in the 12th century from Flanders and Zeeland to the delta of Holland, and from there, further north. During the 13th century, the fishery moved further from the shoreline to meet the herring on its migration through the North Sea. At first, the herring was brought ashore after each catch. For the Hollanders, this could be their own home port or the harbours on the east coasts of England and Scotland. The ships and nets gradually increased in size. The crew sometimes formed a partnership with the owner of the ship (they were called *volgers*, 'followers', or *gezellen*, 'companions') by supplying some of the nets. They would receive part of the catch as their reward.

In the 13th and 14th centuries, several types of herring were distinguished: basket herring (*korfharing*), smoked herring (*bokking*), and gutted herring. *Korfharing* is fresh herring that was placed in baskets after it was caught, and sprinkled with salt. The salt that was used initially was peat salt, produced by burning saline peat. *Bokking* was created by smoking the herring. In gutted herring, the gills and the intestines, prone to decay, were removed with a knife. This type of herring was packed in layers in a barrel, with salt between the layers. The blood of the herring mingled with the salt, creating a brine that preserved the herring from decay.

In the 13th and 14th century, an international trade in gutted herring from the island of Skåne (southern Sweden) existed. The trade in herring from Schonen was strongly regulated by the Danish king and increasingly by the German Hanseatic League. Fishermen worked under the authority of the Hansa merchants and were not allowed to further process or sell the herring. Processing took place ashore, in specially created trading posts (called *vitten*). After Albrecht of Sweden had conquered Schonen in 1368 and subsequently gave the people from Brielle the right to create their own *vitte* on the island, the Hansa attempted to oppose the competition from the herring fishermen from Holland. Several conflicts occurred as a result. Around 1400, significant changes in the herring trade occurred. Because of the monopolising measures of the German Hanseatic League, Hollanders started to expand their own herring fishery in the North Sea. The shoals of herring off the south coast of Sweden declined at this time, while they increased in the North Sea. Herring suitable for packing in brine was not found near the coast of Holland, but it could be found off the English and Scottish coasts. This is why the herring was now gutted on board, instead of ashore. Larger ships were needed now, partly to transport the barrels necessary for storing fish and salt. A new type of ship was developed at this time: the *haringbuis*. Because the owners of fishing boats tried to reach the highest yield possible, the fishing season was started earlier and the boats were forced to travel longer distances to meet the herring on their migration. This was another reason why larger ships were needed. Instead of the native peat salt, sea salt imported from France and the Iberian Peninsula was now used more and more.

The fishing fleet was escorted by armed ships to defend them against piracy or other hostilities. The owners of the ships and the herring traders had to pay for this so-called *buiskonvooiering*: the *lastgeld* (*last* money).[28] The amount was charged per *last* of herring. One *last* consisted of 14 barrels of herring. For each *last* of herring, around 5 barrels of salt were needed. After the herring that had been gutted on board was brought ashore and sold, it was repacked in new barrels with fresh salt. The herring packers (or *leggers*) were supervised by a cooper. The herring was tightly compressed during packing. One *last zeestucx* of 14 barrels was packed into one *last* of 12 land barrels. When the barrel was fully packed and branded, it had become an internationally marketable product.

In the 15th century, Brielle was the largest herring fishing port in the Netherlands and played a key role in the herring trade. It also owned the largest *buizen* fleet of the Netherlands. In 1423, the Count of Holland even declared the Brielle herring barrel to be the standard measure. Numerous English, German (especially from Cologne) and Flemish traders were active on the herring market in Brielle. The herring trade, as well as the supply industries (salt trade and preparation, cooperies, shipbuilding, roperies, etc.) played an important role in the flourishing of Brielle in the 15th century.

The hustle and bustle in Brielle at this time must have been tremendous. The testimonies recorded in the *Informacie* of 1527 say "*dat de stad te nauwe was voor den harinckman ende coopman van buyten*". ("that the city was too small for foreign herring merchants.")

The landlord of the inn Den Engel described how "*over zeeckere jaeren zoeveel gasternije in zijn huijs...van overlanders (Duitsers, AC) ende van andere coopluyden, dat hij soms op eenen dach mijnde (veilde, AC) hondert last harinx voor zijn gasten ende hadde van elcke last een pont Hollants*".[29] ("A few years ago, he had so much custom from Germans and other merchants that he sometimes sold a hundred *last* of herring on one day for his customers, and received 1 *pont Hollands* per *last*.")

From the latter, it appears that the landlords in Brielle also looked after the business interests of their customers, and sold fish for merchants who were not burghers of Brielle.

The town council obviously had a large interest in a flourishing trade in gutted herring. This explains why various regulations on this subject were recorded in the municipal statutes. In this way, an attempt was made to guarantee the quality of herring and to maintain the good relations with foreign merchants. Apart from protecting the merchants and supplying facilities to fishermen to sell their catch, the municipal statutes also intended to generate income for the town itself. For instance, the municipal statute of 1446-1455 mentions a *kercken goidspennynck*. The *godspenning* was a tax on the sale of herring, to benefit the Brielle churches. To understand the text on the waxed tablets it is necessary to go into a little more detail.

Godspenning

In the statute books from Brielle, the herring trade is regulated quite extensively. Stipulations are included on the location and layout of the fish market for various kinds of fish, on the quality and the branding of herring barrels, on the quality of salt, etc.

The municipal statute of 1446-1455 also includes several lines on the *godspenning*.

14. Van dat elc, die vorschen haring off tonharing voir den stoel coept, der kercken goidspennynck mit reden gelde betalen sall. Item dat alle dieghene, die harinck vercopen voir den stoel, off die harinck gehouden wort, hetzy vorscharinc off tonnharingk, die sal rechtevoirt der kercken trede gelt geven, op een boete van III pond Hollans, rechtevoirt off te panden.[30]

("14. Everyone who buys fresh or barrelled herring on the fish market shall pay the church a *godspenning* in cash. This also applies to the sellers. Evasion will be fined with 3 *pond Hollands*.")

Both buyers and sellers of (fresh and barrelled) herring were obligated to hand over a kind of ecclesiastical sales tax to the person charged with collecting the *godspenning*. This tax had to be paid at the location where the fish market (*voir den stoel*) was held.

More information on the *godspenning* can be found in an act by Frank van Borsselen from 1437, in which he grants the town council permission to levy a tax on fish for the benefit of the local churches. The amounts for several different kinds of fish are regulated in the record.

*"(…)om nutscip ende profijten onser kerken onser stede vanden Briell voirs. der selver kerken goidspennigen van corfharing, van cabbeliau, van heylbot, van lever, van smout, van vorsschen harinck ende van tonharinck te verhueren tot haren scoensten (..)".*31
("(…) to lease a similar *godspenning* on *korfharing*, cod, halibut, *lever*, *smout*, fresh herring and barrelled herring, for the benefit of the churches in Den Briel.")

Regarding barrelled herring we read:
"Ende alsomen van elker last tonharinck pleget te geven VI gr., so ist overdragen datmen, om oirbair der kercken voirs. voirtan geven sal acht gr. van elker last tonharinck, hij sij gescoten of ongescoten of vol. Ende wes beneden een last tonharinck is, sal geven vier g."
("For every *last* of herring, six *groten* used to be transferred, now it has been decided to charge eight *groten* for the benefit of the church. For less than a *last* of barrelled herring, four *groten* are to be paid.

From the above, it appears that before 1437 six *groten* (a currency unit) had to be paid as a *godspenning* on every *last* of herring (=14 barrels), and that this amount was now increased to eight *groten*. At Schiedam a similar arrangement was in force, and the amount was increased at the same time. The municipal statute from Schiedam from 1434 reads:

*"Eerst soe sal die kerck ende stede ('ende stede' was later added, AC) van Schiedamme hebben van elck las tonharijnx vols harijnx 8 ('8' substitutes something else, AC) groot, dat elke stierman vercoopt, ende van elc last yels harinx desgelijcks oic ('desgelijcks oic' substitutes a deleted phrase, AC) 8 (the figure was changed from 4 to 8, AC) gr., van den coper rechtevoirt te betalen(..)".*32
("The church of Schiedam and the town ('and the town' is a later addition, AC) shall receive eight (the number was changed from 4 to 8, AC) *groten* from the herring merchant and from the purchaser for every *last* of barrelled herring.

When we return to the act issued by Frank van Borsselen, we read:

Ende dese verhoginge van den tonharinck sal dueren thien jaer achter een na datum 'sbriefs ende dairen t'enden sullen onse gerecht dien goidspenninge vanden voirs. tonharinck mogen verminderen of zij willen twee gr. van elker last ende niet meer, mit voirwarden dat die kercmeesters voirs. deze voirn. goidspenningen bij onsen gerechte alle jaere verpachten sullen ons leven lanc gedurende ende die gelden alle jaere up te bueren ende t'ontfangen om die te beleggen ter kerken behoef an tymmeringe ende anders als des van noode oirbairlijc zijn sal. "
("And the increase on barrelled herring shall last for 10 years. After that period, the amount may be decreased, but by no more than two *groten* per *last*. The church wardens who receive the money and spend it on, amongst other things, the maintenance of the churches, shall lease out their right to collect the *godspenning*.")

The increase of the *godspenning* was valid for ten years. After that period, it could be reduced, but not by more than two *groten*. The church wardens who received the money, and answered to the town authorities, would then lease out their right to collect the *godspenning*.

Text: commentary and interpretation
Commentary
Waxed tablet A, line 1 (A,1: *dit is den heige gest*) can be read as "this is the holy ghost". "The Holy Ghost" refers to a *Heilig Geesthuis*, i.e. a hospital, three of which were in existence in Brielle around the middle of the 15th century: the Zuideindse hospital, the Noordeindse hospital and the previously mentioned hospital on Maarland-Noordzijde. The line can be read as "this is part of, belongs to, or is delivered to the Holy Ghost hospital".

Line A,2 (*cloten 1 toen herinc*) mentions - keeping in mind the following lines - a (sur)name 'Cloten'. Further in the same line are the words 'toen herinc', meaning 'barrel of herring'.
Five names (A,2-5 en B,1) are followed by the number '1'. The names are likely to have referred to (herring) merchants (from Brielle), who apparently handed over a barrel of herring. Two of these names are known from the records: Peter Rosert (A,4) and Mes (i.e. Bartholomeus) Huge (A,6).

These two men were summoned to The Hague on 26 March

1443, together with others from Brielle. There, they heard the verdict in a dispute between themselves and the captain Ailbrecht van Buedinchuysen. The source in case mentions a "*Mathiis Jacob Cupersz. (and his companions) Jacob Boyezoen, Pieter Roesart, Meeus Huge Wittersz., Walraven van den Briele ende Willem Bone van der Goede Reede*". [33]

The men whose names precede the figure 1 probably delivered or paid one barrel of herring to the hospital.

Three more names seem to have been written on waxed tablet B. Only B,2 is legible: Jan Jacopz. The previously mentioned record from 1443 shows that on 26 March of that year, a man called Jan Jacobsz is also summoned to The Hague, together with others, to appear as a witness in a case that again involved the captain Ailbrecht van Buedinchuysen. Jan Jacobs, however, is from Schiedam. It is doubtful whether this person is the same as the man mentioned on the waxed tablet, also because this was a very common name. The name in line B,1 has been only partially preserved.[34]

Most of the text is written on waxed tablet C. Line C,1 (*xiiii tonen herinc iiii soten*) refers to 14 barrels of herring, which is precisely one *last* of herring. It is not clear how we should read "iiii soten". Possibly, four of the 14 barrels of herring were salted. Another explanation is that it is an indication of the quality. For each *last* of herring, five barrels of salt should be used; it is possible that this phrase indicates that only four barrels were used for this *last* of herring.

Lines C,2 ((*(.)en gheven iiii p(.)stelae*) and C,3 (*(.) xvi gheven om xxxii pont*) mention several currencies and quantification units. The meaning is unclear. Line C,2 refers to 4 '*p(o?)stelae*'. This word almost certainly refers to postulate guilders. A postulate guilder is a gold guilder of a low standard, minted by Rudolf van Diepholt, postulate (1423-1432) and later bishop of Utrecht (1432-1455). After this time, the word was used for coins that had roughly the value of half a Rhenish guilder.[35]

At the court of Frank van Borsselen (1436-1470), Lord of Voorne, who was resident at Brielle for most of the year, postulate guilders were in use around the middle of the 15th century. The city pipers of Rotterdam, for instance, received two postulate guilders as a reward for their performance at the Brielle court.[36]

Line C,5 can be read as "*en nog i toe* (or *ton*) *Arnt Monchzoon*". This last name almost certainly refers to Arent Montschoenzoon or Montsszoon (several variants of his name occur). Arent Montschoenszoon was sheriff of Brielle, and appears as such in the so-called *Correctiebouck* of Brielle (1404-1474).[37] He is associated with this position once in 1426, once in 1447, several times in 1450, and once in 1452. Arent Montschoenzoon also appears in a record from 1447, that lists complaints and demands from merchants from Holland, Zeeland and Friesland because of the damage caused by cizitens of Prussia and Livonia.[38] Merchants from Brielle lived in these regions on the Baltic Sea and were actively involved in the herring trade there. The record states that "*Aernt Montschoensoen van de Brielle*" is owed 650 marks by a Peter Joorden from Gdansk.

Why Arent Montschoenzoon is allocated anything, keeping in mind the text on the waxed tablets, is unclear. It is possible that he was involved as the leaseholder of the *godspenning*, and was entitled to receive part of the collected lease.

Line C,6 can possibly be read as "*4 penningen*".

The text on waxed tablet D is difficult to read and cannot be transcribed. No text was written on waxed tablet E.

Interpretation

It is unlikely that we shall ever know exactly how the text on the waxed tablets should be interpreted. The lines are after all personal notes, reminders that could be copied on paper or parchment at a later stage. Furthermore, part of the text is missing or illegible. At least we know that the text refers to the herring trade. (Herring) merchants from Brielle are mentioned, two of whom are referred to in a record from 1443 as companions of Mathijs Jacob Cupers. Apparently, the sheriff Arend Montschoensoen had business interests in the Baltic region, which can be concluded from the record from 1447. The text also refers to the Holy Ghost, which seems to indicate a connection with one of the hospitals of Brielle. As far as we can tell for now, the combination of 'herring trade' and 'holy ghost' seems to indicate that the text relates to the collection or administration of the *godspenning*.

The writer of the text must have been a practised scribe, considering the regularity of his handwriting. Perhaps he was the clerk or leaseholder charged with the administration of the collection of the *godspenning*? Or perhaps this is the handwriting of one of the church wardens of Brielle? Or perhaps it is the memo of a hospital warden? Or ……

Back to the excavation

In the historical introduction to the excavation location at the beginning of this paper, the *Kathelijn meyster* Jan Emonts made an appearance. His name is recorded in 1397 and 1426 as the owner of a property located on the west side of the Kerkstraat, adjacent to another property to the north. This description of the location of the premises of Jan Emonts could refer to the property on the Maarland-Zuidzijde where the cesspit was found, but several other locations also meet this description. When 'Kathelijn meyster' is read as 'Katherijn meyster', then this function could be regarded as the church warden of the St. Catharijnekerk. It is possible that a church warden was involved in some way in the administration of the *godspenning*, and if so, that the waxed tablets were his. However, the contents of the cesspit are dated to the middle of the 15th century, as are the records of the people that could be traced in archives. Considering these dates, it is not very likely that Jan Emonts was the owner.

A second observation is related to the fact that archaeological excavations show that brickwork was present at a relatively early date on Maarland-Zuidzijde, while buildings on the Kerkstraat were still built in wood. A brick cesspit of a striking size was found here (the wooden houses in this area all have small wooden barrel wells, reused as cesspits and rubbish pits). Large brick cesspits from the 15th century are usually associated with either large houses with rich households or specific institutions (monasteries, hospitals, etc.). However, the location within the town and the contents of the cesspit do not indicate a rich household. It is therefore most likely that the cesspit was used by some kind of institution.

It is very well possible that the cesspit belonged to a branch of the nearby hospital, which was located across the dam in the Maarland. In that case, the location on Maarland-Zuidzijde, where the cesspit was found, could have been used by the hospital, for instance as sleeping quarters and/or a refectory. We cannot be sure about this. However, from the earliest annual accounts of the Heilige Geesthuis in Maarland from 1523/24 we can conclude that this institution possessed land in the Kerkstraat at this time. The annual accounts mention an item which is described as '*maken van een kamertje en overal te inspecteren in de Kerkstraat*' ('building a small dwelling and *overal te inspecteren in de Kerkstraat* ').[39] Unfortunately, the precise location of this building, which belonged to the hospital, cannot be reconstructed.

Conclusion

The archaeological excavation between the Langestraat and the Kerkstraat in Brielle uncovered various barrel-lined rubbish pits containing 15th-century finds, which belonged to timber-built houses on the Kerkstraat. In the back yard of a building on the corner of Maarland-Zuidzijde and the Kerkstraat, a large brick cesspit (diameter 260 cm) was found. The cesspit appears to have belonged to the premises of some kind of institution. In the cesspit, a fragment of a leather case with a stylus and five (partially) inscribed waxed tablets were found.

The text on the waxed tablets – relating to the transfer of barrels of herring and to (herring) merchants from Brielle – can be associated with the so-called *godspenning*: a tax levied on the sale of fish, benefiting the churches and hospitals in Brielle. It is suggested that the cesspit belonged to an annexe of the Heilige Geesthuis, which was located across the Maarland. However, this is not certain.

Notes

1. A.J. Guiran (BOOR) was in charge of the archaeological excavation. The excavation was carried out by employees of BOOR under the supervision of C.Y. Burnier (Jacobs en Burnier, Archeologisch Projectbureau). An extensive report on the excavation results can be found in: Carmiggelt and Burnier 2004. This paper on the waxed tablets previously appeared - in a very limited edition - in *BOORrapporten* 206 (Carmiggelt 2004). The illustrations in this article were produced by M.F. Valkhoff (BOOR).
2. Alkemade and Van der Schelling 1729, p. 249. More on the history of the water mill and sluice can be found in: Guiran 1998.
3. On the (mainly later) history of Verloren-Kost: Van Rooijen 1992.
4. See Jacobs, Kempenaar and Van Trierum 2002.
5. Klok 1967 and Gallas 1986, p. 73-74.
6. Opinions differ on the precise foundation date. Klok (1967) mentions 1467 and Gallus (1986) 1473. However, the Women's Hospital would not have been established until after Geertruid's death.
7. Gallas 1986, p. 77.
8. *De middeleeuwse keuren der stad Brielle* (edition H. de Jager) 1901, p. 97.
9. Van der Gouw 1986, p. 195, no. 66.
10. Van der Gouw 1986, p. 237, no. 143.
11. Klomp 2004, p. 22.
12. The identification and additional information were supplied by C. Smeenk (Naturalis, Leiden).
13. Identifications were made by E. Esser (Archeoplan Eco). Several fish vertebrae were identified by F. Laarman (ROB).
14. The botanical analysis was carried out by O. Brinkkemper.
15. Writing tablets from the Roman Period in the Netherlands are known from Valkenburg (Zuid-Holland), Tolsum and Woerden, see: Glasbergen 1967, Boeles 1917 and Vos and Haalebos 2000.
16. Lalou 1992 and Krüger 2002.
17. Büll 1977.

18. De Vrie and Janssen 1997, p. 104 (fig. 34.7) and p. 127.
19. Krüger, p. 63.
20. Klomp s.a.
21. Goubitz 1996.
22. Various leather cases for waxed tablets are described in Goubitz 2007, p. 87-96.
23. Van de Walle 2002, p. 6.
24. See for example Bull 1977, p. 849 and O'Connor and Tweddle 1992. The latter authors describe the find from York of a 14th-century leather container for eight small, probably unbound, waxed tablets. Six of these were covered with wax on both sides. For a survey see also Krüger 2002, 83 ff.
25. Identification of the wood and additional information was provided by O. Brinkkemper.
26. The waxed tablets were transcribed by the author (in collaboration with the people mentioned below) by inspection of the original and by the use of macro-photographs of the tablet - taken with skimming light. The text was also inspected by A. van der Schoor (Municipal Archive Rotterdam), A.A. van der Houwen (Regional Archive Voorne-Putten) and especially by M. Moree (Vlaardingen). The author is grateful to them. The presented transcription is the outcome of the – in detail not always concurrent - results of the various inspections.
27. Several studies have been published on the history of the herring fishery and trade. For a good summary, see: De Hoog 1986 (with extensive references) and also Boelmans Kranenburg 1954 and 1976.
28. On the use of convoys, see Degryse 1974.
29. Quoted by and taken from Haak 1907, p. 48-49.
30. De Jager 1901, p. 154.
31. Transcription by A.A. van Houwen, certificate C98 (1437, 13 June).
32. Heeringa 1904, p. 232.
33. Poelman (ed.) 1917, no. 1646.
34. In theory, the text could even refer to the previously mentioned Mathijs Jacop Cupersz.
35. Van Gelder 1965, p. 267.
36. Lingbeek-Schalekamp 1992, p. 32.
37. Regional archive Voorne-Putten; ORA Brielle, inv. no. 9. *Regesten op het correctiebouck* have been supplied by S.M. Auwerda-Berghout.
38. Poelman (ed.) 1917 no. 1853.
39. Regional archive Voorne-Putten, inv. no. 135. Annual accounts of the Heilige Geest in Maarland 1523/24, fol. 7. With thanks to M. Moree (Vlaardingen) who took a quick look through the accounts.

References

Alkemade, K. van, and P. van der Schelling 1729: *Beschrijving van de stad Brielle en den Lande van Voorne*. Rotterdam.

Boelmans Kranenburg, H.A.H. 1954: Het afslagwezen voor de visserij in het Beneden-Maasgebied 1400-1600, *Zuid-Hollandse Studiën* 4, 72-92.

Boelmans Kranenburg, H.A.H. 1976: Visserij van de Noordnederlanders, *Maritieme geschiedenis der Nederlanden* 1, Bussum, 285-294.

Auwerda-Berghout, S.M. 2003: *Regesten op het Correctiebouck der stede van Den Brielle 1404-1474 (R.A. Brielle inv. Nr. 9)*. Brielle.

Boeles, P.C.J.A. 1917: Eene Romeinsche koopacte uit de terp te Tolsum, *Bulletin van de Nederlandsche Oudheidkundige Bond* 10, 275-278.

Brown, P. 1994: The role of the wax tablet in medieval literacy. A reconsideration in light of a recent find from York, *Journal of the British Library* 20, vol. 1.

Büll, R. 1977: *Das grosse Buch vom Wachs: Geschichte, Kultur, Technik*. München.

Carmiggelt, A. 2004. *Notities uit middeleeuws Brielle. Een 15de-eeuws leren etui met beschreven wastafeltjes uit een beerput bij de Maarlandse haven* (BOORrapporten 206). Rotterdam.

Carmiggelt, A., and C.Y. Burnier 2004: *Archeologisch onderzoek in Brielle tussen Langestraat, Maarland-Zuidzijde, Kerkstraat en Coppelstockstraat* (BOORrapporten 183). Rotterdam.

Casparie, W.A., and J. Schoneveld 1991: Een pseudo-leienboekje van het Martinikerkhof in Groningen (Gr.), *Paleo-Aktueel* 2, 140-142.

Clevis, H. and J. Kottman 1989. *Weggegooid en teruggevonden. Aardewerk en glas uit Deventer vondstcomplexen 1375-1750*. Kampen.

Degryse, R. 1974, De Zeeuws-Hollandse buisnering en konvooiering omstreeks 1439-1440, *Holland* 6, 57-86.

Gallas, J.P. 1986: *De stedebouwkundige ontwikkeling van Brielle in de Middeleeuwen* (Amsterdam, unpublished dissertation).

Gelder, Enno van, 1965: *De Nederlandse munten*. Antwerpen.

Glasbergen, W. 1967: *De Romeinse castella te Valkenburg Z.H.. De opgravingen in de dorpsheuvel in 1962*. Groningen.

Goubitz, O. 1996: hout, leder en textiel, in: E. Vrenegoor en J. Kuipers (eds.), *Vondsten in Veere. Middeleeuwse voorwerpen uit een beerput van huis 'In den Struys'*. Abcoude, 79-90.

Goubitz, O. 2007: *Purses in Pieces. Archaeological finds of late medieval leather purses, pouches, bags and cases in the Netherlands*. Zwolle.

Gouw, J.L. van der 1986: *De regulieren van Rugge*. Alphen aan den Rijn.

Grol, H.G. 1940: *Het Stedelijk Museum te Vlissingen*. Vlissingen, 61-69.

Guiran, A.J. 1998: *Archeologisch onderzoek van de stadsmuur bij de Langestraat te Brielle* (BOORrapporten 36). Rotterdam.

Grassmann, A. 1986: Das Wachstafel-Notizbuch des mittelalterlichen Menschen, *Zeitschrift für Archaeologie des Mittelalters*, Beiheft 4, 223-235.

Haak, S.P. 1907: Brielle als vrije en bloeiende handelsstad in de 15de eeuw, *Bijdragen van de Vaderlandsche Geschiedenis en Oudheidkunde*, 4de reeks, no. 6, p. 7-66.

Heeringa, K. 1904: *Rechtsbronnen der stad Schiedam* (Werken de Vereeniging tot Uitgave der Bronnen van het Oud-Vaderlandsche Recht, 2de reeks, no. 6). Den Haag.

Helfrich, K., J.F. Benders and W.A. Casparie 1995: *Handzaam hout uit Groninger grond. Houtgebruik in de historische stad*. Groningen.

Hoog, M. de 1986: *De haringtrafiek van Dordrecht* (Kwartaal en teken Extra 3). Dordrecht.

Jacobs, E.J., G.F.H.M. Kempenaar and M.C. van Trierum 2002: *Brielle Maarland NZ. 87: een doorsnede van een dijk en Brielle-Kruithuisstraat: een bakstenen fundering* (BOORrapporten 91). Rotterdam.

Jager, H. de 1901: *De middeleeuwsche keuren der stad Brielle* (Werken de Vereeniging tot Uitgave der Bronnen van het Oud-Vaderlandsche Recht, 2de reeks, no. 2). Den Haag.

Klok, J. 1967: Vrouwe Geertruid en de parochie Maarland in Brielle, *Spiegel der Historie* 2, afl. 2, 288-291.

Klomp, M. s.a.: *Van mestplaats tot woonwijk. De geschiedenis van het Eiland in Zwolle vanaf de 15de eeuw tot het midden van de 20ste eeuw* (unpublished Master's dissertation).

Klomp, M. 2004: *Van opgaand hout en eenige perken. Archeologisch onderzoek op het Broerenkerkplein in Zwolle (Archeologische Rapporten Zwolle 15)*. Zwolle.

Kranenburg, H.A.H. 1954: Het afslagwezen voor de visserij in het Beneden-Maasgebied, 1400-1600, *Zuid-Hollandse Studiën*, 72-92.

Krüger, K. 2002: *Archäologische Zeugnisse zum mittelalterlichen Buch- und Schriftwesen nordwarts der Mittelgebirge*. Bonn.

Lalou, E. 1992: Inventaire des tablettes médiévales et présentation générale, in: E. Lalou (ed.), *Les tablettes a écrire de l'antiquité a l'époque moderne*. Turnhout, 234-288.

Lingbeek-Schalekamp, C. 1992: Muziek aan het hof van Frank van Borselen, *Brielse Mare* 2, no. 1, 28-42.

O'Connor, S., and D. Tweddle 1992: A set of waxed tablets from Swinegate, York, in: E. Lalou (ed.), *Les tablettes a écrire de l'antiquité a l'époque moderne*. Turnhout, 307-322.

Olivier, R. 1994: *Bodemvondsten uit Goeree-Overflakkee*. Ouddorp.

Poelman, H.A. (ed.) 1917: *Bronnen tot de geschiedenis van den Oostzeehandel, Rijks Geschiedkundige Publicatiën* 35 (deel 1). Den Haag.

Rooijen, J.P. van 1992: *De ontwikkelingsgeschiedenis van "Het Verloren Kost", het einde van de Langestraat en aangelegen gronden te Brielle*, (typescript Brielle).

Sarfatij, H. 1984: Dordrecht: Voorstraat, in: D.P. Hallewas (ed.), Archeologische kroniek van Holland over 1983, 2, Zuid-Holland, *Holland* 16, 319-322.

Thijssen, J.R. 1996: De Hessenberg ondergronds, in: *Geschiedenis van de stedelijke weeshuizen te Nijmegen*. Nijmegen, 74-82.

Vliet, A.P. 1994: *Vissers en kapers. De zeevisserij vanuit het Maasmondgebied en de Duinkerkse kapers (ca. 1580-1648)*. Den Haag.

Vos, W.K., and J.K. Haalebos 2000: Woerden-Molenstraat, *Archeologische kroniek provincie Utrecht* 1998-1999, 196-200.

Vrie, D.M. van de, and H.L. Janssen 1997: Het archeologisch onderzoek van de middeleeuwse bebouwing op het Sint Janskerkhof, in: H.W. Boekweit en H.L. Janssen (eds.), *Bouwen en wonen in de schaduw van de Sint Jan*. 's-Hertogenbosch, 48-139.

Vries, S.G. de 1895: Het gebruik van 'wastafeltjes' in de Nederlanden, *Oud-Holland* 12, 1-6.

Walle, T.Y. van der 2002: Een middeleeuwse woonterp onder de Winston bioscoop, *Hoorn onder ons*, no. 1 (Maart 2002).

Toying with miniatures

Finds of 'doll's-house items' from Alkmaar

Peter Bitter

Alkmaar and Jan Thijssen
It was in the early 1990s that I as the newly appointed municipal archaeologist prepared a publication on my very first excavation in Alkmaar: the excavation near the Wortelsteeg in September 1991. During the processing of the finds, I decided to join a small group of archaeologists who were employing the *Classification system for late and post-medieval ceramics and glass*, also known as the 'Deventer system'. The report, entitled 'Geworteld in de bodem', was to be published by the Society for the Promotion of Archaeology (SPA).[1] Since then this system has been used for the description of all ceramic and glass finds in Alkmaar. During this first project in particular, there was much contact with Jan Thijssen and Hemmy Clevis, who had started the classification system. The archaeological service of Nijmegen played their part in the production of the publication, not only through Jan's welcome advice and comments, but also through the participation of Rob Mols as the photographer of the finds. After this project, several other publications followed, but these were produced by our own team from Alkmaar. Jan Thijssen is one of the very few archaeologists in the Netherlands with an extensive knowledge of post-medieval ceramics. I have frequently made use of his publications on the subject and will of course continue to do so.

In this contribution I will focus on a special find category: toys of ceramics and glass that in the classification system we have rather unspecifically labelled 'min' for 'miniature'. The majority of the finds discussed here are from cesspits, mainly dated between 1550 and 1800. These finds often can be attributed to a specific house, which enables us to link the finds to information from other sources on the house and its occupants. In the archeological collection of Alkmaar there are a great number of miniature objects from several excavations. This contribution deals with about 140 miniature items excavated up to 2005. In the conclusion of her famous research on children's toys, Annemarieke Willemsen calls for closer analysis of the find contexts of such archaeological material.[2] This contribution will be a modest first attempt to do so.

Cesspit research in Alkmaar
In Alkmaar, brick cesspits were built from as early as the 13th century, at first only near the wealthiest houses. After the 16th century, however, most houses in Alkmaar had a brick cesspit, albeit that among the poorer dwellings, cesspits were usually shared by two or three households. For whatever reason, for centuries it was uncommon in Alkmaar to construct a sewer instead of a cesspit. The earliest cesspits contained only little rubbish. Perhaps the maintenance of cesspits was not yet professionally organized, while the emptying and repairing of waste-filled cesspits and clogged chutes only became a specialist profession after 1500. In written sources from the 18th century these professionals were called 'night workers' (*nachtwerkers*). It must be noted that only a small proportion of all rubbish was deposited in cesspits. The oldest remaining town Ordinances, surviving as an incomplete copy from the mid-15th century, contain several regulations on waste disposal.[3] There were specific locations where the town's inhabitants were permitted to dump their waste, namely in the town's refuse pits (*vuilniskuilen*). Most of these were located near the town walls, often close to the town gates. In the 16th century these rubbish pits were round or rectangular constructions with a brick floor and a low wall on three sides. There were official inspectors who would fine anyone disobeying the rules. But the town also employed refuse collectors who, for instance, cleaned up the streets after market days. Waste was sometimes buried in a pit in the back yard of a house, but the number of such waste pits excavated in Alkmaar so far is quite modest. In these pits, the sherds of a single object often are found dispersed throughout the pit. This might be caused by the waste having been collected in a rubbish heap first. Only rarely (e.g. during spells of bad weather) would the rubbish from such a heap not be taken to the town's refuse pits but be buried in the back yard.

In the first half of the 16th century, refuse collecting was reorganized, and the town owned a refuse barge to collect the waste from the quays on regular weekdays. People had a rubbish bin in the house, which was put on the quayside when the collectors came. In the whole town, rubbish was collected on regular weekdays: on Tuesdays, Thursdays and Saturdays. The refuse barge remained in use for centuries. The efficiency of the system is demonstrated by the almost complete absence of waste pits in back yards after 1550. The waste was separated into on the one hand materials that could be sold to farmers as fertilizer (ashes and dung) and, on the other, coarse debris like bone, fragments of ceramics, glass and metal.

In 1881 Alkmaar introduced a 'barrel system' (*tonnenstelsel*), with barrels placed in latrines, to be changed once or twice a week by the municipal 'barrel-collectors' (*tonophalers*). In the town centre most cesspits were then abandoned. The terminology of the 'cesspit' however persisted into the 1950s for septic tanks and in the name for the sanitation taxes (*beerputbelasting*). A modern sewerage system was constructed only in the course of the 20th century.

In Alkmaar the cesspit finds by far outnumber those from other contexts. As shown above, the digging of waste pits largely predates the 16th century. We also have some other find contexts, such as filled-in ditches or raised levels. In Alkmaar the raising of the level of houses and streets was only minimal. After the first development of a site, only very little soil was later added. The use of waste for these raised levels was connected to the clearing-out of the town's refuse pits and (after the 16th century) to the dumping of rubbish from the refuse barges. The coarse debris that remained after sorting out the ash and dung from the waste was re-used for this purpose. In the finds from our raised levels, the two 'boom periods' of Alkmaar's town expansion are reflected in the age of the majority of the archaeological material, which dates from the 14th and 16th centuries.

In the cesspit finds there is a marked peak in the late 16th and first half of the 17th century, which can be related to changes in the population figure. From the late 15th century, the town went through a period of steady growth, from about 4,000 inhabitants in 1500 to about 8,000 in 1550 and about 12,000 in 1625. The 16th century saw several town extensions, but after the construction of new fortifications in 1573-1595 all the available space within the town became densely filled in with buildings. After about 1650 an economic recession set in and the population figure rapidly decreased to about 8,000 by 1725. In this period many houses became uninhabited, especially the smaller, single-room dwellings (*kamers*) which often were converted into stables, sheds and warehouses, with their cesspits going out of use.

The systematical research of cesspits started in Alkmaar as early as 1987, when a group of amateur archaeologists founded the *Stichting Behoud Alkmaarse Bodemvondsten* (Society for the Preservation of Archaeological Finds from Alkmaar). By

01 The excavation Wortelsteeg 1991. Below to the right a cesspit, the chute of which was connected to a garden wall.

02 Excavation of a cesspit behind Huigbrouwerstraat 3 in 1995. The find layer is collected in plastic buckets to be washed on a sieve later.

1991 they had salvaged some 20 cesspit assemblages.[4] They developed an efficient and accurate method for excavating and processing cesspit finds by collecting complete find layers in big plastic buckets with airtight lids and then washing the contents on a sieve with a 6 mm mesh. Bartels has named this 'the Alkmaar method'.[5] Since 1991 about 150 cesspits have been excavated, yielding some 25,000 objects, complete or in fragments, approximately 4,000 of which have been restored to museum quality. The majority are ceramics, but we also have many glass objects. From 1998 to 2003 the description of the contents of about 125 cesspits was undertaken by Rob Roedema and Sebastiaan Ostkamp, with help from volunteers, in the so-called Cesspit Project. The project has resulted in some publications and a major exhibition in the Stedelijk Museum of Alkmaar in 2004.[6] So far, however, only few data have been digitalized. We have not yet finished the analysis and evaluation of these assemblages and much has not yet been published or otherwise made accessible to other researchers. Meanwhile the contents of 26 cesspits have been published in detail.[7] The Cesspit Project has made possible the analysis of specific themes in the material culture of historical Alkmaar.[8]

Child's play with miniature objects

In the *Classification system for late and post-medieval ceramics and glass* the three-letter code 'min' is used to denote miniature items. These objects usually were used by children imitating the household activities of adults. The traces of wear and of use on a fire of the prototypes of course are absent on these toys. These miniature objects were named *poppegoed* ('doll's items') in written sources, as they were associated with young girls playing with dolls. From the 16th century this theme was

03 Girls playing with dolls and doll's items, boys playing soldier, detail from the engraving 'Ex nugens seria' by Experiens Sillemans for the publication Houwelick by Jacob Cats, 1625.

depicted in paintings and engravings of child's play that often also had a moralizing connotation, e.g. as illustrations to the very popular emblemata poetry by Jacob Cats.[9]

In the 17th and 18th centuries, miniature objects were also used in doll's houses. Some of these were not intended for child's play but were on display as precious showpieces, under the care of the lady of the house. Some doll's houses were even constructed as a scale model of a real house, containing many dozens of miniature objects. Such doll's houses were very costly, sometimes even comparable in value to real buildings.[10]

From the late 17th century, miniature items were also put on display in special furniture, such as a cabinet with glass-panelled doors or a buffet. These showpieces were usually made from precious materials, especially silver. Important written sources on these collections are probate inventories. The majority of these inventories were made up for the division of an inheritance. The possessions of the deceased were listed with great accuracy, from loans and debts and cash money to real estate and the furniture and other items of his or her household. The latter was often listed room by room, going through the house. For the more wealthy households, probate inventories were drawn up and registered by a notary. In Alkmaar 451 probate inventories from the period 1689-1734 have been digitalized by Jan Klinkert.[11] *Poppegoed* was listed in 59 of the 451 inventories. Of these, 44 are recorded as silverware, 10 objects are without the fabric mentioned and only a few such items of other materials are described. Clearly, ceramics, glass and the like were not considered worth mentioning in these lists. In a few cases the silver weight is noted or the estimated value.[12] Frequently the description is limited to the number of silver miniature items, sometimes even just 'some silver doll's items' (*'eenig silver poppegoed'*). Other materials are scarcely mentioned, like a collection made of pewter, or once 'two bedpans, a pair of tongs and an ash shovel, doll's items' made of copper, or a collection of 14 porcelain 'doll's bottles' and once 'some doll's items of basketry'.[13] Numbers vary from a few objects to many dozens of silver items. Some even mention 40, 70 or 99 silver miniatures and these must have been silver collections on display.[14] As silverware is usually listed separately in the inventories, it is in most cases unknown where the objects were located in the house. If the room is mentioned, it usually is a living room.[15] Only rarely is any information found on the way in which the objects were displayed. Sometimes a glass showcase (*'glaskastje'*) is mentioned, or a rack or a wall cupboard (*'muurkastje'*, a small cupboard hanging on the wall). Only twice does a doll's house get mentioned, but here we should remember that a simple doll's house with cheap contents probably was not worth recording in a probate inventory.[16]

In the inventories we may find silver miniature objects of many types; for example, in a large collection of miniature silver objects registered in 1702: '...a tea table, a warming stand with a teapot, a calabash, 3 boxes, a kettle, a cup with a spoon, a bucket, a cannon, 6 spoons, a skater, a child with a hoop, a snuffer, a tray, a violin with a fiddlestick, a carriage and two horses, a sergeant, a fountain, 3 Magi with the star, a spinning top, 5 silver buckles, 3 pieces of old silver, a gold hoop, a booklet with silver locks, another booklet with silver, another almanac with silver mounts, a silver signet'.[17] From museum collections and archeological finds elsewhere it is known that a great variety of miniature household utensils were made from pewter, which might also be characterized as 'poor man's silver', as many pewter objects were close imitations of silver ones.[18] Amongst the archaeological finds, silver is extremely rare, while pewter and ceramics prevail. The finds from Alkmaar include miniature items of red earthenware, white earthenware, Weser earthenware, majolica, faience, stoneware, porcelain, industrial redware, fine whiteware (*pijpaarde*, 'pipe-clay'), pewter, glass and wood. The archaeological finds illustrate the great variety of materials. Without doubt these were also present in the households of our sample of probate inventories. Therefore our various sources of information are highly complementary, with only little overlap.

With the archaeological finds it is not always clear whether we are indeed dealing with doll's items, as some customary household utensils too are of a small size. Examples are the small, 15th- and 16th-century two-handled jugs of salt-glazed stoneware that might have been perfume bottles or inkwells,[19] or the small 15th-century skillets of red earthenware that usually are much worn and sooted and probably served for frying small pancakes (*poffertjes*) or some kind of omelette.[20] Small bowls of glass, red or white earthenware, majolica, faience, porcelain and other ceramics were used as salts. We may also find very small cups and saucers in tea-sets. Minuscule glass bottles may have held perfume but might equally have been children's toys. It can be difficult to recognize such an archaeological find as a miniature.

The majority of small items, however, are fairly exact miniature copies of well-known household utensils. Minor differences due to the small size occur for example in the profile of rims or when a footring is replaced by a flat base, or a rod handle by a strap handle. Frequently the model can even be recognized in detail and be determined down to type in the *Classification system*.

The miniatures seem to have been produced roughly on two scales: the pewter items are very small, on a scale of 1:5 to 1:10. They measure only a few centimeters. In our archaeological

04 Small jug, possibly an inkwell or perfume bottle, of saltglazed stoneware (s2-kru-2), probably from Cologne or Frechen, diameter 4,5 cm and height 6,5 cm, late 16th century, from a ditch behind the Hof van Sonoy, a former monastery that was changed into a house (01HOF9A).

05 Small jug, possibly an inkwell or perfume bottle, of iron-washed and salt-glazed stoneware, probably from Langerwehe, diameter 6.5 and height 7.5 cm, late 15th century, excavated at Langestraat no. 16 (00LANBP2K).

06 A collection of sooted and worn small skillets of red earthenware, second half of the 15th century, from a cesspit excavated at Langestraat 103 in 1993 (93LANXBP6). They have a diameter of 8-9 cm and a height of 2-2,5 cm.

07 Miniature skillet of white earthenware with brown-stained yellow lead-glaze, diameter 7 cm and height 3 cm, late 17th or first half of the 18th century, excavated at Koningsweg no. 29/31 (03KWE39BO).

10 Pewter jug, from a 14th-century raised level at Laat to the west of Ruitersteeg (94LAA20).

08 Miniature skillet of white earthenware with dark green lead-glaze (imitating type w-stk-9), diameter 9.5 cm and height 5.5 cm, late 17th or first half of the 18th century, found at Luttik Oudorp no. 18 (94LUTBPAV).

11 Pewter miniature dripping pan, length 4.5 cm and width 2.5 cm, found in a mid-16th-century ditch at the Kwakelkade (95KWAK13).

09 Small glass bottles that may have served as perfume bottles or as doll's items, diameter 2,5 and 3 cm and height 4 and 5 cm, late 17th or first half of the 18th century, excavated at a house in the Breedstraat on the western corner of Pastoorsteeg (90BRE88BP4).

12 Pewter miniature bowls, diameter 3-4 cm and height 1-2 cm, late 17th or first half of the 18th century, found at Luttik Oudorp no. 18 (94LUTBP).

collection, however, the miniature ceramics and glassware are executed in a larger size, to a scale of roughly 1:2 to 1:3. In the above-mentioned precious doll's houses, items are found in both scales.

Pewter objects are not found in great numbers in Alkmaar, which is in part due to the high salt content of the soil in part of the town and the arid conditions in other parts, which makes for poor preservation. The earliest find of a pewter doll's-house item from Alkmaar dates from the 14th century. It is a pewter miniature jug that was excavated in a mid-14th century layer in the street Laat.[21] From elsewhere in the Netherlands, pewter miniatures of all kinds of household utensils are known, dating from the 13th century onward.[22] The pewter toys bear no maker's marks. In Alkmaar there is very little material from the 15th and 16th centuries. A rare find is the pewter miniature dripping pan from a mid-16th century find context.[23] Most pewter finds are from the second half of the 17th and the18th centuries. There is a wide range of pewter miniature tableware, with dishes and bowls, a goblet, teapot, chafing dish, etc. By contrast, there are almost no miniature kitchen utensils of pewter. An extraordinary find is a 17th- or 18th-century miniature version of a bovine phalanx I, measuring only 1,7 cm.[24] Such knucklebones were used by children in a throwing game called 'jacks' or 'huckle' ('*kootspel*' or '*bikkelen*' in Dutch); our pewter miniature jack or huckle ('*koot*' or '*bikkel*') therefore represents 'a toy for a doll'! The earliest ceramic miniature items in Alkmaar date from the 13th century. They are a jug of pale yellow Andenne-type earthenware with green lead glaze and the lower half of a red earthenware tripod pipkin, both found in a well near the Laurenskerk (church of St. Lawrence) in 1970.[25] From the moat of castle De Nieuwburg near Alkmaar comes the lower half of a miniature tripod pipkin of white earthenware with green-spotted yellow lead glaze, presumably a 14th-century

13 Pewter haul, length 9,5 cm and width 4,5 cm, excavated at Schermerweg 80-82, presumably from the raised level of circa 1590 (04SCHW37).

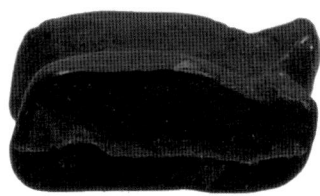

14 Pewter or lead miniature huckle or jack, a miniature item of only 1.7 x 0.7 x 0.7 cm, second half of the 17th or 18th century, excavated at Luttik Oudorp no. 100 (88LUTBP)

15 Pewter miniature brazier, width 8 cm and height 6 cm (one of the legs is broken off), second half of the 18th century, excavated at Turfmarkt (89TURBPAH).

import from the Rhineland (in the *Classification system* labelled 'Hafner earthenware').[26] From a cesspit at Voordam we recovered a miniature chamber pot and a pipkin of red earthenware from the second half of the 15th or the early 16th century.[27] The majority of the ceramic miniature finds from Alkmaar date from the 17th and 18th centuries and imitate all kinds of kitchen- and tableware and utensils like chamber pots, oil lamps and some porcelain vases and bottles. There are also small-scale fire covers of red earthenware, white earthenware and even one of polychrome majolica. A special group of miniature objects from the mid-17th century is made of a very fine-textured white earthenware (*pijpaarde* or pipe-clay), to imitate

16 Miniature jug of Andenne-type earthenware with green leadglaze, diameter 5,5 cm and height 5 cm, from a 13th-century well, excavated to the west of the Church of St. Lawrence in 1970 (70GRK Well II).

18 Red earthenware miniature pipkin (after the type r-gra-22), diameter 5,5 cm and height 6 cm, second half of the 15th or early 16th century, from the excavation at Voordam 13/15 (05VDA270B).

17 Red earthenware miniatures: three pipkins (left behind: after r-gra-41), skillet (after the type r-bak-2), basket and chamber pot (after the type r-pis-5), second quarter of the 17th century, from a waste pit at Oudegracht 182 (05ODG23).

19 Miniature faience dish with a decoration imitating 'kraakporcelain' with a bird on a rock surrounded by flowers, the backside decorated with lines and circle-and-dots, diameter 11 cm and height 1,5 cm, first half of the 17th century, found at Koorstraat 37 (98LAA160BP1AS).

21 Miniature (chamber?)pot of Weser earthenware (after the type we-pot-2), diameter 7 cm and height 5,5 cm, late 16th or early 17th century, excavated at Bierkade 17 (02BIE 3BPK).

22 Miniatures from a mid-17th-century find complex: a white faience jug (after the type f-kan-2; diameter 4,5 cm and height 6 cm), a roemer of dark green glass (diameter 3,5 cm) and a red earthenware pipkin with internal leadglaze (diameter 7 cm and height 7,5 cm), found at Verdronkenoord 139 (95HBSIICJ, 95HBSIIAAE and 95HBSIICQ).

20 Miniature faience cup, decorated on the outside with a crow on a branch in a Chinese style, diameter 4,5 and height 2,5 cm, late 17th of early 18th century, excavated at Zijdam 5/6 (02ZDABPL).

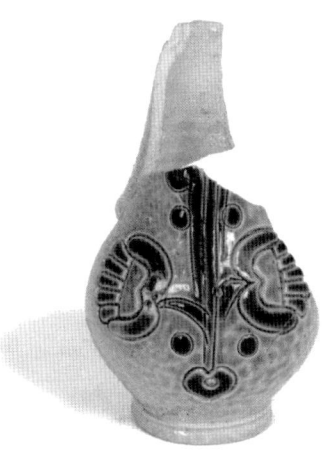

23 Miniature jug of saltglazed stoneware (after the type s2-kan-68) decorated with flowers above a heart in cobalt blue and sgraffito, diameter 10,5 cm and height 3 cm, late 17th or first half of the 18th century, excavated at a house in Breedstraat on the western corner of Pastoorsteeg (90BRE88BP4ACA)

24 Two miniature vases and a small bottle of Chinese porcelain, with flowers in underglaze dark blue and in red and gold paint, vases diameter 4 and 3,5 cm and height 7 and 7,5 cm and bottle diameter 4 cm and height 7 cm, second half of the 18th century, excavated at Langestraat 73 (97LAN7BP5AGC, -AGD and -AGB).

27 Miniature lobed dish and jug of pipe-clay with traces of red paint on the jug (imitations of faience, after the types f-plo-3 and f-kan-1), dish diameter 6 cm and height 1 cm and jug diameter 4 cm and height 5 cm, middle of the 17th century, found at Luttik Oudorp 18 (94LUTBP).

25 Miniature fire cover (without airhole) of red earthenware, decorated with white earthenware appliques with yellow and green leadglaze, width 14,5 cm and height 18,5 cm, waster of pottery 'De Properepot' at Luttik Oudorp 36, shortly before 1620 (91WOR3).

28 Miniature items of red earthenware and of white earthenware with brown-stained yellow leadglaze, first half of the 18th century, excavated in a ditch near a house of a shipyard at Schermerweg 82 (04SCHW25).

26 Polychrome majolica miniature fire cover, 13,5 x 7,5 x 3,5 cm, first half of the 17th century, from a cesspit to the west of Ruitersteeg (94LAA12BP2AZ). Unfortunately it could not be established which house the cesspit belonged to.

29 White earthenware oil lamp with brown leadglaze (after the type w-oli-2), diameter 5,5 cm and height 5 cm, second half of the 17th century, excavated at Luttik Oudorp 100 (88LUTBP

30 Miniature berkemeier of green glass, diameter of footring circa 2 cm, second half of the 16th of early 17th century, excavated at Langestraat 73 (97LAN3BP2AD).

31 Miniature glass beaker of colourless glass on blue feet (after the type gl-bek-15), middle of the 17th century, width 4 cm and height 3,5 cm, excavated at Oudegracht 26 (02ODG46AAE).

32 Wooden miniature bowl, diameter 5 cm and height 2,5 cm, second half of the 18th century, excavated at Luttik Oudorp 58 (89LUTBP).

faience or pewter wares. In this material we have lobed dishes, jugs, a bowl, a cuspidor and a tray.[28] Most miniatures are made of red or white earthenware. These were locally produced at Alkmaar in the 17th century, but later they were imported from different regions in the Netherlands. Judging by the fabric, which includes dark grey grains of contaminating material, some of the 18th-century objects of red earthenware probably come from the province of Friesland. There are various fabrics of 18th-century white earthenware, which most probably come from different regions of the Netherlands. However, as still little is known of the products of the western Netherlands in this period, this question for now remains unresolved. Amongst others, there are finds of a specific white earthenware with yellow lead glaze that is decorated with dark brown stains (possibly through the addition of iron or manganese to the lead glaze), which is quite common in 18th-century Alkmaar. A particular type of 18th-century white earthenware was used for a miniature oil lamp and a jug, which are covered with a mottled orange-brown lead glaze.[29]

We complete this brief overview by mentioning a few finds of miniature drinking glasses and a wooden miniature bowl.

Rich and poor children

Presumably there were great differences among the toys of children from different social groups in town. These might reflect differences in wealth, in education and in mentality. Children of the poorer social classes will have had less, and other types of formal education, and they also started to work at an earlier age. It is unknown whether this influenced the use of miniature items in various social groups. For a better insight, we must largely depend on several non-archaeological sources of information. Archaeologically, it is, however, possible to investigate differences between households of dissimilar wealth.

For most of our cesspits it is possible to determine to which houses they belonged. Ideally we should like to link the finds to particular citizens. In Alkmaar it is possible to identify the owners of many houses after the 16th or 17th century with the aid of several written sources. The owners, however, often were not the residents of these houses, as many were rented. Rent was not registered officially and we largely depend on only a few tax lists that give us all the town's residents at a specific moment in time. Matters are further complicated by the loose dating of most archaeological objects. In this contribution, another method is applied. We can distinguish differences in wealth between households on the basis of the real-estate value of the houses.

Since the late Middle Ages, real-estate taxes were levied, the so-called *Verpondingen* that were collected from the house owners in favour of the sovereign authority, in this case the Council (*Staten*) of the County of Holland. The tax was based on the so-called 'rent value' (*huurwaarde*). This was the annual rent of the house or, if it was owner-occupied, an estimated figure. Following a decree of the Council of Holland in 1627, a re-evaluation of these taxes was executed, the so-called *Redres*, which was completed for Alkmaar in 1632. This included a house-by-house reassessment of the rent values. From then on the owners were to pay 1/8 of the rent value each year. In 1730 a new *Redres* was performed, after which the taxes were reduced to 1/12 of the rent value. For Alkmaar a complete list is available of the *Redres* of 1730.[30] Changes in individual house values, caused by for instance demolition, alteration or improvements, meanwhile had been written down in separate lists, of which only the 'Records of newly built and renovated houses' of 1654-1665 have been preserved.[31] Now and again new tax lists of all houses were compiled, of which only the list of 1718 is preserved.[32] The *Verpondingen* were levied on all buildings in Alkmaar except public buildings. Listed are the rent or the estimated rent value, the old and the new figure (in 1730), the owner, and a rough indication of the type of building. Fortunately these lists all were digitalized some years ago and the administration of the *Verpondingen* was cross-referenced with the Land Registry of 1832.[33] By overlaying the very accurate Land Registry maps (*Kadastrale Minuut*) of 1832 onto the present-day map of Alkmaar, all these data can be connected to current addresses. These data from the *Verpondingen* could be retrieved for more than three quarters of the premises in the Cesspit Project.[34] We shall compare the data from the houses in our Cesspit Project with a 10 % sample of all buildings in Alkmaar.[35]

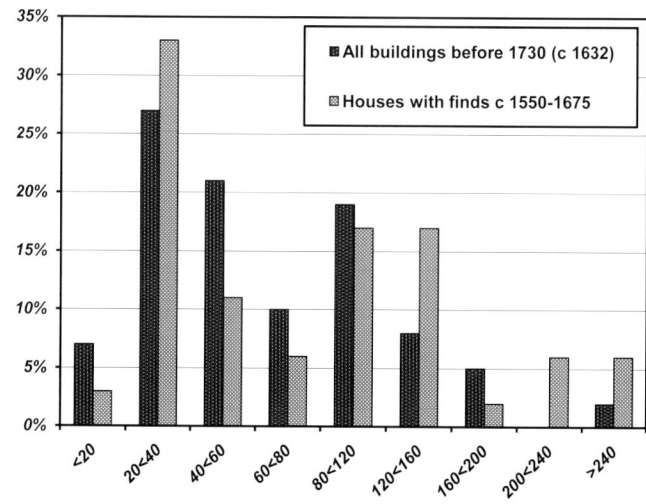

Table 2. Rent values of all houses in 1730 compared with the rent values of houses with assemblages from circa 1675-1825. The sample of all houses contains 244 addresses, the assemblages come from 66 houses (none counted double). Rent values in guilders.

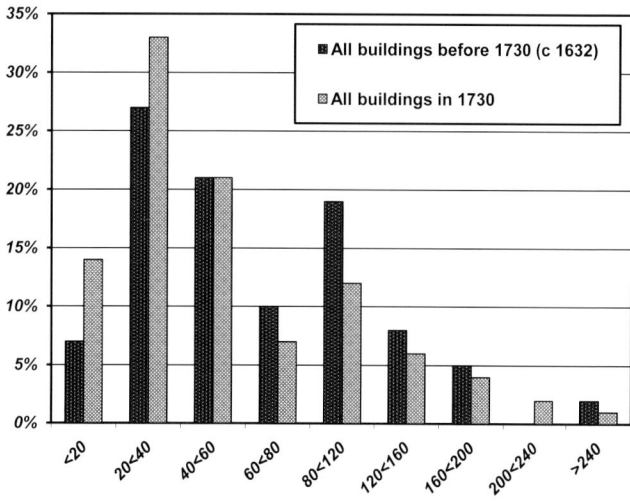

Table 1. Rent values of a sample of the Alkmaar buildings before and after the new taxes levied in the *Verpondingen* in 1730. The sample of all rent values before 1730 (i.e. the rent values of 1632) contains 220 buildings, the sample of the new rent values of 1730 contains 236 buildings. Rent values in guilders.

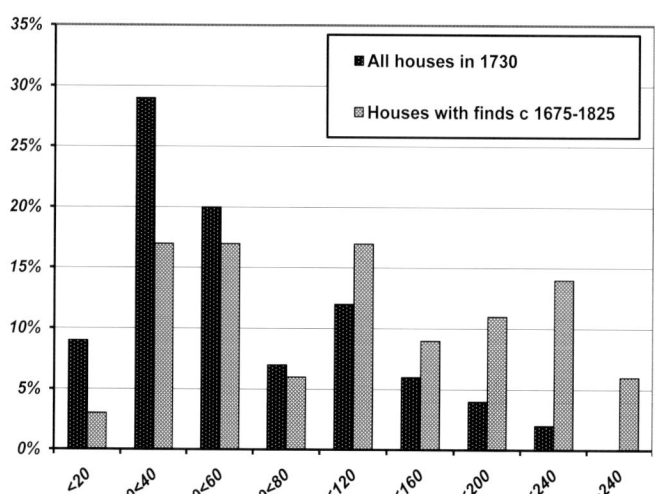

Table 3. Rent values of all houses from before 1730 (i.e. the rent values of 1632) compared with the rent values of houses with assemblages from circa 1550-1675. The sample of all buildings contains 220 addresses, the assemblages come from 35 houses (of which twice a cesspit in the category of 20<40 guilders was counted double for being shared by two *kamers*). Rent values in guilders.

In 1730 no less than 48% of all houses were rented. It is unknown whether this had been any different a century earlier. It appears that in 1730 the majority of the rented houses belonged to the cheaper categories, but some expensive houses were rented as well. These proportions are not known for the *Redres* of 1632. It can be argued that when it comes to wealth the difference between rented or owner-occupied homes is barely significant for the more expensive houses. If such a house is seen as a means to express status and to underline one's social position, it may not have mattered much whether a house was owned or rented. Moreover, there was of course no linear relation between house value and the wealth of the occupants. Differences in wealth must have been far greater than can be made visible in the value of the houses, with the very rich investing heavily in other displays of wealth, such as the decoration and furnishing of houses, the possession of carriages (and horses, stables and mews), and mansions in the countryside.

The different tax categories of the *Verpondingen* will roughly run parallel to the principal house types in Alkmaar during the period, but it should be borne in mind that this is a crude simplification of the actual variation in buildings. The simplest house was a single-roomed dwelling (*kamer*) with a rent value between 10 and 30 guilders. A standard house with two or three rooms at ground level and an attic was valued at 20 to 60 guilders. For the higher categories it is increasingly unclear what the higher rent value really stood for. Here we find several addresses where not only a house but also the adjacent industrial buildings accounted for the rent value. Hence the houses with rent values above, say, 100 guilders would be a mixture of really expensive residential houses and the less expensive houses with adjacent outbuildings. The description in the tax list is too concise to distinguish these groups.

The archaeological finds here are divided into two chronological groups. The first period is from ca 1550 until 1675. The houses with finds from this period will be compared with rent values of all houses from before 1730 (largely unaltered since 1632). The second period concerns finds from 1675 until 1825 and a comparison will be made with the rent values of 1730. There was a general decline in house values from the early 17th until the early 19th century, which after 1780 was accelerated by the economic crises caused by war and the French invasion of 1795. The economic depression continued well after 1813 and even the construction of the Noordhollands Kanaal (connecting Amsterdam with the sea via Alkmaar) around 1822 failed to improve the economic situation. From sales figures of houses[36] it seems that after the great prosperity of around 1625 a slow but steady economic recession caused house values to decline by about a quarter in the following century. In the late 18th century many houses were sold at only half to two-thirds of their prices in the early 17th century. Meanwhile the population figure had dropped from about 12,000 in 1625 to about 8,000 in the early 18th century. The smallest houses especially were abandoned. There also was a change in the distribution of wealthy households across the different parts of town. The value of houses in the eastern part of town, which were predominantly inhabited by traders and craftsmen, decreased, and in the 18th century the wealthy households became concentrated in the western half of the town centre, especially in the vicinity of the town hall.[37] The effects are also visible when we compare the rent values of 1632 with those of 1730 (table 1). In 1632, 55% of the houses had a rent value below 60 guilders, but by 1730 this percentage had risen to 68%. Remarkably, there seems to be a bipartition in rent values, with a distinctly low number of houses with a rent value between 60 and 80 guilders. In 1730, 11% of all buildings were uninhabited. The

rent value	number of houses	number of find com-	r	w	we	m	f	py	gl	number of
20<40	2	2	2	1						3
40<60	4	4	3	1					1	5
60<80	3	2	1	1			1			3
80<120	9	9	7	1	1			5		14
120<160	4	4	5				1		2	8
160<200	0	0								0
200<240	4	4	4						1	4
>240	2	2	2						1	3
unknown	4	4	6	1	1	1		3		12
total:	32	31	30	5	2	1	2	8	5	53

Table 4. Miniatures from 31 assemblages from circa 1550-1675, compared with the rent values from before 1730 (i.e. the rent values of 1632); r = red earthenware, w = white earthenware, we = Weser earthenware, m = majolica, f = faience (Netherlands), py = pipe-clay and gl = glass. Listed are the numbers of objects. Rent values in guilders.

percentage of the 17th century is unknown, but we may assume that in 1632 almost all buildings were occupied.

If we compare the data relating to the houses with cesspit finds with the data of all houses, we can test whether the sample of cesspit finds may be considered as representative. One might for instance question if all houses indeed did have cesspits. From excavations and written sources is appears that especially the single-room dwellings (*kamers*) often shared cesspits - two or three *kamers* would make use of a single cesspit. For this reason the tables are based on the numbers of houses and not just cesspits.[38] For each cesspit it has been established as well as possible whether it was shared, and if so, by how many households (see the Appendix). Such a shared cesspit thus represents more than one dwelling/*kamer*.

The distribution of rent values from all buildings before 1730 (i.e. of 1632) is compared with the distribution of houses with finds from circa 1550-1675 (table 2). These prove to correspond quite well, with only a minor deviation when it comes to the more expensive houses.[39] This implies that the cesspit finds from this period are a fairly reliable sample of all households. If we make a similar comparison between all houses[40] in 1730 and houses with finds from 1675-1825 (table 3), the interpretation becomes more complicated. There proves to be a marked discrepancy between 'all houses' and 'houses with cesspits'. Presumably there were also many houses in the cheaper categories that lacked a cesspit but perhaps already used some kind of barrel system, or shared cesspits were more common than expected![41]

After all these considerations we can at last address the archaeological find contexts of the doll's-house items (tables 4 and 5). It becomes clear that ceramic miniatures were widespread among a broad range of households! These fail to show any differentiation between poorer and wealthier households. Apparently these toys were quite common and affordable for almost everyone.

The numbers of finds illustrate the popularity of these toys. Strikingly, even the materials that would be considered more expensive, such as faience, glass and porcelain (possibly also pewter) turn out to be omnipresent.

Final remarks

The archaeological research and analysis of waste deposits such as those found in cesspits contribute to our understanding of the material culture of the past, for different reasons. One is that much of the archaeological material is almost completely absent in the written sources, as the objects were too inexpensive to record. Secondly, a large proportion of our ancestors remains almost invisible in the written sources. For instance, of all those inhabitants of Alkmaar who rented their homes, most of them belonging to the poorer households, our archives hold very little in terms of their material culture, often even the location of their rented homes remaining unknown. However, for interpreting the archaeological finds, a comparison, confrontation or completion with a variety of non-archaeological sources proves indispensable.

There is still much to detect for researchers of historical material culture. I hope that Jan will continue to contribute in this field for many years to come!

Photography

Cor Prins and Peter Bitter, municipality of Alkmaar

rent value	number of houses	number of find com-	s2	r	w	f	p	ir	pewter	wood	number of objects
20<40	3	3		3	3		1				7
40<60	1	1					2				2
60<80	1	1	1		1						2
80<120	4	4		1	4		1	1	9	1	17
120<160	3	3			4	1			3		8
160<200	3	3		1	3				2		6
200<240	0	0									0
>240	2	2			2				2		4
unknown	7	7	1	8	10	1	1				21
total:	24	24	2	13	27	2	5	1	16	1	67

Table 5. Miniatures from 24 assemblages from circa 1675-1825, compared with the rent values of 1730; s2 = salt-glazed stoneware, r = red earthenware, w = white earthenware, f = faience (Netherlands), p = porcelain, ir = industrial redware. Listed are the numbers of objects. Rent values in guilders.

Notes

1. Bitter 1995.
2. Willemsen 1998, 291. She has also drawn attention to the presence of dolls and miniature items in some 16th- and 17th-century family portraits (Willemsen 2003).
3. Written sources about waste disposal in Alkmaar are summarized by Vis 1992. Similar regulations and organisations are known to have existed in Amsterdam, Gouda, Leiden and Haarlem, from as early as the 14th century (Hulshof 1995).
4. Roedema/Bruin 1992.
5. Bartels 1999, 35-36.
6. Bitter et al 2004.
7. Bitter 1995; Bitter, Dijkstra, Roedema and Van Wilgen 1997; Ostkamp et al 1998; Ostkamp, Roedema and Van Wilgen 2001; Roedema 2004; Bitter, De Jong, Roedema and Van Wilgen 2007. The finds from 11 rubbish pits have also been published.
8. Cf. Bitter, Ostkamp and Roedema 2002; Ostkamp, Roedema and Van Wilgen 2002; Ostkamp 2003; Bitter et al. 2004; Bitter in preparation (2008).
9. There are a multitude of authors on the subject, see for instance Schama 1988, 480-514. There appear to have been no medieval representations of girls playing with miniature items (compare Willemsen 1998), probably because the emblemata were linked to 16th-17th century Humanism.
10. Compare Pijzel-Dommisse 2000. She for instance mentions a doll's house on which 1700 guilders were spent, while the showpiece of Petronella Oortman (now in the Rijksmuseum, Amsterdam) seems to have cost a prodigious 20,000 to 30,000 guilders (Pijzel-Dommisse 2000, 13).
11. These probate inventories are in the Regionaal Archief Alkmaar (ONA inv.382 - 487). I owe many thanks to Jan Klinkert for making this valuable documentation available to me.
12. In one inventory, four silver miniature items are assessed at 1 guilder and 5 stuivers (ONA inv. 411 akte 59) and in another, seventeen pieces at 39 guilders (ONA inv.421 akte 14), without further specifications, however.
13. There are 37 pewter objects described in ONA inv.385 akte 58; 'twee bedpanneties, tangh and asschop poppegoet' made from copper in ONA inv.420 akte 98; 14 porcelain 'poppeflesjes' in ONA inv.416 akte 113; 'eenigh poppegoed van mandewerk' in ONA inv.403 akte 50.
14. There are 41 silver miniature items in ONA inv.466 akte 4; 70 pieces in ONA inv.441 akte 41; 99 pieces in ONA inv.414 akte 10.
15. Silver miniature items are listed in a basement kitchen (kelderkeuken), downstairs room (benedenkamer), upstairs room (bovenkamer), 'best room' ('beste camer'), back room (achterkamer) and inner room (binnenhuis) (ONA inv-akte: 385-58, 403-50, 413-1, 419-45 and 437-68).
16. In ONA inv.441 akte 26: '2 poppekasjes'; in ONA inv.485 akte 203: '1 poppegoeds kasje' (kasje = kastje or cupboard).
17. 'Een thee tafeltje, een comphoirtje with een thee potje, een cabasje [kalebas], 3 doosjes, een keteltje, een kopje met een lepeltje, een emmertje, een canonnetje, 6 lepeltjes, een schaets rijdertje, een hoepelaertje, een snuijtertje, een schaalbortje, een phiooltje met een strijckstockje, een wagentje met twee paertjes, een chercheantje [=sergeant], een fortuijntje [=fontijntje], 3 koningen met de star, een treck tolletje, 5 silvere gespen, 3 stuckjes out silver, een goude hoepringh, een boekje met silvere slootjes, nogh een boekje met silver, nogh een almanackje met silver beslagh, een silver signet' (ONA inv.466 akte 4).
18. Compare Willemsen 2000.
19. In the Classification system: s2-kru-2. In an early-16th-century painting such a jug is hanging on a wire beneath a bookshelf with books and a stationery box (Bitter, Ostkamp and Roedema 2002, 26). For a long time these small jugs were interpreted as 'jars for ointment' supposedly used on the fingers during spinning, but this assumption has been rejected (Groeneweg 1999). The interpretation as an inkwell is already found in an article by H.J.E. van Beuningen in 1948 (see Kicken, Koldeweij and Ter Molen 2000, 40-44).
20. De Jong-Lambregts 2004, 34-36. In the Classification system these are the types w-bak-8, r-bak-14, -26 and -30. They are the simple version of the triple pancake-skillet (drieling-poffertjespan) of the types r-bak-36 and -42.
21. Registration number 94LAA20. A badly damaged, pewter miniature pipkin, possibly of the same period, was excavated in a mid-16th-century ditch behind some 14th-century dwelling mounds at the Kwakelkade in 1995 (95KWAK13).
22. Compare Willemsen 2000.
23. Registration number 95KWAK13.
24. Registration number 88LUTBP.
25. The Andenne-type jug (from Well II: registration number 70GRKE A70-57) is published (Cordfunke 1972, 125-126 and 136-137), the red earthenware pipkin (70GRKK A70-140) is unpublished. Nothing is known about the house connected to this well.
26. Registration number 76NBG376.
27. Registration number 05VDA270BP, excavated at Voordam 13-15 in 2005. We could not link the cesspit to a specific contemporary premise.
28. They are found in registration numbers 94LUTBP and 94LAA12BP2.
29. Registration numbers 88LUT (oil lamp) and 94LAA4BP1AH (jug).
30. The complete records are kept in the Rijksarchief Noord-Holland acc.no. Kop.Coll.528-530, but there is also a copy in the Algemeen Rijksarchief, acc.no. Archief Financie Holland 515. The Regionaal Archief Alkmaar keeps an incomplete draft version: acc.no. Archief Stad Alkmaar voor 1815, no. 742.
31. Kohier van nieuwgetimmerde en vernieuwde huizen, in which changes in house values since 1654 were recorded until 1665 (Regionaal Archief Alkmaar acc.no. SA 715). Apparently a new draft was made in 1665, but this was lost in later times.
32. Regionaal Archief Alkmaar, acc.no. Archief Stad Alkmaar voor 1815, nos. 716 and 717.
33. This was the result of the project 'Historisch Kadaster Alkmaar' carried out by W.J. Van den Berg (Van den Berg 1998). Nowadays it is also available on the website www.archiefalkmaar.nl. In this manner also several other written sources and tax lists are accessible, starting from current addresses. I wish to thank Theo Peters and Gerard Laan of the municipal department of 'Geo-Information' (afdeling Geo-Info gemeente Alkmaar) for overlaying the map of 1832 onto present-day maps.
34. In a number of cases it proved impossible to link a cesspit to a specific house, for instance when it was found at the very end of a back yard, or on one of the often irregularly shaped plots near a street corner, or when the boundary of a plot was unclear for other reasons.

35. The sample was taken from every 10th plot number in the Land registry of 1832, which produced a total of 244 addresses. Thus the sample not only is representative statistically but also spatially. For a small number of buildings it proved impossible to match the 18th-century Verpondingen with the Land Registry of 1832. The sample therefore is of 220 buildings before 1730 and of 236 buildings in 1730 (of the latter, 218 buildings were described as a 'house').
36. This is a general impression based on sales figures of dozens of houses, but the data were gathered unsystematically in the course of several research projects.
37. This process of 'social segregation' was studied by Van den Berg, Van Leeuwen and Lesger 1998; and Van den Berg, Van Leeuwen and Lesger 2000.
38. There is yet another reason for the use of the numbers of houses rather than cesspits. Sometimes the relocation of a latrine (on account of building activities or changes in the garden lay-out) meant the construction of a new cesspit and we then excavate more than one cesspit belonging to a single house. Such changes are more frequent in the wealthier houses.
39. The deviation might be related to a small number of cheap buildings being used as stables, sheds, mews or warehouses. There is possibly also an underestimation of the number of small dwellings that shared cesspits.
40. In this table the comparison is made not with a sample from all buildings in 1730, but with the buildings that were actually described as houses (huis or kamer) in the Verpondingen. The other buildings were referred to as stables, sheds, mews, warehouses or industrial facilities such as a brewery, a tannery or a flour mill.
41. In this period, the sales contracts that were registered by a notary tend to describe the properties less accurately than in the 17th century, the mention of shared cesspits perhaps being omitted more often. The total quantity of cesspit finds seems to decrease in the 18th century. There might also have been a link with the disappearance of private alleys between the houses in favour of built-in corridors. These corridors and entrance halls became more representative, with neatly laid marble floors and fashionable wall decorations, e.g. with stucco. In this situation the emptying of a rubbish-filled cesspit and transporting the smelly waste through the corridor was more troublesome than it previously had been through the alley - perhaps this made people more reluctant to deposit rubbish in cesspits. The effect of such a process, however, would have resulted in fewer finds from the expensive premises rather than from the cheaper ones.

References

Berg, W.J. van den (1998). *Historisch Kadaster Alkmaar, 1: 1700-1914*. Utrecht (cd-rom).

Berg, W.J. van den, M.H.D. van Leeuwen and C. Lesger (1998). Residentiële segregatie in Hollandse steden. Theorie, methodologie en empirische bevindingen voor Alkmaar en Amsterdam, 16^e-19^e eeuw. *Tijdschrift voor sociale geschiedenis* 24. 402-436.

Berg, W.J. van den, M.H.D. van Leeuwen and C. Lesger (2000). Verschillen in kaart gebracht. De sociaal-ruimtelijke structuur van Alkmaar, 17de-19de eeuw. *Oud-Alkmaar* 24. 1-13.

Bitter, P. (1995). *Geworteld in de bodem*. Publikaties over de Alkmaarse Monumentenzorg en Archeologie 1. Alkmaar.

Bitter, P., J. Dijkstra, R. Roedema and R.P. van Wilgen (1997). *Wonen op Niveau; archeologisch, bouwhistorisch en historisch onderzoek van twee percelen aan de Langestraat*. Rapporten over de Alkmaarse Monumentenzorg en Archeologie, 5 and 5A. Alkmaar.

Bitter, P., S. Ostkamp and R. Roedema (2002). *De beerput als bron. Archeologische vondsten van het dagelijks leven in het oude Alkmaar*. Alkmaar.

Bitter, P., e.a. (2004). *De verborgen stad. 750 jaar Alkmaar onder de grond*, Alkmaar (tevens themanummer *Vormen from Vuur* 186/187).

Bitter, P., N. de Jong, R. Roedema and R. van Wilgen (2007). Rapporten over de Alkmaarse Monumentenzorg en Archeologie, 12, in preparation.

Bitter, P. in preparation (2008). Wealth and waste- aspects of a luxurious lifestyle in Alkmaar. In: M. Gläser (red.). *Lübecker Kolloquium zur Stadtarchäologie im Hanseraum, VI: Lifestyle. Luxus in der mittelalterlichen Stadt*. Lübeck.

Cordfunke, E.H.P. (1972). *Alkmaar, van boerderij tot middeleeuwse stad*. Alkmaar.

Groeneweg, G. (1999). Het 'spinpotje' van Hoeven: tijd voor een nieuwe visie. *Westerheem* 48. 121-130.

Hulshof, M. (1995). Om het gemeyne welvaren behoeff. Het leefmilieu in Gouda, Haarlem en Leiden circa 1400-1700. *Skript* 17. 226-275.

Jong-Lambregts, N. de (2004). Koken, braden en eten met aardewerk. In: P. Bitter e.a. *De verborgen stad. 750 jaar Alkmaar onder de grond*. Alkmaar. 30-47.

Kicken, D., A.M. Koldeweij and J.R. ter Molen (2000). *Gevonden voorwerpen. Opstellen over middeleeuwse archeologie voor H.J.E. van Beuningen; Lost and found. Essays on medieval archaeology for H.J.E. van Beuningen*. Rotterdam Papers 11. Rotterdam.

Ostkamp, S. e.a. (1998). *Afval van gorters, brouwers en een hospitaal. Archeologisch onderzoek aan het Wortelsteegplein*. Rapporten over de Alkmaarse Monumentenzorg en Archeologie 6. Alkmaar.

Ostkamp, S., R. Roedema and R. van Wilgen (2001). *Gebruikt en gebroken. Vijf eeuwen bewoning op drie lokaties in het oostelijk stadsdeel*. Rapporten over de Alkmaarse Monumentenzorg en Archeologie 10. Alkmaar.

Ostkamp, S., R. Roedema and R.P. van Wilgen (2002). The introduction of majolica in Alkmaar. In: J. Veeckman e.a. (red.). *Majolica and glass from Italy to Antwerp and beyond. The transfer of technology in the 16th- early 17th century*. Antwerpen. 449-464.

Ostkamp, S. (2003). De introductie van porselein in de Nederlanden. *Vormen uit vuur* 180/181. 14-29.

Pijzel-Domisse, J. (2000). *Het Hollandse pronkpoppenhuis. Interieur en huishouden in de 17de en 18de eeuw*. Amsterdam/Zwolle.

Pluis, J. (1979). *Kinderspelen op tegels*. Assen.

Roedema, R. (2004). 'Een beerput bij de Zijpse kamer'. Een archeologische verkenning van de stadhuistuin. In: J.C.M. Cox e.a.. *"Onse heerlijcke Stadt-huijs binnen Alckmaer". De geschiedenis van het stadhuis van Alkmaar*. Alkmaar. 83-94 and 174-176.

Schama, S. (1988). *Overvloed en onbehagen. De Nederlandse cultuur in de Gouden Eeuw*. Amsterdam.

Vis, G.N.M. (1996). Van *'vulliscuyl' tot Huisvuilcentrale; vuilnis en afval en hun verwerking in Alkmaar en omgeving van de middeleeuwen tot heden*. Alkmaar.

Willemsen, A. (1998). *Kinder delijt. Middeleeuws speelgoed in de Nederlanden*. Nijmeegse Kunsthistorische Studies VI. Nijmegen.

Willemsen, A. (2000). Poppegoed precies bekeken. Verzameling van, herkomst en functie van loodtinnen miniatuurtjes. In: D. Kicken, A.M. Koldeweij and J.R. ter Molen. *Gevonden voorwerpen. Opstellen over middeleeuwse archeologie voor H.J.E. van Beuningen; Lost and found. Essays on medieval archaeology for H.J.E. van Beuningen*. Rotterdam Papers 11. Rotterdam. 347-355.

Willemsen, A. (2003). 'Poppe-goed en anders niet'. Speelgoed in Holland in de 16de en 17de eeuw. *Holland* 35. 80-91.

List of find assemblages from the 17th and 18th centuries (until 2005).

The excavations are listed chronologically, as the site identification code starts with the year of excavation. Summarized are: the current house adress connected to the assemblage, the Land Registry code of 1832, the rent value before and in 1730, find registration number and a brief mention of the miniature items (dates in brackets).

s2 = salt-glazed stoneware, r = red earthenware, w = white earthenware, we = Weser earthenware, m = majolica, f = faience (Netherlands), p = porcelain, ir = industrial redware, py = pipeclay, and gl = glass; min = miniature. Sometimes the prototype can be determined as a type in the *Classification system for late and post-medieval ceramics and glass*.

site registration code Alkmaar	present-day address	find complex (find registration number: date)	Land Registry 1832	rent value	miniature objects (date)
86DST	Doelenstraat 1	cesspit (86DSTBP: 17)	Kad.A291	rent value house before 1730 fl.200, in 1730 zero (since 1699 corn grinders' guildhouse)	r-min colander (after r-lek-5; 17A); r-min jug (17A); w-min pipkin (after w-gra-23; 17B); f-min jug (17B)
88LUT	Luttik Oudorp 100	cesspit (88LUTBP1: 17-18A)	Kad.B176	house rented in 1730 fl.150	w-min oil lamp (17B); pewter miniature huckle (17B-18A)
88VRO	Vrouwenstraat 6	waste pit (88VRO1: c 1650-1670)	Kad.A1138 +A1136 +A1141 +A1142	rent value before 1730 fl.149,40 (inn Sint Hubertus)	r-min oil lamp (after r-oli-2; 17c)
89ADA2	Achterdam 2	cesspit (89ADA2: 17ac)	Kad.B116	rent value house before 1730 fl.85,60	r-min cooking pot (after r-gra-47; 17bc)
89LUT58	Luttik Oudorp 58	cesspit (89LUTBP: 18B-19a)	Kad.B215	rent value house 1730 self-used estimated at fl.85	pewter miniature dish, teapot, 3 bowls, brazier; wooden miniature bowl (18B)
89TUR	Turfmarkt 1	cesspit (89TURBP: 17c-19a)	Kad.B1153 +B1108 +B1109 +B1110 +B1111	rent value 1730 self-used estimated at fl.460 (house and brewery De Lelie, since 1707 Starrecroon)	two w-min teapots (18A); pewter miniature chafing dish and dish (18)
90BIE	Bierkade 18/19	cesspit (90BIEBP: 17bc)	Kad.B584	rent value house before 1730 fl.100	r-min fire cover (17bc)
90BRE	Breedstraat / western corner of Pastoorsteeg	cesspit (90BRE88BP4: 17d-18c)	Kad.A664a bis	rent value of kamer unknown (tax combined with main house on Langestraat)	r-min skillet (after r-bak-19); r-min colander; 3x r-min tripod skillet (after r-stk-2); s2-min jug (after s2-kan-68): all 17d/18A
90BRE	Langestraat 57	cesspit (90BRE70BP3: 18b-	Kad.A663 +665+666	rent value house 1730 self-used estimated at fl.180	w-min cuspidor; w-min chafing dish (both 18bc)
90MAR	Marktstraat (formerly Korte Nieuwesloot)	cesspit (90MAR2: 18th-century layer)	unknown	unknown	p-min jug or vase (18a)
90VER	Verdronkenoord 53-55	cesspit (90VERBP: 17B-18A)	Kad.B655	rent value house before 1730 fl.104	r-min skillet (16d-17A)
92LAN	Langestraat 113	cesspit (92LANBP2: 16d-19)	Kad.A751	rent value house before 1730 fl.152, in 1730 rented fl.160	gl-min berkemeier (16d-17a); r-min chamber pot (18A); w-min brazier (18A)

site registration code Alkmaar	present-day address	find complex (find registration number: date)	Land Registry 1832	rent value	miniature objects (date)
92LAN 93LAN	Langestraat 115/117	cesspits (93LANBP5B: 15,	Kad.A750	rent value house before 1730 fl.78 (was rented), in 1730 rented fl.110	93LANBP5A: r-min pipkin (15d-16A); 92LANBP1: r-min fire cover (16d-17A) 93LAN BP1: w-min porringer; p-min vase (both 18A)
92VDA	Dijk 29/31	cesspit (92VDA2:	Kad.B104-O+105	rent value house before 1730 fl.120	r-min dish; r-min colander (both 16bc)
92WOR	Wortelsteeg	cesspit (92WORBP1: 18)	Kad.B248g	rent value of kamer unknown (tax combined with brewery Het Lam)	r-min chamber pot (18)
92WOR	Wortelsteeg	cesspit (92WORBP2: 16d-17A)	Kad.B248b	rent value before 1730 fl.88 (house and grain mill)	r-min tripod cooking pot (16B-17A)
93LAN	Langestraat 119	cesspit (93LANBP2: 17b-18d)	Kad.A749	rent value house before 1730 fl.44	gl-min beaker (after gl-bek-15; 17bc)
93LANX	Langestraat 103	cesspit (93LANBP6: 15A-18B)	Kad.A754	rent value house before 1730 fl.80	r-min skillet (after r-bak-4; 16B/17a)
94FNI	Luttik Oudorp 79	cesspit (94FNIBP: 17A-18A)	Kad.B288 +B306	rent value house before 1730 fl.92	w-min porringer (17)
94LAA	Oudegracht 218	cesspit (94LAA4BP1: 17A-18B)	Kad.A879 +A854	rent value house in 1730 fl.264	w-min jug (17B)
94LAA	Ruitersteeg (eastern side)	cesspit (94LAA12BP2: 17ac)	unknown	unknown	m-min majolica fire cover (17A); r-min porringer (after r-kop-2; 17ac); fragments of pipe-clay lobed dish, jug and handle of a bowl (all 17bc)
94LUT	Luttik Oudorp 18	cesspit (94LUTBP: 17b-18d)	Kad.B241 +B241	house rented in 1730 fl.100	r-min teapot and lid (after r-the-6 and r-dek-22); w-min green tripod skillet (after w-stk-9); w-min skillet; f-min chamber pot; pipe-clay: lobed dish, jug, garden vase and fragments of cuspidor, bowl and tray; 3 pewter bowls (all
94RTV	Ritsevoort 16-18	cesspit (94RTVBP: 17A-18B)	Kad.A1132	house rented in 1730 fl.72	w-min fragment; s2-min jug Westerwald (both 18)
95HBS	Verdronkenoord 139	cesspit (95HBSIIBP: 15ac en 17bc)	Kad.B722	rent value house before 1730 fl.136	r-min pipkin; r-min colander; f-min jug (after f-kan-2); gl-min roemer (all 17bc)
95LIN	Vrouwestraat	waste pit (95LIN5: 16c)	unknown	unknown	w-min fire cover fragment (16c)
97LAN	Langestraat 73	cesspits (97LAN3BP2: 16a-17a; 97LAN7BP5: 18ad)	Kad.A657	rent value house before 1730 fl.144, in 1730 self-used estimated at fl.120	97LAN3BP2AD: gl-min berkemeier (16B-17a) 97LAN7BP5: w-min lightgreen warming stand with teapot and lid; 5x p-min vases/bottles; 2 pewter bowls and 1 dish (all 18)
98BLO	Bloemstraat (eastern side)	waste and ash pit (98BLO45: 17A)	Kad.B936	rent value house before 1730 fl.21,60	r-min pipkin fragment (17A)
98LAA	Koorstraat 37	cesspits (98LAA160BP1: 16d/17a, 98LAA174BP3: 17)	Kad.A783	rent value house before 1730 fl.70	98LAA174BP3: w-min green colander (17a) 98LAA160BP1: f-min dish (after f-bor-10; imitation of kraakporcelain; 17a)
99BLO	Bloemstraat (eastern side)	waterput (99BLO12: 18B-19a)	Kad.B929	house rented in 1730 fl.22	r-min porringer (Friesland?; 18B)
99BLO	Bloemstraat (eastern side)	waste pit (99BLO29: 17a)	Kad.B930	rent value kamer before 1730 fl.24,80	w-min pipkin (after w-gra-10 green); r-min skillet (both 17a)
99RUI	Laat 221	waste in former well (99RUI5BP3: 17c)	Kad.A840	rent value house before 1730 fl.52	w-min porringer (17c)
00LAN	Langestraat 16	cesspit (00LANBP1: 17-19A)	Kad.A470	rent value house before 1730 fl.136; rent value of self-used house in 1751 lowered to fl. 72,93	r-min fire cover (17A); w-min skillet (18B); ir-min cup (19A)
01LAN	Langestraat 64-66 (midden)	cesspit (01LAN104BP8:	Kad.A448	rent value big house before 1730 fl.328,56	r-min porringer (after r-kop-2; 17A)
01VDA	Voordam 13A	cesspit (01VDABP2: 17b-19a)	Kad.B146	rent value house in 1730 self-used estimated at fl.160 (from before 1737 until 1817 silver	pewter miniature dish and goblet (17B-18)
02BIE	Bierkade 17	cesspit (02BIEBP: 17B-18)	Kad.B583	rent value house before 1730 fl.159, house rented in 1730 for only fl.45 (!)	we-min pot (16d-17a); r-min tripod cooking pot (17d/18a)
02HKS	Hekelstraat 19	cesspit (02HKSBP: 17)	Kad.B428	rent value house in 1730 self-used estimated at fl.42	w-min pot (17); 2x p-min vases Kangxi (17B)
02KRS	Koorstraat 59	cesspit (02KRSBP1: 17ac)	Kad.A850 +A849	rent value before 1730 fl.210 (house and inn De Rode Leeuw)	r-min skillet (17A); r-min dish (after r-bor-6; 17ac)

site registration code Alkmaar	present-day address	find complex (find registration number: date)	Land Registry 1832	rent value	miniature objects (date)
02ODG	Oudegracht 26	cesspits (02ODG43BP: 16d-17c; 02ODG46BP: 17a-18c)	Kad.B918 +B891-Z	rent value before 1730 fl.739,80 (house and brewery Het Zwaard/Wapen van Haarlem)	02ODG43BP: w-min jug (after w-kan-16); w-min pipkin; r-min pot (all 17bc); 02ODG46BP: r-min colander (after r-lek-5); r-min tripod cooking pot (after r-gra-70); gl-min beaker (after gl-bek-15)(all 17bc)
02ZDA	Zijdam 5/6	cesspit (02ZDABP: 17-18A)	Kad.B137	rent value house before 1730 fl.114, in 1730 house rented fl.120	r-min porringer (after r-kop-2; 17bc); f-min cup (after f-kop-9 crow's cup; 18A)
03KWE	Koningsweg 35	cesspit (03KWE11/12BP1: 17d-18a)	Kad.A203-oost	house rented in 1730 fl.40	r-min fragment (17d-18a)
03KWE	Koningsweg 29/31	cesspit (03KWE39BP3: 16d-19A)	Kad.A204+205	two kamers under one roof with a shared cesspit; in 1730 A205 rented fl.22 en A204 self-used fl.25.	r-min tripod cooking pot (17d/18); r-min porringer (after r-kop-4; 17B/18A); w-min skillet (17d/18A); w-min soap/salt (17d/18A); w-min porringer (18); p-min vase (17B/18a)
04LAA	Oudegracht 230	cesspit (04LAA9BP1: 17a-18d)	Kad.A844	rent value house before 1730 fl.67	r-min jug (17)
04SCHW	Schermerweg (82)	ditch next to house (04SCHW25: 18A)	unknown	unknown (house and shipyard in 17th and 18th century)	w-min chafing dish (after w-kmf-4); w-min bowl; 2x w-min porringers; w-min chamber pot; w-min colander; w-min chafing dish; 3x r-min porringers (all 18A)
04SCHW	Schermerweg (82)	waste pit (04SCHW40: 17a)	unknown	unknown (house and wood saw mill 1593-c 1640)	we-min pipkin (after we-gra-2; 16d-17a)
05ODG	Laat 215 or Laat 217	waste pit (05ODG15: 18B)	unknown	unknown (backyard behind two houses)	w-min brazier (18B)
05ODG	Oudegracht 182	waste pit (05ODG23: 17b)	Kad.A876	rent value big house before 1730 fl.212,15	r-min pipkin (after r-gra-41); 2x r-min pipkins; r-min skillet (after r-bak-2); r-min chamber pot (after r-pis-5); r-min basket (all 17b)
05VDA	Voordam (13)	cesspit (05VDABP6)	unknown	unknown	r-min pipkin (16d/17A)
05VDA	Voordam (13)	cesspit (05VDA270BP)	unknown	unknown	r-min pipkin (after r-gra-22), r-min chamber pot (after r-pis-3) (both 15d/16a)

Late medieval bling-bling

A collection of decorated leather and metalbase mounts in the National Museum of Antiquities in Leiden

Annemarieke Willemsen

with contributions by Jasper Luijendijk and Marieke van Werven

*Alle gemene menschen draghen
hare gordele met silver beslagen.*

(All common people wear their belts mounted with silver)
Spiegel der Sonden (15th century), vs. 11563 ff.

Introduction
When groups of reenactors dress up to look 'medieval' they often unintentionally create a kind of 'eco' look of that period: coarse, fairly colourless, unadorned fabrics with accessories such as belts and bags of unworked leather, in their natural shades of brown, and everything kept simple. Illustrations and surviving clothing and accessories however present an entirely different picture of medieval fashion: bright, contrasting colours, costly, lavishly decorated fabrics and belts and bags adorned with all kinds of golden and silver-coloured mounts (fig. 1). Many of those illustrations of course had a (double) meaning, just like texts such as the *Spiegel der Sonden* (Mirror of Sins) quoted above: to scorn people who decked themselves out in such finery, or at the very least present such behaviour as typical of a specific group such as courtiers or *nouveaux riches*. A large, and so far unpublished, collection of belts and belt mounts made of modest materials that were found in the southern part of the Netherlands shows that even common late medieval men and women decorated their accessories with a lot of shiny mounts, with which they deliberately or unintentionally impressed the people they met in the street. Their adornments varied from rivets via fake coins and imitation coats of arms to entire texts: the 'bling-bling' of the Late Middle Ages.*

The Mackenbach collection
In the spring of 2006 the *Rijksmuseum van Oudheden* (National Museum of Antiquities) in Leiden purchased a large collection of 'belt mounts' from P. Mackenbach, a resident of the Dutch town of Breda. The collection comprises 62 belts and other pieces of leather adorned with metal mounts (fig. 2) and 1002 isolated mounts, all differing from one another (fig. 3).[1] The remains date from the 14th, 15th and 16th centuries. About 90% of the finds come from the Dutch province of Zeeland, the remaining approximately 10% from the Dutch town of Dordrecht. The collection was created by Mr Mackenbach, an enthusiastic amateur archaeologist who spent many decades exploring the Verdronken Land area of Zuid-Beveland (in the province of Zeeland) with his metal detector. Between 200 and 300 mounts in his collection he found himself – in his words mainly around Nieuwlande, Tolsende and Oud-Rilland. The majority he however bought or obtained through exchange with other searchers. Those finds come from other parts of Zeeland, too, and possibly from elsewhere. In

view of the tremendous quantity of small metal finds known from Nieuwlande it is likely that many of the mounts will come from that area. Many of the leather finds come from piles of dumped soil from an excavation that was carried out in the context of a building project in Statenplein in Dordrecht in 1997. After the soil of the top six metres had been investigated by the *Dordts Archeologisch Centrum*, the rest of the soil was removed and dumped; it is known that several metal-detector searchers found a lot of objects in that soil.

At the time of the collection's purchase the museum considered the ethical aspects of a collection obtained with the aid of a metal detector, consulted various experts and had some off-the-record talks. In the end it was decided to purchase the collection because of its importance, the comprehensive survey it provides and the fact that it would make the Dutch archaeological finds accessible to the public and available for study. It was also felt that this collection of late medieval 'belt mounts' would constitute an interesting supplement to the museum's existing collection, which includes many early medieval belt mounts; the Mackenbach collection shows that belt mounts continued to be made and used for many more centuries. Mr

02 Belts with mounts shortly after the purchase of the collection. Photo: A. Willemsen.

01 The people in this wedding procession are wearing lavishly decorated belts, jewellery and a belt pouch adorned with mounts, as tokens of their wealth. Simon Bening *et al., Breviarium Grimani, c.* 1510. Venice, Biblioteca Marciana, ms 7531, f 4 ff. Photo from *The Grimani Breviary* 1972: Plate 7.

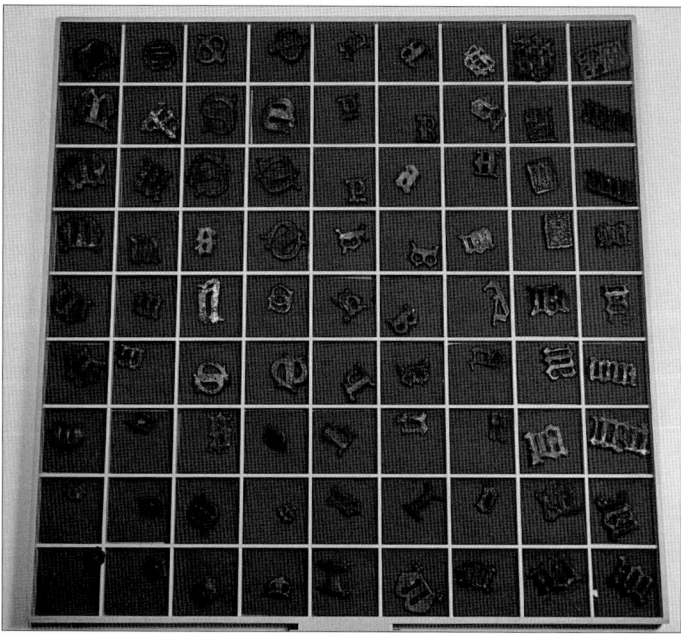

03 A drawer with mounts (letter combinations) shortly after the purchase of the collection; the entire collection has meanwhile been repacked. Photo: A. Willemsen.

Mackenbach himself moreover very much wanted his collection to go to a museum.

For this article we pushed the discussion about metal detectors aside and decided to value the remains as they are – an important group of finds which has so far received insufficient attention, but which gives an impression of the tastes and imagery of common people in the Late Middle Ages. Here we want to present the vast quantity of ornamental mounts – which, it was soon found, did not all adorn belts –, determine their function and place them in an archaeological and iconographical context. To this end we compared our collection with the large collections of metal finds from the Verdronken Land area in the *Provinciaal Depot van Bodemvondsten Zeeland* and Museum Boijmans Van Beuningen[2] (fig. 4) and with more precisely dated finds from the city centre of Amsterdam. We used the chapter entitled 'Mounts' in the publication focusing on the Dress Accessories in the Museum of London as our guide.[3] Using a number of standard works we made a survey of illustrations of mounts in late medieval art and we consulted the *Digitale Bibliotheek der Nederlandse Literatuur* (Digital Library of Dutch Literature)[4] to obtain a first impression of the role played by these objects in Middle Dutch literature. All this is but a start: in the future we hope to extend our study of this tremendous reference collection of late medieval Dutch ornamental mounts to comparable finds elsewhere, our ultimate aim being to obtain more, and more finely tuned answers to the most interesting questions raised by these objects: who wore them and why?

The find context
Mounts from the Verdronken Land area

Als men schreef duysent vijf hondert ende dertich, den vijfden dach Novembris, 't wordt u ontdeckt,
Doen ghebeurder jammer ende druck seer smertich, ten tijden van de Keyser Carolus die vijfde effect,
Eenen grooten hooghen vloedt isser ghestreckt over geheel Zeelandt, deur 't groot mishagen,
Sach men menich mensche weenen, kermen, en deerlijck klagen
(On the fifth day of November in the year one thousand five hundred and thirty a sorrowful affliction occurred during the reign of the Emperor Charles the Fifth; a tremendous flood covered the whole of Zeeland and the catastrophe caused many people to cry, wail and moan bitterly).[5] This quote from the chronicle of Jan Jansse Reigersberg of 1551 refers to the storm flood of 1530, which took place on *Sint Felix quade saterdag* (Saint Felix's ill-fated Saturday) and wiped the greater part of Zuid-Beveland off the map. The great majority of the small metal (belt) mounts in the Mackenbach collection come from this area, which was later to become known as *het Verdronken Land van Zuid-Beveland* (the Drowned Land of Zuid-Beveland).

The history of this area reflects the occupants' long struggle against the water. The earliest mention of a storm flood dates from 838. After the storm floods of 1014 and 1134, systematic dike construction began in the eastern part of Zuid-Beveland and on the island of Rilland. A separate department was established to manage the dikes, their maintenance, land reclamation and drainage. The villages were obliged to cooperate and to pay for the dikes' construction and maintenance under the principle of *elc sinen dike* (each his own dike). Landowners were made responsible for the maintenance of the stretches of dike placed under their care and the associated land.[6]

Between 1134 and 1530 Zeeland, parts of the province of Zuid-Holland and Flanders were ravaged by more than 45 storm floods. The St Felix flood of 5 November 1530 affected the area to the west of Bergen op Zoom, all the polders from Bergen op Zoom down to Antwerp and the islands of the provinces of Zeeland and Zuid-Holland. In total, 117 villages were drowned; the town of Reimerswaal also suffered the consequences of the catastrophe; for decades after the flood it was an island contained within its own walls until the last occupants moved elsewhere in 1631.[7] Salt marshes formed in the eastern part of Zuid-Beveland and conditions in this area have remained virtually unchanged until today. The drowned villages are only accessible at low tide.[8]

The remains of the drowned villages and the town of Reimerswaal and incidental finds aroused the curiosity of amateurs and scientists. In 1971 and 1972 the *Nederlandse Jeugdbond tot Bestudering van de Geschiedenis* (NJBG; Dutch Youth Organisation for the Study of History) carried out research at the site of Reimerswaal, and since 2002 the *Stichting Cultureel Erfgoed Zeeland* (SCEZ; Foundation for the Cultural Heritage of Zeeland) has been conducting archaeological and historical research in the context of its Drowned Villages Project.[9] The *Archeologische Werkgemeenschap voor Nederland* (Archaeological Association of the Netherlands) performs research in collaboration with the SCEZ and also carries out projects independently – mostly augering and ground surveys, for example in the villages of Valkenisse and Rilland.[10] Archaeological activities have been carried out in Zuid-Beveland outside the official organisations, too. Day trippers and 'treasure hunters' have explored several villages in the Verdronken Land in search of skulls and interesting ancient objects. The introduction of metal detectors in particular prompted the formation of private collections, with the associated loss of valuable information on the finds' contexts. In 1990 parts of Zuid-Beveland were placed under the protection of the Conservation Act and the public was no longer allowed access to them. And in 1991 the Rijksdienst voor het Oudheidkundig Bodemonderzoek (ROB, State Service for Archaeological Investigations) banned the use of metal detectors there.

Although most areas are no longer accessible for archaeological research or treasure hunting, the drowned villages have lost nothing of their original appeal. Even today, the church spires which for many years projected above the surface of the water and served as beacons for sailors (the only one still surviving today is the Stompetoren on Schouwen-Duiveland) appeal to people's imagination. In 2009 a monument commemorating the drowned villages in Zeeland will be erected on the Oosterscheldedijk, near Colijnsplaat. The monument – a tall tower that will at specific times emit the sounds of a storm and people shouting – was inspired by the church towers. The times in question are symbolic interpretations of the years in which the floods took place, for example 14.21 (St Elizabeth flood), 19.53 (North Sea flood) and also 15.30, referring to the year of the St Felix flood.[11]

Leather from Statenplein in Dordrecht

Most of the belts and other pieces of leather in the Mackenbach collection come from the dumped soil from an excavation that the department of archaeology of the municipality of Dordrecht (DAC) carried out in 1997 under the supervision of Johan Hendriks at Statenplein, a square in the town centre.[12] The square was undergoing redevelopment to turn it into a shopping centre incorporating new buildings and an underground car park. The deep digging work implied large-scale excavations, because this part of town was assumed to contain remains from its earliest history. In the 13th and 14th centuries Dordrecht evolved into the largest and most important town in Holland – the western part of what is now the Netherlands. Its great wealth it owed to tolls and other privileges that Count Floris V granted the town around 1300. Dordrecht is of great importance for medieval archaeology. Many excavation campaigns, including several large-scale projects, have been carried out in the city centre, where vast quantities of remains have been recovered from waterlogged contexts and the thick layers of soil that have been deposited here over the centuries to raise the ground level. Among the remains are notorious amounts of leather: between 1969 and 2004 alone, 25,000 shoes were found.[13]

The deepest layers investigated at Statenplein contained remains of timber houses from the first half of the 14th century. The houses had a back yard enclosed by a ditch. It is thought that a house-*cum*-workshop of a leather craftsman that was found here along with its yard and a refuse pit date from the same occupation phase. This pit yielded many leather finds, some of them quite spectacular, such as a circular cover of possibly a small shield or a drum, decorated with mythical creatures,[14] and waste from the manufacture of knife sheaths. In addition, vast quantities of metal objects were found in Statenplein – both during the official excavation and in the dumped soil – and some slates with drawings scratched in them. Analysis of the botanical remains has yielded an impression of the wealth of the earliest occupants of this town square. When the large-scale research, whose results have not yet all been published, had been completed, more soil was dug out to a depth of several metres below the lowest examined horizon and dumped elsewhere in Dordrecht. It is that dumped soil that contained the pieces of leather discussed here. Like the lowest occupation remains, they can be dated to the period 1300-1350. The pieces of leather were found with the aid of metal detectors, which responded to the metal mounts adorning the leather. We may assume that the dumped soil also contained quite a lot of leather without mounts, which was not traced by the detector users.

The leather collection

The leather collection comprises 58 belts and parts of belts plus four pieces of leather that did definitely not form part of belts, and will be discussed separately below as possible parts of bags. The remains do not include any complete belts, but there are many belt ends with a strap end or a buckle (fig. 4). This is probably due to the way in which they were found – with detectors that responded to the metal – and the collector's interest in the mounts on the belts. It is moreover quite common for belts found in excavations to be damaged in one way or another, because they were discarded for a reason, and it is known that the belt parts worn on the front of the body were adorned more than those worn on the back. The fragmentary condition makes it difficult to infer the functions of the individual belts. In this article pieces smaller than 7 cm will be called 'parts of belts' and the term 'belt' will be used for longer pieces. A remarkable feature of the collection is the wide diversity of mounts, forms of attachment and dimensions. They will be discussed per category below.

Buckles and strap ends

All but four of the pieces of leather are adorned with mounts. One of the exceptions is part of a belt with a length of 3.0 cm and a width of 0.8 cm and the others are three parts of belts with a buckle. One of the latter, with a length of 5.3 cm (number 4.15), has a circular buckle with a diameter of 3.0 cm and a pin; the buckle is attached to the belt by means of two rivets that are finished with a small plate on the inside of the belt (fig. 5). The leather strap has been stretched heavily; it might well have been part of a dog's leash. One thin belt (4.17) with a length of 15.8 cm and a width of 1.05 cm has a double looped buckle with oval loops and a pin. Buckled leather belts were often used for fastening bags, purses and shoes. Of a somewhat more luxurious design is a belt with a circular buckle decorated with two oval lobes; there is no pin (4.18b). The associated plate has an engraved ornamentation (fig. 6) and twelve small holes set at equal distances from one another. The collection also contains a belt with an oval buckle and one with a square buckle (4.36b and 4.37). Both buckles are attached to a plate that is fixed to the belt with two and one rivets. The square one has a short pin, that held the hanging belt end in place. Three belts have a strap end at the end; two are of lead/tin (4.36a and c, see fig. 50) and one is of a copper alloy (4.11a); in this case the spot where the belt was bent downwards is still visible. The strap ends are rectangular and taper to a point. The copper strap end consists of two plates between which

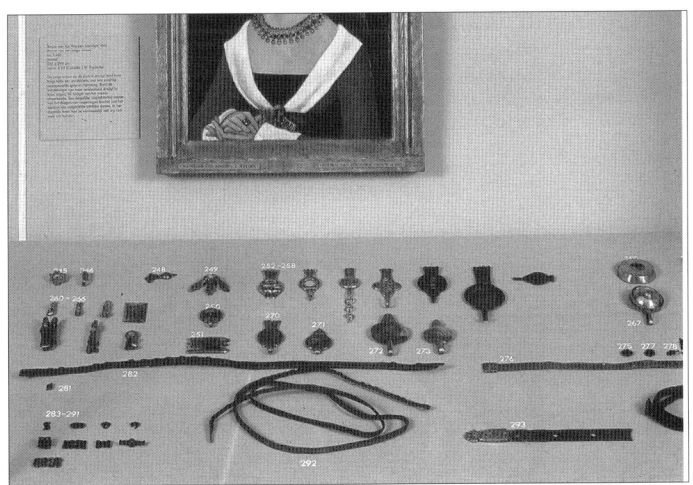

04 Dress accessories and belts adorned with mounts from the Van Beuningen-de Vriese collection at the exhibition entitled *Haken en ogen* in Museum Boijmans Van Beuningen in 1994. Photo: BVB/Tom Haartsen.

06 Belt with a decorated buckle and plate (4.18b). Photo: RMO/Anneke de Kemp.

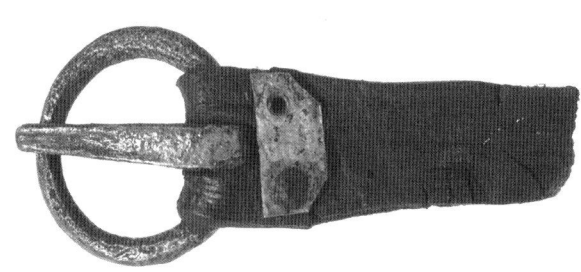

05 Belt with a buckle (4.15). Photo: Restaura.

07 Belt end adorned with a brass heart-shaped mount (4.11b). Photo: RMO/Anneke de Kemp.

the belt is clamped; one layer or leather survives between them, with room for a second layer that is now lost. Two other strap ends are rivetted. A fourth short end piece has a heart-shaped mount (4.11b) attached by means of integrated pins (fig. 7) beaten down on the inside of the belt. This heart must have been heavy enough to pull the belt end down. A similar heart-shaped mount from Amsterdam is known to date from 1575-1600;[15] this mount was not found in association with any leather remains.

Reinforced belts

One leather belt with a length of 16.5 cm and a width of 0.95 cm (4.26, fig. 8) is adorned with eleven copper ornamental rivets that are held in place by a plate on the inside of the belt. An unusual feature of this belt is the bone ring at the end. The ring has a diameter of 2.35 cm and is decorated with a horizontal line along its entire outer side. There is also a notch on the outer side. We assume that this is a connecting ring, used to link different parts of belts or to suspend something from, for example a knife (sheath) or a purse. A different system is represented by a belt with a length of 16.5 cm and a width of 0.8 cm (4.24) with two rectangular mounts with a rectangular hole in the middle. Under the mounts are two short leather ends with anchor-shaped reinforcements that can be inserted back through the groove and twsited; they were held in place with a hinged bar on top of the mount. Something could then be inserted through the resulting loop, or suspend from it (fig. 9). One of the broadest belts in the collection is 2.1 cm wide and 16.5 cm long (4.33). Two rectangular mounts are set on the belt around openings that are also rectangular. Also visible on the belt are the equidistant impressions of four bars, of the same width as the belt. The rivets and plates have survived on the inside of the belt. The mounts around the openings and the bars were both primarily intended as means of reinforcement (fig. 10), maybe because something pended from this part of the belt. How holes in a belt were reinforced can be seen in what is known as the Nuremberg *Hausbuch*; on the bench in the depiction lie belts with holes in them, the belt maker is busy attaching a ring and hanging next to him is a finished reinforced belt (fig. 11). A narrower variant (4.23f) is part of a belt measuring 3.6 cm x 1.0 cm that is reinforced with three bar-shaped mounts that are likewise of the same width as the belt.

Belts with rivetted patterns

Very common are belts with mounts shaped like hobnails made of a copper alloy cap attached with a rivet. Characteristic of these belts is that the mounts usually span the entire width of the belt and are attached to the belt close together or even without any space between them. This was observed on a number of belts and on some 0.5-cm-wide parts of belts whose mounts are affected and discoloured by corrosion (4.30a - 4.30j). These belts were found together in the same pit; several parts were tied together, suggesting intensive reuse (fig. 12). The most complete belt in this category is 37.2 cm long and 0.7 cm wide

09 Belt with a loop that can be opened and closed (4.24). Photo: RMO/Anneke de Kemp.

08 Belt with ornamental rivets and a bone ring (4.26). Photo: RMO/Anneke de Kemp.

10 Belt with rectangular reinforced holes and impressions of bar-shaped mounts that were attached on the inside (4.33). Photo: RMO/Anneke de Kemp.

(4.32). It has 31 square mounts hammered into round caps; eight mounts are missing because they slipped off the thin nails. Here again the mounts are of the same width as the belt; their golden colour is still intact. The aforementioned belt with a bone ring (4.26, fig. 8) is also a good example of this category.

The hobnails of some belts are creatively arranged in patterns (4.20 and 4.35, fig. 13). The belts in question are 10.0 cm and 39.0 cm long and 0.9 cm and 1.1 cm wide. The mounts on both belts are small caps attached to the belt with nails. The caps have a diameter of 0.4 cm. On both belts the hobnails are arranged in a pattern of flowers with six petals and a heart. The spaces between the flowers are filled with between two and six hobnails. These finds again underline the importance of surviving leather belts; without the leather we would have had only a handful of rivets and would not have known about the patterns. Find number 4.20 is also a belt end, with two oval rings attached to the belt by means of a plate. The rings may have served as a kind of buckle, with the belt being passed back through them, or they may have been connecting rings.

Belts with mounts

Belts were adorned by using functional mounts for decorative purposes. Decorated belts can be admired in medieval sculptures, in which the mounts are often rendered in relief, for example on the figures of the Well of Moses carved by Claus Sluter (fig. 14). As we can infer from isolated mount finds, flower designs were very popular in the Middle Ages, and we find this theme expressed on belts in different forms. Part of a belt (4.23i, fig. 15) with a length of 5.8 cm and a width of

11 A belt maker reinforces the holes in a belt. *Hausbuch der Nürnberger Zwölfbrüderstiftung*, 15th/16th century. Nuremberg, *Stadtbibliothek*, Amb. 317.2°, f 27r. Photo: Stadtbibliothek Nuremberg.

12 Parts of belts, some of them knotted, with rivetted ornamentation (4.30). Photo: Restaura.

13 Belt with hobnail patterns and a double ring (4.20). Photo: RMO/Anneke de Kemp.

14 Moses wearing a belt adorned with rectangular plates; visible on the left is Isaiah wearing a belt with circular mounts and a pouch and holding a book decorated with mounts. Claus Sluter, *Well of Moses*, 1395-1403; Dijon, Chartreuse de Champmol. Photo from Ridderbos & Van Veen 1995: 244.

2.4 cm contains two ornamental rivets. Beneath the rivets is a thin metal plate shaped like a flower with eight petals. There are also flowers with four petals attached to a belt with a rivet (4.34). The belt in question is 34.3 cm long and 0.9 cm wide and has 16 mounts set at varying distances from one another. It is the end of a belt of which only the engraved plate and the pin survive; the buckle loop has disappeared (fig. 16). The collection contains a few parts of belts adorned with circular mounts with a finely beaded edge. There are also several isolated finds of such mounts. Worthy of separate mention within this category is find number 4.22a (fig. 17) – part of a belt consisting of two layers of leather with stitching holes along the edges; the stitching may have been meant to reinforce the small strap of thin leather. Still surviving on the leather is one circular mount with a beaded edge that was attached via an integrated pin. Square mounts, bars on rectangular engraved plates and triangular mounts surviving on parts of belts are all differently shaped variants of the ornamental mounts.

One belt has pendant mounts (4.25, fig. 18). The belt is 14.5 cm long and 0.7 cm wide and has four bar-shaped mounts. Beneath two of those bars is a metal loop from which is suspended a three-lobed ring pendant, possibly connected to a purse;[16] the bars are attached to the belt by means of a rivet. The longest belt in the collection (4.39) is 86.0 cm long and

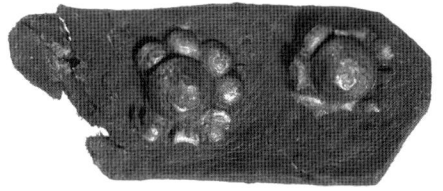

16 Belt with four-lobed flower-shaped mounts (4.34). Photo: RMO/Anneke de Kemp.

15 Belt with flower-shaped mounts (4.23i). Photo: RMO/Anneke de Kemp.

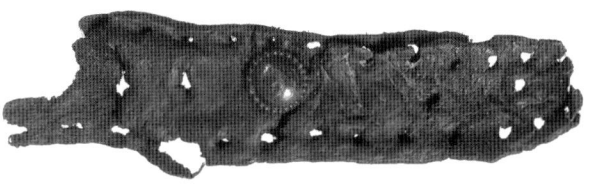

17 Belt with stitching holes and a mount with a beaded edge (4.22a). Photo: RMO/Anneke de Kemp.

1.4 cm wide. Attached to the belt are six openwork rectangular mounts. The remains of another five similar mounts are still visible. The mounts are attached to the belt by a rivet and a plate. The collection contains isolated mounts of this type, too. Interestingly, the belt has been cut 'right through' at six points. On average, the notches are 2.5 cm long (fig. 19).

Belts with figurative mounts

The finds of isolated figurative mounts (rendered below) outnumber the figurative mounts surviving on belts. Only one belt and two parts of belts in this collection are adorned with figurative mounts. The belt (4.9) is 9.2 cm long and 1.2 cm wide. Its five circular mounts are decorated with a star; the sixth mount is ring-shaped. A remarkable feature of this belt is the way in which the mounts are attached; the circular mounts are held in place by a rivet and two finishing plates are visible on the inside of the belt. The ring is attached by two rivets. Stars also adorn another part of a belt (4.14, fig. 20) that is 4.8 cm long and 4.8 cm wide. The two stars alternate with three moons and have a cross-section of 0.8 cm. The mounts are attached by means of integrated pins. At the bottom of the surviving leather is a metal loop with a hooked pin. Two of these pins together will have hold some kind of purse. The loop is attached by a pin and a plate at the back of the leather. The other part of a belt is adorned with mounts shaped like letters made of tin lead (see fig. 32) and discussed with the letters.

20 Leather adorned with star- and moon-shaped mounts with metal pins (4.14). Photo: RMO/Anneke de Kemp.

18 Belt with pendant mounts and bars clamped to the belt (4.25). Photo: RMO/Anneke de Kemp.

19 The longest belt (68 cm) with rectangular mounts and notches (4.39). Photo: J. Luijendijk.

Pieces of purses

At least four pieces of leather with mounts in the collection are too wide and too weak to have belonged to a belt. They are mostly calf or goat skin and more likely to be parts of pouches or cases. Most clearly indicative of a pouch is number 4.40 (fig. 21), a piece of leather that is 13.8 cm wide and 7.9 cm high, shaped like two semicircular 'lobes' with an edge at the top and a mount at the centre. The stitching holes along the edges of the two 'lobes' do not correspond, indicating that the two parts were not sewn together, but that the entire piece was sewn to something else. This is indeed also evident from the position of the mount, that is on the 'back' side of the piece. These are probably the remains of the flap of a belt purse.[17]
A triangular piece of leather (with a length of 7.2 cm and a greatest width of 4.9 cm) with mounts along the long edge and loose straps (4.19, fig. 22) may also be part of the flap of a purse – it merely coincidentally resembles a patten. A supple piece of reddish leather (possibly deer skin) with mounts (4.43, fig. 23) most likely belonged to the covering of a small circular box, indicated by the serrated edges and puckering.
An elongated piece of supple leather measuring 5.9 x 4.2 cm (4.16, fig. 24) shows two wheel-shaped mounts with a cross-section of 2.5 cm. Stitching holes are visible along all the sides of the leather. The mounts are shaped like six-spoked wagon wheels; the wheels have a beaded edge. The mount is attached to the leather by two coarse rivets, representing the 'axles' of the wheels; the rivets are held in place by a plate on the inside of the leather. The collection includes a comparable isolated find of a six-spoked wheel mount (4.57) and another is contained at the centre of a T-shaped piece of leather with a second mount and a leather thong passed through it; the latter's

22 Triangular piece of leather with elongated mount and straps (4.19). Photo: Restaura.

23 Piece of puckered red leather with mounts (4.43). Photo: RMO/Anneke de Kemp.

21 Two-lobed part of a pouch with a mount (4.40). Photo: RMO/Anneke de Kemp.

24 Piece of leather with wheel-shaped mounts (4.16). Photo: RMO/Anneke de Kemp.

function is not clear.[18] The surviving piece of leather is too small to allow us to say from what type of pouch it may derive, but it has an interesting parallel in a badge made of lead tin (fig. 25) shaped like a rectangular belt purse with two loops on which are represented four wheel-shaped mounts and letters (EARB?).[19] Other badges show decorated purses on a belt with mounts, and a recent find from Bois-le-Duc even shows a purse with a dagger on a belt adorned with letters that is wrapped around it; this miniature object is three-dimensional and was probably once mounted on a stick (fig. 26).[20] The interpretation given by Van Beuningen and Koldeweij for the purse badge holds for the pouch with its mount, too: 'With their designs, which are often quite striking, these [purses] underline their owner's wealth.'[21] In the words of Olaf Goubitz: 'No purse, no prestige!'[22] Pouches were worn visibly, on the outside of people's clothing, so they were particularly suitable for ornamentation. The leather itself was decorated, with patterns that were cut or impressed in relief. Some pouches were painted or adorned with embroidery, textile or tassles. The metal mounts often served a double function, as a means of reinforcement and decoration (fig. 27);[23] that's why they are usually placed along edges, in particular on the flap for opening the pouch and on the fastening strap. Being shiny, metal made a pouch an even more conspicuous eye-catcher. Large mounts, and especially buckles and strap ends are often missing from (parts of) bags and purses that are found in excavations; those bags and purses will mostly have been discarded, and their metal parts could be reused. Such metal parts do however occur in our collection, so in that respect it complements the book by Olaf Goubitz.

25 Badge in the shape of a purse with wheel-shaped mounts and letters that was found in Dordrecht, 1375-1425. Photo from Van Beuningen & Koldeweij 1993: no. 811.

26 Miniature object in the shape of a purse on a belt adorned with letters that was found in Bois-le-Duc, before 1450. Photo from Janssen & Thelen 2007: 118.

27 Belt purse with mounts on the 'false' flap and belt that was found in Dordrecht. Rotterdam, Museum Boijmans Van Beuningen, inv. no. F 8359. Photo: A. Willemsen

The ornamental mounts

The collection was split up into twenty typological groups on the basis of the objects' shape and content (see the table). No distinctions were made within the groups on the basis of employed materials or forms of attachment.

Ornamental rivets

The great majority of the ornamental rivets are cap-headed with a pin. On the inside, the rivets are concave or flat. Many of the ornamental rivets have a beaded edge (4.130). Others are steeple-headed with one bead in the centre. This is the end of the pin, which, besides being decorative, is necessary for attachment (4.150). Most of these ornamental rivets are black, a few are golden. They usually have one pin for attachment. Some of the pins are more than 1 cm long. The point of the pin may be quite sharp, which could mean that the rivet in question was used to attach leather to wood, for example a chest. But as we can infer from some pieces of leather in our collection such sharp rivets were also inserted through leather, after which the pin was beaten sideways (4.22c, fig. 28).

Circles

The collection contains a lot of circular mounts. They comprise rivets with three-dimensional heads (hobnails), open circular mounts and circles that are filled in and sometimes decorated. The majority of the ornamental rivets are black (66%), a smaller proportion is golden (29%) and a few are silver-coloured (5%). The inside may be either concave or flat, but the rivets all have one attachment pin. The open circular mounts can be split into circles with an attachment shank and circles with pins, usually two. Mount 4.341 has an open circular shape, the circle itself consisting of a wreath of flowers. The circular mounts have cross-sections of between 1 and 2 cm. The filled-in circles are decorated with figures, such as a 'Tudor' rose (4.268), a deer (4.251) or a complex pattern of fine linear motifs (4.257).

Flower-shaped mounts

The great majority of the flower-shaped mounts have six lobes or petals (69%) The backs of these mounts are flat, with a single pin attachment. Most are black. Such flower-shaped mounts occur in large quantities in other collections, too, for example in the collection in Middelburg, from an excavation at Nieuwlande.[24] Some have a hole at the centre (4.385); they may have served to reinforce a belt hole.

Bar-shaped mounts

The collection contains 84 bar-shaped mounts. Many of them have an circular hole in the middle. Some are copper-coloured (4.17), others black (4.15, lead tin). Another common bar-shaped mount is rectangular with two small holes for its attachment at the ends (4.682). Mounts of this type were also found on some of the parts of belts; they were then attached across the entire width of the belt (for example 4.23f), held in place by a rivet and a plate.

Angular mounts

The common characteristic of the mounts of this category is that they all have three or more corners. They are triangles, quadrangles, hexagonals and octagonals. The decoration on these angular mounts varies tremendously, as does their form of attachment. One square mount (4.474) has a flat reverse and a shank for its attachment. One octagonal mount (4.492) is concave inside and has a hole at the centre, through which the pin was originally inserted.

Figures

The collection includes 45 'figures' – mostly stars (fig. 29); one star (4.756) was originally attached at four points. Most of the star-shaped mounts are concave on the inside; they are made of different materials and have parallels that are known to derive from Nieuwlande.[25] Other mounts in this category are crescents and an arrow (4.111).

28 Hobnails with long pins, hammered down on the back of the leather (4.22c). Photo: RMO/Anneke de Kemp.

29 Star-shaped mount with a rivet (4.1010). Photo: RMO/Anneke de Kemp.

Object	Letter				
Specification	Letter A	Letter B	Letter C	Letter D	Letter E
Number	8	11	1	3	1
Depicted on object	1				
Object shown	4.733	4.734	4.873	4.741	4.914

Object	Letter				
Specification	Letter I	Letter J	Letter M	Letter O	
Number	5	1	28	3	
Depicted on object			1	1	
Object shown	4.743	4.731	4.751	4.4	

Object	Letter			Lettercomb.	M + crown
Specification	Letter Q	Letter S	Letter U		
Number	3	19	2	20	2
Object shown	4.891	4.896	4.892	4.838	4.887

Object	Utensils				
Specification	Purse	Horseshoe	Rake	Jug	Barrel
Number	6	1	1	1	1
Object shown	4.49	4.53	4.54	4.55	4.56

 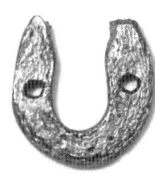   

Object	Figures				
Specification	Star	Sun	Moon	Heart	Arrow
Number	21	3	8	2	1
Object shown	4.1011	4.1022	4.1006	4.71	4.111

Object	Plant				
Specification	Twig + leaves	Twig + grapes	Grape	Flower	Leaf
Number	1	2	1	8	4
Object shown	4.344	4.345	4.346	4.353	4.963

 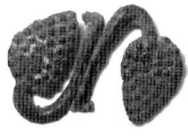   

Object	Animal			Buildings	
Specification	Bird	Hound	Lion	Tower	Arch
Number	2	4	10	4	4
Depicted on object	2				
Object shown	4.82	4.997	4.88	4.104	4.107

Object	Human		Status	
Specification	Face	Vera Icon	Crown	
Number	5	5	6	
Object shown	4.68	4.70	4.63	

Object	Shield			
Specification	Flower	Lion	Eagle	Empty
Number	6	2	3	10
Object shown	4.600	4.608	4.612	4.609

Object	Religious symbols				
Specification	Tunic	Banderole	Coin + cross	Shell	Crown + wings
Number	3	1	7	8	6
Object shown	4.100	4.112	4.234	4.79	4.60

  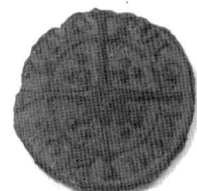  

Object	Ornamental rivet		Bar-shape
Specification	Button + rivet	Button-head	
Number	91	40	84
Object shown	4.124	4.182	4.682

 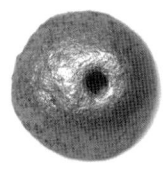 

Object	Angular mount				
Specification	Square	Rectangle	Diamond	Hexagon	Octagon
Number	75	63	9	5	7
Object shown	4.464	4.1025	4.653	4.336	4.492

Object	Circle			Oval
Specification	Circle + hole	Ring	Decoration	
Number	44	3	121	4
Object shown	4.201	4.233	4.257	4.597

 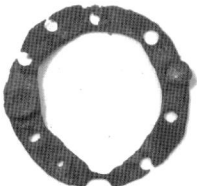  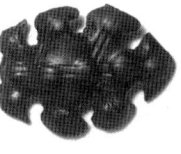

Object	Flower-shape			
Specification	3 petals	4 petals	5 petals	6 petals
Number	3	9	21	99
Object shown	4.358	4.365	4.372	4.423

Object	Flower-shape			Adornment
Specification	7 petals	8 petals	12 petals	Pearls
Number	3	5	3	2
Object shown	4.565	4.401	4.515	4.340

Object	Pyramid	Ornament	Book mount	Various
Specification				
Number	12	18	3	21
Object shown	4.451	4.617	4.659	4.598

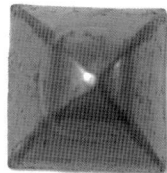   

Utensils

This small group consists of mounts shaped like purses (4.51), a rake (4.54), a horseshoe (4.53), a jug (4.55) and a cask (4.56). These mounts were attached in different ways and some even miss any trace of attachment, such as the barrel. Also many badges represent such utilitarian objects.[26]

Buildings

The category of mounts shaped like buildings comprises framed and unframed buildings (4.107); they have flat reverses and two attachment pins.

Plants

The small group of plant-shaped mounts consists largely of variants of the French lily with flat reverses (4.351). Exceptions are a golden twig with two leaves and a piece of fruit (4.344) and a silver-coloured bunch of grapes (4.345). The golden twig is concave on the inside and there are holes in the leaves through which nails could be hammered. The bunch of grapes has two attachment pins.

Animals

Some mounts indisputably represent an animal that is not portrayed on a different form such as a shield or circle. The animals in question are dogs (various sorts), lions and birds. A fine example is a large silver-coloured eagle (mount 4.82, 2.1 x 1.65 cm.) A mount of such large dimensions may have been worn on a pouch or a hat.

Faces

Twelve mounts represent faces. They are made of different materials, including copper sheet (4.68). Some show Christ's face and were interpreted as 'Vera Icons' (4.70). All of these mounts were attached by means of a single pin, which was in some cases inserted through the mount.

Shields

Shield-shaped mounts were categorised as heraldry. The shields show different motifs, some of which are included in the collection as separate mounts, such as an eagle (4.612) and a plant: mount 4.599 is a 'shield variant' of mount 4.345.

Letters

There is a great diversity of letters, including several combinations of letters. Most common is the letter M (31 mounts). We know of parallels that indisputably came from Nieuwlande, and hence date from before 1530.[27] The M-shaped mounts were attached with one or two square pins and in one case (4.877) with three pins. There are also mounts in which the letter M is represented in mirror image (4.878), as can be inferred from the direction of the ends of the legs of the letter. Other frequently encountered letters are S (19 mounts) and B (11 mounts). Also quite common is a combination of the letters Y and S.

Religious symbols

The religious mounts comprise representations on coins and isolated representations. The great majority are crosses. Some of the crosses are on a coin (4.234). These imitation coins are mounts with a flat reverse and one or two attachment pins. A banderole bearing the name MARIA (4.112, fig. 30) was attached with two pins. Some scallop-shaped mounts (4.73) probably refer to Saint James, who is venerated in Santiago de Compostela.

Book mounts

The category of book mounts comprises three finds (4.658, 4.659 and 4.660) that were interpreted as such on the basis of comparison with other collections; parallels are for example known from the soil dumped along Kousteensedijk in the town of Middelburg, dating from 1530-1570.[28] One of the mounts (4.660) has two small holes on either side, through which the attachment pins were presumably inserted. Books represented in illustrations are often clearly adorned with mounts, and sometimes also small ornamental rivets (fig. 31).

The imagery

Talking belts

One part of a belt, consisting of the end with the strap end (4.38), is adorned with mounts representing the letters A and M alternately arranged (fig. 32). There are also many letters (90) among the isolated mount finds in the collection. Most present is the letter M (29 x), of which there are also two

30 Banderole made of tin lead bearing the name 'Maria' (4.112). Photo: RMO/Anneke de Kemp.

crowned variants. Besides, there are dozens of Bs and Ss and many letter combinations including an M, R and A. The Ms and many of the letter combinations (fig. 32) seem to refer to the name of Mary or to the Ave Maria prayer (fig. 33), while some interwoven combinations of Y and S or I, H and S appear to be abbreviations of the name of Christ. Belts with letters are also known from other collections: part of a belt bearing an A and a B from Amsterdam (fig. 34)[29] and part of a belt adorned with a monogram (representing a Christ monogram) from 's-Hertogenbosch (fig. 35). All these letters are made of a tin-lead alloy. Some show remains of paint on their reverse, indicating that the belts to which they were attached were painted.

These belts can be interpreted as cheap imitations of luxury waistbands that were often made of leather lined with velvet or some other coloured material, and were adorned with letter-shaped mounts or plates of precious metal bearing words.[30] A good example is a 14th-century belt from Colmar. This belt, which was lined with silk, was over its entire length adorned with punched-out rosettes in the shape of four French lilies surrounding a rivet, between which were gold-plated and enamel plates bearing the words AMOR (love), LIEB (love), HAIL (health) and ANCH (also?). Other luxury waistbands from the same workshops show a series of plates bearing the word AMOR, pendant letters B, or alternating women's heads and rosettes. The latter were attached to a delicate silk band that was probably worn around the head.[31] The workshops that produced these waistbands made ornaments for wealthy citizens, but there is nothing to suggest that their clientele was restricted to the highest echelons of society.

From iconographic sources it is also known that belts were regarded as suitable media for communicating a message. The mourning Mary Magalen on the right in Rogier van de Weyden's Deposition from the Cross in Madrid is wearing a low-slung belt, fastened at the front, bearing the words IHESUS MARIA (fig. 36).[32] In some cases such illustrations refer to real text-bearing belts, but often the artist will have used the belt area to seemingly inconspicuously write something such as a maxim or even his signature; widely known is that Michelangelo carved his name in the shoulder strap worn by Mary in the Pietà sculpture in the Vatican. That he should have chosen a belt for this purpose indicates that text-bearing belts were indeed a common phenomenon. As long, narrow bands, both belts themselves and representations of belts were very suitable for use as a 'line' for text.

The part of a belt bearing the letters A and B from Amsterdam's city centre has survived only to the point at which the next letter was attached; the belt seems to have broken

31 Book adorned with mounts (front right); the man on the right is wearing a pouch adorned with mounts on his belt; the horse gear is also adorned. *A delegation from Tournay visits the Bishop of Noyon*, stained-glass window in the cathedral of Tournay, after 1500. Photo: KIK/IRPA Brussels, slide no. b180305.

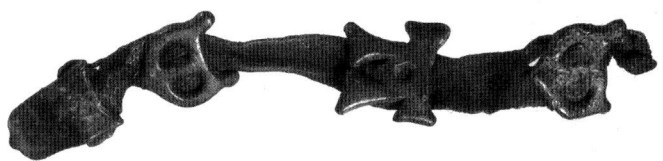

32 Strap end bearing letters A and M (4.38). Photo: RMO/Anneke de Kemp.

along the line of that mount. So unfortunately we don't know whether the belt was adorned with alternating As and Bs, or perhaps the succession A-B-C, representing the beginning of an entire alphabet. Belts bearing the alphabet are known from various sources; they will have been intended to help people learn the letters. From the *vita* of Saint Lubin we know that, when he was a boy, a monk made a belt with the alphabet for him; this is represented in a 13th-century stained glass window in Chartres Cathedral. Lubin's belt was for a long time cherished as a relic in the cathedral's treasury.[33]

Besides as mounts, letters and letter combinations are also quite common as badges. The same letters dominate both groups, M being the most common among the letter badges, too. In some cases it is even impossible to say whether a find represents a letter mount or a letter badge. Badges have been found in the same contexts as mounts. In the case of the Mackenbach collection, finds were selected on the basis of technical characteristics, and metal letters with unambiguous remains of a brooch pin or lips or loops were interpreted as badges, and were not included in the collection.[34] The letters

33 Letter combination AM (4.842). Photo: RMO/Anneke de Kemp.

34 Belt bearing the letters A and B that was found in Amsterdam, 1450-1500. Amsterdam, Dienst Archeologie en Bouwhistorie, find no. NES-239. Photo: DAB/Wiard Krook.

35 Belt bearing monograms, found in Bois-le-Duc, 1500-1550. Bois-le-Duc, Bouwhistorie, Archeologie en Monumenten, inv.no. i 11513. Photo: BAM/G. de Graaf.

36 Belt bearing 'IHESUS MARIA' worn by Mary Magdalen. Rogier van de Weyden, *Deposition from the Cross*, c. 1430-1435. Madrid, Museo del Prado, inv. no. 2825. Photo from De Vos 1999: 17.

that were interpreted as mounts have pins or no attachment point on their reverse. In terms of meaning the two categories are closely related: belt mounts and badges were both worn on the body, on top of clothing, and were hence used as 'means of communication', to literally express an opinion.

So in our opinion, the letter mounts had more or less the same meaning as letter brooches, which can (also) be subdivided into initials, abbreviations of maxims, mottos or slogans, fancy letters without meaning and 'exotic letters'. Many of the crowned letters are initials, referring to someone's Christian name. The crowned M will usually refer to Mary, but it may also stand for a ruler, such as Maximilian or Mary of Burgundy, who had the letter M minted on coins. An initial may also refer to the name of a town: the crowned Gothic letter B has since the 14th century symbolised the Flemish town of Bruges.[35]

Hounds

The collection includes a golden hound with a length of 3.1 cm and a width of 1.75 cm (4.997, fig. 37). The dog's stance shows that it is running. This mount bears a striking resemblance to running hounds that have survived on two dog collars from Amsterdam; a similar hound was recovered as a stray find at the same findspot as one of the collars, the Weesperstraat site along the course of the new metro line. It can be dated to the last quarter of the 16th century.[36] Besides two hounds, the remaining part of this collar shows two ornamental rivets and there is a hare between the hounds; at the end is a hexagonal star alongside a shell-shaped eye via which the collar could be fastened (fig. 38).[37] The other collar, of which only part of the fastening is missing, shows various hunting elements: a horseman between two swines and two hounds chasing a hare. In the middle of the collar is a small bell. The fastening is the same as that of the other collar – a ring attached to the collar with a shell-shaped mount (fig. 39). Both collars were decorated with an apt iconography of a hunting scene with hounds; they may have been worn by hounds. Hounds and other domestic animals represented in illustrations also often wear lavishly decorated collars (fig. 40).

Memento mori

Late medieval man was constantly aware of the transience of earthly life and the unpredictability of the time of death. Symbols of transience reminded the faithful to make efforts to secure their salvation; this powerful theme even had an impact on belt mounts. Besides two copper ornamental rivets and a copper loop, a narrow leather belt with a length of 22.5 cm and a width of 0.8 cm (4.28) has a four-lobed metal plate bearing two small heads (0.85 x 0.9 cm). The head on the left is an 'ordinary' head, that on the right is a skull and the two are facing one another (figs. 41 and 42). The scene is what's known as a *memento mori* ('remember that you are mortal'). Parallels are known from for example prayer beads, which sometimes include beads with the head of a woman on one side and a skull on the other[38] – this theme is also omnipresent in iconography. The prayer beads were a means for private contemplation. The small dimensions of the *memento mori* heads on the belt make it likely that this symbol of transience was also primarily intended to subtly remind its wearer to be focussed on his salvation.

37 Running hound cast in brass (4.997). Photo: RMO/Anneke de Kemp.

38 Part of a collar adorned with hounds and a hare that was found in Amsterdam, 1575-1600. Dienst Archeologie en Bouwhistorie, find no. MWP4-1. Photo: DAB/Wiard Krook.

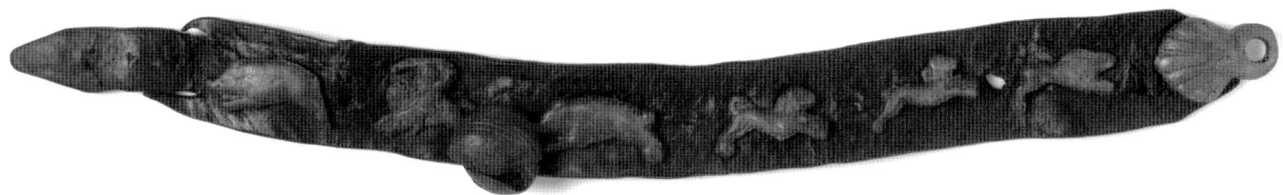

39 Collar with hunting scenes and a bell that was found in Amsterdam, 1575-1600. Amsterdam, Dienst Archeologie en Bouwhistorie, find no. WE2-8. Photo: DAB/Wiard Krook.

41 Belt with gold-coloured mounts (4.28). Photo: RMO/Anneke de Kemp.

40 The dog at the front right is wearing a collar adorned with silver-coloured mounts; even the horse gear of the hobbyhorse in the background is adorned with golden mounts. Jan Anthonisz. van Ravesteyn, *Portrait of a Boy*, 1628. Private collection. Photo from Bedaux and Ekkart 2000: 23.

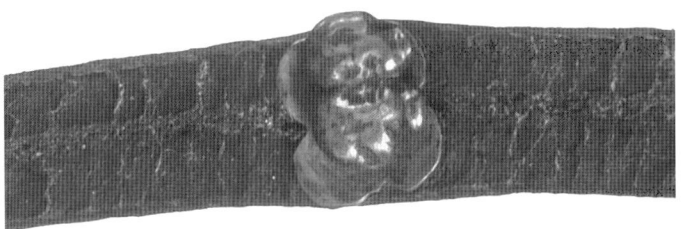

42 Two heads on the belt in fig. 41 (4.28). Photo: RMO/Anneke de Kemp.

Material and production

Tin-lead cast mounts

The belt mounts are made of copper or tin alloys. The alloys' composition has not been analysed; in some cases it even proved to be difficult to distinguish between copper and tin, partly because many of the finds have been thoroughly cleaned, preserved and treated.

More than half of the collection of belt mounts (642 in total) consists of mounts made of tin lead with a flat reverse. In at least 265 cases the burr was still clearly visible (fig. 43). These mounts were cast in flat, possibly single moulds. A burr is also observable in the case of at least 68 (of the 232) mounts with a concave reverse, including all the circular mounts with an integrated cast pin, which look as though a nail was hammered through them; they seem to be imitations of caps that were attached with rivets. The concave mounts (such as 4.455, 4.470 and 4.477) were also all cast. Threedimensional moulds must have been used for these mounts.

Most of the mounts were cast flat, in self-releasing moulds, using the same technique as employed in the production of badges. The alloy of 50 badges has been (scientifically) analysed, but the outcome was that there is actually little sense in carrying out such analyses – there seems to be no standardisation: all ratios of tin and lead were encountered.[39] A discussion as to how tin-lead miniatures were made led to the same conclusion. The casters probably assessed the fluid mass with an expert's eye, and will have added an extra tin spoon if it appeared to be too soft or an insufficient quantity. They did not use pure tin and lead in precisely weighed quantities, but whatever was available. The process must have been extremely practical and pragmatic. The evidence suggests that such mounts were made more or less everywhere where tin was cast. Some of them may well have been produced by itinerant casters, travelling from one place to another, who combined their casting activities with the sale of their products. Moulds for such small objects could be easily transported – indeed, they were not even essential – and (collected old) material needed for the alloy was available anywhere.[40]

Mounts punched out of copper sheet

The thinnest mounts (92 in total) were cut or punched out of thin sheets of copper. Many of these are convex caps with a hole at the centre, but three crowns (4.63-4.65), three dogs (4.83-4.85, fig. 44) and for example a thistle with two serrated leaves (4.344) were also made in this way. As this technique always yields thin objects, these mounts do not have any fixed attachment pins, but almost always tiny holes (also punched), via which the mount was attached with golden nails. Most

43 Tin-lead mount with an integrated pin and a burr (4.580). Photo: RMO/Anneke de Kemp.

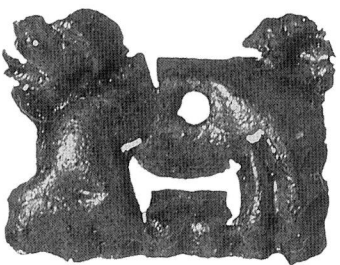

44 Dog punched out of copper sheet with a hole at the centre (4.85). Photo: RMO/Anneke de Kemp.

45 Reverse of a mount showing remains of textile (4.614). Photo: RMO/Anneke de Kemp.

mounts have a single hole at the centre, but the holes of the thistle-shaped mount are in the leaves, so this mount was attached by two nails; the mount has at some point broken along the right nail hole.

Punching from thin sheets is a quick way of producing large quantities of flat, very uniform mounts. Some metal sheet always remained, but that could be melted down and reused – and sometimes waste was even minimized, as indicated by the square mounts on 4.32 (fig. 46), hammered in the shape of caps to resemble hobnails. In 2003 a 14th-century workshop where mounts for clothing or chests were made in this way was excavated in the Rue des Archives in the centre of Paris. In total, 726 remains of bronze sheet and 176 mounts were recovered. On the basis of the remains of the working places and the required material the excavators estimated that a workshop like this, with four people working in it, will have been capable of producing around 10,000 mounts a month.[41] The cast and the punched mounts both tell us that we are dealing with a collection of mass-produced objects that will have been very cheap, and hence affordable for a large group in late medieval society. This further supports the assumption that the belts were everyday variants of the belts with imagery that were common elements of the fashion for humans and animals in the Late Middle Ages.

Functions and dates

The Mackenbach collection was originally compiled as one of 'belt mounts' and we assumed that the majority of the belts will have been worn around the waist; in works of art belts around the waist are indeed often represented as decorated with rivets or other ornamentation. But some pieces of leather did indisputably not form part of a belt. The dimensions, shape and form of fastening of other belts suggest that they were part of some structure involving straps, for example for hanging pouches, cases or sheaths from a belt.

Microscopic examination of the isolated mount finds showed that some have textile remains on their reverse (fig. 45), so they must have been attached to textile, or to leather that was lined with fabric. Others showed remains of paint on their reverse, indicating that they were attached to a painted belt. Both aspects show that the belts and pouches must have been more colourful than the state in which they were recovered from the soil would suggest.

The vast majority of the belts with mounts were decorated with simple golden mounts that were punched out of copper sheet (figs. 46 and 47). Many are round caps that were attached by thin nails in lines or patterns, to make the belt look as though it was rivetted. The longest surviving parts of belts contain large quantities of such ornamental hobnails, in some cases more than 120 on a single belt (4.30a-j). Some belts were adorned with series of flower-shaped mounts that were attached by nails hammered through a hole at the centre. These belts were dated to the first half of the 14th century on the basis of their provenance (Statenplein Dordrecht, fig. 48). Comparison with other collections gives no reason to doubt this date (and hence the belts' provenance). The French workshop where mounts of the same shapes were made in the same way was also dated to the 14th century. The belts and pouches of a trader who was portrayed in this period are also all decorated with mounts; they are presented as suitable gifts for a gentleman to give to a lady (fig. 49). Although some figu-

46 Belt with a row of ornamental caps (4.32). Photo: RMO/Anneke de Kemp.

47 Belt with ornamental hobnails arranged in patterns (4.35). Photo: RMO/Anneke de Kemp.

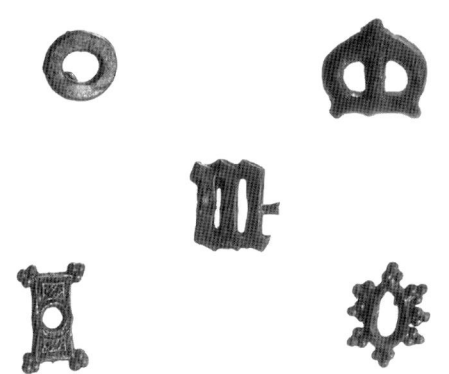

48 The only five isolated mounts in the collection from Statenplein Dordrecht (4.1-4.5). Photo: RMO/Anneke de Kemp.

rative mounts were made with this technique, too, most of the copper-sheet mounts are of a simple shape and were used in large series of the same shapes. All in all there is enough reason to assume that all the mounts that were punched out of copper sheet date from the 14th century. So in terms of fashion they represent the 'early' phase in the collection.

Most, by far, of the isolated mount finds are made of tin lead, cast in moulds, often with integrated attachment pins. According to the collector many of the objects come from the Verdronken Land area, in particular from Nieuwlande. Comparison of the mounts with other objects from the Verdronken Land and with mounts of similar shapes from well-dated contexts confirms the date, because almost all the comparative objects also date from the second half of the 15th and the first half of the 16th century. The technique that was used to attach these mounts differs from that employed for the copper-sheet mounts, which were attached by separate gold-coloured nails hammered through holes in the mounts. Almost all the tin-lead mounts have integrated pins, with which they were attached to the leather. Some mounts were clamped to the leather, without pins. Both techniques are represented by a few parts of belts adorned with tin-lead mounts in the collection: the mounts of the parts of belts decorated with letters and with stars and moons and those of the part of a pouch adorned with wheels were attached with pins, while the grey triangular 'rivets' on one belt were clamped in place, so they were not inserted through the belt. There seem to be sufficient comparative finds to assume that all the belts adorned with tin-lead mounts (fig. 50) date from the late 15th and early 16th century – so they probably come from Zeeland. This represents a 'later' phase in fashion, which is also illustrated in miniatures

49 Dietmar van Ast tries to gain access to his lover's castle disguised as a belt and pouch trader. *Codex Manesse*, 1305-1340. Heidelberg, Universitätsbibliothek, Cod. Pal. germ. 848, f 64r. Photo via http://digi.ub.uni-heidelberg.de/diglit/cpg848/0123.

50 Belt with tin-lead triangular rivets (4.36). Photo: RMO/Anneke de Kemp.

from the southern part of the Netherlands (see fig. 1) and in early Netherlandish painting.

A few mounts, such as the running hound (ill. 37), were cast in copper or brass. We know of well-dated parallels from the last quarter of the 16th century, a time when increasing use was made of copper alloys, in particular brass, as a raw material for utensils and dress accessories. A well recognisable type of brass loop intended to connect two belts also dates from the last quarter of the 16th century. On the basis of this, brass mounts may be dated to the end of the 16th century. They represent fashion from the period of the Dutch Revolt, which can no longer be classed as medieval, and feature in the portraiture of this period. This date makes it unlikely that the copper and brass mounts come from the Verdronken Land. Such mounts have however been recovered in large quantities during the digging of Amsterdam's metro lines and Rotterdam's railway tunnel, so the few copper and brass mounts may have ended up in our collection via all the metal-detector searching that was done there.

Conclusion

Belts and pouches were in the Late Middle Ages lavishly decorated with shiny mounts, which simultaneously reinforced and adorned the leather. These accessories were worn on top of clothing, and were hence visible when the wearer moved. The golden or silver-coloured metal mounts reflected the light and attracted attention, making the wearer look wealthy. There was a large range of mounts of cheap materials, so everyone could choose what message they wanted to convey. In terms of content the figurative mounts are very similar to the badges. They closely resemble one another in terms of function, too, though an individual badge will have been more deliberately chosen, and was also more conspicuous. The imagery of the badges is hence on the whole more explicit than that of the mounts, which are moreover smaller.

Some of the messages conveyed by the ornamental mounts were unambiguous enough to be understood by people who saw them. This was for example the case with the letters and words on the belts. But even in those cases we can not be certain whether the wearers deliberately intended to 'communicate' via their accessories. Letters and combinations of letters that are known as mounts, like the M and the Christ monogram, also often occur in paintings and on utensils; they belong to the standard imagery of this period. Messages will more often have been implicit, the shields, coins, animals and heavenly bodies chosen not as individually interpretable objects, but as elements of a decorative pattern. Because of the collection's referential character – the outcome of efforts to collect as many different mounts as possible – it is tempting to regard the mounts as isolated images, but they were always used in combinations on the belts.

Of some mounts, such as the tiny 'memento mori', it is fairly certain that other people will have been unable to make out what they represented from a distance. Such finds show us that late medieval man's common imagery, in which religion played a distinct role and which is also known from other sources, had an impact on even the smallest details in life, and was generally understood, even when no specific message was being conveyed. But in spite of the great attention paid to details, the key concern will have been the mounts' overall effect. Like the well-to-do gentlemen (and ladies!) with all their gold and silver, medieval commoners could with all kinds of this cheap mass-produced bling-bling make themselves (and their pets) look dazzling – and perhaps appear to be more than they actually were.

Notes

* Dr A. Willemsen is the curator of the medieval department of the Museum of Antiquities in Leiden. Jasper Luijendijk and Marieke van Werven, both students at Leiden University, inventoried, documented and analysed the museum's collection of belt mounts in the context of a traineeship project in 2007. The authors would like to thank Museum Boijmans Van Beuningen in Rotterdam (Alexandra van Dongen and Christel van Hees), the *Dienst Archeologie en Bouwhistorie* in Amsterdam (Wiard Krook), the *Provinciaal Depot voor Bodemvondsten* in Middelburg (Henk Hendrikse), the afdeling *Bouwhistorie, Archeologie en Monumenten* in Bois-le-Duc (Ronald van Genabeek), Carol van Driel-Murray, Jos Koldeweij and the staff of the Leiden museum for their help.
1. Leiden, Rijksmuseum van Oudheden, inv. nos. i 2006/4.1-4.1047.
2. See Van Dongen 1993.
3. Egan & Pritchard 1991: 162-143.
4. See http://www.dbnl.org/zoeken/zoekeninteksten/ (22/02/08).
5. See http://www.scez.nl/index2.php?/pagina.php?nummer=911~mainFrame (28/01/08).
6. Dekker 1971: 83-84, 99, 578, 595-600.
7. Kuipers 2004: 27-35, 48-49.
8. *Schatten uit de Schelde* 1987: 13.
9. Kuipers 2004: 61-67.
10. See http://www.awnzeeland.nl/index.html (11/02/08).
11. See http://www.scez.nl/index2.php?/pagina.php?nummer=911~mainFrame (29/01/08).
12. See http://cms.dordrecht.nl/dordt?waxtrapp=vjqboDsHaKnPvBQHTC (24/01/08).
13. Goubitz 2007: 115.
14. De Ridder & Willemsen 2004: 29.

15. Amsterdam, Dienst Archeologie en Bouwhistorie, find no. MH7-520 (Leprozengracht/Nieuwe Amstelstraat 1975).
16. See Lightbown 1992: 336 (silk girdle with trapezoid pendants suspending from bars, Danish/North German, early 15th century, now in the National Museum of Danmark in Copenhagen).
17. See Goubitz 2007: 15-35.
18. This piece belongs to a group of leather objects with mounts that were at P. Mackenbach's request restored by Restaura, but not sold with the Mackenbach collection; see Kempkens & Lupak 2004: 11.1.
19. Van Beuningen & Koldeweij 1993: 286, fig. 811.
20. Janssen & Thelen 2007: 117-118; see also 131-134 (decorated belts and mounts from Bois-le-Duc, before 1450).
21. Van Beuningen & Koldeweij 1993: 286.
22. Goubitz 2007: 13.
23. See also Koldeweij 2006: 121, numbers 7.78 and 7.79 (leather purses with tin-lead mounts that were found in Bruges, 13th/14th century), and Goubitz 2007: 33, fig. 42 (pouches with metal mounts from Sluis and Den Bosch).
24. Middelburg, Provinciaal Depot voor Bodemvondsten, find number 928-11.
25. Middelburg, Provinciaal Depot voor Bodemvondsten, find number 928-13, from Nieuwlande.
26. See Van Beuningen & Koldeweij 1993: 286 (pouches), 300 (rake), 303 (horseshoes), 308 (jugs); Koldeweij 2006: 121 (pouches) and 122 (horseshoes); see also Van Dongen 1995.
27. Middelburg, Provinciaal Depot voor Bodemvondsten Zeeland, find numbers 1489-231-243.
28. Middelburg, Provinciaal Depot voor Bodemvondsten Zeeland, find numbers 1992-A549-556, see *Geld uit de belt* 1994: 61.
29. Amsterdam, Dienst Archeologie en Bouwhistorie, find no. NES-239, from the Nes/Rokin find assemblage, dated 1450-1500
30. See Lightbown 1992: 326 (silk girdle with As and lions, Paris 1330-1340, now in the Zähringen Museum in Baden-Baden); see also idem 519-521 (silver collars made of letters) and Hackenbroch 1979: 300 (English Stuart pendants with the Christ monogram).
31. Paris, Musée National du Moyen Age, belts and belt mounts from 14th-century hoard finds from Erfurt and Colmar; see Descatoire 2007: 76-80.
32. Madrid, Museo del Prado, inv. no. 2825, see De Vos 1999: *passim*.
33. Chartres, window representing the life of St. Lubin, bay 45, dated 1205-1215; see Manhes-Deremble 1993: 103, notes 376-377 and fig. 37.
34. The majority of the badges found by P. Mackenbach ended up in the collection of H.J.E. van Beuningen; they are discussed in Van Beuningen & Koldeweij 1993.
35. Koldeweij 2006: 132-141.
36. Baart 1977: 165.
37. Amsterdam, Dienst Archeologie en Bouwhistorie, find number MWP4-1(Weesperplein).
38. Koldeweij 2006: 254d.
39. Van Beuningen & Koldeweij 1993: 24-25.
40. Willemsen 2000: 347-348.
41. Paper presented at the 'Medieval Europe 2007' congress in Paris in September 2007 by Nicolas Thomas (Institut National des Recherches Archéologiques Préventives, INRAP): 'La fabrication de masse et en série des objets de parure en alliage à base de cuivre au Moyen Âge.' See Thomas & Bourgarit 2006.

References

Jan Baart et al., *Opgravingen in Amsterdam, twintig jaar stadskernonderzoek,* Amsterdam 1977.

J.B. Bedaux & R. Ekkart (eds.), Kinderen op hun mooist. Het kinderportret in de Nederlanden 1500-1700, Ghent/Amsterdam 2000 (exhibition catalogue, Frans Halsmuseum Haarlem/ Koninklijke Musea voor Schone Kunsten Antwerp).

H.J.E. van Beuningen & A.M. Koldeweij, *Heilig en Profaan, 1000 laatmiddeleeuwse insignes uit de collectie H.J.E. van Beuningen*, Cothen 1993.

C. Dekker, *Zuid-Beveland: de historische geografie en de instellingen van een Zeeuws eiland in de Middeleeuwen*, Assen 1971.

Tim de Ridder & Annemarieke Willemsen, *Gat in de stad, Ontdek de stadsarcheologie van Nederland*, Leiden 2004.

Christine Descatoire (ed.), *Trésors de la Peste Noire, Erfurt et Colmar*, Paris 2007 (exhibition catalogue, Musée National du Moyen Age, Paris).

Dirk de Vos, *Rogier van der Weyden, Het volledige oeuvre*, Amsterdam 1999.

Geld uit de belt, Archeologisch onderzoek in de bouwput van de gemeentelijke parkeerkelder en het belastingkantoor aan de Kousteensedijk te Middelburg, Vlissingen 1994.

Geoff Egan & Frances Pritchard, *Dress Accessories c. 1150-c. 1450*, London 1991 (Museum of London cat.).

Olaf Goubitz, *Purses in Pieces, Archaeological finds of late medieval and 16th-century leather purses, pouches, bags and cases in the Netherlands*, Zwolle 2007.

Olaf Goubitz, *Stepping through time: archaeological footwear from prehistoric times until 1800*, Zwolle 2001.

The Grimani Breviary, Reproduced from the illuminated manuscript belonging to the Biblioteca Marciana in Venice, Venice 1972.

Yvonne Hackenbroch, *Renaissance Jewellery*, Munich/New York 1979.

Jean Helbig, *Corpus Vitrearum Medii Aevi: Les Vitraux Médiévaux conservés en Belgique, 1200-1500*, Brussels 1961.

H.L. Janssen & A.A.J. Thelen (eds.), *Tekens van leven, Opgravingen en vondsten in het Tolbrugkwartier in 's-Hertogenbosch*, Utrecht 2007.

Jo Kempkens & Ton Lupak, 'Restauratie in de archeologie, Restauratierapporten diverse archeologische voorwerpen. In opdracht van Patrick Mackenbach', Haelen 2004.

Jos Koldeweij, *Geloof en geluk, Sieraad en devotie in middeleeuws Vlaanderen*, Arnhem 2006.

Jan J.B. Kuipers, *Sluimerend in Slik, Verdronken dorpen en verdronken land in zuidwest Nederland*, Goes 2004.

Ronald W. Lightbown, *Mediaeval European Jewellery, with a catalogue of the collection in the Victoria & Albert Museum*, London 1992.

C. Manhes-Deremble, *Corpus Vitrearum Medii Aevi, Les vitraux narratifs de la Cathédrale de Chartres, Étude iconographique*, Paris 1993.

Bernhard Ridderbos & Henk van Veen (ed.), *'Om iets te weten van oude meesters.' De Vlaamse Primitieven - herontdekking, waardering en onderzoek*, Nijmegen 1995.

Schatten uit de Schelde, Bergen op Zoom 1987 (exhibition catalogue, Markiezenhof, Bergen op Zoom).

Nicholas Thomas & David Bourgarit, 'Une industrie médiévale du bronze', *La Recherche* 403 (12/2006) 56-58.

Alexandra van Dongen, 'Haken en ogen, kledingaccessoires 1450-1650', Rotterdam 1993 (exhibition sheet, Museum Boijmans Van Beuningen).

Alexandra van Dongen, 'Het gebruiksvoorwerp als draagteken', in: A.M. Koldeweij & A. Willemsen (eds.), Heilig en profaan, laatmiddeleeuwse insignes in cultuurhistorisch perspectief, Amsterdam 1995, 75-87.

Annemarieke Willemsen, 'Poppengoed precies bekeken. Verzameling, herkomst en functie van loodtinnen miniatuurtjes', in: D. Kicken, A.M. Koldeweij & J.R. ter Molen (eds.), Gevonden voorwerpen, Opstellen over middeleeuwse archeologie voor/ Lost and found, Essays on medieval archaeology for H.J.E. van Beuningen (Rotterdam Papers 11), Rotterdam 2000, 347-355.

Early medieval glass linen smoothers from the *emporium* of Deventer

A comparative study of the context and use of glass linen smoothers in Deventer, the Low Countries and north-western Europe (AD 700-1200)

Michiel H. Bartels

Introduction
It was in the summer of 1992 at Susteren in central Limburg, where the ROB (now RACM) were excavating the site of a convent. Henk Stoepker and Alexandra Mars had been referring to Jan Thijssen as 'the Oracle'. The Oracle was called on to pronounce on the huge amount of finds, especially ceramics, that emerged from the convent's moat. On a hot afternoon in the sea-freight containers crammed full of finds, the Oracle did pronounce. I was astounded at what I heard, and all I could do was to watch closely, listen intently, take notes and understand that I still had a very long way to go. In the evening hours, discussion focused on the broader connections, material from production sites and assemblages from other find spots, and expertise poured from Jan apparently without effort: this was knowledge of material culture handled by a big-time player.
A good year later, within the ROB scheme Deltaplan Cultuurbehoud, the project 'Rubbish pits and Cesspits' (1993-1996) was initiated, which meant working through almost a thousand boxes of pottery, glass and other materials. Apart from a lot of medieval ceramics, there was a huge amount of post-medieval pottery: industrial wares. The only person with real in-depth knowledge of this material and its archaeology once more proved to be Jan. He rapped me over the knuckles, took me by the hand and put things right. So after my apprenticeship, the project went successfully, while Jan's helpful advice, solicited and unsolicited, has continued to come in. Jan infected me with a zest for researching any subject down to the last detail and an unabashedly critical approach. Thus it is that in this study of glass linen smoothers, I follow Jan's lead as I put a modest class of finds under the spotlight and place them in a broader framework.

Definition: a glass linen smoother is of a round or nearly round, plano-convex shape, i.e. a bun-shaped object, made of solid glass. It generally measures 4 to 8.5 cm across and 2.5 to 6 cm in height. The underside of the object is convex and entirely smooth, without angular edges. The sides are generally rounded, with a smooth finish. On the upper side, the smoother has a centred kick with a pontil scar.
Synonyms in English are: smoother, linen smoother, glass smoother, slick-stone; in Dutch: strijkglas, gliedesteen, gliede, strijksteen; in Frisian: glêdstien; in German: Glättglas, Gniedelstein; in French: lissoir; in Danish: sømglätter.

The problem
In almost every excavation in the town centre of Deventer, features and structures from the AD 800-1200 period have yielded glass linen smoothers or fragments of them. These objects come to light both close to the river IJssel and further a field. Sometimes they are found in a primary context, in a distinct feature such as a sunken-floored hut or a pit. But fragments turn up also in secondary contexts, e.g. in excavated soil reused elsewhere in the settlement. Finally, linen smoothers also surfaced in the past, from early medieval but not properly documented findspots in the trading settlement. This study will concentrate on the following questions:
A. Why does so little glassware, i.e. glass tableware, personal ornaments, and window glass occur in early medieval Deventer while there are numerous glass linen smoothers? Is this a common state of affairs, or is Deventer different from other early medieval settlements?

B. In what context and period do glass linen smoothers occur in Deventer? What does this tell us about their use?
C. In what context and period do glass linen smoothers occur elsewhere in the Low Countries and north-western Europe? Is the picture in Deventer and the Low Countries the same or different from that in other parts?
D. What is the economic and cultural background of these objects in the light of socio-economic developments?

In this study I shall not go into the aspects of chemical composition and glass production, although this survey may prompt such a study in the future. Therefore only general statements can be made about the provenance of the smoothers. Smoothers from late medieval and post-medieval contexts will on the whole be left aside. It is assumed that these were mostly used for smoothing delicate textiles. Glass smoothers are known from many excavations and shipwrecks.

Research history of the early medieval linen smoother

From the earliest documented archaeological excavations in the mid 19th century, linen smoothers have been recovered throughout north-western Europe and especially in funerary contexts. The first examples were documented in Ireland, Scotland, Norway and Sweden, almost without exception from Viking burials. In the Netherlands, the first recovered linen smoothers came from the dwelling mounds along the coast of Friesland and Groningen, as many of these mounds were quarried from the 19th century onwards. The numerous archaeological finds from them, including some glass linen smoothers, generated a great deal of scholarly interest. The sites of emporia such as Dorestad, York, Birka, Helgö and Haithabu (Hedeby) yielded countless specimens. In recent decades, glass linen smoothers have turned up not only in Deventer and the rest of the Low Countries, but in many other areas as well.
In general, linen smoothers are found in settlement contexts. This includes rural settlements, trading centres and ecclesiastical sites. As yet, funerary contexts are known only from the Viking heartland and Viking-colonised regions.

Early medieval glass finds at Deventer

Since town-centre archaeology was put on a systematic footing at Deventer, only a few glass finds predating the 14th century have turned up. The wide range of glassware found at centres such as Haithabu, Dorestad and Birka is absent. There, many remains of drinking vessels, such as funnel beakers and palm cups are recovered; also jugs, bowls and cup-beakers are

01 Deventer in the Netherlands.

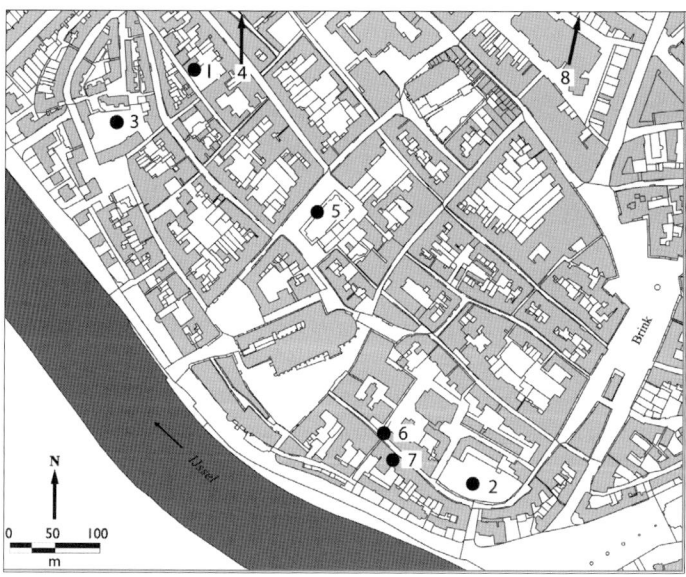

02 The distribution of glass smoothers in Deventer, 850-1200, 1. Bruynssteeg, site 223, 2. Polstraat, site 199, 3.Muggeplein, site 262, 4. Smedenstraat, site 236, 5. Stromarkt, site 34, 6. Polstraat 1957, next to Oude Manhuis, 7. Polstraat 21, 8. Molenbelt, site 239.

encountered on a regular basis. Window glass turns up as small sherds of thick pane glass. Moreover, at Dorestad and certainly at Haithabu, large numbers of glass beads in many shapes and sizes are found. However, the glass finds come mostly from late Merovingian contexts rather than 9th- to 12th-century features. Yet at Deventer there are barely a handful of glass beads pre-dating 1400. Sherds of drinking vessels are virtually absent. Fragments of window glass, cup-beakers, jugs and bowls are not known to have ever appeared. The only kind of glass that turns up with any degree of regularity is the glass linen smoother. So far, eight sites have produced some ten specimens from 9th- to 12th-century contexts (see Table 1). The absence of drinking ware in 9th- to 12th-century contexts is mainly due to the decline in long-distance trade in luxury goods. This also applies to Niedersachsen and Nordrhein-Westfalen in Germany, as well as to the eastern Netherlands and Friesland.[1] At the town of Zutphen, located 17 km to the south, glass from the post-Merovingial period up to the 14th century is equally scarce. Yet whether the excavated amount of glassware is a true reflection of the actual amount present in the soil archive, is doubtful. The method of find gathering in the field must have played a role. At Haithabu, for instance, very many features were sieved, so that even quite small items such as glass sherds and beads were recovered. In the Netherlands there was no systematic sieving of archaeological contexts until well into the 1990s, especially in medieval town centres. Systematic sieving was done only at stone-age sites. Still, despite intensive searching with shovels and trowels, little glass has been found. On occasions when soil samples were taken, there usually was no time to fully sieve and sort them. When sieving did take place, the sample volume often proved to be far too small to contain adequate amounts of material. When in coming years sieving will be done more frequently and on a larger scale, especially of early medieval features, the find picture may yet be altered. A similar development occurred when metal detectors were introduced at excavations in the Netherlands: the number of recovered small metal objects soared exponentially. Using the shovel and trowel in rabotage fashion, we will find only the larger and more recognisable pieces of glass.

Glass linen smoothers from early medieval Deventer

In Deventer, most specimens and fragments have been found within the early medieval settlement.[2] Just a single fragment derives from a medieval context outside the boundaries of the medieval town centre.

The eight smoothers found in Deventer are the following:

1. Bruynssteeg 10 (V 223-236, 2003)

Part of the artisans' quarter, situated on one of the axes of the early medieval trading settlement, was excavated in 2003. Rubbish pits, ditches and a row of parallel postholes were found, dating from the earliest phase of occupation, between 825 and 900. These postholes are part of an unknown structure associated with the earliest parcelling system. A smoother came from one of its postholes. The smoother was in such poor condition that it had already disintegrated in the soil and crumbled irretrievably upon excavation.[3] Still it could be established that the dark green smoother was of a usual size. About one third, 120 grammes of it, survived. In the same level no remains were encountered of loomweights, leatherworking waste or other materials that might be clearly linked to artisan activity. From subsequent centuries, such activities are well documented at this site.

2. Polstraat (V 199-763, 1999)

In the course of excavations in the early medieval commercial quarter on the Polstraat, two linen smoothers were recovered from a pit in the bottommost level.[4] Both are intact. The condition of the smoothers in the field and after excavation has remained unchanged; indeed, they could still be used. The first, with a diameter of 8.3 cm and a height of 3.6 cm, and weighing 405 grs, is somewhat smaller than the second. The glass is opaque black in colour and contains some small white inclusions and air bubbles. Lizard skin is absent. The underside is not evenly convex but rather flat on the flanks The edge, however, is nicely rounded. As a result of the smoothing, the entire underside has become dull. On the surface there is evidence of micro-wear in the form of short, straight lines running across the edge towards the middle of the smoother. This suggests that a to-and-fro, rather than a circular movement was made with the lower side of the glass. The surface of the top around the kick is not neatly horizontal, but undulates slightly. On the top, use-wear is hard to identify, but the glass has become dull here. This suggests that not only the bottom but also the top was used for smoothing, possibly with a circular motion. The centre of the top has a kick 1.4 cm deep and within it a pontil scar 1.5 cm across. The sloping surface surrounding the kick clearly shows the torsion of the production process. The gob of glass was twisted into a mould with the pontil iron, producing a tornado-shaped coil. The pontil scar was neatly finished and shows hardly any burrs. On the slopes of the kick, the glass is smooth and glossy.

The second smoother, with a diameter of 9.2 cm, a height of 4.2 cm and a weight of 630 grs, is the larger of the two. Its colour is a deep dark green. The underside is perfectly convex, as are the sides. On the bottom, the glass shows a slight degree of iridescence but no sign of this progressing into a flaky 'lizard skin'. As on the first smoother, short straight wear marks running across the centre can be observed. Apart from the diagonal lines there also are wear marks. Once more the smoother is not quite horizontal at the top, which here too indicates that the top was not carefully finished. On the upper surface, heavy wear-marks suggest that abrasion may have worn down the surface by 0.5 to 1 mm. The sides display a clear gloss, while the rest of the object is dull. The torsion around the pontil scar is slight. The pontil scar measuring 1.1 cm is fairly small and poorly finished.

On either side of the pit lay the remains of large, rectangular, timber-built cellars. To the west lay cellar S212, 4 m wide and 10 m long, and 2 m deep when built. This cellar belonged to a half-timbered house from the period 965-1050.[5] To the east lay another wooden cellar, S213, also belonging to a half-timbered house. This even larger cellar (5 x 10 m) like its western neighbour contained many finds, and also functioned in the 965-1050 period.[6] Given the large amounts of loam floors, carbonized grain, sherds of relief band amphorae and loom-weights, both houses may be linked to the trade in grain and wine, and the production of woven textiles. The interjacent pit containing the smoothers must also date from the period 965-1050.

03 Two glass smoothers found in a pit near the timber-built merchant's house on the Polstraat (Deventer), dated 965-1050. 4.1: from above (left 9,2 cm Ø, right 8,2 cm Ø), 4.2, torsion inside pontil, 4.3, from below, 4.4 ware marks on edge, 4.5, section 9,2 cm Ø.

3. Muggeplein 10 (V 262-244, 2005)
In the bottommost floor layers of a half-timbered house with loam/wattle-and-daub walls, dating from the period 890-910, a quarter of a black linen smoother with lizard skin was found. The earliest identifiable houses on the river side of the Noordenbergstraat may even date from as early as ca AD 900. The floor layers and the pits and holes around them contain large amounts of pottery, including the earliest kind of Pingsdorf ware and tephrite quern fragments. Also the remains of a possible oven structure were uncovered.[7] A second smoother (V 262-308, 2005) occurred in a domestic context dating from AD 1000-1100.

4. Smedenstraat 38-44 (V 236-C13, 2003)
For the construction, shortly after 882, of a protective rampart against the Vikings, soil from the burnt-down settlement was used. Settlement waste thus ended up within the rampart. After 1050, the original body of the rampart (Wal 1) was slightly levelled to broaden the base for a second rampart (Wal 2). Finds from this layer also derived from the pre-882 settlement. The smoother found here had been broken in half, was severely affected by lizard skin and upon excavation crumbled entirely. It had been 10.4 cm across and 3.2 cm high. The fairly coarse black to green glass contained many (15-20%) small, white inclusions and a single air bubble with a diameter of 2-6 mm.[8]

5. Stromarkt 17-19 (V 034-000, 1966)
The Stromarkt lies at the heart of medieval Deventer and reckoning from the river IJssel is about 150 m beyond the bishop's palace. The location is generally thought to have been within the episcopal immunity. The excavations of 1966 uncovered a huge number of features belonging to the early medieval settlement. At a depth of a few metres, a sunken-floored hut of 5 x 5.5 m appeared. It possessed a double floor. The bottom floor consisted of loam and lime mortar, the upper floor just of loam.[9] On the latter lay a quantity of waste that could be dated to the late 11th and early 12th century. Among this waste was a smoother with a shallow kick, a diameter of 6.2 cm and a height of about 3 cm.[10] In his overall analysis of the excavated finds, Spitzers noted that the 9th- to 12th-century features produced very many clay loomweights, at least 18 of them. A number of these were found in the immediate vicinity of the sunken-floored hut.

6. Polstraat 1957
Making an observation close to Polstraat 1, beside the Manhuis, ROB correspondent Alex Dorgelo at a considerable depth recovered a complete smoother. Its exact context is unclear. Given the other finds from the close vicinity, this probably is a smoother from the 900-1200 period. Curiously, the glass does not have smooth flanks from the smooth underside upwards, but consists of a thick, imperfectly compressed glass spiral. A kick with a pontil scar is lacking. We may be dealing with a reject, which during its manufacture was never properly finished.

7. Polstraat 21, 22-3-1984 (Stanlein V 290)
In 1984 large parts of the town centre of Deventer were redeveloped. The premises on the uneven side of the Polstraat were provided with new cellars. volunteers carried out a monitoring

04 Glass smoother found in the body of the 'Viking rampart' (Deventer), 882-890. 5.1 fragments, 10 cm Ø, 5.2 section with white pebbles in structure.

project here (Project 095).[11] Prior to the monitoring, ROB correspondent Jules H. Stanlein made some observations as the building excavation progressed. Among the many features and archaeological finds in the excavation at Polstraat 21, about 2 m below the surface, a shallow cesspit containing mollusc shells and Pingsdorf ware came to light. Here too were a biconical spindle whorl about 3 cm high, and a loomweight or netweight made of a reused, square piece of tuff (about 15 x 15 x 8 cm). The tuff had a small, straight perforation through the centre. Beside these finds, in the same context, appeared half a smoother, broken across the centre. The black glass smoother had a diameter of 7.2 cm, and a height of 3.3 cm. The entire smoother must have weighed about 180 grs, as the recovered half weighed 90 grs. The bottom is evenly convex and again showed short, straight wear marks diagonally along the centre. The wear marks appear specifically on the flank and not on the edge. The rounded top is barely abraded. The pontil scar, 0.9 cm across, is quite small. The surface is dull all over and shows some flaking. Given its context, the smoother may be dated to the period AD 900-1200.

In 1984 a second smoother (Stanlein V 257) was found in a deep cable trench beside Polstraat no.1.[12]

8. Molenbelt (V 239-45, 2005)

This fragment was excavated on a very high coversand rise, about 800 m east of the church of St. Lebuïnus, far outside the rampart-enclosed settlement. The fragment of greyish glass was found at the interface of the prehistoric and early medieval surface and the overlying *plaggen* soil. It constitutes roughly one-eighth of a black smoother with an original diameter of about 8 cm. Its height cannot be reconstructed. As a result of erosion in the sand, the surface had become pale grey and pitted. In its immediate vicinity were found sherds of Walberberg, Pingsdorf, Paffrath and Kugeltopf ware, also none of these associated with any features. This dates the fragment to the 850-1100 period.[13] Possibly this was an area of large production farms serving the town. Town waste may have been used as manure even at this time, which would explain how this fragment ended up in a rural context.

Other early medieval glassware from the centre of Deventer

The amount of glassware recovered in the early medieval centre of Deventer is very modest. A rim sherd of a beaker comes from a settlement predating the Viking raid of 882; it was found on the excavation at the Noordenbergschild.[14] From Muggeplein no 10, a round bead of red glass with a double, wavy trail of white glass was found in the 10th-century cellar of a half-timbered house.[15] In the course of the large-scale redevelopment of the medieval artisans' quarter Noordenberg, Stanlein found some 20 plain blue glass beads with diameters of 5-8 mm in various places, including Muggeplein. The contexts of the beads were always of the 9th or early 11th century.[16] It was not until the 14th century that glassware found its way to the local elite, before becoming increasingly widespread in the 16th century.

Early medieval linen smoothers in the Netherlands

In the eastern Netherlands, linen smoothers from early medieval contexts remain exceptional. The only other find known so far is from the Town Hall excavation at Zutphen. This smoother came from a context within the settlement, datable between 900 and 1100. The linen smoother of green-blue glass has a diameter of 8.8 cm and is 4.4 cm high. The pontil scar is very distinct.[17] In the eastern part of the province of

05 Glass smoother found in the Polstraat (Deventer) in 1957, 7 cm Ø.

Gelderland, glass linen smoothers are as yet unknown.[18] In the Noordoostpolder (Flevoland), on the Oude Emmeloorderweg (*kavel* P14), a linen smoother came from a medieval house platform. The associated pottery dates it to the 12th or 13th century.[19]

In the central Netherlands, the supra-regional emporium Dorestad occupies prime position in terms of early medieval trade. Here, in contrast to Deventer, luxury glassware has been found on a large scale.[20] The bulk of this material could be dated to the 7th and 8th centuries, the Merovingian period. Most of the glassware comes from the site Hoogstraat I; Hoogstraat II, III and IV produced fewer glass finds.[21] The glassware consisted of funnel beakers, the rare squat jars, and bowls. One funnel beaker was decorated with gold leaf; hence this is interpreted as a luxury vessel possibly for liturgical use. The amount of window glass is small. This consists of mainly small, flat fragments with grozed (clipped-off) edges. There were huge numbers of glass beads, of great diversity. The number of linen smoothers was low in comparison with the glassware, but, given the early context, may still be called considerable. From Hoogstraat I came thirteen linen smoothers. These were dark green in colour and mostly showed a dull weathering. One smoother contained white and yellow streaks and 'pebbles'.[22] From Hoogstraat II came seven linen smoothers, from Hoogstraat III four, and a single one from Hoogstraat IV. This brings up to 25 the total so far from the ROB excavations at Dorestad. Some of these linen smoothers are in the collection of the Rijksmuseum van Oudheden (Leiden); part of the Dorestad collection are stray finds.[23]

In 2004, a linen smoother was recovered from a 12th-century watercourse in the newly developed area called Leidse Rijn, 20 km north of Dorestad and 5 km south of the city of Utrecht. It has a diameter of 7 cm and a height of 3.6 cm. The glass is grey, almost black, and has a density of 2.48. The watercourse skirted a large settlement of the 10th-11th century.[24] So far, no early medieval linen smoothers have been found in the old centre of Utrecht.[25]

This lack of smoothers curiously also applies to the early medieval town centre of Tiel, located on the rivers Waal and Linge, between Nijmegen and Dordrecht. Like Utrecht and Deventer, Tiel in the late 9th to 12th centuries played an important role in the trade and the power politics of the Ottonian aristocracy. Although in this period various trades were plied at Tiel, and the recovered material may be called exceptionally rich, glassware was virtually absent among the finds.[26]

06 The distribution of early medieval glass smoothers in the Netherlands, 650-1200 and places mentioned in the text.
1. Deventer, 2. Zutphen, 3. P 14, NOP, 4. Dorestad/Wijk bij Duurstede, 5. Utrecht-Leidse Rijn, 6. Tiel 7. Malburg, Kerk-Avezaath, 8. Stenen Kamer, Zoelen, 9. Oost-Souburg, 10. Burgh, 11. Domburg, 12. Borssele, 13. Aardenburg, 14. Haarlem, 15. Oud-Diemen, 16. Medemblik, 17. Alblaserdam, 18. Dorkwerd, 19. Wirdum, 20. Kollumerland, 21. Ried (near Franeker), 22. Someren, 23. Bakel, 24. Gassel, 25. Beek en Donk, 26. Dommelen, 27. Ittervort, 28. Venray.

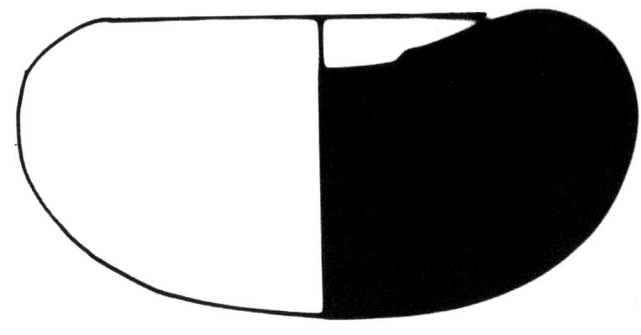

07 Zutphen, 900-1100, 8,8 cm Ø (Illustration Archeologie Zutphen).

In contrast to the trading centre of Tiel, no fewer than four linen smoothers were found 3 km upstream in a 10th- or 11th-century context at Huis Malburg (near Kerk Avezaath) on the river Linge. The linen smoothers from this settlement can be roughly dated 750-1250, but given the associated finds may be put in the 10th-11th century. Their colours are blackish brown (2), dark green (1) and blue-black (1). The smoothers have curious opaque white streaks enclosed within them.[27] From the contemporary settlement at Stenen Kamer (near Zoelen) on the river Linge, 900 m from Huis Malburg, there is no smoother from the same period.[28] This contrast is surprising. No linen smoothers are known from the Merovingian cemeteries along the river Rhine, such as Rhenen, Wageningen and Krefeld-Gellep.[29]

In the western Netherlands (provinces of Zeeland and North and South Holland), linen smoothers are known only from the ring fortresses in Zeeland. A dark brown or green linen smoother with a diameter of 8.8 cm was found in the excavation at Oost Souburg in 1970, in a context dated 880-1000.[30] In 1952, a linen smoother with a diameter of 7.7 cm and a large pontil scar was recovered within the castle mound of Burgh on the island of Schouwen. It was dated to 885-950.[31] Beneath the ring fortress of Domburg, in an archaeological excavation at the Badhotel in 1991, a spurious foundation sacrifice was uncovered. It was the skeleton of a woman aged 45-50, buried in a coffin.[32] Close to her were potsherds (Badorf, Pingsdorf and Paffrath ware), the nether stone of a tephrite quern and a complete linen smoother.[33] Another specimen was found at Borssele in 1961, but remains undated.[34] In excavations at Aardenburg in the 1950s and 1960s, linen smoothers turned up on a regular basis in the cultural layers and rubbish pits, but these were late medieval and fall outside the scope of this inventory.[35]

In terms of linen smoothers, North and South Holland are rather empty provinces. In the excavation on the Grote Markt (Brinkman site) in the centre of Haarlem, a linen smoother was found in a 1100-1250 context,[36] hence presumably associated with the 12th-13th-century timber-built phase of the town. At Oud-Diemen, a village now completely engulfed by new development east of Amsterdam, a rather flat linen smoother emerged from a raised layer on a 13th-century pioneer toft. Its diameter is 6.5 cm and its thickness 1.2 cm; overall height is 1.8 cm. The dark green glass is heavily weathered, has opaque white streaks and a pearly sheen. On the top were some carved lines.[37]

In the western coastal zone, early medieval linen smoothers are so far unknown.[38] In the early medieval trading town of Medemblik a single linen smoother was recovered, at the site Oude Haven-Sint Maartenshof, in a context dated 725-900.[39] A probably early medieval linen smoother was found on the sea floor off the island of Texel.[40] This object may well have spilled out of one of the many 16th- to 18th-century shipwrecks here. No glass linen smoothers are known from the early medieval settlement of Den Burg on Texel.

In South Holland, retting pits and many remains of flax have been found within the marshland pioneer settlement of Alblasserdam-Lange Steeg. These are directly related to the production of flax fibre from flax. The availability of fresh water without lime and iron and its position on the river Alblas will have attracted flax industry to the site in the 13th century. Two linen smoothers were recovered at the settlement. From a ditch in area 2 comes a virtually intact specimen with a diameter of 7 cm and a height of 2.5 cm. A little further on, in area 3, half of a well-preserved linen smoother with a fairly high pontil scar was found *in situ*; 7 cm across and 2.5 cm high.[41] A link is likely between the linen smoothers, flax cultivation, and the flax processing and fibre production, in which the linen smoothers probably played a part in the finishing phase: the smoothing of the fibres.[42]

In the north-eastern coastal region of Groningen and Friesland, linen smoothers are known from several dwelling mounds. At Dorkwerd (Groningen) a linen smoother was excavated in 1908, measuring 7.6 cm across and 3.6 cm in height.

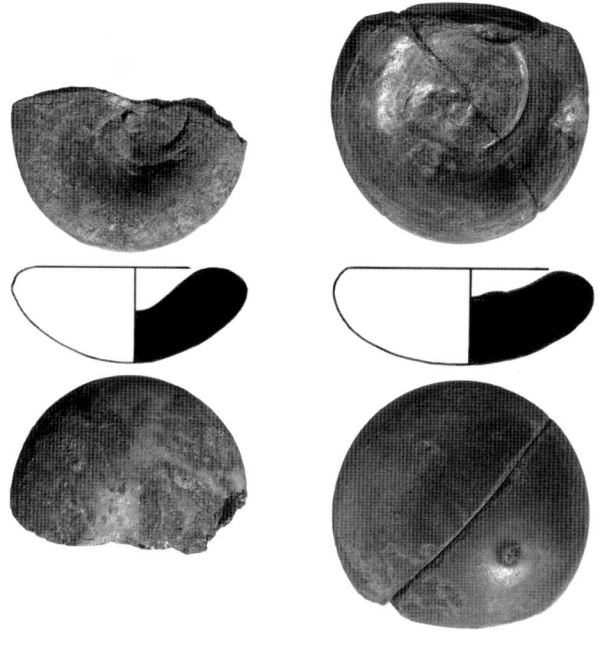

08 Glass smoothers from Alblasserdam, 1200-1300. 8.1, Site 1, 7 cm Ø, 8.2, Site 2, 7 cm Ø (Illustration ADC Archeoprojecten).

In Miedema's analysis of early finds kept at the Groninger Museum, this dark-green to black specimen was placed in the 700-1000 period.[43] Two specimens derive from the village dwelling mound of Wirdum (Groningen) east of Loppersum. These linen smoothers, excavated in 1920, have diameters of 7.4 and 3.7 cm and are 6.7 and 4 cm high, respectively. Both are dark green to black.[44] As yet, no smoothers have been recorded in the city of Groningen.[45]

From the dwelling mound of Wijnaldum, north of Harlingen on the Frisian coast, the most extensively investigated dwelling mound in Friesland so far, a large amount of Merovingian glassware was found. But linen smoothers are lacking. The systematic sieving there did allow a fair amount of broken glass to be recovered. On this 'elite' site, glass beads were made from semi manufactured glass, and various fragments of palm cups and bell beakers were identified. Elzinga catalogued undated linen smoothers from Kollumerland and Ried, near Franeker.[46] Elzinga remarks that well into the 18th century these smoothers were used not only for smoothing textiles, but also in dairying, to smooth down the tops of tubs of butter. A lot of butter was produced in the dwelling-mound region. Yet in the dwelling-mound excavations of Oldenhove at Leeuwarden, smoothers are absent. Nor are any other sites in Leeuwarden known to have produced such finds.[47]

Apart from one remarkable post-medieval exception, no smoothers have been found in the province of Drenthe.[48] Flax growing was an integral part of farming here between the 8th and the 13th centuries.[49] Maybe the people of Drenthe, on grounds of efficiency or economy, preferred smoothers of natural stone. Erratic pebbles are well suited to the job and even today are easy to find throughout the province. A 'yellow' glass smoother comes from a 15th- or 16th-century bronze pot, found in a peatbog near Eelde in July of 1868. Nothing else was found within the pot.[50] Although the find falls outside the period investigated here, depositions of metal vessels outside settlements in the Middle Ages and later in the rural north-east of the Netherlands are interpreted as contexts reflecting remnants of a ritual procedure. The linen smoother in this pot may well have played a ritual role.

In the southern Netherlands, linen smoothers occasionally appear in medieval settlements, somewhat more frequently than in the northwestern provinces. Smoothers turn up fairly regularly in the early medieval settlements on the sandy soils of eastern Noord Brabant. In 1992, a grey-brown linen smoother was uncovered in the excavation Warerdael at Someren. It came from a posthole of a timber building that was dated 1125-1150.[51] The site Bakel-Achter de Molen, yielded a small, thick piece of window glass and part of a small green glass bowl, as well as a linen smoother broken in two. This green smoother has a diameter of 7.4 cm, is neatly convex on the underside, and at the top has a normal kick and pontil scar.[52] The linen smoother came from a demolition trench of a timber building measuring 18 x 8.2 m, which on the basis of a Badorf-like sherd was dated to the 9th or 10th century.[53] In the development area Het Rad van Avontuur at Gassel, south of the river Meuse and east of Cuyk, seventeen features were found in a building excavation, and among them a linen smoother. By the associated Pingsdorf, Paffrath and Andenne ware it could be dated to the 12th century.[54] At Beek en Donk, north of Helmond, investigations were carried out in 1990-1991 into a settlement of the period 900-1100/1200. Here various house plans, wells and a linen smoother were uncovered.[55] At Dommelen, south of Eindhoven, another linen smoother was found, in association with a globular Mayen pot and sherds of Paffrath and Pingsdorf ware.[56]

Among the finds from the excavated aristocratic convent at Susteren (Limburg) which dates from the 9th century, there were no linen smoothers.[57] In the early Middle Ages, Maastricht already was the principal city of Limburg. Much research has focused on this period. Yet glass linen smoothers turn out to have been absent. The full inventory of the glassware from the cemetery of the basilica of St Servaas in Maastricht fails to mention a single linen smoother.[58] At Ittervoort on the west bank of the Meuse a linen smoother was found in a 12th- or 13th-century context. Also in the excavation of Venray-Sint Antoniusveld a late-Carolingian linen smoother came to light.[59]

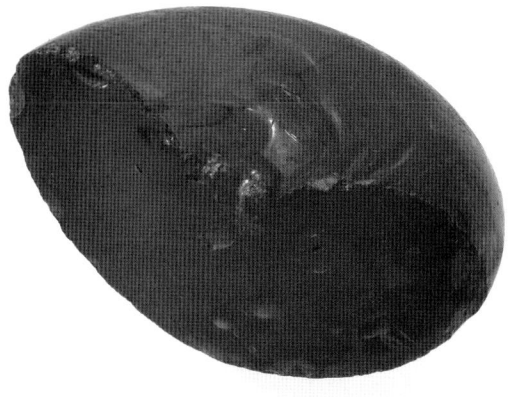

09 Glass smoother from Bakel-Achter de Molen, 9th-10th century, 9.1, from above 7,4 cm Ø, 9.2 from the side (Illustration Archol Leiden)

Glass linen smoothers elsewhere in Europe
Germany
No detailed investigation was made of the occurrence of linen smoothers in Germany, because several useful studies are available. Stepphun compiled inventories of finds from Haithabu (1998) and the town of Schleswig (2002).[60] In 1999, Stepphun published an interpretation of such finds from the literature covering Germany and a large part of north-western Europe. The Low Countries, however, were not considered in his survey, though he does discuss and interpret smoothers from Norway, the environs of St. Denis and Paris (France) and Winchester (UK).

In his research, Stepphun concentrates on the interpretation of the context and the use of the smoothers. The best published site for smoothers in Germany is the emporium of Haithabu. Of the 600 smoothers that Stepphun tracked down throughout north-western Europe, in 1999 no fewer than 103 were counted at Haithabu.[61] These can all be dated to the 7th to 11th centuries. There is little evidence of any typochronological evolution of the linen smoother. At Haithabu, clear dark green as well as dark-green-brown and black smoothers occur. All of them are solid and opaque, but some transparent ones are also present. At Haithabu too, the glass contains air bubbles and coloured streaks, which show that the glass is not homogeneous. About 70% of the smoothers are corroded through and through which is due to the poor quality of the glass. At Haithabu the diameter of the smoothers is between 7 and 10 cm; about half of them have the standard size of 8 cm. Their average diameter is 8.24 cm. Their height varies between 2.7 and 5.1 cm. An average-sized specimen will weigh 400 grs. Hollow smoothers are rare and are only found in 7th- to 9th-century contexts. The distribution of the many smoothers in the emporium shows no particular hotspots, though small clusters may be observed in two areas with some further evidence of textile production and processing. The smoothers turn up in domestic contexts as household implements.[62] Some were recovered in the Great Hall of Haithabu.[63] On the opposite bank of the river Schlei lies the trading settlement of Schleswig. Stepphun described its linen smoothers of the 11th-17th centuries. Of the total of 13 specimens, three come from the 11th- to 13th-century period, and were found in the excavation of Schleswig-Schild. Their dimensions are similar to those of the smoothers from Haithabu.[64]

The exact distribution and the associated contexts in Germany were not investigated. Yet it is clear that the smoothers occur both in rural settlements, e.g. 'Hambach 500' east of Aachen, and in the trading centres mentioned above.[65] As in the Netherlands, linen smoothers are quite common in towns after 1200. So far, two sites in Germany have produced evidence of smoother production. Besides other glassware such as finger rings, window panes and drinking vessels, six linen smoothers dating from 1200-1240 were found at the Waldglashütte (glasshouse) Steimke in the Bramwald forest near Göttingen, Niedersachsen.[66] A second 13th-century production centre was identified at Schriersheim, north of Heidelberg.[67]

Switzerland
When it comes to Switzerland, there is an important publication by Schmaedecke. He conducted a survey of finds in the cantons of north-western Switzerland. As this inventory was more object- than context-focused, it fails to provide evidence for his later assertions relating to process and context. Their distribution around the upper reaches of the Rhine shows that linen smoothers occur in rural settings, i.e. mountain villages, as well as in the towns of Zürich and Basel. At Basel six smoothers turned up in the 11th- and 12th-century artisans' quarter on the Petersberg.[68] Schmaedecke's argument however does not so much focus on the local cultural context, as on his attempt to prove that linen smoothers were in fact 'glasscakes', semi products intended for further processing. This different function attributed to the objects certainly opens up surprising perspectives.

Belgium, Luxemburg and France
Apparently - as far as this survey could ascertain - just a few smoothers come from either Flanders or Wallonia. In Flanders, an early medieval smoother was found in the *portus* of Ename (Oost-Vlaanderen) on the river Scheldt. Other early medieval smoothers are known from Beveren-Waas, Jabbeke, Snellegem-Meerbeelsestraat, Oudenburg-Ter Beke and Oostkamp-'t Zwarte Gat.[69]

In Wallonia smoothers were found at any rate in the early medieval settlement of Namur.[70] Another - late medieval - smoother, of black glass, comes from the living quarters of the castle of Beaumont (Esneux) in the Ardennes.[71] The fortress of Luxemburg-city, the capital of the grand-duchy, yielded a fairly small smoother, 5 cm across and 2 cm high, from a 13th-century context.[72]

Most of the French linen smoothers have been recovered in the region of Paris and Saint Denis.[73] These can be dated from the 8th century up to 1000, and come both from the civilian settlement and the abbey of St. Denis.[74] Also, ten linen smoothers were found in the 9th- and 10th-century context of the castle of Blois, close to Paris. A single outlier is datable to the late 8th or early 9th century. The smoothers' diameters lie between 7.9 cm and 8.1 cm.[75]

Scandinavia

In Scandinavia, linen smoothers occur in Norway as well as in Sweden and Denmark. It would take us too far to discuss them all here, but in the debate about their interpretation an important point is that the earliest smoothers come from Viking contexts, both settlements and cemeteries, and date from the 7th century onwards. Smoothers are known from the Swedish Viking sites of Sigituna, Helgø and Birka. At Birka, the large emporium west of Stockholm, smoothers come both from male (1) and female (5) graves.[76]

Smoothers also regularly turn up in Viking settlements in Norway. In Denmark is Ribe in particular where they are found with some frequency.[77]

The British Isles

In the British Isles too, the earliest smoothers appear in Viking contexts. At Kilmainham-Islandbridge, west of Dublin, a smoother was found in one of the thirty male or nine female burials. The Viking (i.e. Norse-period) cemetery as a whole is dated to between 841 and 902.[78] Also in the context of a Viking grave, but on the most south-westerly Scottish island of Islay, woman's burial at Ballinaby contained a black glass linen smoother. Together with a tinned bronze needle-case, a bronze ladle, a necklace with twelve beads and a silver pin, this grave, presumably of the 8th or 9th century, was a very rich one.[79] A remarkable find in this grave was an iron heckle for flax processing.[80] In the Orkneys three 9th-century smoothers were found.[81] On the southeast coast of the Isle of Man near the village of Cronc ny Merriu, a smoother was contained in the wall footing of a Norse house.[82] Both in Norway and on the Scottish islands, not only glass linen smoothers but also so-called whalebone plaques are found. These plaques were used for pressing linen pleats into shape. In Scotland these plaques are quite rare; a single one was found in 1992 in Ruisgarray on the island of Berneray, between North Uist and Lewis.[83] A combination of whalebone plaques and linen smoothers is occasionally found in the Viking world. About forty glass smoothers are known from the Norse period in Scotland, roughly as many as we have from Norway, which means that they are quite rare.[84] Apart from the 8th- to 10th-century finds in the Scottish isles, glass smoothers also occur in 12th- to 14th-century domestic contexts, in towns such as Perth.[85]

In England, linen smoothers are largely an early urban affair. The Peter's Street excavation in Northampton produced four specimens from Saxon-period layers. The early 11th-century smoothers are of the usual size; the later, 14th- to 15th-century ones gradually increase in size to a diameter of 9 cm.[86] At Thetford (Norfolk) three smoothers are known from various excavations, their contexts being pits and sunken-floored huts. One can be dated as pre-10th century; a second, from a sunken-floored hut, is dated to the 12th century at the latest.[87] North of the river a third was found, coming from an 11th- or 12th-century context.[88]

So far, York has been the place richest in smoothers. From a Viking-period context on Clifford Street, a number of smoothers were recovered, of which two were in good shape. One has a rather high kick and another is fairly conical.[89] Since the late 1950s up till 1997 as many as 41 linen smoothers were found in 10th- to 14th-century contexts. Ninth-century smoothers are quite rare at York. The average diameter in this period lies between 7 and 7.5 cm, with heights of 2.3 to 4.1 cm. Many smoothers display fine wear marks, mostly radiating from the centre. Many of the smoothers were broken down the middle, and show a glossy break, which indicates good-quality glass. These smoothers were presumably produced at York-Coppergate in the 10th to 12th centuries.[90] Of the 41 smoothers, 25 date from the Anglo-Scandinavian period. Besides, also three stone smoothers were found. One is of sandstone, another of mudstone or siltstone and finally there is one of an unidentified, glossy black rock.[91] At York, the frequent occurrence of smoothers is linked to innovations in textile manufacturing and an increase in the output of linen and woollen fabrics.[92]

In London, four linen smoothers have turned up in 9th- and 10th-century contexts.[93] The earliest smoothers date from the Viking period, which in the London context is related to changing fashions and the wearing of smoothed, shiny linen fabrics.[94] Finally, in the large-scale excavations at Winchester, thirteen linen smoothers were recovered up till 1990, their dates ranging from the first quarter of the 10th century well into the 15th century. Twelve of them are of the 13th century or later; there is no evidence of a gradual increase in diameter.[95]

Interpretation

There is some controversy about the interpretation of the smoothers in early medieval contexts. Globally, there are three views:

- smoothers were used for smoothing textiles and leather (Stepphun)
- smoothers were semi manufactures in the glass working industry (Schmaedecke)
- smoothers were ritual objects (Gratuze)

This last opinion is voiced in French quarters. Most of the smoothers in France, York and Haithabu are made of wood-ash glass, but a minority consist of a quite rare silica-lime-lead glass. At Melle, southwest of Poitiers (France), glassmaking waste was found with this very composition, marked by the presence of barium, aluminium and lead-silver components. In view of this unusual composition, Gratuze wonders whether this chemically distinct minority might not have served an apotropaic rather than a merely utilitarian purpose. He does not exclude the possibility that these special glass smoothers were traded by the Vikings. He rejects the idea of their being semi manufactures for further glassworking.[96] Still, the absence of ritual cultural contexts of early medieval smoothers does pose a problem. The single postmedieval ritual deposition is convincing and underlines the special nature of these objects, but is not enough to validate Gratuze's proposition. It must be concluded that Gratuze's proposition is not supported by the Dutch and other northwest European finds. From Switzerland comes the opinion that smoothers are semi manufactures for further glassworking, such as the production of small window panes and beads. Even in the light of Swiss finds, the cultural evidence supporting the assertion is very thin. In association with smoothers, there should also be small kilns for remelting, where the glass was next to be processed. As far as this survey has been able to establish, these are totally absent. Other semi manufactures look very different.[97] They consist of thick glass plates, easy to break up for weighing out the correct amount and for transportation. Globular pieces would not be so amenable. Indeed, people generally used broken glass, both in early- and late-medieval contexts. For both Dorestad and Ribe, travelling glassblowers have been postulated, who would make new glassware out of old sherds. Hence broken glass was considered a valuable commodity.[98] A glassblowing industry has been demonstrated in 10th-/11th-century York. In Groningen (the Netherlands) a 17th-century glass kiln was investigated that used broken glass as its raw material.[99] Moreover, the composition of many smoothers seems to be so impure that making them into fine clear or coloured drinking vessels or brightly coloured beads would be a tall order. Beads were fashioned from glass rods rather than from massive gobs of dark glass.

Moreover, in Carolingian buildings incorporating quite a lot of window glass, such as the palace at Paderborn, batches of broken glass were found but no smoothers.[100] The bulk of the glass from the Paderborn excavation dates from the period 750-850. The finds include 1600 fragments of window glass, and funnel beakers, but no smoothers. Gai believes that probably *Fritte-Klumpen* or semi manufactured glass were supplied from which panes and vessels were made locally. No evidence of such semi manufactures was recovered at Paderborn. Still, a small, domed kiln was found in which new glass had been made. This predated 778. Here were are probably dealing with travelling glassblowers who plied their particular trade for short periods at any site.[101] The rough glass presumably came from central and southern Europe; only after 800 did the amount of locally produced glass increase. This was made from wood ash, quartz sand and lime. For one kilogram of glass, some 200 - 250 kg of beech wood would be required.[102] Given the poor reusability of glass in the shape of smoothers for making glass vessels, Schmaedecke's suggestion seems hardly tenable. Also, the general lack of glass in 9th- to 12th-century contexts prompts the question why we should be finding semi manufactures in the form of smoothers but no finished products such as drinking ware.

The third proposed use of these artefacts is for smoothing textiles, particularly wool and linen, and also in fibre production. At the end of the manufacturing process of flax fibres or woollen or linen textiles, these would usually be dyed and finished. The finishing treatment of woollen material entailed the removal of surplus fibres, known as shearing, and pressing, also called calandering. The latter made the fabric more compact and less apt to absorb dirt. Originally this was done with a smoother; from the 18th century on, a calandering press was used.[103] After heated iron and ceramic smoothers came into use in the 17th century, the use of glass smoothers declined. Flax fibres and linen too were smoothed, in order to crush and remove impurities.

The smoother was hand-held and moved to and fro on the fabric or the fibres. The glass was not heated but became warm through the friction. The radial wear marks indicate that the movement was unidirectional; no circular movements were made.[104] The microwear on the smoothers was not made by the actual fibre or fabric, but by sand and other impurities engrained in it. Some deeper grooves may come from the mould in which the smoother was shaped.[105] Woven material as well as items made of felt or lace were smoothed. Seams and pleats in linen garments especially required smoothing.[106] Smoothers were used also for finishing starched linen. From the Viking funerary contexts it is evident that linen was worn by the wealthier women in particular. The damp pleated material would be wound around whalebone plaques, and thus be left to dry.[107] In the British Isles, the fashion of wearing linen was directly related to the introduction of flax, which was its source. The new dress style coincided with the arrival of the Vikings in these parts. The link between flax cultivation, fashion, immigration, and the use of smoothers is obvious. An equally obvious connection is that of smoothers with textile production in the form of wool spinning (recovered spindle whorls) and of weaving on vertical looms (loomweights and weaving battens). Besides, smoothers were used for smoothing thin leather and suede, and for grinding seeds and herbs.[108]

In the case of Deventer, the cultural context of the smoothers seems mostly associated with pits, sunken-floored huts and cellars of the trading settlement, in which spindle whorls or large numbers of loomweights or horn cores may be found, items directly linked to the production of textiles or leather. It is unclear whether we are dealing with just wool, or linen as well. The production and supply of wool is certain.[109] Flax production around Deventer in the 9th-19th centuries was a definite possibility, given the occurrence of flax in the excavations of 6th- to 8th-century Odoorn and the presence of clumps of this plant at several early medieval sites.[110] Given the contexts, it seems evident that we are not just dealing with merchandise of the wealthier merchants in the 11th- and 12th-century Polstraat district, but also with smoothers from 9th- and 10th-century features relating to artisans in the early urban settlement. There was no evidence of a local shift in fashions towards the wearing of linen fabrics. As yet no textiles have been recovered from this period. But it seems more than likely that people came into touch with new fabrics and fashions through foreign cultural influences; for instance, given the friendly and less friendly contacts, from the Vikings. The Vikings in the Low Countries often belonged to the elite, entertaining relations with the local headmen, and with them may well have set the fashion trends. However, the linen smoothers should not simply be regarded as reflecting a process of cultural exchange with the Vikings: linen smoothers were used in the Netherlands well before the latter's arrival and long after their departure. Still, at Deventer the earliest smoothers did occur in the period of closest contacts with the Vikings, the 9th century. Subsequently, they remained in use well into the 12th century.

In the Netherlands, the earliest medieval smoothers turned up at Dorestad. Here also the largest number have been found. Dorestad is known as a location for the exchange of prestige goods and a residence for the elite. The same goes for small early-medieval trading centres like Medemblik. From the late Carolingian trading centre of Tiel, but also from Utrecht, no smoothers are known, while in a place like Deventer, comparable in development and economic potential, they do appear. Remarkably, both at Tiel and Deventer utensils of whale bone have been found and it is very likely that fresh whale meat was eaten locally.[111] Whale bone plaques have never turned up in the Netherlands. In settlements outside the large emporia a few smoothers may appear (Marburg and Zutphen) or not appear (Stenen Kamer). Sometimes smoothers occur as single finds (Leidse Rijn). In the carefully investigated settlement of Limmen near Castricum, a great deal of imported pottery but just one fragment of a glass funnel beaker was found; loomweights too are few in number (5) whilst spindle whorls and glass smoothers are absent.[112] Flax growing is demonstrated here, but given the brackish water at the site its processing must have taken place out in the open air (retting in the field, retting in dew) or elsewhere altogether. Leaden spindle whorls and sheep or goat bones attest to the presence of wool in the settlement.

In the late medieval villages on the sandy soils of Noord-Brabant and along the river Meuse we occasionally find smoothers, although there are no major trading settlements close by. Smoothers are found also in the dwelling mounds of Groningen and the ring fortresses of Zeeland. Twente, Drenthe and the eastern part of Gelderland, as well as the hilly parts of Utrecht seem devoid of smoothers. It remains hard to pinpoint what underlies this pattern of distribution.

Possibly settlements on aristocratic estates were assigned specific tasks, which resulted in some implements being restricted to particular sites. Maybe in these villages the presence of a smoother reflects some degree of wealth, or merely the absence of natural pebbles suitable for smoothing. On the current evidence, any idea of smoothers being gender-specific items must be rejected, for the Low Countries at any rate. The convent of Susteren is a well-investigated site, which specifically accommodated aristocratic ladies in the early Middle Ages; yet it failed to produce a single smoother. The use of smoothers as semi manufactures for glassware production can also be ruled out for Deventer and the Netherlands in general. Any glassware, such as drinking cups, simply is lacking (Deventer) or quite

10 A Viking maid using a glass smoother on linen cloth wrapped around an 'ironing board'. Drawing by Virve Kiil, 2007, DK.

different in colour from the smoothers. No ritual or occult associations can be attached to the early medieval Dutch finds. Given the slight amount of glass circulating in early medieval communities, smoothers must be regarded as luxury products with a special purpose. In the early medieval Netherlands, they were used in fibre production, for finishing fine, fashionable textiles and for making certain garments shiny and stiff. This means that smoothers were implements for special uses. Why we have a relatively small number of smoothers in the 13th to 15th centuries is still an open question. In post-medieval times, the 16th to 18th centuries, smoothers are found in ample numbers. They served the purpose of laundering irons. It seems that the use of fibre smoothers had been abandoned by this time.

At a few trading sites in Europe, like Haithabu and York, access to smoothers for domestic or craft purposes presumably was a different matter: 'Any laundress, needlewoman would not have to go far, as there was a workshop using high-lead glass at Coppergate'.[113]

Acknowledgements

I wish to thank sincerely all colleagues who assisted me in my search for linen smoothers; in the Netherlands: Michel Groothedde for our discussions and for critically reading the text, Jules Stanlein, Emile Mittendorff, Bart Vermeulen, Herre Wynia, Pim Verwers, Wim van Es, Fiet van Lidt, Jaap Kottman, Stijn Cornelissen, Margje Vermeulen, Gerrit Groeneweg, Annemarieke Willemsen, Egge Knol, Adri Ufkes, Vincent van Vilsteren, Eric van der Kuijl, Peter de Boer, Alexandra van Dijk, Henk Stoepker and many other Dutch colleagues;
in the UK: Andrew Nicholson, Nicola Rogers, Jackie Kelly and Jane Cowgill;
in Belgium: Koen de Grote and Yann Hollevoet;
in France: Bernard Gratuze and Geert Verbrugghe;
in Switzerland: Andreas Heege and Michael Schmaedecke;
and in Sweden: Matias Bäck.

All illustrations are courtesy of Archeologie Deventer, Gemeente Deventer; except the following: Utrecht-Leidse Rijn: Gemeente Utrecht; Alblas: ADC Archeoprojcten; Bakel: Archol Leiden.

Notes

1. In fact drinking vessels were present, but only in very small numbers . An exception can be made for churches and monastic institutions where some flat window glass may occur (pers. comm. Sveva Gai, LWL Paderborn).
2. For the extent of the early medieval settlement, see: Bartels 2005, Vermeulen 2006, Mittendorff 2007.
3. Mittendorff & Vermeulen 2004, 17.
4. Area 1A, level 5, no feature number; a smoother was erroneously labelled 1065. Spitzers 2000, 125; the feature is the pit in the south section between cellars S 212 and S 213.
5. Mittendorff 2004, 13, 70.
6. Mittendorff 2004, 14, 70.
7. Bartels & Vermeulen 2005, 16-18.
8. Bartels 2006, 76, 81.
9. Sarfatij 1973, 389-390.
10. Spitzers 1996, 122 (fig. 4), 123-124.
11. Mittendorff 2007, 119-132.
12. Stanlein s.a., 32, 64.
13. Hermsen 2005, 31.
14. Bartels 2006, 141-142.
15. Bartels & Vermeulen 2005, 29.
16. Identification was at the time performed by Hein Wijnman, glass specialist at the Rijksdienst voor het Oudheidkundig Bodemonderzoek (now Rijksdienst Archeologie Cultuurlandschap en Monumenten).
17. Henkes 3003, 4. Find number ZU-ST V758-01.
18. In the eastern part of the province of Gelderland, glass linen smoothers do not make a regular appearance until the 17th century (pers. comm. Eric van der Kuijl, Ruurlo).
19. Archis no. 27860; the find is associated with early grey-firing ware and Kugeltopf ware (author's observation 1993).
20. Isings 1980; Roes 1965, 42-43.
21. Isings, *in prep*.
22. Isings 1980, 233.
23. In the collection of the Rijksmuseum van Oudheden, Leiden. These finds turn out not to be from the cemetery.
24. Pers. comm. Herre Wynia; Archeologie Gemeente Utrecht: Hoge Weide site, find no. LR 48. v 257.
25. One linen smoother comes from a 17th-century cesspit on the Eligenstraat, find no. ELI00-391.
26. In the available and accessible literature, no early medieval glass items are mentioned. Nor are any such objects known to the author from his own observations in the years 1994-2006. The grey literature (company reports) from the period 2000-2005 was not fully scrutinized for this survey. See also Bartels & Oudhof, 2007.
27. Kleij 2000, 195-196.
28. Kleij 2000, 320. The author was project manager on this site of the Betuweroute project, closely followed the finds from both sites and is able to confirm the difference.
29. Van Dijk-Van der Moolen 1997 and written comm. Alexandra van Dijk, August 2006.
30. Van Heeringen 1995, 170, fig. 113.
31. Van Heeringen 1995, 36, fig. 27.
32. Van Heeringen 1995, 28.
33. Archis no. 26544. The burial itself held no finds (pers. comm. Robert van Heeringen, RACM).
34. In the collection of the RMO, acc. no. i1961/1.3.
35. Trimpe Burger, 1965, 216. Trimpe Burger does note a link between 13th/14th-century cloth production in Brabant and the occurrence of smoothers.
36. Archis no. 18566.

37. In the collection of AWN Amsterdam, acc. no. DM 87-1011, with thanks to Piet van Reenen and Paul Hoogers.
38. These are absent at the large-scale excavations at Limmen (North Holland) and other sites(pers. comm. Menno Dijkstra, AAC-University of Amsterdam).
39. Archis no. 30964.
40. Archis no. 17696.
41. De Boer 2006, 52, 115 (The dates from the catalogue were adhered to.)
42. De Boer 2006, 97.
43. Miedema 1983, 296 and fig. 263. Groninger Museum, acc. no: 1908-IX-20/7.
44. Miedema 1999, 326, 433, fig. 188-1 (Wirdum7Ez/En84, 1920/V7) and fig. 188-2 (Wirdum7Ez/En84, 1920/VI 23).
45. Gert Kortekaas (municipal archaeologist, Groningen) notes that smooth erratic pebbles were sometimes used for this purpose. In Groningen, plenty of erratics are found locally.
46. Archis nos. 238700 (Ried, Friesland) and 300446 (Kollumerland, Friesland).
47. Pers. comm. Jan Willem Oudhof (Gemeente Leeuwarden).
48. Written comm. Vincent van Vilsteren (Drents Museum, Assen) and Adri Ufkes (ARC Consultancy, Groningen), January 2006.
49. Spek 2004, 535-538.
50. Van Vilsteren 1998, 115; Van Vilsteren 2000, 117.
51. Someren Warerdael, find no. SMR II 92-3-1239-1. Building 12. Eva Kars (ADC Archeoprojecten, Amersfoort) notes that this smoother was made from French glass waste. From the same context comes a smoother made of stone.
52. Arnoldussen 2003, 166-168.
53. Arnoldussen 2003, 50-51, 173-175. Other finds from the plan are a fragment of a tephrite quern, a piece of sandstone and a flint blade.
54. Archis no. 38750.
55. Archis no. 21664.
56. Archis no. 14215. Dated by the pottery to the 9th-11th century.
57. Pers. comm. Henk Stoepker (Maaswerken project).
58. Pers. comm. Sophia van Lith. Van Lith here refers to an unpublished survey by Sablerolles and Van Lith, 1994.
59. Pers. comm. Jacob Schotten (RACM); both are as yet unpublished.
60. Stepphun 1998; 1999; 2002.
61. Stepphun 1999, 114; Stepphun 1998, 74.
62. Stepphun 1998, 74-76.
63. Jankuhn 1943, 110.
64. Stepphun 2002, 100-101.
65. Heege 1997, 174-175 and *Tafel* 131, no. 1590. Two smoothers come from Hambach 500: one from a ditch and one from a posthole of a 12th-century building.
66. Stephan 1992, 103.
67. Schmaedecke 1998, 95, note 18.
68. Schmaedecke 1998 110-114.. Concerning the rest of Europe, the survey must be regarded as very patchy, and is based on rather dated literature.
69. Pers. comm. Yann Hollevoet (Vlaams Instituut voor het Onroerend Erfgoed).
70. Schmaedecke 1998, 114-115.
71. Eubelen 1997, 31.
72. Bis-Worch 1999, 338.
73. Stepphun 1998, 135, plate 20; Maquet 1990.
74. Cuisinier& Guadagnin 1988, 287-288.
75. Gratuze 2000, 109, 150-151.
76. Sigituna: Henricson 1996; Uppland: Henricson 1993; Helgö: Henricson 1990; Birka: Arbman 1937 and Schmaedecke 1998, 105. Danmark: Sode 2007.
77. Lund Feveile 2006. The smoothers are mentioned but not described.
78. Ó Flóinn 1992, 320.
79. Graham-Campbell & Batey, 1998, 122.
80. Ritchie 2001, 89.
81. Ritchie 2001, 60. The three smoothers are antiquarian finds and not well provenanced (e-mail communication Anne Brundle, The Orkney Museum.
82. Cubbon 1983, 18 and note 19. A linen smoother was excavated in the 1950s by P.S. Ceiling of Birmingham University.
83. Batey 1994, 109.
84. Batey 1994; Ritchie 2001, 46.
85. Bowler *et al.* 1995, 970, 976, plate 561.
86. Williams 1979, 82. Williams also mentions English finds at Great Yarmouth in Norfolk. Norfolk) in an 11th-century context; at Hangleton (Sussex), 13th century; and at Lyveden (Northants.), 15th century.
87. Rogerson & Dallas, 1984?, 27. The smoothers are of a very dark colour.
88. Talbot 1999, 44.
89. Waterman 1959, 96, nos 36 and 37.
90. Walton-Rogers 1997, 1772, 1775-1776.
91. Mac Gregor 1999, 2534, 2626.
92. Mac Gregor 1976, 102.
93. Pritchard 1992, 173. Meanwhile, this number has significantly risen (pers. comm. Paul Courtney), Leicester).
94. Pritchard 1992, 173.
95. Charleston 1992, 240-241.
96. Gratuze 2002.
97. Stepphun 1998, 76.
98. Isings, *in prep.*; Lund Feveile 2006, 253.
99. Van Gangelen 1988, 175-176.
100. Gai 1999, 212-213.
101. Gai 1999, 214.
102. Wedepohl 1999, 219-220.
103. Bitter 1999, 20.
104. Walton-Rogers 1997, 1775.
105. Stepphun 1999, 113.
106. Pritchard 1992, 173.
107. Ritchie 2001, 46.
108. Stepphun 1999, 113-114. From the 19th century on, smoothers were also used for smoothing wet paper, as paperweights, as implements for darning socks and the like (see Stepphun 1999), and for the smoothing of butter in tubs (remark by Elzinga).
109. From every excavation in the town centre come large numbers of sheep and goat bones.
110. Spek 2004, 536.
111. Holthuis, Smeenk & Laarman 1998. Tiel: A barnacle that grows on the skin of northern whale and a vertebral epiphysis of a Eubalena glacialis, used as a dish with cutting marks on the top. Bartels & Oudhof, 2007, 444-445. Tenth-century layers in the 1980-1981 Polstraat excavations at Deventer also produced whale bones.
112. Dijkstra, De Koning & Lange 2006, 108, 212-213.
113. Walter-Rogers 1997, 1772.

References

Arbman, H., 1937.Karolingiosche Glasindustrie und die Einfuhr von Glaswaren nach Skandiavien, in: *Kungl. Vitterhets Historie och Antikvitets Akademiens Handlingar* 14-3-10. Stockholm

ARCHIS, archaeological database operated by the Dutch State Service for Archaeology and Monuments (formerly ROB, now RACM).

Arnoldussen, S., 2003. Middeleeuwse bewoning te Bakel Achter de Molen (*Archol Rapport* 16). Leiden.

Bartels, M. H., 2005. Deventer anno 882, van *tabula rasa* tot de phoenix van het IJsseldal. Vikingagressie als kans voor een nieuwe ruimtelijke ordening in een Karolingische handelsplaats. In: *Madoc* 19, 74-84.

Bartels, M. H. & B. Vermeulen, 2005. *Rapport inventariserend veldonderzoek Muggeplein, Deventer*. Interne Rapportage Archeologie Deventer.

Bartels, M. H. & J-W Oudhof, 2007. Tiel, opkomst, bloei en ondergang van (het onderzoek naar) de vroegmiddeleeuwse handelsnederzetting, in: *Westerheem* 56, 440-452.

Batey, C., 1994. A Viking whalebone plaque fragment and a linen smoother, in: *Glasgow Archaeological Journal* 19, 109-113.

Bis-Worch, C., 1999. Lissoir ou lingot de verre, in: NN: *Le passé recomposé, archéologie urbaine à Luxembourg*. Luxemburg. 338.

Bitter, P. 1999. *Goed gevonden, textielvondsten uit de archeologische opgravingen in de Grote- of St. Laurenskerk te Alkmaar* (=Rapportages over de Alkmaarse Archeologie en Monumentenzorg 7). Alkmaar.

Bowler, D. et al. 1995. Four excavations in Perth, 1979-84, in: *Proceedings of the Society for Antiquities in Scotland* 125, 917-999.

Charleston, R. J., 1990. Slick stones 'linen smoothers', in: Biddle, M. (ed.). *Object and economy in medieval Winchester, artefacts from medieval Winchester* (=Winchester Studies 7ii), Oxford, 240-241.

Cubbon, M.,1983. The archaeology of the Vikings on the Isle of man, in: C. Fell et al. (eds.) *The Viking age in the Isle of Man*. London.

Cuisiner, J. & Guadagnin, R., (red.), 1988. - *Un village au temps de Charlemagne. Moines et paysans de l'abbaye de Saint-Denis du VIIe sièce à l'an Mil*. Catalogue de l'exposition du Musée National des arts et traditions populaires, 29 novembre 1988 - 30 avril 1989 ; Paris.

Dijk – Van der Moolen, van, 1997. *Merovingisch glas in Nederland, een inventarisatie*. Typescript Vrije Universiteit Amsterdam.

Eubelen, M., 1997. Fouilles de château de Beaumont (Esneux), in: *Archeo-contact, cercle archeo-historique Ardenne-Condroz* 25.

Gai, S., 1999. Karolingische Glasfunden der Pfalz Paderborn, in: C. Stiegmann & M. Wemhoff (Hrsg.) *799 Kunst und Kultur der Karolingerzeit* III, Mainz, 212-217.

Gangelen, H, van, 1988. De Glasblazerij, in: P. H. Broekuizen (red.) *Kattendiep Deurgraven, archeologisch en historisch onderzoek aan de noordzijde van het Gedempte Kattendiep te Groningen*, Groningen, 175-176.

Graham-Campbell, J. & C. E. Batey, 1998. *Vikings in Scotland, an archaeological survey*. Edinburgh.

Gratuze, B., 2000. L'Étude des verres à vitre carolingiens de Blois, in: *Blois, un château en l'an mil*, Paris.

Gratuze, B. 2002, Les lissoirs carolingiens en verre au plomb: mise en évidence de la valorisation des scories issues du traitement des galènes argentières de Melle (Deux Sevres) (*abstracts and internet papers from the 33rd International Symposium on Archaeometry*, April 22-26, 2002, Amsterdam, The Netherlands, VU-University)

Haevernick, Th. E. & W. Haberey, 1963. *Glättsteine aus Glas, in: Beiträge zur Geschichte des antiken Glases*. (= Jahrbuch des Römisch-Germanischen Zentralmuseums Mainz 10).

Heege, A., 1997. Hambach 500, Villa rustica und früh- bis hochmittelalterliche Siedlung Wüstweiler (Gemeinde NIederzier), Kreis Düren, in: *Rheinische Ausgrabungen* 41, Keulen.

Heeringen, R. M. van, P.A. Henderikx & A. Mars (red.) *Vroeg-Middeleeuwse ringwalburgen in Zeeland*. Goes/Amersfoort.

Henkes, H. E., 2003. Glaswerk uit kleine glascomplexjes, opgraving Zupthen Stadhuis, in M. Groothedde & H. E. Henkes (red.) *Zutphens glas zonder glans*. Zutphen (CD-publication), 2-4.

Henricson, L. G., 1986. *Glaset i Birka : en material- och tillverkningsteknologisk studie Stockholms universitet*. Stockholm.

Henricson, L. G., 1990. Glas i svensk forntid, in: *Arkeographica* 4.

Henricson, L. G., 1990. Glasfragment och Helgö : identifikation/rekonstruktion, in: *Laborativ arkeologi* 4, 57-64.

Henricson, L. G., 1993. Late Viking period and early medieval glass and glass beakers of an „oriental" origin from recent excavations in Uppland, Eastern Central Sweden. in; G. Arwidsson *et al.* (eds.) *Sources and resources : studies in honour of Birgit Arrhenius*. Lund, 491-504.

Henricson, L. G., 1996. Bysantinska och venetianska glasbägare i Sigtunas svarta jord. in: *Vikingars guld ur Mälarens djup*. Sigitua, 29-31.

Hermsen, I., 2005. *De bodem onder de belt, archeologie en geschiedenis van een agrarisch gebeid in de Voorstad van Deventer*. (Interne Rapporten Archeologie Deventer).

Holthuis, L. B., C. Smeenk & F. J. Laarman, 1998. The find of a whale barnacle, *Cetopirus complanatus* (Mörch 1853) in 10th century deposits in The Netherlands, in: *Zoölogische Verhandelingen Leiden* 323, 349-363.

Isings, C., 1980. Glass finds from Dorestad, Hoogstraat I, in W. A. van Es & J. Verwers (eds.) *Excavations at Dorestad* 1 (= Nederlandse Oudheden 9), 225-238.

Isings, C., Glass, in: W. van Es, J. Verwers & J. van Doesburg (red.) *Excavations at Dorestad* 2 (in process, pre-print)

Jankuhn, H, 1939. *Die Ausgrabungen in Haitabu 1937-1939*. Berlin.

Kleij, P., 2000. Glas, in: J. W. M. Oudhof, J. Dijkstra & A. A. A. Verhoeven (red.) *'Huis Malburg' van spoor tot spoor, een middeleeuwse nederzetting in Kerk Avezaath* (= Archeologie in de Betuweroute/ Rapportages Archeologische Monumentenzorg 81). Amersfoort. 195-199.

Kleij, P., 2000. Glas, in: A. A. A. Verhoeven & O. Brinkkemper (red.), *Twaalf eeuwen bewoning langs de Linge bij Stenen Kamer in Kerk Avezaath* (=Archeologie in de Betuweroute/Rapportages Archeologische Monumentenzorg 85). Amersfoort. 319-340.

Kock,J. & T. Sode 1993. *Glas, glasperler og glasmagere I Nordindien*. Esbjerg.

Mac Gregor, A., 1976. *Anglo-Scandinavian finds from Lloyds Bank Pavement and other sites* (= York Archaeological Trust vol. 17, facsimile 3) York.

Mac Gregor, A., 1999. *Craft, industry and everyday life, finds from Anglo-Scandinavian York* (= The archaeology of York Small Finds 17/14). York.

Margeson, S., 193. *Norwich households: the medieval and post medieval finds from Norwich survey excavations*, 1971-1978 (= East Anglian Archaeology Report 58).

Maquet, C., 1990. Lissiors en verre, approche de technique et bibliographique, in: *Archéologie Medievale* 20, 319-334.

Miedema, M., 1983. *Vijfentwintig eeuwen bewoning in het terpenland ten noordwesten van Groningen*. Dieren (Thesis Vrije Universiteit Amsterdam).

Miedema, M., 1999. West-Flivelgo 600 vC – 1900 nC, archeologische kartering en beschrijving van 2500 jaar bewoning in Midden-Groningen, in: *Paleohistoria* 41-42, 237-445.

Mittendorff, E. S., 2004. *Kelders vol scherven. Onderzoek naar keramiekcomplexen uit de 9de-11de eeuw afkomstig uit de Polstraat te Deventer* (=Rapportages Archeologie Deventer 13).

Mittendorff, E. S. & B. Vermeulen, 2004. *Ambachtslieden arme vrouwen en arbeiders. Archeologisch onderzoek naar de Vroegmiddeleeuwse ambachtswijk en latere periodes aan de Bruynssteeg 6-10 te Deventer* (= Rapportages Archeologie Deventer 14).

Ó Floínn, R., 1992. Group of female grave-goods, in: E. Roesdahl & D. M. Wilson (eds.) *From Viking to crusader, the Scandinavians and Europe 800-1200*. New York.

Pritchard. F., 1992. Textile implements, in: A. Vince (ed.) *Finds and environmental evidence, Aspects of Saxo-Norman London* 2 (= London & Middlesex Archaeological Society, special paper 12), 173.

Ritchie, A., 2001. *Viking Scotland*. Batsford.

Rogerson, A. & C. Dallas, 1984. *Excavations in Thetford, 1948-59 and 1973-80* (= East Anglian Archaeology Report 22).

Roes, A.,1965. *Vondsten van Dorestad*. Groningen.

Sarfatij, H., 1973. Digging in Dutch towns: Twenty five years of research by the ROB in medieval towns centres, in: *Berichten van de Rijksdienst voor het Oudheidkundig Bodemonderzoek* 23, 367-420.

Schmaedecke, M., 1998. Glasbarren oder Glättsteine, Beobachtungen zur mittelalterlichen Glasherstellung und Glasverarbeitung, in: *Beiträge zur Archäologie des Mittelalters* 1998. 93-120.

Sode, T. 2007. Glattesten, in: *Skalk* 121, 9-13.

Spek, Th., 2004. *Het Drentse esdorpenlandschap, een historisch geografische studie*. Utrecht.

Spitzers, T.A., 1996b. De opgraving aan de Stromarkt (1966/1967), in: J. R. M. Magdelijns (*et al.*) (red.) *Het Kapittel van Lebuïnus in Deventer: nalatenschap van een immuniteit in bodem, bebouwing en beschrijving*, Nieuwegein, 115-126.

Spitzers, T. A. 2000. *Archeologisch onderzoek Polstraat69/71 te Deventer 1998-1999. 1100 jaar bouwen en leven in de Polstraat* (= BAAC-rapport 99.006). 2 delen ongepubliceerd typscript.

Stephan, H-G, K. H. Wedepohl, G. Hartmann, 1992. Die Gläser der hochmittelalterlichen Waldglashütte Steimcke. Berichte über die Grabungsergebnisse, in: *Zeitschrift für Archäologie des Mittelalters* 20, 89-123.

Stepphun, P., 1998. *Die Glasfunde von Haitabu*. Neumünster.

Stepphun, P., 1999. Der mittelalterliche Gniedelstein: Glättglas oder Glasbarren? Zu Primärfunktion und Kontinuität eines Glasobjektes vom Frühmittelalter bis zur Neuzeit, in: *Nachrichten aus Niedersachsens Urgeschichte* 68, 113-139.

Stepphun, P., 2002. Glasfunde des 11. bis 17 Jahrhunderts aus Schleswig, in: *Ausgrabungen in Schleswig Beichte und Studien* 16.

Steuer, H., 1987. Der Handel der Wikingzeit zwischen Nord- und Nordwest Europa aufgründ archäologischer Zeugnisse, in: K. Düwel, H. Jankuhn, H. Siems & D. Timple (Hrsg.), *Untersuchungen zur Handel und Verkehr der vor- und frühgeschichtlichen Zeit in Mittel- und Nord Europa, Teil IV, Handel der Karolinger und Wikingerzeit*, 113-197. Göttingen.

Talbot, L. 1990. The glass, in: Andrews, P. & K. Penn (eds.) *Excavations in Thetford, North of the river; 1989-90* (= East Anglian Archaeology Report 87), 44.

Trimpe Burger, J. A., 1965. Korte vondstberichten uit Aardenburg 2, in: *Berichten van de Rijksdienst voor het Oudheidkundig Bodemonderzoek* 15-16, 211-220.

Walton Rogers, P., 1997. *Textile production at 16-22 Coppergate* (= The archaeology of York Small Finds 17/11). York.

Waterman, D. M., 1959. Late Saxon, Viking and Early Medieval finds from York, in: *Archaeologia* 97, 59-106.

Wedepohl, K. H., 1999. Karolingisches Glas, in: C. Stiegmann & M. Wemhoff (Hrsg.) *799 Kunst und Kultur der Karolingerzeit* III, Mainz, 218-222.

Williams, J. H., 1979. *St Peter's Street Northampton excavations 1973-1976*. Northampton.

place	location	year of find	number	date	gewicht	diameter (cm)	hight (cm)	colour	misc.
Deventer	Bruynssteeg	2003	233-236	825-900	>120			dark green	in posthole
Deventer	Polstraat	1999	199-763-1	965-1050	630	9,2	4,2	dark green	
Deventer	Polstraat	1999	199-763-2	965-1050	405	8,3	3,6	black	
Deventer	Muggeplein	2005	262-244	890-910					
Deventer	Muggeplein	2005	262-308	1000-1100	>75			grey	
Deventer	Smedenstraat 38-44	2003	236-C13	<882	>182	10,4	3,2		white inclusions
Deventer	Polstraat 3-5	1957		900-1200	>250	7	4,2	grey	small air pockets
Deventer	Polstraat 21	1984	(095-)290	900-1200	>90	7,2	3,3	black	
Deventer	Polstraat 1	1982	257	900-1200	>180	8,7	4,4	brown grey	
Deventer	Stromarkt	1966		1050-1150					
Deventer	Molenbelt	2005	239-45	1000-1200	fragment			ligt grey lizard skin	
Zutphen	Stadhuis	1997	Zu-st-V758-01	900-1100		8,8	4,2	green blue	from post hole
NoordOosPolder P14	Oude Emmeloordweg		Archis 27860	1000-1100					
Wijk bij Duurstede	Hoogstraat I					8	2,8	grey, ware marks	pontil mark
Wijk bij Duurstede	Hoogstraat1					8	3,5	dark green	pontil mark
Wijk bij Duurstede	Hoogstraat1					8,2	3	dark green	pontil mark
Wijk bij Duurstede	Hoogstraat1					7,2	4,6	dark green, with yel-	pontil mark
Utrecht	Leidse Rijn	2004				7	3,6	black grey	
Kerk Avezaath	Malburg	1997	12-422-5342	900-1225		6,2	4,5	dark green	opaque white slings
Kerk Avezaath	Malburg	1997	5-5000-1384	900-1250		7,2	3,3	brown black	opaque white slings
Kerk Avezaath	Malburg	1997	15-78-5865	900-1250		6,9	3,4	bue black	opaque white slings
Kerk Avezaath	Malburg	1997	1-1-327	900-1250		6,7	3,5	blue black	opaque white slings
Oost-Souburg		1970		880-1000		8,8		dark brown - green	
Burgh op Schouwen		1952		885-950		7			large pontil mark
Domburg	Badhotel	1991	Achis 26544	900-1100					
Haarlem	Grote Markt-Brinkman	1978	Archis 18566	1100-1250					
Diemen	Oud Diemerlaan	1987	DM 1011	1200-1300		6,5	1,2	dark green	mother of peal shine
Medemblik	Oude Haven St.	1970	Archis 30964	725-900					
Alblasserdam	Lange Steeg	2004	site 2	1200-1300		7	2,5		
Alblasserdam	Lange Steeg	2004	site 3	1200-1300		7	2,5		
Dorkwerd		1908		700-1000		7,6	3,6	dark green - black	
Wirdum		1920				7,4	3,7	dark green - black	
Wirdum		1920				6,7	4	dark green - black	
Ried	Franekaradeel	1958	Archis 238700						
Someren	Warerdael	1992	SMR-92-3-	1125-1150				grey brown	building 12
Bakel	Achter de Molen	2003		875-1050		7,4		green	
Grave-Gassel	Rad van Avontuur	1992	Archis 38750	1100-1250					
Beek en Donk		1990	Archis 21664	1150-1250					
Dommelen		1978	Archis 14215	900-1100					
Ittervoort	Maaswerken			1100-1300					
Venray	Sint Antoniusveld	1996		800-900					

List of Dutch early medieval glass smoothers (situation 2006)

A peek into the kitchen cupboard

The grange of *De Kranenburg* in the 20th century

Michael Klomp

In 2004 an assemblage containing various 20th-century objects was recovered from a rubbish pit during excavations at the *havezate* (aristocratic seat) and later country estate De Kranenburg in Zwolle. Twentieth-century finds are often immediately put aside by archaeologists. To some extent, this is due to the limited time that archeologists have for studying this material. But, on the other hand, it is also caused by a gap in our knowledge of the artefacts of this period. In the Netherlands, recent years have fortunately seen a growing interest in 20th-century objects from an archaeological perspective. In the 1990s Jan Thijssen already demonstrated the historical and archeological value of material from the first half of the 20th century in various assemblages at the Piersonstraat site in Nijmegen. Recently, excavated material from this period has received increasing attention in archeological publications.[1] In addition to pottery, the assemblage from De Kranenburg contained quite a number of glass objects. The majority of the latter bear a text in relief and had served as packaging material. In this article we first discuss the glassware, followed by the ceramics.

Glassware

Among the glassware we can distinguish bottles, jars, drinking glasses, and objects used for decoration or display. The bottles and jars served as packaging material and in most cases are inscribed. Three jars lack an inscription but have tin screw-top lids bearing a text. The texts allow us to discover what the various vessels were used for. The majority of the glass objects appear to have been containers for pharmaceutical products.

Oils and condiment
It is immediately clear that one bottle made of brown glass was used as packaging for Maggi sauce. Maggi is the name of a condiment prepared from soy protein, which was first put on the market by Julius Maggi in 1886. The bottle was designed by Maggi himself, and has been the symbol of the product for over a century. The shape of the Maggi bottle has in the course of time undergone only minimal changes; the characteristic four-pointed star is missing from the present-day bottles, and the transition from belly to neck is more rounded. The same goes for the size indication in the form of a number on the neck. The name "Maggi" however is still present on the transition to the neck. The virtually unchanging shape of the bottle makes it impossible to date the object closely.

Medicines
The majority of the recovered medicine bottles are cylindrical in shape. The bottles are mostly cork-mouthed or drip-mouthed. These medicine bottles come in sizes from 15 ml. to 250 ml., and were closed with a conical cork over which the pharmacist folded a piece of coloured paper that was held in place by an elastic band. Medicine bottles of this cylindrical model were used until 1950/1960.
Until the 1950s it was very common for the standard medicine bottles to be returned to the pharmacist for reuse. Almost every pharmacy had a back room where an assistant would wash out bottles in a bowl of hot water. This space was often separated from the store by a rubber curtain. Many fragments of this sort of standard bottle were found in the assemblage from De Kranenburg. One of them showed the number 50 on the bottom, which stood for 50ml.
A little blue jar with a screw top might also have been used as a medicine bottle. Blue glass however was also used for poisons and ink. On the bottom is an inscription reading *"patented 1909."*
A small bottle made of clear glass was, according to the inscription, used as a container for quinine drops from the Amsterdam Quinine Factory (the later ACF). The Amsterdam Quinine Factory was established in 1881. Quinine drops were a remedy advised for treating anaemia, paleness, malaria and lack of appetite. The principal ingredient of the substance is quinine. In addition to quinine drops, quinine wine was used as a medicine in the 1920s. Quinine wine was manufactured by

allowing quinine bark to soak in red wine for some time. The wine had an alcoholic content between 14 and 16% and was also sold in wine shops.

Quinine is made from the bark of the Cinchona tree. Cinchona plantations could be found especially in African countries such as the Congo, in India and in South and Central American countries such as Bolivia and Guatemala, and in the Dutch East Indies (Indonesia). A "quinine agreement" between planters and manufacturers was negotiated in 1913. The official executive agency was the Quinine Bureau in Amsterdam. The purpose of the agreement was the creation of stable conditions on the raw materials market, to avoid price fluctuations. These fluctuations were caused especially by the long growth cycle of the trees. The Dutch played a prominent role in the production of quinine. The majority of quinine plantations and the manufacture of quinine remained in Dutch hands until the end of the Second World War.

So-called "peptone" is another product that was used to improve the appetite and digestion. Peptone is a protein compound that is easily absorbed in the blood. The conversion of proteins to peptone involves the addition of peptin and the use of hot water or quick lime. Peptone was discovered in the late 19th century by the pharmacist of the Hospital of Diest (*Gasthuis van Diest*), Louis Cornelis. At the exhibition in Ghent in 1899, the inventor of the remedy was awarded the highest distinction, the so-called Honour Diploma. Peptone was sold in glass jars with the inscription *PEPTONE DIEST HOPITAL* (Peptone Diest Hospital) in relief.

01 A brown glass bottle was used as packaging for Maggi Sauce since 1886. On the sides are the characteristic four pointed star.

Three more jars with screw tops were found at the site. One of these little jars is complete, and besides a glass stopper has a metal screw top. The inscription *Van Ledden Hulsebosch Amsterdam,* and the description *onder controle van het laboratorium,* (under laboratory supervision) are clearly legible on the top. Christian Jacobus van Ledden Hulsebosch was an important police expert in the field of chemistry and was nick-named 'the Sherlock Holmes of Amsterdam'. He was born in 1887 as the son of the pharmacist and inspector of public health Marius Quirin van Ledden Hulsebosch and Jansje Gerardina Koek. Father Marius ran a pharmacy on the Korte Nieuwendijk in Amsterdam, and carried out many investigations for the police and the judiciary. As a result, Christian came into contact with this sort of investigation at quite an early age and was soon charged with assignments. Eventually he took over his father's pharmacy, which he kept going until around 1910. In 1910 he converted the pharmacy into a laboratory, where until 1950 he carried out analyses for industry, private clients and the judiciary.[2] The little jar from De Kranenburg is presumably connected to research for a private person. It can be dated to the period 1910-1950.

The find of two tin screw-top lids with different inscriptions shows that not always the same laboratory was called in. Oxidation has rendered the inscriptions illegible, but presumably they refer to a laboratory in The Hague. This is suggested by an inscription on the bottom of an accompanying jar: *J. Hofman 's Gravenhage.* Like Van Ledden Hulsebosch, Hofman was a pharmacist who applied himself to laboratory diagnostics. He worked as a pharmacist for the Coolsingel Hospital in Rotterdam. In 1892, he established himself in The Hague, where in addition to a pharmacy he ran a general laboratory and a factory, *ter bereiding van Nectar Essences en Hofman's Kunstmatige Kunstzouten* ("for the preparation of Nectar Essences and Hofman's Artificial Salts"). Hofman is a typical representative of the modern, scientific pharmacist. He was active until the late 1930s, after which the firm was taken over by his son L.J.J. Hofman, who continued its activities until 1955.

The three little screw-top jars were probably used by private laboratories, which mainly engaged in bacteriology, serology, and clinical chemistry.[3] They can be dated between 1910 and 1950. This period was characterized by a decline in the market position of private laboratories, as many factories, hospitals, central government and local authorities established their own laboratories. This did not mean that the private laboratories disappeared; after all, the demand for laboratory research did not decrease in this period. Essential changes took place in Dutch laboratories, and as a consequence many private laboratories disappeared from the scene. These changes included the establishment of countless government and regional laboratories, an increase in scale and the automation of laboratory work.[4]

The private laboratories used jars that often were manufactured to their own specifications. At the laboratory of Van Ledden Hulsebosch in Amsterdam also little jars from the *NV BronwaterFabriek Holland* ("Spring-Water Factory") were used. The work included analysis of urine, saliva, blood and faeces. Another important research theme was the testing of milk.

The question remains whether the jars from De Kranenburg were indeed used for medical research. If this was the case, then a link with the recovered medicine bottles seems obvious.

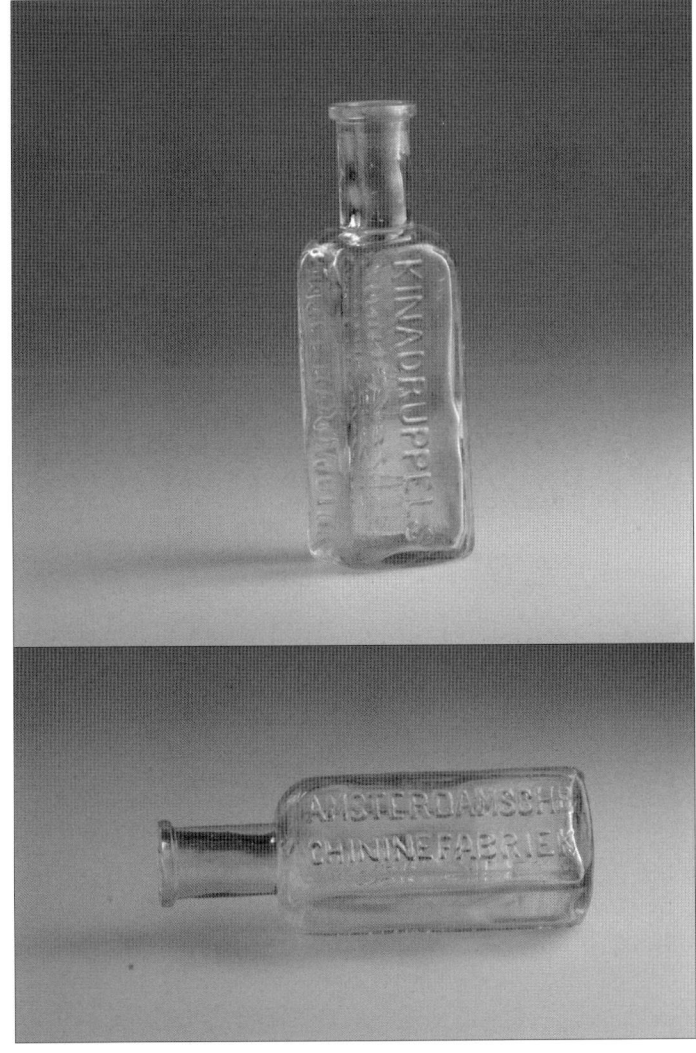

02 Glass container for quinine drops, from the "Amsterdamsche Chinine Fabriek".

Perfume and cosmetics

A small octagonal bottle with six ridges on the neck was presumably used for perfume. The bottle is closed with a cork. The text "L&T" is legible on the bottom.
Among the special finds is a rectangular glass box that was presumably used for a skin cream or toothpaste. There was probably a paper label on the lid, which mentioned the brand name.

Ink

Among the finds were two containers for holding ink. Ink bottles come in all sorts of shapes. In addition to the usual round and square ones, we know, among others, pyramidal, igloo-shaped, octagonal and turtle-shaped bottles. Some ink bottles have recesses in which one or more dip pens could be rested.

Milk glass

Five tumblers were made of milk glass. The tumblers have ridges on the bottom (cold ridges) displaying a number. The numbering suggests that the tumblers were part of a series of six. Tumblers made of milk glass are no everyday finds. In the first half of the 20th century, milk glass was principally used in the manufacture of lamp glass and shades for petroleum lamps. Occasionally milk glass was also used for packaging: for example, the surrealistically-shaped "Odol" mouthwash bottle of the 1920s.

Art Deco glass

Six fragments that were part of a decorative vase from the 1900-1940 period were found in the refuse pit. Art Deco is a style in architecture, interior decoration and applied art. Much glass from this period originated in Germany, Bohemia (Czechoslovakia), England, Belgium, France, Italy and the Netherlands. Well-known designers and/or manufacturers include Loetz, Kralik, Rindskopf, Walther, Davidson and Schneider.
The decorative vase from De Kranenburg was made of blue, pink and green mould-pressed glass in the form of a flower calyx.

Earthenware

Among the earthenware products were found three plates with the so-called "big Sphinx mark". The mark is of the "Polling logo 86" type .[5] This mark is almost identical to "logo 80" but the square frame around the text is absent. The text *Made in Holland* that occurs with some variants of logo 80/logo 86 is also absent. According to Polling, logo 80/logo 86 is associated especially with products of the "*GRANIET*" quality. Earthenware of this quality was mainly manufactured in the period 1900-1910 in Maastricht.
The recovered pottery included also two coffee filters and a fragment of a coffee jug. One of the filters has a brown surface

03 Left: Laboratory bottle with a metal screw top; right container for Peptone.

04 Tumblers made of milk glass.

and two handles. The other coffee filter is white throughout. It is difficult to date them. Given the associated finds, the filters can be placed in the period 1910-1950.

Conclusion

The finds from the grange of De Kranenburg come from a period when the grange buildings at De Kranenburg were still inhabited. The overseer of the municipal nursery of the city of Zwolle lived in the still standing house from the late 1920s on. It is not clear whether the other dwelling was occupied at that time. The latter was partially demolished in 1865; the southernmost part remained in use as a summer house until the 1990s. The objects offer a glimpse of society in the first half of the 20th century, a period that saw two world wars as well as great unemployment and economic recession. It is also a period when a wide diversity of remedies for physical complaints were on the market (quinine drops, cod-liver oil, etc.) and large laboratories became the norm. Ever more institutions such as hospitals, companies and local autorities established their own laboratories. The private laboratories progressively receded into the background. However, they continued to perform many analyses for private households and for firms without laboratories.

In addition to clues about drinking habits (coffee), the objects also offer a possible hint about the health of the occupants or users of the grange. The quinine drops and peptone were used principally to improve the appetite and digestion. The small jars point to laboratory analyses. As mentioned above, these may have been for medical purposes or for testing milk or drinking water. The analyses were probably carried out in 1923.

Notes

1. Hoorn; Schrickx 2006, 94-95 en 103-105, Deventer
2. Snelders 2007
3. Private laboratories are laboratories that fulfil two criteria: 1) the results of the laboratory research are made available to external clients in exchange for payment; and 2) the laboratory is not part of a larger organization: Vledder, Houwaert and Homburg 1999, 253
4. Vledder, Houwaert and Homburg 1999, 252
5. Polling 2001, 38, logo 86

References

Polling, A. 2001. *Maastrichtse ceramiek, merken en dateringen* (6^e druk)

Schrickx, C.P. 2006. Het onderzoek op het terrein van de voormalige Winston bioscoop te Hoorn (campagne 2004). De opgraving op de percelen Grote Noord 4 en 6. *Verslagen van de Archeologische Dienst Hoorn 3.*

Snelders, H.A.M. 2007. Ledden Hulsebosch, Christiaan Jacobus van (1877-1952). In: *Biografisch Woordenboek van Nederland*.

Vledder, I., E.S. Houwaert en E. Homburg, 1999. Particuliere laboratoria in Nederland. Deel 1: opkomst en bloei, 1865-1914. In: *Jaarboek Nederlandsch Economisch Historisch Archief 62*, 247-290.

05 Two coffee filters 1910-1950.

Gothic book clasps and mounts from excavations in Eindhoven and their contexts

Nico Arts

This article deals with metal book clasps and mounts dating from the 15th and 16th centuries. It is a category of finds that, so far, has received scant attention in the archaeological literature. Finds of book furniture are usually only generally described and illustrated, and, in the Netherlands and in Belgium, are often compared with those in the Dutch handbook on (post-)medieval material culture in Amsterdam.[1] The lack of more attention probably originates from the fact that metal book fittings are usually found only in small numbers during excavations. If any are excavated, these are individual pieces, usually not more than a handful per site. Apparently this is both true for the Netherlands[2] and for elsewhere in northwestern Europe, such as in Bruges in Belgium,[3] and London[4] and York[5] in England. Even in North America such artefacts have been found.[6]

Metal book claps and mounts are not only known as finds from regular excavations. In the past twenty-five years hundreds of such artefacts have been discovered by private persons through the frequent use of metal-detectors. In the Netherlands, these finds generally come from fields in the countryside, while those found during excavations almost always come from ecclesiastical sites and sites in medieval towns. Regrettably, though some of these finds are regularly published in detector-magazines,[7] there is no accurate and systematic registration of the metal finds found by private persons using metal-detectors.

It is reasonable to suggest that the majority of the clasps and mounts that are found during excavations accidentally broke from the books they belonged to, and were subsequently lost and discarded close to the place where the books were stored or used. The way in which book furniture was littered on farmland is less obvious. One possibility is that they were part of urban waste, which was removed from towns and spread on the fields, but generally there are few historical notes on waste disposal in medieval and post-medieval times.

As far as evidence is available, the moats of the former Eindhoven Castle (fig. 1) seem to have produced the largest number of book clasps and mounts known so far in northwestern Europe. At this site, various excavations in the years 1989-1992 yielded a total of 53 pieces.[8]

Especially the finds from Eindhoven Castle are the topic of this article. After two brief introductory paragraphs, the evidence relating to medieval books in Eindhoven is summarized. The

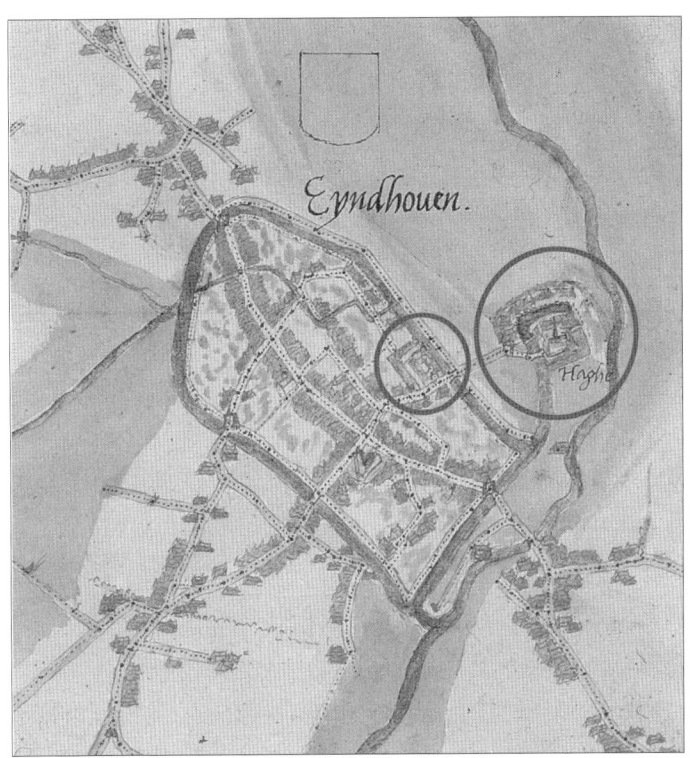

01 The town of Eindhoven according to Jacob van Deventer's map of 1560. The large circle indicates the site of the Abbey of Mariënhage, the small circle is around Eindhoven Castle.

clasps and mounts from Eindhoven Castle are briefly described and an explanation is given about how all those book fittings might have been lost and discarded at this site.

Clasps and mounts

From about the 9th to the end of the 16th century, clasps were commonplace on wooden board bindings of hand-written codices (fig. 2). Mounts were less commonly used, but they were typical of ordinary Gothic wooden board bindings. Unlike clasps, mounts were not integrated into the construction of books, but helped to protect the leather cover from damage. They were usually found only on the larger books. Clasps were used to prevent dust from entering between the leaves of the book. They also stopped boards from warping and kept the pages flat. In the usual Germanic style, the book clasps fasten from the back of the volume and catch on the front, the opposite of Italian and English binding practices.[9] After the introduction of printing in Europe in the mid 15th century, book production increased considerably, which in the long term negatively affected the quality of the binder's work. Book clasps and mounts gradually fell from general use from circa 1525 onwards. Though printing was introduced around 1450, hand-written books were common into the early 16th century.

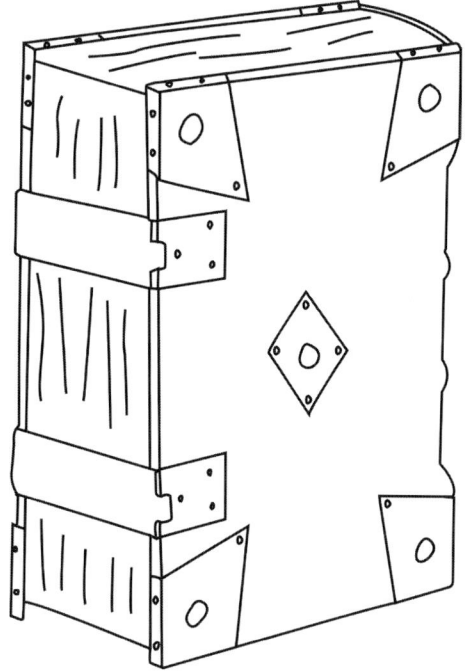

02 Schematic drawing of a 15th-century book with hook-clasp fastenings, corner pieces and a central boss on the board.

Most Gothic bindings of manuscripts and the earliest printed books had hook-clasp fastenings. In the Netherlands, the earliest Gothic examples date from the 15th century. They are made of sheet brass, 1 to 2 mm thick, with bevelled edges, simple engraved lines and ornamental perforations. In contrast to the sparsely decorated fastenings of the 15th century, those of the 16th century are usually embellished with engraved lines, stamped ornaments and concentric circles. Their wide distribution suggests that they may have been products of German (Nuremberg) brass manufacture, exported all over Europe.[10] However, there are various typological differences among geographical areas across Europe, which suggests that book furniture was produced in different areas.

Except in archaeology, there is not much literature on book furniture. There are some references in art-historical works,[11] or descriptions of technological production,[12] but these are quite exceptional. The main source, however, is the handbook of medieval bookbinding written by J.A. Szirmai, already cited above,[13] but it does not yield any archaeological reference. Also Kristina Krüger's dissertation is of importance.[14] This study is to be considered the first attempt in archaeology to look beyond individual sites, though it is mainly a typological and descriptive catalogue without much synthesis. Unfortunately, the works of Szirmai and Krüger are barely known in Dutch archaeology.

Archaeological sites

During the Middle Ages, books were valuable and were found only in the possession of religious and other elites. The majority of book clasps and book mounts found in north-western Europe come from ecclesiastical sites (cathedrals, churches, monastic institutions), although examples from secular sites also regularly occur (table 1). Most secular sites are in medieval town centres. Other kinds of context, such as rural sites, seem on the whole to be lacking. However, as mentioned above, quite a lot of examples of book furniture are known from fields in the countryside, and it is suggested that these might originate from deposits of urban waste.

At all sites, clasps outnumber book mounts. Probably the main reason for this is that the clasps were attached to leather straps which became detached through frequent use; book mounts are much more difficult to remove from wooden boards. Besides, clasps were used much more than mounts.

Worth mentioning in this context are two rural examples from the countryside near Eindhoven, which have words engraved in the surface. Both are clasps (fig. 3). One was found in 2003 in a field between the villages of Hoogeloon and Casteren

Site	context	number	reference
Aalst (NL)	church(yard)	3	Arts 1998, 58.
Eindhoven (NL.)	church(yard)	7	Arts & Van den Broek 2009.
Wharram Percy (UK)	church(yard)	3	Goodall 1987, 173; 2007, 306-307.
St. Mary, Coventry (UK)	cathedral/priory	2 or 3	Rylatt et al. 2003, 126-127.
Wells (UK)	cathedral	3	Rodwell 2001, 522-523.
's-Hertogenbosch (NL)	abbey	11	Nijhof & Jansen 2007, 216-217.
Oldenzaal (NL)	abbey	4	Wiggers 2004.
Carmarthen, Wales (UK)	abbey	10	Brennan 2001, 25-26, 67-68.
Beaulieu, Petegem (B)	abbey	11	De Groote 1992, 386-387.
Helmond, Binderen (NL)	abbey	1	unpublished.
Øm Kloster (DK)	abbey	40	Madsen 2003.
The Hague (NL)	town centre	7	Jacobs 1995,
Groningen (NL)	town centre	5	Adolfs & Kortekaas 1988, 76-77.
Bourtange (NL)	town centre	2	Hasselt et al. 1993, 441-442.
Middelburg (NL.)	town centre	13	Hendrikse 1994.
Bremen (D)	town centre	3	Rech 2004, 208.
Oldenzaal (NL)	town centre	22	Ostkamp n.d. (2005).
Eindhoven, Vrijstraat (NL)	town centre	1	unpublished.
Eindhoven, Smalle Haven (NL)	town centre	1	unpublished.
Eindhoven (NL)	castle	53	Arts 1992c, 177-178.

Table 1. Some archaeological sites yielding book clasps and book mounts (with their numbers) by context.

03 Two clasps from farmland near Eindhoven. No. 1 (length: 62 mm) was found between Hoogeloon and Casteren and is engraved with the name 'IANSEN'; no. 2 (length: 72 mm) was found near the Castle of Croy and is engraved with the name 'Calepinus' (a Latin dictionary).

and has the engraved name 'IANSEN.' This name might be that of the owner or the author of the book from which the clasp had become detached. The other exceptional clasp was found in 2002 in a field near the Castle of Croy (municipality of Laarbeek).[15] This one bears the engraved name 'Calepinus', which refers to the Italian monk Ambrogio da Calepino (1453-1511), who wrote the Latin dictionary *Dictionarium* or *Dictionnaire polyglotte*. This dictionary, first printed in 1502 at Reggio (Italy), was very popular and was reprinted twenty times during the 16th century. Even during the 17th and 18th centuries the book saw many reprints, including translations into eleven languages. Because of its popularity, 'Calepinus' became eponymous for the dictionary. The clasp found near Croy had obviously come off a Latin dictionary.

One other category of exceptional finds, which is relevant here, concerns fragments of leather book covers. In the Netherlands, examples are known from two cesspits in Alkmaar, which both are of post-medieval date. One has the imprints of two metal fastenings and the other has parts of such fastenings.[16] Another fragment of a leather book cover, but without traces of clasps, was found in the filled-in moat of a motte-castle at Eindhoven, and dates from the first half of the 15th century or earlier (fig. 4).[17]

04 Leather book cover from Eindhoven, dating from the first half of the 15th century or earlier. Scale 1:1.

05 Model of Eindhoven Castle in the 16th century (Museum Kempenland, Eindhoven).

Clasps and mounts from Eindhoven Castle

Though it is historically documented that in the years ca 1470-1560 writing and book production took place at the abbey of Mariënhage, close to the town centre of Eindhoven (fig. 1),[18] archaeological evidence for writing in Eindhoven is very meagre. To date, only two urban sites have produced a stylus,[19] while a handful of fragments of roof-slates and windowpanes are known with text engraved on them.[20]

Archaeological evidence of the presence of books is more abundant, but is almost entirely limited to one site: Eindhoven Castle (fig. 5, table 1). It seems that castle sites are rather unusual places for archaeological book hardware: table 1 lists twenty sites, of which only one concerns a castle. The finds from Eindhoven Castle comprise 4 corner pieces, 10 bosses, 8 hooks and 31 clasps (figs. 6-9). Three bosses are made of lead, all other book mounts are made of brass. In one of the leaden bosses still two of the originally three brass nails are present, both of which have a length of 9 mm. Hence the wooden boards onto which these bosses were fitted, had a thickness of at least 1 cm. The leaden bosses are ornamented with marks: a 'T' and a large and a small dot. The meaning of these marks is unclear. One of the brass hooks (fig. 6, no. 1) has two pairs of letters: 'SM' and 'ND' stamped in it, in this case too the meaning is not known. Among the 31 clasps, 3 are not complete. The length of the 28 complete ones gives an impression of the thickness of the books they were fastened to. The actual paper or parchment codex must have been considerably thinner, as both boards could have had a thickness of 1 cm. Besides, there was some scope in the length that the clasp had to bridge, because the clasp was fastened to a leather strap, whose length might vary. Usually books had two identical clasps. No two of the 31 clasps from the Castle of Eindhoven are identical and

Length	number
41-45 mm	1
46-50 mm	2
51-55 mm	4
56-60 mm	3
61-65 mm	3
66-70 mm	6
71-75 mm	4
76-80 mm	2
81-85 mm	-
86-90 mm	2
91-95 mm	-
96-100 mm	1

Table 2. The lengths of 28 measurable clasps from Eindhoven Castle.

06 Book furniture (3 corner pieces) from Eindhoven Castle (15th century). Scale 1:1.

07 Book furniture (4 bosses) from Eindhoven Castle (15th century). Scale 1:1.

08 Book furniture (3 hooks) from Eindhoven Castle (15th and 16th century). Scale 1:1.

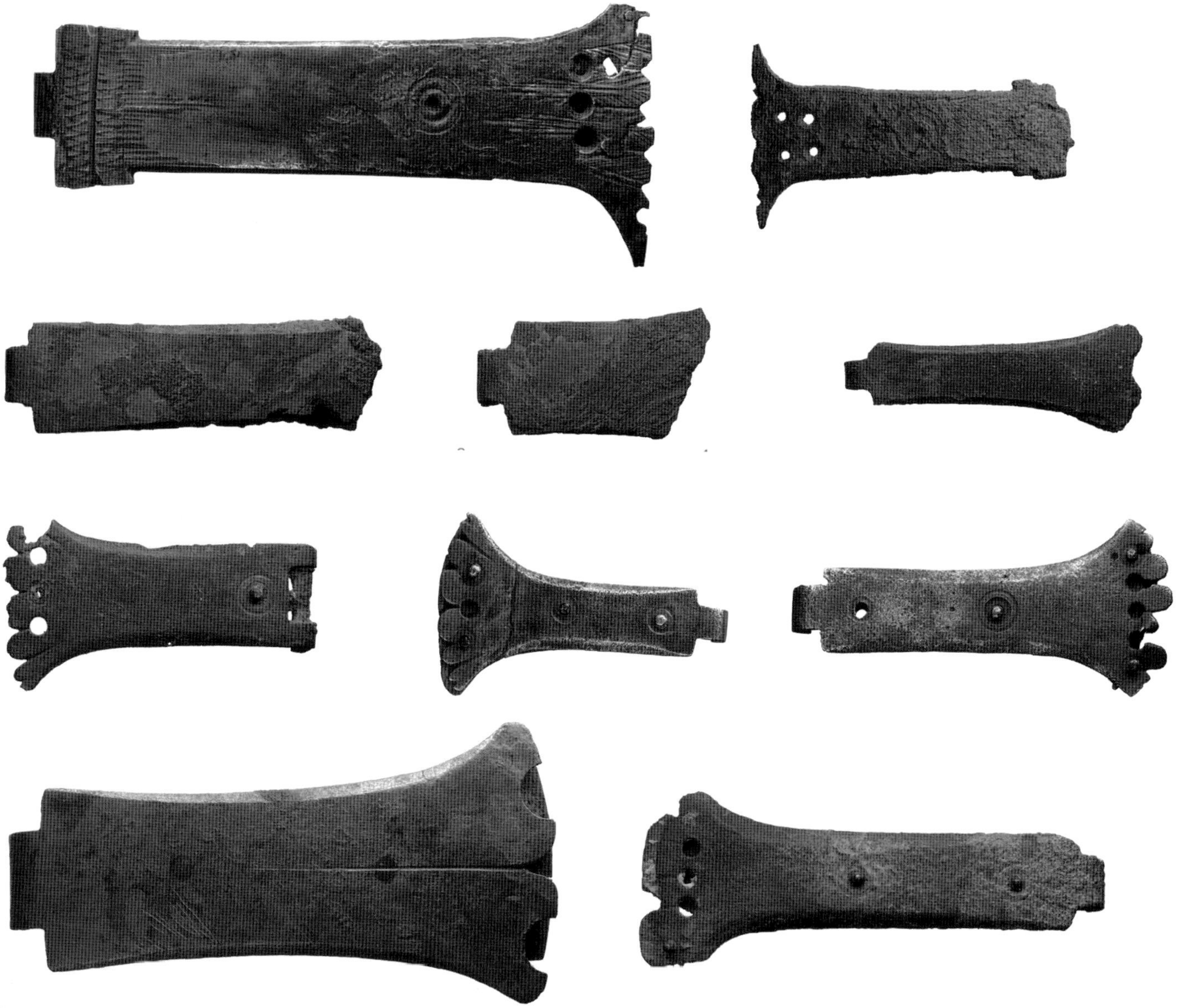

09 Clasps from Eindhoven Castle (15th and 16th century). Scale 1:1

the lengths of the 28 complete clasps vary. This means that the clasps and mounts excavated on the site of the Castle of Eindhoven come from at least 31 different books, whose thickness varied between at least 4 and 10 cm (table 2).

Context

In the history of Eindhoven Castle, there is no evidence of the presence of a library, or indeed the presence of any book.[21] If the owner of this castle was in the possession of at least 31 books, which in the years around 1500 was a huge number, this probably would have been historically recorded. The historical records also lack evidence on the residence of literate people who might have been in the possession of such a number of books.

At a distance of only 200 metres from Eindhoven Castle there was the Abbey of Mariënhage, which did have an extensive library. In the history of this abbey, it is known that faced with warfare in October of 1581, the monks removed their valuable possessions from the abbey. Without doubt these valuables will have included the books from the library. The removal of the treasures happened in a hurry and their storage would have been at the nearest safe place. In the circumstances of the time, this safe place would have been Eindhoven Castle. It is suggested that during the hasty handling of the books from the abbey's library, clasps and mounts broke off and were eventually discarded in the castle's moat.[22]

In November 2008, an exhibition was staged in Eindhoven on the *Florarium temporum*, a world chronicle written at the Abbey of Mariënhage in 1472. In the exhibition also a number of other medieval manuscripts from Mariënhage were exhibited. As the ancient books were displayed in the showcases together with the book furniture from Eindhoven Castle, it was discovered that one of the late-15th-century manuscripts[23] had brass corner pieces identical to one found at the site of Eindhoven Castle (fig. 10 and fig. 6 no. 3). Two of the original corner pieces are missing from the board on the back of the book. Though not absolute proof, this evidence makes it likely that the corner piece from Eindhoven Castle, and probably all other book furniture from the site, originated from the Abbey of Mariënhage. Possibly, the fittings were separated from the books in 1581 in the way reconstructed above.[24]

10 Detail of a late-15th-century manuscript from the Abbey of Mariënhage with a corner piece identical to that in fig. 6, below.

Notes

1. Baart *et al*. 1977, 400-404.
2. See, among others, Baart *et al*. 1977, 400-404; Groeneweg 1987, 69; Olivier 1994, 228; Vrede 1994, 150-151.
3. Vandenberghe 1988.
4. Egan 2005; Wheeler 1940.
5. Ottaway and Rogers 2002, 2898-2899.
6. Luccketti 1994, 26-27.
7. E.g., in the Netherlands: *The Coinhunter Magazine* and *Detector Magazine*; in Germany: *Das Schatzsucher Magazine*; in the United Kingdom: *Treasure Hunting*.
8. Arts 1992c, 177-178 and table on p. 196, with 3 additional finds.
9. Szirmai 1999, 254.
10. Szirmai 1999, 251-260.
11. E.g. Ter Kuile 1986, 294, where five furnishings are shown which evidently originate from one board binding dating from the second half of the 15th century.
12. E.g. Mowery 1991.
13. Szirmai 1999.
14. Krüger 2002.
15. Arts & Van de Wijdeven 2003 (front cover).
16. Bitter & Roedema 1995, 65; Dijkstra *et al*. 1997: 171, 173.

17. Arts & Rooijakkers 2008, 41.
18. Arts & Rooijakkers 2008.
19. Arts & Van den Broek 2009; Debruyne & Nollen 2003, 131.
20. Arts 1992a, 99; 1992b, 107.
21. Melssen 1992.
22. Arts & Rooijakkers 2008, 82.
23. Van de Ven 1990, 74-76: a large-sized Graduale (475x338 mm) dating from the second half of the 15th century.
24. With thanks to Emy Thorissen (keeper of the Brabant-Collectie, University of Tilburg) for her permission to publish the photograph in fig. 10, and to Laurens Mulkens (Archeologisch Centrum Eindhoven) for his photographs of the leather book cover (fig. 4) and the clasps and furniture from Eindhoven Castle.

References

Adolfs, F. & G.L.G.A. Kortekaas 1988: Metalen en benen voorwerpen, in P.H. Broekhuizen, A. Carmiggelt, H. van Gangelen & G.L.G.A. Kortekaas (eds.), *Kattendiep Deurgraven. Historisch-archeologisch onderzoek aan de noordzijde van het Gedempte Kattendiep te Groningen*, Groningen, 62-105.

Arts, N. 1992a: De aard en het belang van de archeologische vondsten, in N. Arts (ed.), *Het Kasteel van Eindhoven. Archeologie, ecologie en geschiedenis van een heerlijke woning*, Eindhoven, 97-100.

Arts, N. 1992b: De glasvondsten, in N. Arts (ed.), *Het Kasteel van Eindhoven. Archeologie, ecologie en geschiedenis van een heerlijke woning*, Eindhoven, 157-160.

Arts, N. 1992c: De variatie aan metalen voorwerpen, in N. Arts (ed.), *Het Kasteel van Eindhoven. Archeologie, ecologie en geschiedenis van een heerlijke woning*, Eindhoven, 161-197.

Arts, N. 1998: Heilig en profaan. De materiële cultuur van het kerkterrein, in A.-J.A. Bijsterveld (ed.), *De schaduw van een heiligdom. De geschiedenis van Aalst en zijn middeleeuwse kerk*, Waalre, 43-58.

Arts, N. & B. van den Broek 2009: De archeologische vondsten, in N. Arts (ed.) *De resultaten van het archeologisch onderzoek van de middeleeuwse Catharinakerk in Eindhoven: het basisrapport met nog wat meer*, Eindhoven.

Arts, N., & G. Rooijakkers 2008: *Het Florarium temporum. Historische en archeologische achtergronden van een middeleeuwse wereldkroniek uit Eindhoven*, Alphen aan de Maas.

Arts, N. en W. van de Wijdeven (eds.) 2003: *Nieuwsbrief Archeologie Kempen- en Peelland* nr. 23, Eindhoven.

Baart, J., et al. 1977: *Opgravingen in Amsterdam. 20 jaar stadskernonderzoek*, Haarlem.

Bitter, P., & R. Roedema 1995: Beschrijving van de vondsten, in P. Bitter (ed.) *Geworteld in de bodem. Archeologisch en historisch onderzoek van een pottenbakkerij bij de Wortelsteeg in Alkmaar*, Zwolle, 50-75.

Brennan, D. 2001: *The small finds and other artifacts* (Excavations at Carmarthen Greyfriars 1983-1990, Topic Report Number 4), Dyfed.

Debruyne, S., & J. Nollen, 2003: *Rapport opgraving Catharinaplein 2001-2002 (gemeente Eindhoven). Projectcode EHV-CP-01/02*, Eindhoven.

Dijkstra, J., D. Duco & R. Roedema 1997: De vondsten uit de beerputten, in P. Bitter, J. Dijkstra, R. Roedema & R. van Wilgen (eds.), *Wonen op niveau. Archeologie, bouwhistorie en historie van twee percelen aan de Langestraat*, Alkmaar, 101-198.

Egan, G., 2005: *Material culture in London in an age of transition. Tudor and Stuart period finds c 1450-c 1700 from excavations at riverside sites in Southwark*, Museum of London Archaeology Service Monograph 19, London.

Goodall, A.R., 1987: Copper-alloy objects, in R.R. Bell and M.W. Beresford (eds.), *Wharram. A study of settlement on the Yorkshire Wolds. Volume III. Wharram Percy, the church of St. Martin*, London, 171-173.

Goodall, A.R., 2007: Non-ferrous metal objects, in S. Mays, C. Harding and C. Heighway (eds.), *Wharram. A study of settlement on the Yorkshire Wolds. Volume XI. The Churchyard*, York, 304-308.

Groeneweg, G. (ed.) 1987: *Schatten uit de Schelde. Gebruiks- en siervoorwerpen uit de verdronken plaatsen in de Oosterschelde*, Bergen op Zoom.

Groote, K. De 1992: Het afval van de Rijke Klaren. Noodonderzoek in de voormalige abdij van Beaulieu te Petegem (gem. Wortegem-Petegem, prov. Oost-Vlaanderen), *Archeologie in Vlaanderen* II, 335-412.

Hasselt, H., J.J. Lenting en H. van Westing 1993: Metaal, in J.J. Lenting, H. van Gangelen en H. van Westing (eds.), *Schans op de Grens. Bourtanger bodemvondsten 1580-1850*, Sellingen, 403-462.

Hendrikse, H., 1994: Boekbeslag, in R.M. van Heeringen, H. Hendrikse en J.J.B. Kuipers (eds.), *Geld uit de belt. Archeologisch onderzoek in de bouwput van de gemeentelijke parkeerkelder en het belastingkantoor aan de Kousteensedijk te Middelburg*, Vlissingen, 60-61.

Jacobs, E., 1995: *Achter kerk en klooster. Opgraven aan de Nobelstraat en de Zuilingstraat*. VOM-reeks 1995-2, Den Haag.

Krüger, K., 2002: *Archäologische Zeugnisse zum mittelalterlichen Buch- und Schriftwesen nordwärts der Mittelgebirge*, Universitätsforschungen zur prähistorischen Archäologie, Band 91, Bonn.

Kuile, O. ter, 1986: *Koper & Brons*. Catalogi van de verzameling kunstnijverheid van het Rijksmuseum te Amsterdam, 's-Gravenhage.

Luccketti, N.M., W.M. Kelso & B.A. Straube 1994: *Jamestown Rediscovery Field Report 1994*, Jamestown.

Madsen, A., 2003: Bøger, bogspænder og bogbeslag fra Øm Kloster, in B. Gregersen & C. Selch Jensen (eds.), *Øm Kloster. Kapitler af et middelalderligt cistercienserabbedis historie,* Odense, 121-134.

Melssen, J. 1992: De geschiedenis van het kasteel van Eindhoven en zijn bewoners, in N. Arts (ed.), *Het Kasteel van Eindhoven. Archeologie, ecologie en geschiedenis van een heerlijke woning,* Eindhoven, 28-61.

Mowery, J.F., 1991: Clasps, Schliessen, Clausuren: A guide to the manufacture and the literature of clasps, *Guild of Bookworkers' Journal* 29 no. 2, 1-58.

Nijhof, E. & H.L. Janssen 2007: Huisraad, in H.L. Janssen & A.A.J. Thelen (eds.), *Tekens van leven. Opgravingen en vondsten in het Tolbrugkwartier in 's-Hertogenbosch,* Utrecht, 190-217.

Olivier, R., 1994: *Bodemvondsten uit Goeree-Overflakkee.* Ouddorp.

Ostkamp, S., n.d. (2005): Een boedel op de schop. 16de eeuwse vondsten uit Oldenzaalse waterput, in H. Clevis, M. Klomp & S. Wentink, *Overijssels Erfgoed. Archeologische en Bouwhistorische Kroniek 2002,* Zwolle, 71-112.

Ottaway, P., & N. Rogers 2002: *Craft, Industry and Everyday Life: Finds from Medieval York.* The Archaeology of York. Volume 17: The Small Finds, York.

Rech, M., 2004: *Gefundene Vergangenheit. Archäologie des Mittelalters in Bremen. Mit besonderer Berücksichtigung von Riga,* Bremen.

Rodwell, W., 2001: *Wells Cathedral. Excavations and Structural Studies 1978-93,* London.

Rylatt, M., P. Mason & I. Soden 2003: The Metal Objects, in M. Rylatt and P. Mason, *The Archaeology of the Medieval Cathedral and Priory of St. Mary, Coventry,* Coventry, 126-127.

Szirmai, J.A., 1999: *The archaeology of medieval bookbinding,* Aldershot.

Vandenberghe, S., 1988: Metalen voorwerpen uit recent archeologisch onderzoek te Brugge, in H. De Witte (ed.), *Brugge onder-zocht. Tien jaar stadsarcheologisch onderzoek 1977-1987,* Brugge, 60-191.

Ven, J. van de 1990: *Handschriften en handschriftfragmenten in het bezit van de Theologische Faculteit Tilburg,* Tilburg.

Vrede, F., 1994: Overige metaalvondsten, in P.H. Broekhuizen, H. van Gangelen, K. Helfrich, G.L.G.A. Kortekaas & R.H. Alma (eds.), *Oudheden onder De Hunze. Archeologisch en historisch onderzoek naar een steenhuis en een boerderij onder een Groninger nieuwbouwwijk,* Groningen, 127-160.

Wheeler, R.E.M., 1940: *London Museum Medieval Catalogue 1940,* London.

Wiggers, J., 2004: Boekbeslagen, in J. Hinke, Y. Hoitink & E. Ulrich (eds.), *Dat coevent toe Oldenzal. De geschiedenis en opgraving van het Agnesklooster te Oldenzaal,* Hengelo, 255-256.

Potter or retailer?

Sixteenth-century ceramic rejects from Zwolle, the Netherlands

Hemmy Clevis

In 2004 an excavation took place at the site 'Achter de Broeren' ('Behind the Brethren') in Zwolle. The aim of the excavation was to investigate the various phases of the town wall and the moat known as 'Kleine Aa'. This investigation revealed a privy vault that had been constructed partly on the foundations of a demolished town wall and partly on a filled-in part of the Kleine Aa.

There is documentary evidence from 1466 about the allocation of a site for the new Broeren monastery. The monastery was to be built outside the town wall. Its construction prompted the municipal authorities to impose a new layout on the area north of the Kleine Aa, known as Het Eiland ('The Island') and to extend the town defences around it. The construction of a new town wall was undertaken along what is now known as the Thorbeckegracht canal. By 1492 this wall still was not finished. It was probably completed around 1500, since from that year on the Broerenpoort gate ceased to function: it is no longer mentioned in the municipal accounts. Whether the wall along the inner side of the Kleine Aa had by then been pulled down is not certain, but it is quite likely. Given this evidence, the excavated privy vault should date from after 1500.

Historical references

From the third quarter of the 16th century, we have no fewer than three references to potters on Het Eiland. These all relate to property transfers. In this period there were as yet no specific street names on Het Eiland, so that it is impossible to locate the premises mentioned in these documents. The earliest reference dates from 23 October 1552 and relates to a property adjacent to that of Johan de Witte, *Potbecker* (potter).[1] The second dates from 15 September 1555 and mentions a transaction by Johan Petersz, *Potbecker*, husband of Gertruidt.[2] The third reference relates to the heirs of Peter Pottebecker in 1569.[3] At first sight there seems to be no connection between these three references, but Johan de Witte may well be the son of Peter and hence identical with Johan Petersz, while the third reference may refer both to himself (as an heir) or to his father. The last instance possibly indicates that the business had closed down.

At the excavated site no traces of a pottery have been found. Neither a kiln, nor pits full of wasters.[4] It is only from the privy vault that a huge number of sherds of wasters and rejects were recovered, representing some 300 items in all. They prompt the question whether this was local pottery waste or rejected material from a pot-seller who bought his wares elsewhere. There is a third possibility, with the potter selling not only his own products, but also crockery bought farther afield. Another possibility is that the potter did not produce his wares where he lived, but only sold them there. An attempt will be made to answer these questions by close examination of the pottery.

Description of the material
Stoneware

The stoneware is not a local product, but was imported from the Cologne/Frechen region. Among the stoneware items are some bearded-man jugs. One of these has a dark brown exterior with a large face mask, a pedestal base and a decoration of upright acanthus leaves alternating with rosettes. The greatest girth of the belly bears a band with an inscription that occurs three times; the text, upside down, reads: WAN GOT VILT SO IST SEIN SI.. (the last two letters are illegible). This type of jug (s2-kan-63) dates from the mid-16th century and probably came from Cologne or Frechen.[5]

A second specimen is of the same type (s2-kan-63), but its glaze displays 'panther spots'. The face mask is large, with a square beard. A third bearded-man jug is globular with a narrow neck and a small, square-bearded face mask (s2-kan-47). The body of the jug is covered with small rosettes. This jug has a flat base and a yellow-brown colour. Reineking-Von Bock puts this type in the mid-16th century.[6]

The fourth stoneware jug, a large example of type s2-kan-19, is decorated with rose sprays. Reineking-von Bock dates this form of decoration to the second quarter of the 16th century.[7] Griffioen and Oostkamp recently presented an overview of jugs decorated with rose sprays and oak-leaf foliage, prompted by a find of an s2-kan-19 jug in a cesspit at Woerden.[8] They do not agree with Gaimster's idea that such decoration occurs before 1500.[9] They note that such motifs are absent on jugs from the Nieuwburg stronghold[10], dated to before 1517, but do appear on traded goods at Bergen op Zoom between 1518 and 1575.[11] At Amersfoort a pot with oak foliage is dated to 1557 by the coins it contained.[12]

The fifth jug is of the type s2-kan-63, which Bartels attributes to the production centre at Raeren.[13] Its handle at any rate ends in a narrow tail on the body and the jug's colour is speckled brown. This type might be described as 'a jug with a high neck on a globular body with a low maximum girth'. Of a sixth item only the base was preserved. A seventh jug once bore medallions and a text band besides a decoration of acanthus leaves (s2-kan-48).

There are a further 40 sherds (450 grs) of stoneware jugs, whose form suggests a 16th-century date. But two sherds belonged to an older funnel beaker, made at Siegburg. Because of their fragmentary condition, these 40 sherds were not considered in establishing the Minimum Number of Specimens. Most of the sherds were very small.

01 Three 16th-century stoneware jugs.

Majolica

There are two unusual items. One is an imitation *snelle* tankard with a 1-mm-thick clay ring accidentally burnt onto the bottom, which shows that there was no abrasion through use. The tankard, an imitation in majolica of a stoneware type, is decorated all over in blue, yellow and a watery orange (see photo). The tin glaze is thin, allowing the orange body to transpire faintly pink.

The stoneware tankard of which this majolica tankard is an imitation, originated in Cologne. It was here that in the second quarter of the 16th century the squat beaker form[14] evolved from the beer mug or pint, which had a larger diameter. Around the mid-16th century the squat shape gradually became taller, to attain its greatest height by about 1575, now produced not only at Cologne but above all at Siegburg. The tall tankard saw its heyday in the final quarter of the 16th century. Hence the majolica copy probably dates from the mid-16th century or somewhat later.

The bottom of the one-handled bowl shows a design of a man with a flower, in blue, yellow, green and orange. His costume resembles that depicted on plates of Werra ware from around 1600. The high rim displays a slip-trailed design in white, spared out in a blue band. The body of the vessel is cream-coloured.

According to Ostkamp, both items are of German manufacture and were probably made at Großalmerode.[15] He mentions a

02 Two majolica objects from Großalmerode.

tankard from Gorinchem (the Netherlands) that is identical to this one.

A tiny sherd of majolica belongs to neither of these pieces and hence must be part of a third item. The sherd, bearing a polychrome decoration, measures about one square centimetre; the bottom shows a dent and the top a boss. It may be part of a plate or bowl with a serrated rim and a circle of round bosses.[16]

Red ware

The red ware comprises a wide range of forms. There are skillets, plates, lids, tripod cooking pots, jugs, chafing dishes, bowls, cups, a strainer, cresset lamps, chamber pots, money boxes, handled ladles, ointment jars, a dripping pan, pedestal dishes and miniature vessels or toys.

Skillets

The type r-bak-18, represented by two skillets, has a simple, upright rim. In this it resembles type r-stk-6. Type r-bak-21 has vertical sides with decorative rilling and a rim flattened outward ending in a ridge. Of both types one specimen had been used.

One skillet measures only 11 cm across (r-bak-14). Its bottom is sooty, which means it was used. At Alkmaar an excavated cesspit on the Langestraat produced several such items. According to Bitter they were not toy pans. These small pans were used over a low fire for cooking egg dishes.[17] As an example, Bitter mentions a *flan* or *vlade* (sweet omelet). He dates these pans to the first half of the 15th century.

03 Three plates with a white slip coating and sgraffito decoration.

Plates
Ten plates with a broad rim and three lug feet on the base belong to the type r-bor-1. Four of them had a white slip coating which has turned a yellowish green. They have a sgraffito decoration. The body being red, so is the design. A curious feature is that the underside of these plates too is washed with white slip, like some of the cups. This gives them the appearance of more expensive white ware.

One of the plates shows a central decoration of three fishes lying across each other; the three others have phantasy coats-of-arms. A fish design is often accompanied by the inscription 'MARIA'. The motif refers to the biblical miracle of the loaves and fishes.

One of the coats-of-arms resembles the coat-of-arms of Frederik van Baden, who according to HCO (Historisch Centrum Overijssel) was a bishop of Utrecht in the early 16th century. However, the coat-of-arms is unlikely to be his, as the shield is topped with a crown, whereas a bishop would have a mitre.

Plates of this type were made mainly in the 15th and 16th centuries. They occur throughout the Netherlands, be it in modest numbers. At Zwolle another such unusual plate was found earlier, decorated with the *arma Christi*, the tools of Christ's passion (cross, ladder, spear, sponge). Indeed plates of this type may bear three kinds of design: religious, heraldic (including castles) or ornamental motifs

Two plates with sgraffito decoration have a cream-coloured slip coating only in certain parts of the design on the centre and rim. These designs are non-figurative. One of them may incorporate initials at the centre, which could begin with a P. It is clear also that these plates were useless for marketing: during firing, some areas have broken out of the surface where the decoration was incised too deeply.

Four specimens have slightly differing, simple slip-trailed designs made up of swags and arches on the rim and centre. The plates were rejected because they turned out warped or overfired. Only a few sherds have survived of another seven

04 Two plates with a slip-trailed design.

large plates. These were plates with simple slip-trail decoration. One undecorated plate is of the type r-bor-6 and has a diameter of just 16 cm. At the centre is an ugly scar left by burnt-on debris. A miniature plate, a mere 10 cm across, has an unsightly pool of glaze in the centre.

Lids

By far the majority of the lids are unglazed and belong to the type r-dek-1. Their diameters range from 14 to 26 cm. Thirteen lids are more or less complete. In all, there are sherds of 31 lids, often of a greyish appearance, which suggests that they were underfired. One fragment belongs to type r-dek-2 and could be the lid of an extinguisher. Three fragments are too small for attribution to a specific type, but definitely do not belong to those mentioned above.

Grapen

Intact, *grapen* or tripod cooking pots are quite voluminous. It is not easy to distinguish the various types. Bitter has made a start by subdividing the type r-gra-8, which features in many publications and comprises a wide variety of forms. He recently defined type r-gra-34. This is the most common type in the Zwolle complex, if we take the carination more broadly than as a 'thick ridge' and allow the space between the carination and the rim to contain more than two rills or ridges. Six specimens of this type have a so-called scallop rim: the collar, below the edge, is marked with a full band of thumb impressions. This leaves us with only four specimens of the original r-gra-8 type. Curiously, just these r-gra-8 pots turn out to have been used; all other types of *grapen* are rejects. Besides r-gra-34 there is r-gra-41: a situation similar to that at Alkmaar. Another type is r-gra-80, which previously had been found only at Veere.[18] The

01 Grape and cups.

only difference from type r-gra-34 is that the rim lacks a collar. In date, the pots from Veere are comparable to those from Zwolle. Therefore it seems that this (r-gra-80) was a common type. If we take a closer look at the Veere assemblage, dated to the last three quarters of the 16th century, it is clear that all items in the stoneware assemblage there have a frilled footring.[19] These should be dated mainly to the second quarter of the 16th century.

Yet another cooking pot form is the type r-gra-18, which has a carinated belly and barely any rilling on the upper part of the pot. This type also occurs at the Cele-complex site in Zwolle, which dates from the same period. Some pots of this type have a curved handle. A variation on this is a vessel of type r-gra-62, which looks similar but has a collared rim with a lid support. The interior of a single pot of type r-gra-43 has a slip coating containing copper oxide, which gives it a mottled green colour.

Jugs
Two near-complete jugs of type r-kan-20 were recovered. These are tall jugs on a footring that have a collared rim with a lid support, a round-section handle and accentuated rilling on the upper half of the vessel.

Chafing dish
Chafing dishes, which were mostly used for keeping food hot, barely feature in the assemblage; there is just a single fragment of one.

Bowls
The remains of six bowls provide us with complete profiles. Five of these are of the type r-kom-7. One is a type r-kom-6 bowl with a pair of horizontally placed round-section handles, a moulded rim and a frilled footring. Among the sherds, some 22 further bowls can be identified as belonging to the type r-kom-7, with sloping sides, a pouring lip and a footring. It is clear that a large majority of these bowls were spoilt by glaze discolouration.

Cups
Dozens of cups were discarded as rejects. They contained a pool of glaze or had been overfired, the glaze had blistered, there was burnt-on debris on the surface, they had broken or cracked during firing or become warped to some extent. Moreover, a few had probably been secondarily exposed to fire.

Forty-two bowls are largely complete and belong to the type r-kop-2. Four rim sherds are of the same type. Also there are eight cups of this type with a white slip sponged onto the outside and a yellow glaze on the interior, and a ninth with a green glaze inside. One specimen can be classified as r-kop-1, also with a white-sponged exterior and a yellow glaze inside. These white-sponged vessels are believed to have been produced in this area. The only examples known so far are from Zwolle and Kampen. The sponging makes the cups look like white ware; the purpose was to make them appear more expensive.

Nine cups belong to the type r-kop-17 and have no handle. One is also sponged white outside with a yellow glaze on the inside. Another cup of this shape owing to its omphalos base in fact represents a new type, r-kop-41, even though this new type comprises just a single specimen.

Fragments of 21 cups could not be identified as to type. Another specimen of undetermined type has a slip decoration on the rim and on the flat, triangular handle. The decoration on the handle is a cloverleaf design.

Strainer
The almost complete strainer (r-lek-7) with a moulded rim bore two round-section handles. The vessel has three small feet and has a grey-green, corroded glaze.[20]

Cresset-lamps
The finds include sherds of at least 17 double-shelled cresset-lamps of the type r-oli-2. In eleven of these oil lamps, the lower shell is flattened on one side, below the suspension loop attached to the upper shell: evidently they were wall lamps. The bottom shell of just one lamp is round. The upper shells have a vertical, moulded rim; the rim of the lower shells curves

01 Cresset-lamps.

upwards more gently. Opposite the suspension loop, the upper shells have a lip which - these being lamps - will have held the wick. In the lower shells the pouring lip is rotated 45 degrees to the left or right with respect to the wick lip of the upper shell. This feature is also seen on a cresset-lamp from another excavation on Het Eiland.[21] It is not a phenomenon exclusive to Zwolle, since it occurs also on two lamps from Alkmaar.[22] Contemporary drawings of oil lamps from Amersfoort show it too.[23] In each of the lamps, the bottom shell below the stem has been hollowed out and pared from below.

All of the lamps were unused rejects. There is no sign of wear. Some of the lamps were overfired, leaving the glaze with black, porous patches. Other lamps have minor or major deformations. These often resulted in part of the rim being too low, mostly on the flattened side. Many published double-shelled lamps are shown with their wick and pouring lips one above the other. The purpose of rotating them is not clear; we can offer plenty of speculative explanations, but no hard evidence.

Chamber pots

The chamber pots can be subdivided into three types: r-pis-3 (sixteen specimens including two unglazed ones), r-pis-6 (six including three unglazed ones) and r-pis-4 (a single, glazed specimen). Two fragments could not be assigned to a particular type. Type r-pis-3 may be described as having evolved from type r-pis-1, with a cylindrical neck and a marked shoulder-belly transition. Type r-pis-3 covers a wide range. In some specimens a neck can still be distinguished, but its transition to the rim and belly gradually becomes smoother, until eventually there is no trace of a neck. Types r-pis-3 and r-pis-6 have an omphalos base, whereas r-pis-13 has a footring. The five unglazed specimens were probably biscuit-fired, and discarded before being fired with glaze. This is surprising, as we usually see biscuit-firing only in more costly items. Maybe there was a different reason for their unglazed condition. One specimen of the type r-pis-3 has turned out a bit lopsided; the potter probably had an off day. One pot has a slightly moulded rim, but nonetheless has been classified as type r-pis-6. Another specimen with a moulded rim is of the concave-based type r-pis-4, despite having a carination and a footring.

The reason why these chamber pots were rejected is as varied as with the cups. Only two of the pots show abrasion on the base and calcium scale inside. These are the only two that had actually seen service. They belong to types r-pis-3 and r-pis-13.

Money boxes

Seven money boxes of the breast-shaped type (type r-spa-1) turned up, as well as a pig-shaped (r-spa-5) and a hen-shaped one (r-spa-). The slots in the hen-shaped and one of the breast-shaped specimens clearly were too narrow to take coins, so these must have been wasters. The shape of the others does not explain their rejection. However, the fabric of these items seems very soft, the grey tinge of the body also suggesting that they were underfired.

Tripod pipkins

Among the 29 tripod pipkins, ten are of the type r-stk-6, with a carinated belly and undecorated shoulder. The seven specimens of type r-stk-5 differ from these only in having decorative rilling or horizontal ribbing on the upper part. Such pipkins were already known from a privy vault at the so-called 'Cele-complex' site.[24]

Type r-stk-6 displays a wide range of rim diameters. The most common is 13 cm, but there also is one 17 cm across and even one of 21 cm. Two pipkins of type r-stk-6 saw domestic use.

Ointment jars

Five ointment jars were recovered, all of type r-zal-3. Four of them are small. Three of these have interior glazing but were overfired, which affected the glaze. The fifth, a large specimen, was also glazed, but has a large pool of glaze in the bottom. The fourth small jar should have been unglazed but is spoilt by blotches of glaze. This means that all of the jars were wasters. The bases show no traces of abrasion.

Dripping pan

Two sherds of a dripping pan were found. It probably was an unused reject, as it shows ugly scars of burnt-on debris as well as discoloured patches in the glaze.

Pedestal dishes

The two pedestal dishes have a yellow slip coating on the interior, which has discoloured to a greenish yellow. One of the dishes lost its high foot in firing through shattering. The foot of the other was badly damaged. The outside of the pedestal dishes had been sponged with white slip, like some of the plates and cups.

Miniatures or toys

Clear miniature forms include fragments of as many as three pots with a suspension handle. In two cases, two-thirds of the pot's body survived without the handle, while of a third, only the handle has survived. A few small handle fragments might belong to the first two specimens.

Also two-thirds of two pipkins with a curved handle and feet have survived; of a third specimen there is just a fragment.

Then there are three pots and the base of a tripod form. One miniature plate was recovered. Most of these miniature forms are obviously wasters, and apparently belonged to the regular output of the same potter.

Miscellaneous red ware
The miscellanea first of all include the 12,890 grs of sherds that could not be fitted to any of the described objects. Besides there are 97 rim fragments, which range in size from 1 sq cm to about 30 sq cm. Most of these rims must have belonged to tripod cooking pots, but they were not included in the Minimum Number of Specimens count. The combined weight of these rims is 1200 grs.

White ware
Five items are more or less complete. It is evident that these too were rejects. Two of them are cups (type w-kop-2) with a green glaze on the inside. One of them is lopsided, the other badly warped, with burnt-on red ware and a sherd that blew out, leaving glaze on the broken surface. Two other cups (w-kop-2) have a yellow glaze on the inside that is marred by black blotches; moreover, one of them is slightly deformed. The fifth item is a bowl with two horizontal round-section handles and a pouring lip. Here too, the yellow-glazed inner surface shows black blotches.

At least fourteen further items were represented, but rarely by more than one or a few sherds. They are a chamber pot, two cups (w-kop-7), one of which contains a pool of glaze, a possible brazier, a firepan, a cresset-lamp, a bowl and another cup. Six fragments could not be assigned to any functional category. Finally there are 25 small sherds (50 grs) which belonged to some enigmatic objects. These were excluded from the Minimum Number of Specimens count.

The five more-or-less complete items and a partial w-kop-7 cup were wasters and rejects. This suggests that the white ware was made by a potter who mainly produced red ware. Compared to the red ware, the white ware includes many incomplete objects and unrelated sherds.

Hafner ware
Three objects were made of so-called 'Hafner ware', whose provenance is the Cologne region. These are fragments of a flat base with folded feet belonging to a tripod cooking pot, fragments of a plate with combed decoration and a sherd that probably was a strap handle.

Glass
Glassware is represented by several fragments of a waisted (ribbed) beaker[25] (gl-bek-2c), and remnants of as many as six tubular glasses known in German as a *Stangenglas*, one of which could be fully reconstructed: it had a height of 21 cm, an octagonal opening 4.4 cm across and a foot 8.4 cm wide. This find of six specimens in a single assemblage may be described as - correctly for once - unique. Only twenty years ago, fewer than six had been documented in all of the literature, and even today they may number just a few dozen in all.

The first *Stangenglas* from Zwolle was found in a small sewage barrel during excavations on Het Eiland in 1995. From the same barrel came a Werra plate bearing the date 1608. The *Stangenglas* is however dated to the first half of the 16th century, and will have been an heirloom.[26] It is a fine piece, fairly complete, bluish green in colour with an openwork decoration around the middle. Similar open-work decoration is found on, for instance, a glass beaker from Deventer which may be dated by its context to the second or third quarter of the 15th century.[27] Havers mentions fragments of two *Stangenglas* specimens from a privy vault on the Bloemdalstraat in Zwolle. This assemblage is dated to 1650-1770.[28] In the present case, however, their shape suggests that the *Stangenglas* finds must be dated to the 17th century. Another assemblage from Zwolle (the Voorstraat) also produced fragments of a *Stangenglas*. This assemblage dates from 1375-1760 and comes from a wealthy context.[29] Yet another specimen is known from Werkeren manor house, from a privy vault that was used for many years. It is a foot fragment with a diameter of 11 cm and the rising cylinder section shows the lowermost two *passen*, horizontal glass trails. It must have been a very large glass. The same privy vault yielded a few small sherds of a second specimen. This brings to 12 the total number of *Stangengläser* from Zwolle alone.

The fact that the *Stangenglas* rarely appears in the archaeological literature might suggest that it is rare. In fact, it seems that the type occurs much more commonly than was hitherto assumed. Kottman states that cylindrical and polygonal *Stangengläser* of forest glass first appear in the late 15th century, but mainly from the early 16th century on, and that they are most common in central and northern Germany, where also their production centres will be found.[30]

In paintings, *Stangengläser* make 64 appearances[31] and in engravings 28.[32] In Dutch art-historical descriptions of *Stangengläser* the name *pasglas* is often used. These glasses are described under the heading of 'social drinking ware' or (in German) *Scherzgefäße*. When several circular glass trails, the so-called *passen*, adorn a *Stangenglas*, it is known as a *pasglas* (or dubiously translated as 'pass glass'). The *passen* were not merely decorative. They played a role in a drinking game in which the participants were challenged to drink down exactly to the next *pas* in a single draught; if they failed they had to drink on down to the next one.[33] C. Laan reports that she found just a single 17th-century source that describes the pastime. It is a text on a 17th-century *pasglas* in a museum in Vienna.[34]

German art-historical descriptions refer simply to *Stangengläser*, irrespective of the presence of *passen*.[35] C. Laan notes yet another interpretation of the *Stangenglas*.[36] In many 17th-century images *Stangengläser* are shown in a context of moral wantonness; she believes that here the *Stangenglas* could be a phallic symbol. This in contrast to the *Stangengläser* depicted on Werra ware, where they appear in a context of weddings or as an invitation to toast to good health.[37]

Miscellaneous finds

Metal finds include a fragment of an iron knife with a wooden handle. The end of the handle probably once bore a brass cap. An unidentified brass object has survived. It is semi-spherical with a diameter of 4.5 cm. Below its rim are four small, opposing holes. Finally there are scraps of leading from leaded window panes.

A pipe-clay figurine just 4.8 cm high shows the Christ child clasping a dove to its breast with both hands.[38]

The wooden items are all under restoration and hence can be described only superficially. They comprise two fairly complete wooden plates or *teljoren*, one large platter, two scoops, a small bowl, a lid with a hole in it, three spindles, a knife-handle, three balls, a peg, a small square board and part of a second lid. The wooden items will be described more fully in a future publication.

As for stone, there is a fragment of a whetstone.

Ceramic building materials also turned up. One is an unglazed floor tile measuring 16.5 x 16.5 x 3.0 cm. The remainder are fragments of roof tiles with burnt-on debris or glaze splotches, or both. They probably served as stacking aids in a kiln.

01 Waisted (ribbed) beaker and three tubular glasses (Stangengläser).

Two bone objects were recovered: a seven-toothed haircomb with a remaining length of 16.5 cm (cattle, metacarpal)[39] and a 'coat hook'. The latter consists of part of a red-deer antler; the main tine was sawn off opposite a lateral tine that stuck up at an angle, and drilled through at the top. Attached to a wall, it made a perfect peg for a single garment.

Soil samples

Soil samples were taken from the fill of the privy vault to be analysed for any seeds and fruits and small bone material. This is standard procedure in Zwolle, but if the assemblage covers a timespan longer than 50 years, the samples are discarded. In this case we are dealing with a shorter timespan, and the samples are perfect for analysis. This will take place at a later stage.

Analysis and comparison

The material from this privy vault is closely comparable to the finds excavated at the Wortelsteeg site in Alkmaar in 1991. A potter's workshop was established here between 1552 and 1620, many wasters and rejects from which were recovered. It was a business where, even more clearly than in the Zwolle situation, white ware was produced side-by-side with its main line of red-ware forms. Still, there is one important difference. In the case of Alkmaar no red-ware items were slip-coated or sponged white on the outside. This appears to be a feature typical of Zwolle.

The range of forms shows correspondences but also differences. We could argue that the points of correspondence indicate a nation-wide trend and that deviations point to regional idiosyncracies. In both places there are type r-kom-6 bowls,[40] but it is the r-kom-7 bowl which has been found only at Zwolle, and indeed in large numbers. Dozens of r-kop-2 cups occur in both towns.[41] At Alkmaar we find cups without a handle, in the shape of types r-kop-12 and -13. At Zwolle we find a slightly differing variant with a less globular body and a flattened rim: r-kop-17. The difference between the Alkmaar and Zwolle cups is minimal, and in both cases we are dealing with small numbers. R-bor-1 is the most common in both assemblages and is chronologically succeeded by r-bor-6. At Zwolle more cresset-lamps were recovered than at Alkmaar.[42] In most of the Zwolle lamps the lips of the upper and lower bowl are rotated by 45 degrees. This is not the case in the Alkmaar examples of type r-oli-2. The difference could be due to the Alkmaar lamps being of a later date. In the 17th century this feature no longer seems to occur.

The skillets and the pipkins in the two towns are clearly different. In numbers too, the contrast is considerable. At Zwolle we find just five skillets, of types r-bak-18 and r-bak-21, while at Alkmaar over 100 were recorded, including 88 of type r-bak-4.[43] At Alkmaar there is just one pipkin, as against 29 in Zwolle. That single Alkmaar specimen is a r-stk-5 with a lid support,[44] but one excavated earlier at the Cele-complex site showed that in Zwolle the type occurs also without a lid support.[45] And now the privy vault at Achter de Broeren has produced four such vessels. These finds correspond in terms of dating. The most common type, however, is r-stk-6, with a sharp carination and a smooth upper part, in contrast to type r-stk-5, which does display ribs or rilling in this area. Among the tripod cooking pots, the similarities once more predominate.

Equally important for a comparison as the Alkmaar-Wortelsteeg finds are those from the second deposit (92VDA2) in a cesspit at the Luttik Oudorp site in Alkmaar, which can be dated to the first half of the 16th century.[46] Close by, also material from a 16th-century rubbish pit (89Lut) was recovered (89Lut).[47] Indeed both assemblages were found close to the site of the pottery on the Wortelsteeg.

A comparable range of forms comes from a mid-16th-century cesspit at Gorinchem.[48]

Conclusion

Archaeologically, the find assemblage from the privy vault could be dated to the second and third quarters of the 16th century. On historical grounds, this dating can probably be narrowed down to (part of) the third quarter. That is, if a link is assumed between the recovered material and the documentary references to one or more potters. The excavated area was not the site of a potter's workshop.

Besides the historical references, the following evidence seems to point to a local potter's waste dump. Rejected output was dumped without having been used. Domestic pottery waste made up just a small proportion of the finds. That the dump site was a privy vault is unusual for potters' waste.

The rejected pots of red ware and white ware displayed similar imperfections and hence seem to represent one or a few failed batches produced by a single potter. At any rate the white ware and the red ware were of local manufacture; this is deduced mainly from the presence of red-ware items sponged with a white slip wash, a product so far excavated exclusively in this area.

The majolica tankard and the stoneware jugs display no wear on their bases. Nor do they in any way qualify as seconds. The absence of abrasion on imported ceramics points towards a retailer's stock, but why these items ended up among rejects remains a mystery.

All in all, an unambiguous answer to the question of whether the wasters were dumped by a potter or by a retailer has proved elusive. The most plausible explanation at this point seems to be that a local potter ran a retail business where also imported products were sold, and that this outlet was quite close to his workshop.

Notes

1. RA001 00022, p. 88, 2nd akte.
2. RA001 00022, p. 170, 1st akte.
3. RA001 00023, p. 33.
4. One fragment of burnt loam was recovered with upright clay-pipe stems baked into it. This could be a remnant of kiln waste from a potter who glazed his clay pipes, datable at least a century later. Glazing was done in a second firing, for which the baked pipes, dipped in glaze, would be set upright in a block of loam inside the kiln. After the second firing, the stems would be broken off above the loam, filed smooth and marketed.
5. Reineking-von Bock 1986, 238.
6. Reineking-von Bock 1986, 234, no. 274.
7. Reineking-von Bock 1986, 230-231.
8. Griffioen & Bartels 2005.
9. Gaimster 1997, 191.
10. Ostkamp, Roedema & Van Wilgen 2001, 61.
11. Vandenbulcke & Groeneweg 1988.
12. Sarfatij 1979, 518-519.
13. Bartels 1999, cat.no. 192, found at Dordrecht.
14. Reineking-von Bock 1986, 246, no. 305.
15. Pers. comm. S. Ostkamp, 21 Feb. 2005.
16. E.g., Bartels 2001, cat.no. 950, found at Dordrecht; this is a late specimen.
17. Bitter 2004, 36.
18. Goldschmitz *et al.* 1996, 66-67.
19. Goldschmitz *et al.* 1996, 60-61.
20. Bartels dates the other known type, r-lek-7, between 1530 and 1575. Bartels 2001, cat.no. 628.
21. Klomp 1998, 147 and 152.
22. Bitter 1991, 131.
23. Van Dijk 2004. The oil lamp on 53 clearly has pouring lips rotated with respect to each other, while those of the two lamps on 54 are not.
24. Clevis 2000, 52, cat.no. 29.
25. Henkes 1994, 2.
26. Klomp 2001, 148.
27. Clevis & Kottman 1989, 141.
28. Havers 2003, 67-68.
29. Clevis 2000, 76.
30. Kottman 1999, 264.
31. Vroom 1980.
32. Henkes 1994, 157, remarks that in the Boymans-Van Beuningen documentation system for pre-industrial utensils, 28 illustrations are known from the mid-17th century.
33. Henkes 1994, 158.
34. Laan 1993, 30.
35. See for example Baumgartner 1987, 91-97 and Baumgartner 1988, 312-408.
36. Laan 1993.
37. Pers. Comm., Hans van Gangelen.
38. Pers. comm., S. Ostkamp, 21 Feb. 2005.
39. Van Vilsteren 1987, 39, fig. 41.
40. Bitter 1992, 111.
41. Bitter 1992, 111.
42. Bitter 1992, 112.
43. Bitter 1992, 110.
44. Bitter 1992, 134, cat.no. 58.
45. Clevis 2000, 52, cat.no. 29.
46. Ostkamp *et al.* 2001, 55-56 and 105-138.
47. Ostkamp *et al.* 2001, 11-47.
48. Van den Berg *et al.* 2003, 126 ff.

References

Bartels, M. (1999). *Steden in Scherven. Vondsten uit beerputten in Deventer, Dordrecht, Nijmegen en Tiel (1250-1900)*. Zwolle.

Baumgartner, E. (1987). *Glas des späten Mittelalters. Die Sammlung Karl Amendt*. Düsseldorf.

Baumgartner, E., & I. Krueger (1988). *Phönix aus Sand und Asche. Glas des Mittelalters*. München.

Berge, H. v.d. *et al.* (2003).In Gorcum gebakken. Aardewerk, kleipijpen, wandtegels. Vianen.

Bitter, P. (1992). *Geworteld in de bodem. Archeologisch en historisch onderzoek van een pottenbakkerij bij de Wortelsteeg in Alkmaar*. Zwolle.

Bitter, P. E.A. (2004). *De verborgen stad. 750 jaar Alkmaar onder de grond*.

Clevis, H. & J. Kottman, (1987). Aardewerk en Glas. In: (H. Clevis & J. Kottman eds.) *Weggegooid en Teruggevonden. Aardewerk en glas uit Deventer vondstcomplexen 1375-1750*. 23-60 and 77-142.

Clevis, H. (2000). Het Zwolse Celehuisje. In: (H. Clevis ed.) Zwolle *Ondergronds. Zeven blikvangers van archeologische vondsten in Zwolle*, 37-59.

Clevis, H. (2000). Tussen Melkmarkt en Kalverstraat. In: (H. Clevis ed.) Zwolle *Ondergronds. Zeven blikvangers van archeologische vondsten in Zwolle*, 59-104.

Dijk, M. van (2004). Eindelijk wat verlichting. In: (T. d'Holossy ed.) *Gespaard verleden. 24 vondsten van de maand*. 53-55.

Duysters, K. (2002). Facetten van Glas. *De glascollectie van het Historisch Museum Arnhem*. Arnhem.

Gaimster, D. (1997). *German Stoneware 1200-1900*.

Goldschmitz *et al.* (1996). Catalogus van Keramiek en Glas. In: (E., Vrenegoor en J. Kuijpers eds.) Vondsten in Veere. Middeleeuwse voorwerpen uit een beerput van huis 'In den Struys'. Abcoude. 60-75.

Griffioen & Bartels 2005?

Havers, G. (2003). Werra keramiek uit Enkhuizen. In: (H. Clevis ed.) Handleiding Classificatiesysteem voor Laat- en Post Middeleeuws Aardewerk en Glas. Digitale versie 1.0. Zwolle. 67-75.

Henkes, H. (1994). *Glas zonder Glans. Vijf eeuwen gebruiksglas uit de bodem van de Lage Landen (1300-1800).* Rotterdam Papers 9.

Jong-Lambregts, N. de (2004). Koken, bakken, braden en eten met aardewerk. In: (P. Bitter ed.). *De verborgen stad. Archeologisch onderzoek naar 750 jaar wonen in Alkmaar*. 30-47.

Klomp, M. (1998). Bijzondere glasvondsten in Zwolle. In: (H. Clevis *et al.* eds) Archeologie en Bouwhistorie in Zwolle 4. Zwolle. 141-155.

Klomp, M. (2000). Een beerput vol verrassingen op het Eiland. In: (H. Clevis ed.) Zwolle *Ondergronds. Zeven blikvangers van archeologische vondsten in Zwolle*, 105-172.

Kottman, J. (1999). Glaswerk. In: (M. Bartels *et al.* eds) *Steden in Scherven. Vondsten uit beerputten in Deventer, Dordrecht, Nijmegen en Tiel (1250-1900)*. Zwolle. 261-274.

Laan, C. (1993). *Het pasglas. Een stille getuige van een bruisend verleden*. Doctoraalscriptie Erasmus Universteit Rotterdam. Typescript.

Ostkamp, S., R. Roedema en R. van Wilgen (2001). *Gebruikt en Gebroken. Vijf eeuwen bewoning op drie locaties in het oostelijk stadsdeel*. Rapporten over de Alkmaarse Monumentenzorg en Archeologie 10. Alkmaar.

Reineking-von Bock, G. (1986). *Steinzeug*. Köln.

Sarfatij, H. (1979). Münzschatzgefässe in den Niederlanden, 1. Die Periode 1190-1566. In: Berichten van de Rijksdienst voor het Oudheidkundig Bodemonderzoek jaargang 28, 1979. 491-526.

Vandenbulcke, V. & G. Groeneweg (1988). The stoneware stock of Ja-Peterss and Cornelis-de-kanneman: two merchants of Rhenish pottery at Bergen-op-Zoom (NL) during the 2nd quarter of the 16th century. In: (R.M. Gaimster *et al.* eds) *BAR International Series* 440. pp 343-357.

Vilsteren, V.T. van (1987). *Het Benen Tijdperk. Gebruiksvoorwerpen van been, gewei, hoorn en ivoor, 10.000 jaar geleden tot heden*. Assen.

Vroom, N.R.A. (1980). A modest Message (vols. 1 & 2). A modest message as intimated by the painters of 'Monochrome Banketje'.

List of contents

Stoneware2
S2-kan-19	1
S2-kan-47	1
S2-kan-48	1
S2-kan-63	3
S2-kan	1
subtotal	7
remainder	450 grs

Majolica
d-bek-1	1
d-kom-1	1
m-	1
subtotal	3

Red ware
r-bak-6	2
r-bak-18	2
r-bak-21	3
r-bak	1
r-bak-flan	1
r-bor-1	10
r-bor-6	1
r-bor	6
r-dek-1	31
r-dek-2	1
r-dek	3
r-gra-8	4
r-gra-18	10
r-gra-34	26
r-gra-41	2
r-gra-43	1
r-gra-62	1
r-gra-80	9
r-gra	2
r-kan-20	4
r-kan	2
r-kmf	1
r-kom-6	1
r-kom-7	28
r-kop-1 (sponged with white slip)	1
r-kop-2	46
r-kop-2 (sponged with white slip)	9
r-kop-17	8
r-kop-17 (sponged with white slip)	1
r-kop-22 (concave base)	1
r-kop-41	1
r-kop-	21
r-kop- (clover-leaf handle, slip-trailed decoration)	1
r-lek-7	1
r-oli-2	17
r-pis-3	16
r-pis-4	1
r-pis-6	6
r-pis-8	1
r-pis-13	7
r-pis	2
r-spa-1	7
r-spa-5	1
r-spa	1
r-spr	1
r-stk-5	4
r-stk-6	13
r-stk	12
r-vet	1
r-voe-1	2
r-zal-3	5
r-min (plate)	1
r-min (pot with suspension handle)	3
r-min (tripod pipkin)	3
r-min (pot shaped)	3
r-min	2
r-	10
subtotal	361
remainder	1200 grs

Hafner ware
Ha-bor-1	1
Ha-gra-4	1
Ha-1	1
subtotaal	3

White ware
w-kom-7	1
w-kop-2	5
w-kop-7	2
w-pis	1
w-gat	1
w-tes	1
w-oli	1
w-kom	1
w-	6
subtotal	19
total	**393**

	Ach04 1-10	89Lut	92VDA	Alkm91	Gorinchem
r-bak	1	4		42	
r-bak-1		1	3	3	
r-bak-2		7	2	27	
r-bak-3		3	1		
r-bak-4				60	
r-bak-6	2				
r-bak-5		8		11	
r-bak-8		6		1	
r-bak-17			1		
r-bak-18	2				
r-bak-21	2				
r-bak-26		1			
r-bor	6			5	
r-bor-1	10	6	7	11	*
r-bor-6	1	3	8	3	*
r-bor-29			1		
r-bor-33					*
r-dek	3				
r-dek-1	31		1		
r-dek-2	1				
r-gra	2	3	3	55	
r-gra-8	4	2	19		*7
r-gra-10a			2		
r-gra-18	10				
r-gra-19			3	2	
r-gra-22			4		
r-gra-29		12		29	
r-gra-34	26	13	2	47	
r-gra-35				9	
r-gra-41	2	2	1	6	*
r-gra-43	1				
r-gra-50					*2
r-gra-62	1				
r-gra-80	9				
r-kan	2				
r-kan-20	4				
r-kan-31					*
r-kmf	1				
r-kom			4		
r-kom-2			4		
r-kom-6				2	
r-kom-11			1		
r-kom-12			1		
r-kom-13			1		
r-kom-61			1		

	Ach04 1-10	89Lut	92VDA	Alkm91	Gorinchem
r-kom-62			1		
r-kop	22	6		1	
r-kop-1	1		3		
r-kop-2	55	4	2		
r-kop-10			1		*
r-kop-11				3	
r-kop-12				5	
r-kop-17	9	6			
r-kop-20					*
r-kop-22	1				
r-kop-36					*
r-kop-38					*
r-kop-41	1				
r-lek-1		2			
r-lek-7	1				
r-min	12		2		
r-oli		1		8	
r-oli-1			1		
r-oli-2	17				*
r-oli-4				1	
r-pis	2	4	4		
r-pis-3	16				
r-pis-4	1	1			
r-pis-5			1	1	
r-pis-6	6				*3
r-pis-8			1	1	
r-pis-9		2			
r-pis-13	7				
r-pis-19			4		
r-pis-21			1		
r-pis-27					*3
r-pot		2		1	
r-pot-7			2		
r-pot-9			2	1	
r-pot-24	1				
r-spa-1	7				
r-spa-5	1				
r-spr	1				
r-stk	12				
r-stk-5	7				
r-stk-6	13				
r-stk-16					*
r-tes-1		1	2		
r-tes-4		8	9		
r-tes-10			1		

	Ach04 1-10	89Lut	92VDA	Alkm91	Gorinchem
r-tes-11			1		
r-tes-14					*
r-tes-18					*
r-vet-1		2			
r-voe	1				
r-vog-1			1		
r-vst		2			
r-vst-1		2		14	
r-vst-2				1	
r-vst-3			3		
r-vuu				1	
r-vuu-2				1	
r-zal		1			
r-zal-3	5				
r-zal-4			1		
r-zou-3					*

Tabular comparison of the Achter de Broeren (Ach04 1-10) assemblage with Luttik Oudorp Alkmaar (89lut and 92 VDA, Alkmaar Wortelsteeg (Alkm91) and Gorinchem.

Oosterhout pottery II

Industrial waste from the Leijsenhoek

Piet Kleij

The two foremost centres of pottery production in Brabant were Oosterhout and Bergen op Zoom. In the 17th century, Oosterhout numbered over 30 potteries. From then on, the number fell to about twenty by 1740, sixteen in 1813 and two in 1914. The last pottery closed down in 1942.[1] The firms were spread across the entire municipality.[2] This means that remains of kilns and pits filled with wasters may turn up anywhere in the area.

In 1995, a description was published of pottery waste found in the Rulstraat at Oosterhout.[3] This was the first article discussing such an assemblage from Oosterhout. In subsequent years, several other finds of potters' waste have come to light. The present article, the second about wasters from Oosterhout, will deal with material from the Leijsenhoek site.

During demolition works in March 1999 on the Leijsenhoek at Oosterhout, some pits containing pottery waste were uncovered. Archaeologists of the municipal archaeological service and volunteers carried out a brief salvage excavation, during which further material was recovered. The pottery was described and drawn in the closing months of 1999 and the beginning of 2000. In 2008 an opportunity arose to publish the material.

This article will refer to the history of Oosterhout's pottery industry only when necessary. For more extensive background information about Oosterhout's potteries and their history and about the organisation of the potters' guild, the reader is referred to the article on the Rulstraat finds.[4]

Find conditions

In 1998 a fire destroyed the ice-cream parlour "La Venezia" on the corner of the Leijsenhoek and the Donkerstraat. The owners, the Van Beek brothers, decided to have an apartment complex built on the now empty site. Prior to the building works, the municipal archaeologist Nico Dijk was given an opportunity to carry out an investigation at the site, assisted by some volunteers. This took place on 29 March and the first week of April in 1999. First the topsoil was removed, a layer 40 to 50 cm thick. Below this, the researchers found a pavement of red, blackened bricks, covered with splashes of glaze. Below this floor a second floor appeared, made from red floor tiles which also were covered with spots of glaze. This tiled floor was set in a 10 cm thick layer of soil that overlay the yellow coversand natural. Under the coversand, at a depth of about 1.50 m, lay a clay deposit that probably belongs to the Formation of Tegelen. This formation lies at a shallow depth in western Brabant, and has traditionally been used for making pottery.[5]

To the north of the floor, the top of the coversand had been worked into a grey ploughsoil, from which early medieval (8th-9th century) and late medieval (13th-15th century) potsherds were recovered. Also a semicircular ditch was found here, possibly surrounding a barn with round ends or a round granary.[6] Adjoining this ditch was a waster pit, *feature 13*, in which the bowl of a double-shelled cresset lamp was found. To the west of the floor, waster pit *feature 5* was uncovered, which yielded about ten sherds belonging to a milk tub and to plates decorated with yellow slip. Below this floor appeared waster pit *feature 17*, which contained many fragments of red ware with a green-tinged glaze. *Feature 17* continued to the east of the floor, where it had been dug over and joined up with waster pit *feature 16*. That these features had been merged through digging was evident from the fact that both yielded sherds of the same items. These two features together contained the majority of the finds, hundreds of fragments of all sorts of products such as tripod cauldrons, chamber pots, milk tubs and platters, but also parts of roofing tiles and slates spattered with lead glaze. Several of these sherds too were covered with glaze with a greenish hue. At the edge of both pits a well, *feature 19*, had been dug in the 19th century. To conclude, the coversand close to the northern edge of the floor produced some further sherds, including an almost complete cresset lamp. These finds could not be linked to any particular feature. A curious find, at the centre of the site, was a champagne bottle with its original contents, dating from the 19th or 20th century.

The material and its significance

It was immediately clear to the excavators that the remains of a pottery were being uncovered. The blackened, glaze-spattered pavement was once the floor of a potter's kiln. The bricks had been blackened by the heat of the fire, and during the firings drops of glaze had trickled off the items being fired and onto this floor. The pieces of roofing tile and slate found among the potsherds had served as stacking aids inside the kiln. These too became glaze-spattered during their use.

Another indication that this was waste from a pottery was the presence of distinct wasters among the sherds, such as three-quarters of a platter encrusted with ash and grit and the belly of a badly deformed jug to which parts of another item had stuck. From the 17th to the 19th century, Oosterhout was one of the leading pottery centres in the Netherlands. However, little is known about its actual output. Potters' waste, turning up now and then throughout the municipality, constitutes a very important source of information about Oosterhout's products. From the wasters, we can determine what forms, typical details, ornamental motifs and other traits characterise the pottery from Oosterhout. With this knowledge, Oosterhout ware may be identified in assemblages excavated in other parts of the Netherlands and even further afield.

In this way we can obtain an ever clearer picture of the characteristics, the use and the distribution of Oosterhout pottery. The material from the Leijsenhoek thus is an important source of information about these products and very significant for the study of 17th- and 18th-century assemblages in the Netherlands and beyond.

01 Platter encrusted with ash and grit.

In recent years, the pottery industry of Oosterhout has been the subject of archive research, which has shed light on the location of many potteries in the municipality. However, the presence of a pottery at the corner of the Leijsenhoek/Donkerstraat was still unknown. After its discovery in 1999 a targeted archive search was undertaken for evidence about this workshop, but this still drew a blank. Therefore the archaeological evidence from the excavation is the only available source about the pottery at this site. This clearly illustrates the importance of archaeologically investigating sites from historical times.

A description of the ceramic body and surface finish

At first sight, the pottery from the Leijsenhoek falls into two categories. The fabric of one is a brownish red, with grey in the core of the thicker parts. This means that these items were not oxidised through and through during their firing.[7] This pottery is tempered with very fine, white sand, i.e. grains smaller than 0.1 mm. The fabric is fairly hard, which means that it cannot be scratched with a fingernail – it will abrade the nail. The items are covered with a fairly thick, quite well-fired layer of lead glaze, which gives the pottery a greyish-greenish tinge. On severely overfired fragments, the glaze has acquired a dark green colour. Sherds of this first category come from features 16 and 17.

The fabric of the second category is orange-yellow to orange, and regular, but not always smooth and contains a temper of fine, white sand (grains smaller than 0.1 mm). The lead glaze, applied not particularly thickly, gives the forms a bright orange brilliance. The hardness of this ware is not as great as that of the first category. The second group comprises also slip-decorated items. This decoration consists of whirls and wavy lines which in some cases have been applied thinly and rather casually. apparently in haste. A single decorative wavy line may be made up of three or four short consecutive trails. Fragments have been found of two cups or bowls provided with a slip coating on the inside. In one of these, copper oxide had been added to the glaze, giving the inner surface of the cup or bowl a bright green colour. Fragments of this category turn up in every feature except *feature 19*.

The differences between the two groups need not indicate a difference in technique or production method. It should be remembered that we are here dealing with wasters, so we should first of all consider whether the differences between the two categories might not be attributable to slip-ups in the firing process.

The first group is clearly darker in colour than the second. This group includes a relatively large proportion of overfired material. Some platters in this category are encrusted with ash and soot, the pots are warped and the glaze sometimes contains bubbles due to overheating. Everything indicates that the potsherds in the first category were exposed to excessive heat. The fact that some thick sherds still have a grey core may mean that the potter interrupted the firing process before all items were properly fired through. He may have done so because the temperature in part of the kiln had become far too high, so that some of the contents were becoming overfired while others were not yet ready.

The second category displays far fewer traces of overfiring, but shows other flaws: cracks in the wall or uneven bases. In these cases the firing has been properly conducted. The wasters are not a result of overfiring but of other imperfections in the production process. The dark colour of the pottery in the first category therefore probably does not result from an intentional process, but rather from accidental overheating of the kiln. The wasters from the second category are not a result of overfiring but were discarded for other reasons. The colour and surface texture of the fabrics in this group probably do correspond to what the potter had in mind. We may therefore assume that the pottery in the first category represents the appearance of the same ware when overfired. The second category shows the surface of the ware as the Leijsenhoek potter intended it to be. The similarities between the categories are considerable. The temper and the hardness, the forms and all sorts of details are identical. The differences in colour of the glaze and fabric are mere effects of overfiring. The only difference between the two groups that cannot be explained in this way is that the second category includes platters with slip-trailed decoration and the first category does not. Presumably this difference is merely coincidental.

The forms and their dating

A total of eleven forms were fully reconstructed. Five others could be only partially reconstructed, but enough features of these were present to justify a description. These include the stacking devices. Apart from these, six characteristic fragments were deemed to merit special attention. Together, these forms and fragments offer a fair idea of what sorts of products were made at the Leijsenhoek.

Two sherds of glass, part of a majolica platter, a white faience platter, the rim of a stoneware jug and the rim of a mineral-water bottle do not belong to the pottery waste but are incidental finds. They are described because they are of use for the dating of the assemblage. In the following description, first the complete items are discussed, followed by the incomplete ones, the fragments and the incidental finds.

Complete forms
Platters

Dozens of fragments of at least four different types of platter were found among the wasters. All four types are platters on pinched feet. The largest platter, indeed more a dish, has a diameter of 49.2 cm, a deep profile, and a virtually horizontal flange (cat. no. 2).[8] At the transition from the centre to the flange there is a ridge on the upper surface. The edge consists of a thickened part turned upward and a smaller downturned lip. The upper surface of the flange is decorated with a white, slip-trailed wavy line. The entire upper surface is glazed. Just one specimen of this type was found. This plate is similar to the plates produced at Bergen op Zoom in the second part of the 16th century.[9] Also there are many correspondences to the plates found in a cesspit at Dordrecht.[10] The Dordrecht plates resemble cat. no 1 especially in their profile. The Dordrecht assemblage is dated between 1580 and 1610. The slip-trailed decoration, as on this plate, is in fact a common feature on Oosterhout pottery. The potsherds from the Rulstraat include a great deal of slip-decorated material.[11] At Bergen op Zoom, by contrast, slip-trailed decoration is very rare.[12]

The second platter, of the second type, has a diameter of 44.5 cm and in its profile strongly resembles the first (cat. no. 3

02 Badly deformed jug to which parts of another item have stuck.

and photo 2).[13] A marked difference from the first type is the absence of the ridge on the centre-flange transition. Instead, there appears to be a groove. The rim is thicker and more massive than on the first plate. The upper surface is lead-glazed. a single, undecorated specimen of this type was recovered. This platter too shows similarities to those manufactured at Bergen op Zoom and those found in the Dordrecht cesspit; hence it must date from the same period. The third platter, with a diameter of 37.2 cm, has a flowing, faintly S-shaped profile with a slight ridge at the centre-flange transition (cat. no. 4). The rim seems to be a variation on that of the previously discussed plate. The upper surface is glazed. The flange bears a wavy line in white slip, while the centre has white slip-trailed circles. Some of the circles have lines drawn across them. This design of circles, sometimes with lines across them, is typical of Oosterhout pottery.

This platter too has parallels among the dishes from Bergen op Zoom and the cesspit finds from Dordrecht. Moreover, a similar platter turned up outside Breda, at the site of an army camp which was in use between 1624 and 1637.[14] For these reasons, this platter is dated between 1580 and 1640. Of this type, a single fully reconstructible specimen was found and three rims of other specimens, all decorated with wavy slip trails.

It is notable that the decoration on platter cat. no. 4 strongly resembles that on two platters found at The Hague. These platters have footrings and a different profile, and date from the final quarter of the 17th and first half of the 18th century.[15] This clearly shows that the slip-trailed decoration at Oosterhout was not bound to a particular type of plate or phase, but may occur over a fairly long period and on objects of different types. This kind of decoration indeed also appears on bowls from an assemblage at Breda. This assemblage can only be very broadly dated: between 1650 and 1850.[16]

The final plate has a diameter of 25 cm, an S-shaped profile with slight ridges both on the top and bottom of the centre-flange transition (cat. no. 5). The rim clearly deviates from those of the first three platters. It is somewhat thickened so that it appears round in section. Three grooves are present on the outer edge. The upper surface of the plate is glazed. The finds included no decorated sherds of this type of plate. Although plate cat. no. 4 has a deviating rim, the overall profile still strongly resembles that of the three other types. It is therefore dated to the same period.

Extinguisher

One near-complete extinguisher was recovered (cat. no. 19). Because of its faulty base it is tilted. Its greatest height is about 25.0 cm; its maximum width of 26.5 cm is at three-quarters of its height and a groove adorns the shoulder. The pot has a footring thrown in one piece with the vessel. Two low, semicircular, upright loop handles complete the vessel. The short rim is vertical and rounded. The exterior is entirely glazed.

This extinguisher is of a type about which Groeneweg states that it was introduced at Bergen op Zoom in the course of the 17th century.[17] The type survived into the 18th century. The shape of the handles, and its slight height give it a rather crude appearance. This may be a common feature of early extinguishers.

Tripod cauldrons

Two tripod cauldrons are almost complete; a third is easy to reconstruct. The largest has an unusual shape (cat. no. 7). Its height (29.2 cm) exceeds its diameter (24.6 cm), which affords the vessel an elongated, tall appearance. It is fully glazed both inside and out, and the upper half shows rilling. The cauldron has two vertical loop handles and a groove at the transition from belly to wall. The rim is quite remarkable: from the shoulder it stands up fairly straight, like a stiff collar, slightly everted towards the top. The oval mouth is due to an error in the manufacturing process. A problem with the complete, illustrated specimen is that because of the warped mouth and the uneven rim, no clear representation of the rim profile was possible. Therefore a rim fragment of an incomplete, low tripod cauldron is shown to clarify the typical profile (fig. 1). Besides this cauldron and this rim, fragments of at least three other cauldrons or pots with collar rims of this type were recovered.

The illustrated "tall cauldron" is of a type that at Bergen op Zoom was produced in the final quarter of the 16th century.[18] Bartels describes tripod cauldrons of this type with the same, semicircular handles from a late-16th-century assemblage from

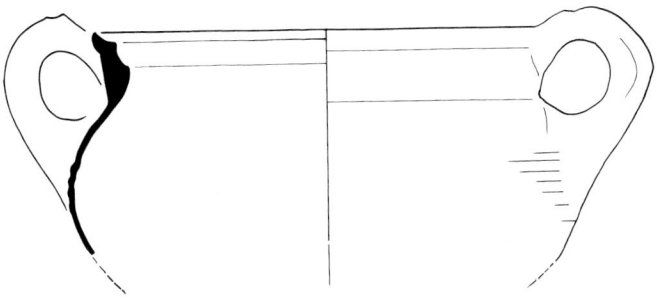

03 Tripod cauldron.

Dordrecht.[19]

The second tripod cauldron is 28.0 cm wide and 20.2 cm high, which gives this vessel a "normal", squat appearance (cat. no. 8). The upper half shows rilling; the two vertically placed handles are somewhat drawn upwards and outwards. The rim profile is interesting: on the inside of the everted rim there is a hollow lid support, and above it, on the inside, is a facet; the top of the rim is rounded. This tripod cauldron too is fully glazed inside and out. This low vessel dates from the first half of the 17th century.[20]

The third cauldron is also a squat one (11.5 cm high; 20.2 cm wide). It is carinated at the transition from base to wall, has rilling on the upper half and two vertical loop handles (cat. no. 9). The rim is fairly flat, thickened at the edge and not unlike that of a chamber pot. This cauldron is fully glazed internally; externally only on the upper half. This specimen like the tall one dates from the final quarter of the 16th century.[21]

Milk tub

One of the largest forms produced by the potters is without doubt the milk tub. Fragments of at least five specimens were recovered, one of which could be almost completely reconstructed (cat. no. 14). The oval bowl has an average diameter of 48 cm, a maximum height of 17.2 cm and a separately made, slightly pinched footring. The two horizontally placed loop handles are elongated. The base of the pouring lip is still present, but the lip itself has broken off. The rim, a distinct example of the fancy, pronounced rims so typical of Oosterhout, is massive, has a downturned lip on the outside, while the top of the thickened upper surface features a broad groove. The interior of the vessel is glazed.

The earliest milk tubs date from the 15th and 16th centuries. Groeneweg states that they no longer occurred in the 17th century but were again produced in the course of the 18th century.[22] The milk tub from the Leijsenhoek (cat. no. 11) has a typical Oosterhout rim associated with the 18th century, which seems to date it to that era.[23] Curiously, it was found in association with several platters from the 1580-1640 period and therefore must definitely date from the late 16th or first half of the 17th century. Groeneweg attributes the absence of milk tubs in the 17th century to a change in the way of dairy processing. Apparently this meant a reduction in the use of milk tubs, but evidently they did not disappear altogether. This is proved by the five milk tubs from the Leijsenhoek site, which definitely date from the late 16th or the 17th century. It is remarkable, however, that they are identical to the 18th-century forms. As a consequence, milk tubs may often have been wrongly dated in the past. Another explanation for the lack of milk tubs identified in 17th-century contexts may be due to lack of research into assemblages from rural sites. In fact, far too little is known about the use of pottery in villages and at farms to allow us to speak with any certainty about the use of "rural pottery". Indeed this type of milk tub may even date from the 16th century. Closer investigation of these milk tubs will have to show what their correct dating is.

Colander

One strainer or colander could be entirely reconstructed (cat. no. 16). This specimen has a diameter of 37.5 cm, three feet and two horizontally placed loop handles. The rim is massive, everted and besides has a downturned, rounded lip. The vessel was perforated from above with a round instrument (an awl or nail?), which produced holes with a diameter of 3 to 4 mm. Grooves appear to have adorned the handles. Only the upper surface of the colander was glazed. This was a long-lived type. It was manufactured from the mid 16th century and survived into the second half of the 18th century.[24]

Cresset lamp

An almost complete cresset lamp was found among the potsherds. It is of the double-shelled type, consisting of a bowl with a lip, from the centre of which rises a thick stem on which is a second, smaller, bowl with a lip (cat. no. 17). An upright loop handle is attached to the upper bowl. The two bowls and part of the stem have a glazed surface. The lips served to hold the wicks. The upper bowl of a second specimen was also recovered.

Cresset lamps of this type occur over a long period, from the 15th to the 18th century. In the course of time, the length of the stem increased. The length of the Leijsenhoek specimen is about 9 cm, which puts the lamp in the late 16th or the 17th century.[25]

Incomplete forms
Platter

Of a fifth plate type (cat. no. 6), only a rim was recovered, so it is not clear whether it had a footring or pinched feet. This plate resembles the second type (cat. no. 2) in that it has a groove marking the transition from centre to flange. But the rim is shaped differently: its upper surface is nicely rounded, as it runs down it turns inward somewhat, and then lower down turns outward again, forming a small lip. This lip projects beyond the upper part of the rim. This contrasts with the rims of the first three types (cat. nos. 1-3), which also are bilobed in section but whose upper part projects beyond the lower. The flange of this fifth type of platter is decorated with short dashes of trailed slip.

It is difficult to date this fragment on the basis of its shape. Since it was found in association with the sherds of the other platters, it presumably dates from the same period: 1580-1640.

Jug (upper half)

The upper part of a jug (cat. no. 12) has a globular belly with a maximum diameter of 18.6 cm, a ribbed neck and a straight, slightly jutting rim, forming a kind of lid support. The outside of the rim is decorated with grooves. The lower end of the large, vertical loop handle was pressed out flat against the vessel body. Both the interior and the exterior are partly covered with a thin layer of lead glaze. Whether the jug ever had a pouring lip cannot be ascertained. The handle is strongly reminiscent of that on an Oosterhout jug from the second half of the 18th century, but since this jug from La Venezia/the Leijsenhoek was only partially preserved, it cannot be dated to this period with certainty.[26]

Cup

The upper part of a one-handled cup was recovered (cat. no. 15). The transition from base to wall is carinated. Its maximum diameter, at this point, is 13.8 cm. The wall is slightly inverted and has a rounded rim. The cup has a semicircular, horizontal loop handle and is glazed on the inside. Sherds of four cups of this type turned up, including one with a yellow-green interior and one coated with yellow slip. At Dordrecht a similar cup came to light in a cesspit, which was dated between 1580 and 1610, while another parallel was found in the excavations at the army camps outside Breda, which had been in use between 1624 and 1637.[27]

The presence of cups among the wasters at Oosterhout is no surprise. Cups were found also among the material from the Rulstraat site.[28] This in contrast to the great competitor, Bergen op Zoom, where no cups were produced.

Kilnware

For the purpose of stacking and supporting the pottery in the kiln, the potters made use of broken roof tiles and pieces of slate. Various supports of this kind, often spattered with drips of lead glaze, were found among the sherds. Besides the obvious wasters, this kilnware is a second proof that we are dealing with waste from a pottery.

Chamber pot

The top part of a simple, one-handled chamber pot also surfaced among the wasters (cat. no. 18). Its greatest diameter, 18.5 cm, lies at the carinated transition from belly to neck. The rim is flat and protrudes outward almost horizontally, allowing the user to sit on it. The vertically placed loop handle protrudes slightly above the rim. The pot was glazed on the inside. The poor condition of the sherd leaves it unclear whether the outside was glazed as well. Besides this specimen, fragments of four more chamber pots were identified by their rims. Chamber pots of this type occur in the late 16th and the entire 17th century.[29]

Skillet

One near-complete skillet or frying pan could be reconstructed from a number of sherds (cat. no. 1) The handle consists of a slab of clay of which the long sides had been folded together. A pouring lip had been present at 90° to the left of the handle; in other words, the pan was intended for a right-handed user. The rim was faceted. The inside is fully glazed. Whether the pan had feet is uncertain. The skillet dates from the second half of the 16th or first quarter of the 17th century.[30]

Fragments

Pot with a suspension handle

A decorated handle belongs to a "pot with a suspension handle" (cat. no. 10). These are small, globular pots with a semicircular handle across the top. Some of them have holes in the bottom. These were used for transporting live coals[31] and are known as "lollepotten". The handle fragment from Oosterhout is fully glazed and decorated with a ridge of pinched clay. Pots with suspension handles with this pinched decoration belong in the 16th and early 17th centuries.[32] With straight handles they even continue into the 18th century.[33]

Jug (handle)

A handle of a jug (cat. no. 11) with presumably the same appearance as the jug described above (cat. no. 11), has three thumb impressions on its lower attachment. The fragment is glazed both inside and out. This handle attachment differs clearly from that of the jug handle described above and is indicative of the range of variation within a potting tradition. A date is hard to give, as too little of the jug has survived.

Brazier

A fragment of a small, unglazed and perforated globular vessel (cat. no. 13) presumably is part of a brazier with an estimated rim diameter of ca 16 cm. The rim is everted and at the very edge is inturned. The holes, pushed into the clay from the outside, have a diameter of about 3 mm. Owing to its fragmentary state, the brazier cannot be dated.

Pot

A fragment of the upper half of a pot or tripod cauldron has a rim profile that differs from that of the other cauldrons (cat. no. 22). For this reason the fragment is presented here. The globular pot has two horizontal loop handles, rilling on the inside and an everted, somewhat thickened rim that has a groove on the outside. The pot is glazed both inside and out. It is unclear as to what kind of pot the rim belonged to. For this reason it is also poorly datable.

Pot

The rim of a large pot (estimated rim diameter 25 cm) with presumably two vertical loop handles is provided with a decorative band consisting of thumb impressions (cat. no. 21). The sherd is decorated both on the inside and the outside. Such thumb-impressed decoration is quite often found on cauldrons and pots.[34] The sherd shows that vessels decorated in this way were manufactured also at Oosterhout. This prominent style of decoration is quite long-lived.
Excavations at Kessel uncovered a pot with a band of thumb impressions that was dated to the 16th century.[35] From Oosterhout comes an 18th-century creamer with similar ornamentation.[36]

Dripping pan

A short end of a dripping pan with a pouring lip indicates that the potters of Oosterhout also produced these massive items (cat. no. 20). A near-complete specimen, which closely resembles the present one but is complete with a handle, three feet and a suspension hole, was found at Dordrecht and dates from the second half of the 16th century.[37] Fragments of this dripping pan were recovered from features 16 and 17.

Incidental finds

From the two pits beside the pavement that were dug over and merged (features 16 and 17) come a few small sherds that should not be reckoned among the pottery waste. The most prominent find is a large part of the neck and the rim of a stoneware jug (fig.*), thickly covered with a dark brown glaze. Maybe this is the neck of a jug of type S2-kan-45, dating from the late 16th or the first quarter of the 17th century.[38] Further there are two body fragments of green glass bottles of the 17th or 18th century, a small rim fragment of a majolica plate of the 17th century or the first half of the 18th, a small rim fragment of a faience plate of the 17th or 18th century, and the neck of a stoneware 19th-century mineral-water bottle.

Dating

Part of the objects, particularly the complete or near-complete forms, can be dated by their appearance to the final quarter of the 16th, or the first four decades of the 17th century. These are the platters, the cauldrons, the skillet, the pot with suspension handle, the cups, the dripping pan and the incidental find, the jug of type s2-kan-45. These items come from features 5, 16 and 17. The chamber pot and the cresset lamp (from features 16 and 17) are datable to a broader period (1575-1700), but may well date from before 1640.
Even looser datings (1600-1800) are assigned to the colander, the milk tub, the extinguisher and some small incidental finds: the sherd of faience, the fragment of a majolica plate, and the two sherds of green glass bottles. These were all found in features 16 and 17. The mineral-water bottle fragment dates from after 1800 and must have become buried during the construction of the well, feature 19.
The closely datable finds all belong in the 1580-1640 period. The more broadly dated items may date from the same period but could also be younger. Some items definitely are not pre-1600 (the extinguisher, the dripping pan and possibly the milk tub). For this reason it can be concluded that the pottery waste from the Leijsenhoek should be dated in the first four decades of the 17th century.

Oosterhout characteristics

The wasters from the Leijsenhoek display several features that seem to be typical of this assemblage. Because of the strong connections that the potters had among themselves, and the exchange of apprentices, these features may well be characteristic of Oosterhout pottery of the 1600-1640 period.
Typical of Oosterhout is the fabric as seen in the second category of finds, those that were not overfired: an orange to reddish fabric with a temper of white grains smaller than 1 mm, and fairly hard – scratching with a fingernail will leave no trace.
Furthermore, fancy-shaped, massive rims like that on the milk tub (cat. no. 9) appear to be typical of Oosterhout. Such rims

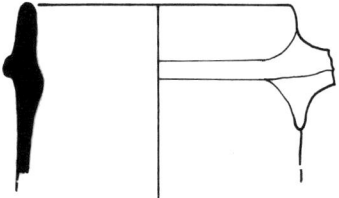

04 Fragment of a stoneware jug.

were also found among the wasters from the Rulstraat site, and are unknown from waster assemblages outside Oosterhout. Also typical of Oosterhout are the slip-trailed circles on the centre of the platter cat. no. 3. Such circles appear also on other wasters from Oosterhout, and some platters with this motif were recovered from the sites of the siege encampments outside Breda. Breda was part of Oosterhout's marketing area.[39] Apart from the circle motif, the thin, casually made slip trail is typical. Probably the same goes for the wavy-line decoration on the flange of the plates, which consists of three or four consecutive trails. Finally, the "collar rim" of the tripod cauldron (cat. no. 7) is quite eye-catching and probably also an Oosterhout feature. Presumably this rim was used not only on tall cauldrons but also on low cauldrons and other pots.

Two phenomena in this assemblage may be used to distinguish products from Oosterhout from those of Bergen op Zoom, the two major pottery centres of Brabant. These are the manufacture of cups and the application of slip-trailed decoration, both of which did occur at Oosterhout but not at Bergen op Zoom. Cups were thrown and slip-trailed designs were applied also at other pottery centres in the Low Countries, so these are not exclusively Oosterhout phenomena.

Besides, forms and details were encountered among the wasters that do not differ from what was customary in the Low Countries. Good examples of these are the cresset lamp (cat. no. 15), the chamber pot (cat. no. 14) and the dripping pan (cat. no. 22). These are such common forms and occur at so many sites that it is most unlikely that they were manufactured at a single production centre. They were probably made throughout the Low Countries. This shows that the Oosterhout potters followed the trends of the times and did not give every product a typically Oosterhout appearance. Finally there are a few details of which it is unclear whether they are typical of Oosterhout or not. These include the slightly inturned rims of the cups (cat. no. 13). In most other assemblages these cups are absent, except in assemblages containing other Oosterhout pottery, such as the siege camps near Breda. The handle of the jug cat. no. 12 has been recognised among other Oosterhout waster assemblages as well. Does this mean it is typical of Oosterhout? Closer investigation of assemblages outside Oosterhout will have to show whether these cups and handles are indeed indicative of an Oosterhout origin.

Conclusion

The pottery waste from the Leijsenhoek site at Oosterhout dates from the period 1600-1640. From the hundreds of sherds, eleven complete forms (four platters, three tripod cauldrons, an extinguisher, a milk tub, a colander and a cresset lamp), five incomplete forms (a platter, a cup, a jug, a chamber pot and a skillet) and six characteristic fragments (of a pot with suspension handle, a jug, a brazier, a chamber pot, a pot and a dripping pan) could be put together.

A hard, orange-red fabric with fine temper characterises the pottery from Oosterhout. Other typical features are the massive, fancy-shaped rim of the milk tub, the "collar rim" of some cauldrons, and the thin, slip-trailed circles and wavy lines on some of the platters. The "collar rim" and the slip-trailed circles may be restricted to the 1580-1650 period. The other features also ocur on 18th-century wasters from Oosterhout. Possibly characteristic of Oosterhout for these decades are the cups with slightly inverted walls, and the base of a jug handle pressed flat against the body. But further research is required on these points. The application of slip-trailed decoration and the manufacture of cups, in any form, distinguish the output of Oosterhout from that of Bergen op Zoom.

The material from the Leijsenhoek offers new insights into the the products of Oosterhout's potters in the first half of the 17th century. This is not to say that all characteristics of Oosterhout's potteries are now known, on the contrary. Much more research will be needed before a clear picture of the 17th-century pottery industry at Oosterhout emerges. It is hoped that the results of the excavation at the Leijsenhoek wil contribute to a greater insight into the distribution of Oosterhout ware, and hence also to an increased understanding of this pottery centre, the archaeology of which has so far remained somewhat underexposed.

Catalogue

Introduction

The pottery was studied and described in accordance with the 'Deventer system' (see Clevis & Kottman 1989, p. 77; Bartels 1999, pp 519 and 526). The numbers in the Deventer-system descriptions stand for the following features:

1. find number / catalogue number
2. type code. This is a code assigned to the object according to the Deventer classification. It allows the object to be compared in a convenient way with finds from other assemblages.
3. date. This refers to the period in which the object was produced.
4. maximum diameter (excluding handles, spouts, etc.), maximum height and maximum diameter of the foot in cm.

5a. fabric
5b. glaze
5c. decoration
6a. base
6b. handle(s)
6c. other
7. function or name
8. production centre
9. literature

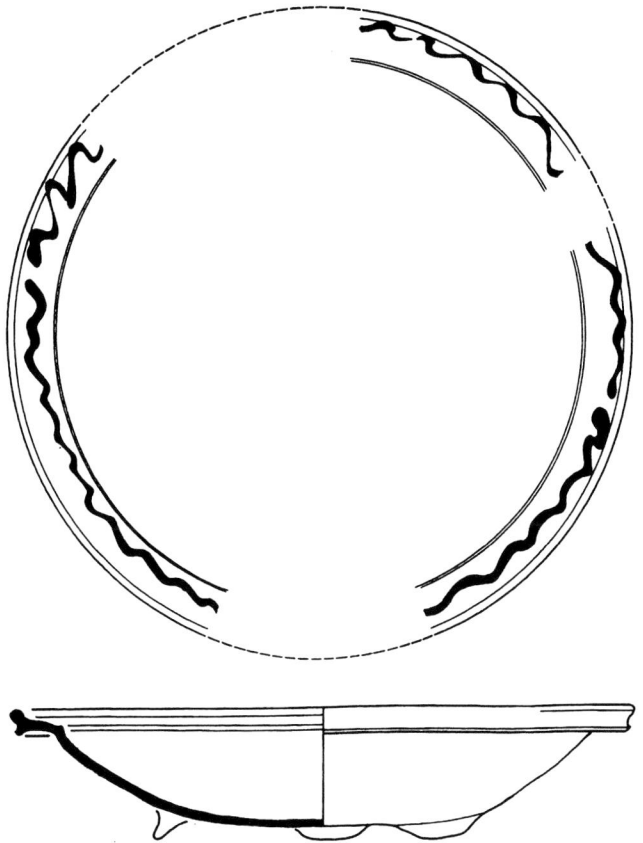

2.
1. OH-LV-2; 2. r-bor-6; 3. 1580-1650; 4. 49.2/10.0/-;
5a. red ware; 5b. lead glaze on upper surface; 5c. series of wavy lines in white slip on the flange; 6a. three lug feet; 6b. -; 6c. -; 7. platter; 8. Oosterhout; 9. -.

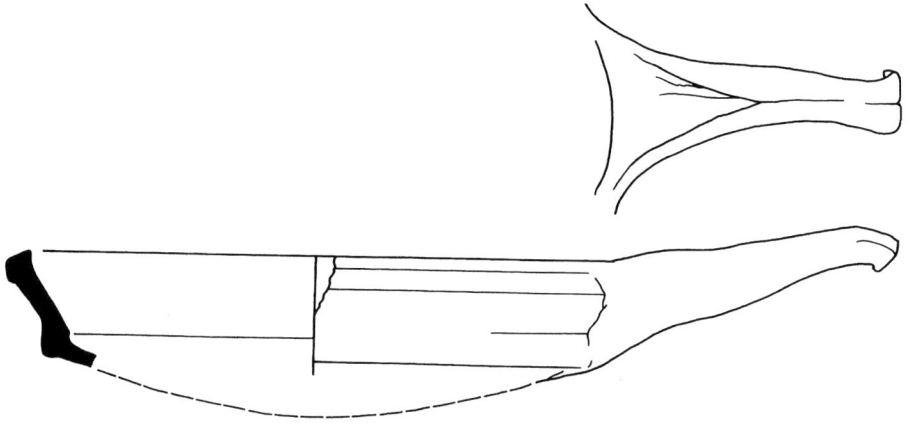

1.
1. OH-LV-1; 2. r-bak-23; 3. 1580-1650; 4. 24.0/-/-; 5a. red ware; 5b. lead glaze on the interior; 5c. attachment of a pouring lip at 90°; 6a. base is missing; 6b. long handle; 6c. -; 7. skillet, frying pan; 8. Oosterhout; 9. -.

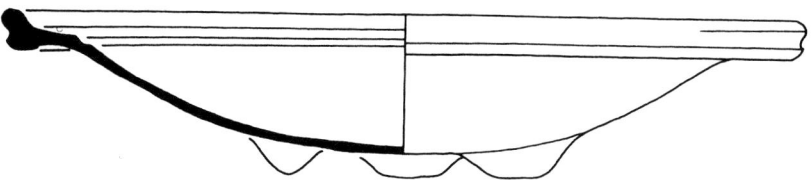

3.
1. OH-LV-3; 2. r-bor-31; 3. 1580-1650; 4. 44.5/8.6/-; 5a. red ware; 5b. lead glaze on the upper surface; 5c. -; 6a. three lug feet; 6b. -; 6c. -; 7. platter; 8. Oosterhout; 9. -.

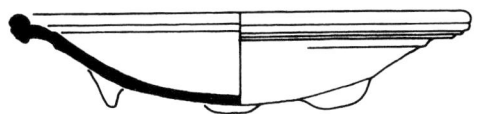

5.
1. OH-LV-5; 2. r-bor-61; 3. 1580-1650; 4. 25.0/5.2/-; 5a. red ware; 5b. lead glaze on the upper surface; 5c. -; 6a. three lug feet; 6b. -; 6c. -; 7. platter; 8. Oosterhout; 9. -.

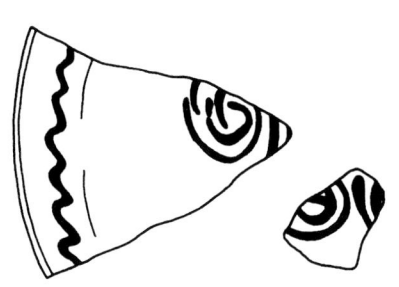

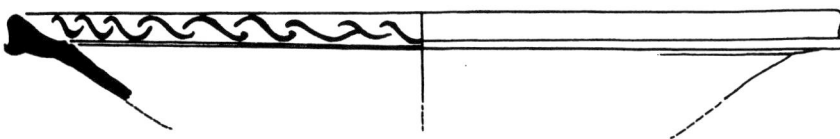

4.
1. OH-LV-4; 2. r-bor-60; 3. 1580-1650; 4. 37.2/-/-; 5a. red ware; 5b. lead glaze on the upper surface; 5c. wavy line on the flange, circles on the centre, all in white slip; 6a. three lug feet; 6b. -; 6c. -; 7. platter; 8. Oosterhout; 9. -.

6.
1. OH-LV-6; 2. r-bor-; 3. 1580-1650; 4. 45/-/-; 5a. red ware; 5b. lead glaze on the upper surface; 5c. dashes of white slip on the flange; 6a. -; 6b. -; 6c. -; 7. platter; 8. Oosterhout; 9. -.

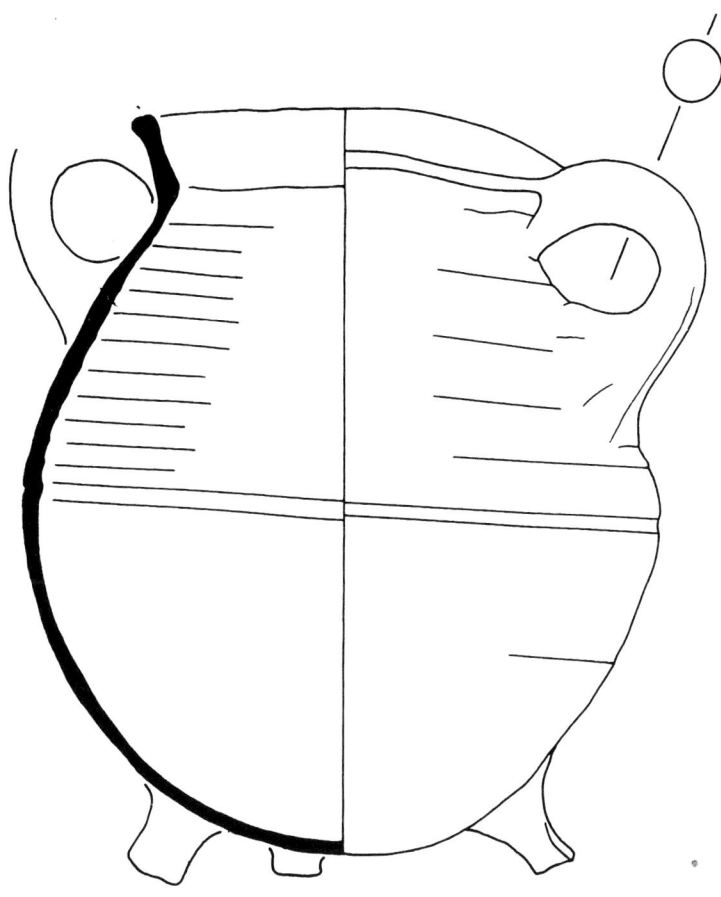

7.
1. OH-LV-7; 2. r-gra-114; 3. 1580-1650; 4. 29.2/24.6/-;
5a. red ware; 5b. olive green lead glaze on the interior and exterior; 5c. -; 6a. three feet; 6b. two vertical loop handles; 6c. -; 7. tripod cauldron; 8. Oosterhout; 9. -.

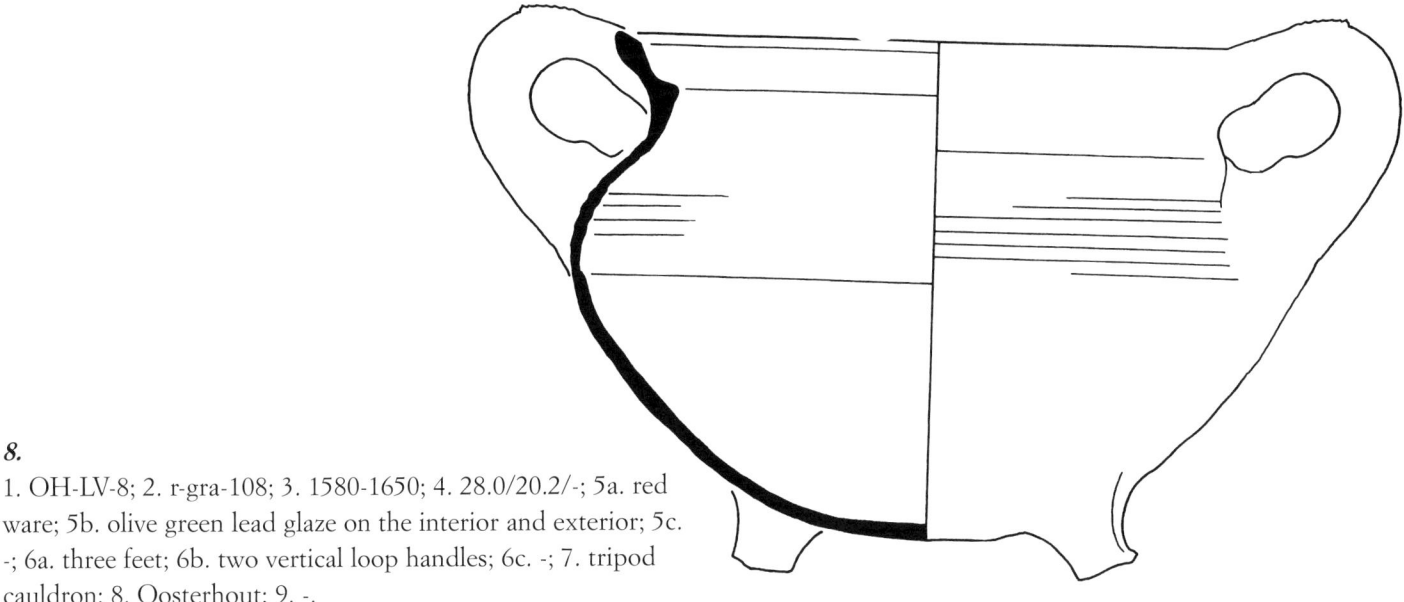

8.
1. OH-LV-8; 2. r-gra-108; 3. 1580-1650; 4. 28.0/20.2/-; 5a. red ware; 5b. olive green lead glaze on the interior and exterior; 5c. -; 6a. three feet; 6b. two vertical loop handles; 6c. -; 7. tripod cauldron; 8. Oosterhout; 9. -.

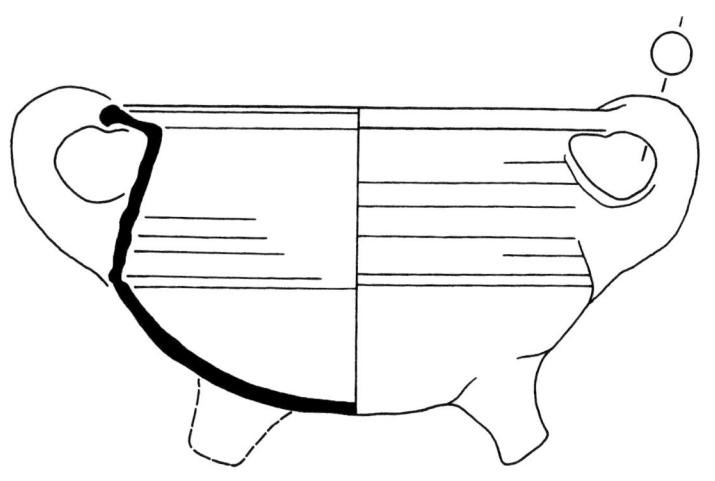
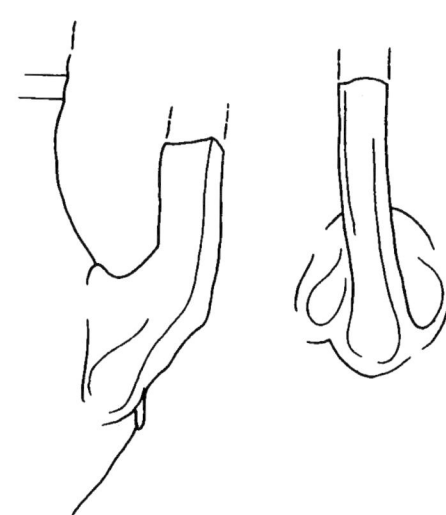

9.
1. OH-LV-9; 2. r-gra-133; 3. 1580-1650; 4. 20.2/11.5/-; 5a. red ware; 5b. olive green lead glaze on the interior (overfired) and half of the exterior; 5c. -; 6a. three feet; 6b. two vertical loop handles; 6c. -; 7. tripod cauldron; 8. Oosterhout; 9. -.

11.
1. OH-LV-11; 2. r-kan-; 3. 1600-1750; 4. -/-/-; 5a. red ware; 5b. lead glaze on the interior and exterior; 5c. thumb impressions on the handle attachment; 6a. -; 6b. vertical loop handle; 6c. -; 7. jug; 8. Oosterhout; 9. -.

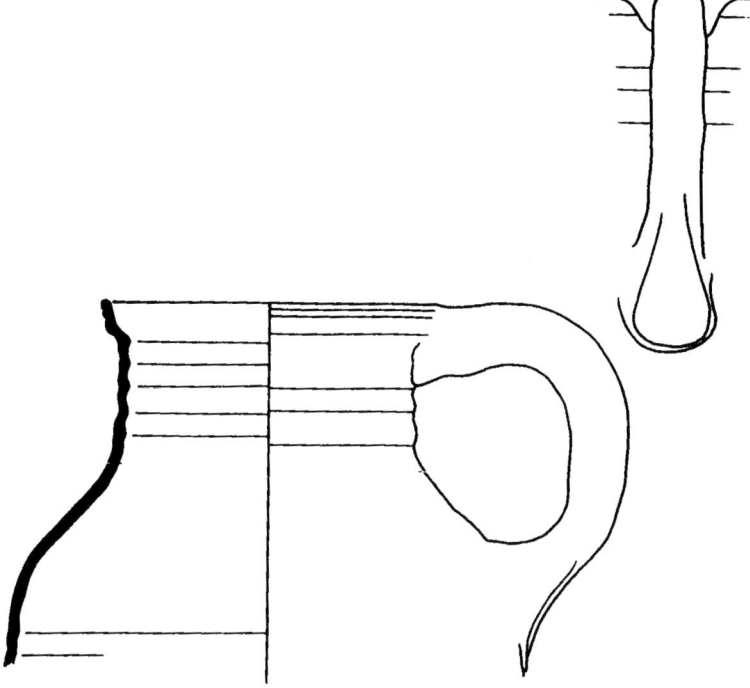

10.
1. OH-LV-10; 2. r-; 3. 1580-1650; 4. -/-/-; 5a. red ware; 5b. fully lead-glazed; 5c. pinched decoration; 6a. -; 6b. handle; 6c. -; 7. suspension handle of a pot for live coals; 8. Oosterhout; 9. -.

12.
1. OH-LV-12; 2. r-kan-33; 3. 1580-1650; 4. 19.8/-/-; 5a. red ware; 5b. lead glaze on the interior and exterior; 5c. -; 6a. -; 6b. vertical loop handle; 6c. -; 7. jug; 8. Oosterhout; 9. -.

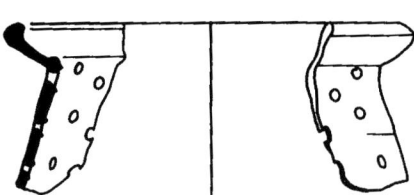

13.
1. OH-LV-13; 2. r-kmf-; 3. 1580-1650; 4. 16.0/-/-; 5a. red ware; 5b. unglazed; 5c. -; 6a. -; 6b. -; 6c. many perforations in the wall; 7. brazier; 8. Oosterhout; 9. -.

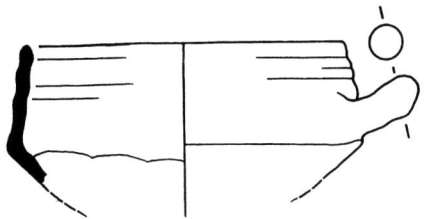

15.
1. OH-LV-15; 2. r-kop-14; 3. 1580-1650; 4. 13.8/-/-; 5a. red ware; 5b. lead glaze on the interior; 5c. -; 6a. -; 6b. one horizontal loop handle; 6c. -; 7. cup; 8. Oosterhout; 9. -.

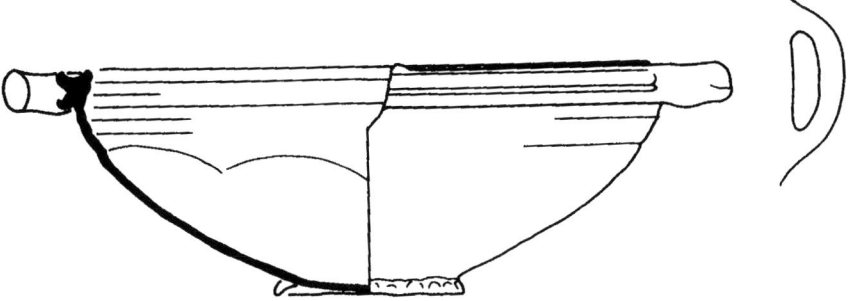

14.
1. OH-LV-14; 2. r-kom-42; 3. 1580-1650; 4. ca 48 (oval)/17.2/14.4; 5a. red ware; 5b. lead glaze on the interior; 5c. pouring lip (almost entirely missing); 6a. footring; 6b. two horizontal loop handles; 6c. pared down internally; 7. milk tub; 8. Oosterhout; 9. -.

16.
1. OH-LV-16; 2. r-lek-1; 3. 1580-1650; 4. 37.5/7.5/-; 5a. red ware; 5b. olive green lead glaze on the upper surface; 5c. many holes 3-4 mm wide; 6a. three feet; 6b. two horizontal loop handles; 6c. -; 7. colander, strainer; 8. Oosterhout; 9. -.

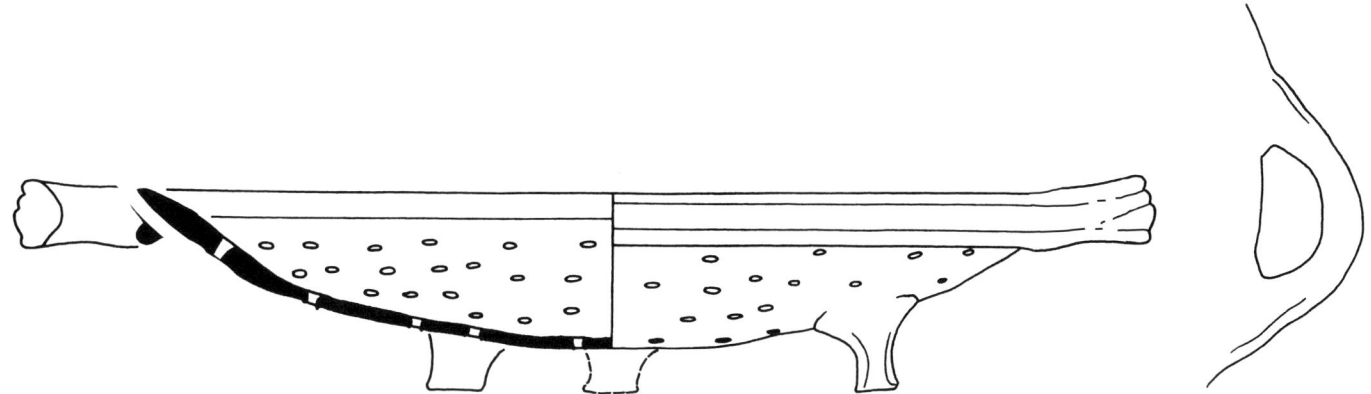

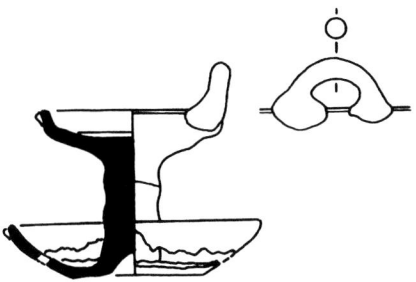

17.
1. OH-LV-17; 2. r-oli-2; 3. 1580-1650; 4. 9.8/9.8/-; 5a. red ware; 5b. olive green lead glaze on both bowls and part of the stem; 5c. -; 6a. -; 6b. one horizontally placed, upright loop handle; 6c. both bowls have a lip opposite the handle; 7. cresset lamp; 8. Oosterhout; 9. -.

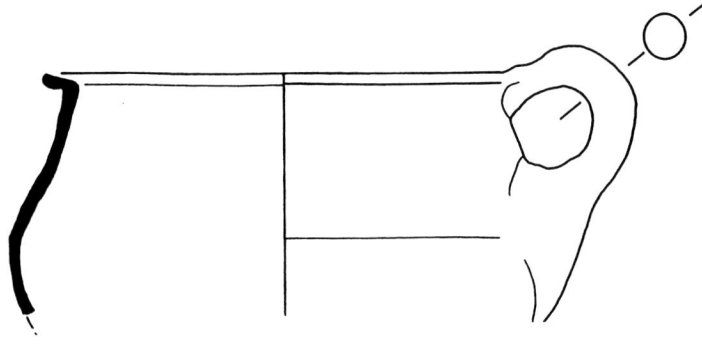

18.
1. OH-LV-18; 2. r-pis-5; 3. 1580-1650; 4. 18.5/-/-; 5a. red ware; 5b. lead glaze on the interior; 5c. -; 6a. -; 6b. vertical loop handle; 6c. -; 7. chamber pot; 8. Oosterhout; 9. -.

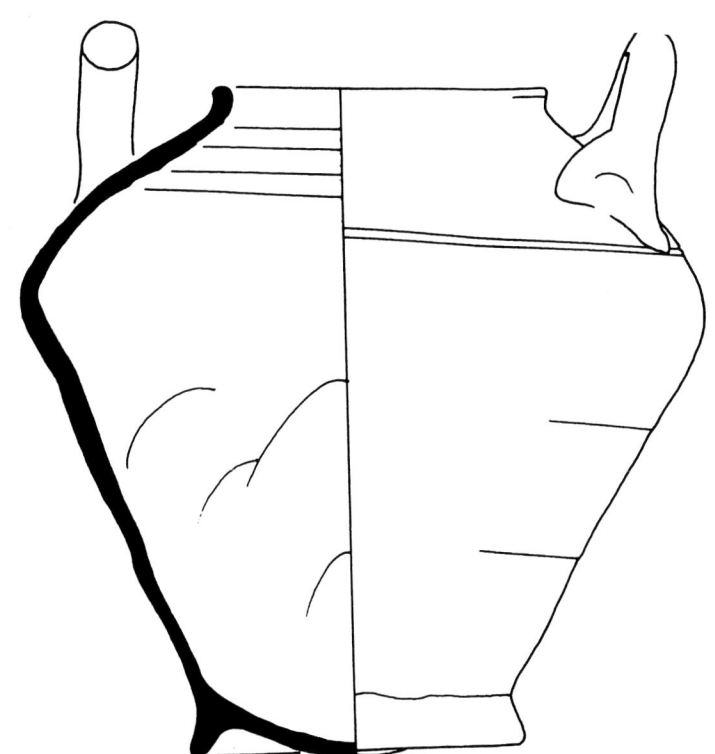

19.
1. OH-LV-19; 2. r-pot-3; 3. 1580-1650; 4. 25.0/26.5/13.1; 5a. red ware; 5b. greeny-grey lead glaze on the exterior; 5c. -; 6a. footring; 6b. two horizontally placed, upright loop handles; 6c. internally pared down; wobbly; 7. extinguisher; 8. Oosterhout; 9. -.

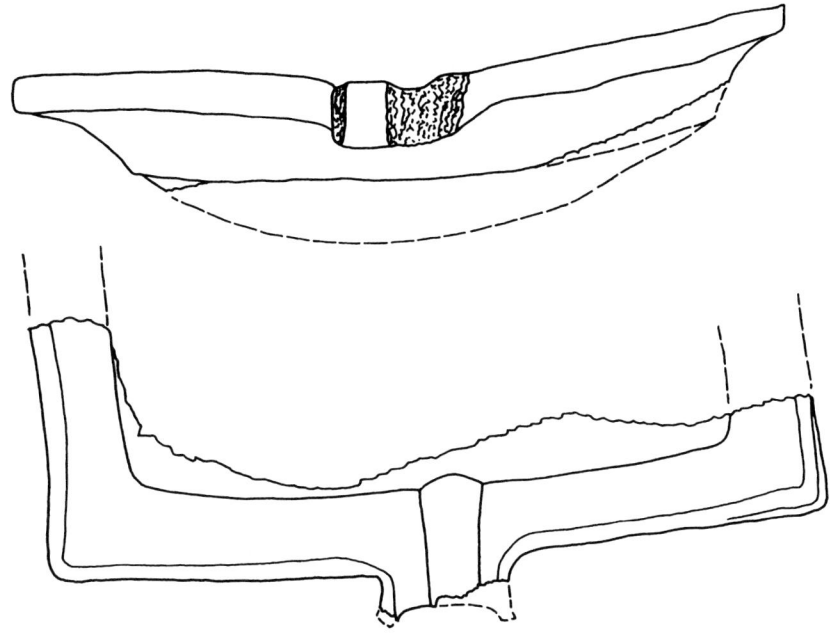

20.
1. OH-LV-20; 2. r-vet-3; 3. 1580-1650; 4. -/-/-; 5a. red ware; 5b. greeny-grey lead glaze on the upper surface; 5c. -; 6a. -; 6b. massive pouring lip; 6c. -; 7. dripping pan; 8. Oosterhout; 9. -.

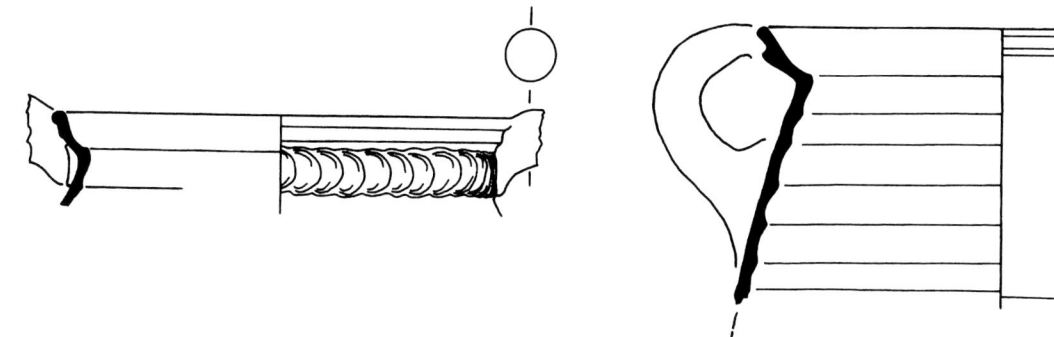

21.
1. OH-LV-21; 2. r- 3. 1580-1650; 4. -/-/-; 5a. red ware; 5b. lead glaze on interior and exterior; 5c. a band of thumb impressions below the rim; 6a. -; 6b. two vertical loop handles; 6c. -; 7. pot or tripod cauldron; 8. Oosterhout; 9. -.

22.
1. OH-LV-22; 2. r-; 3. 1580-1650; 4. 21.0/-/-; 5a. red ware; 5b. lead glaze on the interior and exterior; 5c. -; 6a. -; 6b. two vertical loop handles; 6c. -; 7. pot or tripod cauldron; 8. Oosterhout; 9. -

Notes

1. Kleij 1996, 102.
2. Kleij 1996, 103.
3. Kleij 1996, 101-128.
4. See note 3.
5. Probably the same clay deposit was used by the potters of nearby Bergen op Zoom. Bergen op Zoom also exported this clay to potters in Zeeland and Rotterdam: see Groeneweg 1992, 120-121.
6. A usually timber-built storage shed for cereals, vegetables, fruit or hay.
7. In the process of oxidation firing, the potter allows fresh air into the kiln, which after a while gives the pottery a red colour. In reduction firing, no oxygen-rich air is allowed into the kiln and the pottery wil turn out grey.
8. On a platter three parts can be distinguished: the central area, the flange, which is usually known as the rim, and the edge of the flange, the actual rim.
9. Groeneweg 1992, 62, figs 315-343.
10. Clevis & Sarfatij 1982, 23-34, figs 8 and 11-16.
11. Kleij 1996, 116, figs 4 and 6; 122, fig. 25; 123, fig. 28; and 124, fig. 32.
12. Groeneweg 1992, 72.
13. This plate is the one in the photo and is encrusted with ash and soot. In the catalogue drawing this contamination has been ignored.
14. Hoegen & De Kievith 2004, 454, fig. 2.
15. Carmiggelt & Van Veen 1995, 54-55, figs 22 and 23.
16. De Kievith 1990, 20, fig. F.
17. Groeneweg 1992, 148-149, fig. 87.
18. Groeneweg 1992, 66, fig. 414[KLOPT DIT WEL? cf NOOT 17!].
19. Bartels 1999, 666, fig. 495.
20. Groeneweg 1992, fig. 411.
21. Bult 1992, IHE B11-53 and IHE B1-1.
22. Groeneweg 1992, 180-183.
23. Kleij 1996, 119, fig. 15.
24. Bartels 1999, 702, fig. 624; Kleij 1996, 120, figs 20 and 21.
25. Groeneweg 1992, 184.
26. Kleij 1996, 118, fig. 13.
27. Bartels 1999, 695, fig. 605; Hoegen & De Kievith 2004, 454, fig. 4.
28. Kleij 1996, 120, figs 18 and 19.
29. Clevis & Kottman 1989, 107, figs 11-89; Bitter 1995, 132, figs 49 and 50.
30. Bitter 1995, 121, figs 6 and 7.
31. Groeneweg 1992, 179, fig. 119.
32. Groeneweg 1992, 65, figs 397-401; and 84, fig. 502.
33. Groeneweg 1992, 179, fig. 119.
34. Kleij 1996, 122, fig. 24; Clevis & Kottman 1989, 92, figs 10-51.
35. Clevis & Thijssen 1989, 42-43, fig. 255.
36. Kleij 1996, 122, fig. 24.
37. Bartels 1999, 731, fig. 716.
38. Bartels 1999, 568, fig. 154.
39. Groeneweg 1996, 91, fig. 4.

References

Bartels, M., (e.a.), 1999: *Steden in scherven 1 en 2. Vondsten uit beerputten in Deventer, Dordrecht, Nijmegen en Tiel (1250 – 1900)*. Zwolle/Amersfoort.

Bitter, P., 1995: *Geworteld in de bodem. Archeologisch en historisch onderzoek van een pottenbakkerij bij de Wortelsteeg in Alkmaar*, Zwolle.

Bult, E.J., 1992: *IHE/Delft bloeit op een beerput. Archeologisch onderzoek tussen Oude Delft en Westvest*, Delft.

Carmiggelt, A., en M.M.A. van Veen, 1995: 'Laat- en postmiddeleeuws afval afkomstig uit zes vondstcomplexen te Den Haag' in: *Haagse Oudheidkundige Publicatiesnummer 2*, Den Haag.

Clevis, H en H. Sarfatij, 1982: 'Borden uit een Dordste beerput' in *Rotterdam Papers 4*, Rotterdam, 23-34.

Clevis, H. en J. Kottman, 1989: *Weggegooid en teruggevonden: aardewerk en glas uit Deventer vondstcomplexen 1375-1750*, Kampen

Clevis, H., en J. Thijssen, 1989: 'Kessel, huisvuil uit een kasteel' in: *Mededelingenblad Nederlandse Vereniging van Vrienden van de Ceramiek*, 1989.

Groeneweg, G., 1992: *Bergen op Zooms aardewerk. Vormgeving en decoratie van gebruiksaardewerk gedurende 600 jaar pottenbakkersnijverheid in Bergen op Zoom*, Waalre.

Hoegen, R.D. en H. de Kievith, 2004: 'De sporen van het beleg van Breda in 1625 en 1637' in: C.W. Koot en R. Berkvens, *Bedase akkers eeuwenoud. 4000 jaar bewoningsgeschiedenis op de rand van zand en klei*, Breda.

Kleij, P., 1996: 'Oosterhouts aardewerk' in: H. Clevis, *Assembled Articles 2*, Zwolle, 101-128.

Kievith, H. de, 1990: 'Achter 'Het Wapen van Schotland' in: Keulenaars, A. en H. Muntjewerff, *Amateursverslag Bodemonderzoek Archeologische Vereniging Breda 1990*, Breda, 5-55.

Fields, farmsteads and sherds

The spatial phasing of the medieval cultivation of the Looërenk near Zutphen

Michel Groothedde

Introduction

The VINEX housing development site Leesten Oost (Looërenk) situated to the southeast of Zutphen (province of Gelderland) was archaeologically investigated between 2000 and 2004, the excavation covering virtually the entire area. Not only were Mesolithic sites and dozens of Bronze and Iron Age farmsteads discovered, but a clear picture was also obtained of the medieval cultivation of the *enk* (former open field with *plaggen* soil). Oak woodland, which had regenerated since Roman times, had been felled within a short period of time during the Carolingian period for charcoal production to serve the iron-smelting industry, which was followed by cultivation of the area.

As described below, an effort was made to plot the medieval pottery finds of different kinds, collected during the opening up of 304 trenches, in an attempt to distinguish phases in the cultivation of the Looërenk during the Middle Ages. It is only rarely that this generally overlooked evidence from the topsoil finds bags is analyzed in this way in an investigation. A somewhat comparable attempt to get to grips with late medieval and more recent cultivation areas was carried out during the ROB investigation at Raalte-Jonge Raan.[1] There a random-sample survey was carried out on a large scale when the topsoil was sifted. At the Looërenk site, evidence was not collected in this experimental and expensive way. During the AAO (test trench campaign) in 2000-2001, too few datable finds were recovered from the documented sections to arrive at a precise dating of the layers of the *plaggen* soil.[2] The collected stray finds, however, did produce a fine spatial picture.

Methodology and material

The developmental phases of the Looërenk site in the Middle Ages can be analyzed on the basis of the distribution of the datable ceramic finds from the soil features and the cultivation layers. Most sherds were recovered from the topsoil before the opening up of the trenches, *i.e.* at a somewhat higher level than the actual trenches, which generally produced prehistoric finds and marks. The collecting consistently took place when the shovel bucket of a mechanical shovel uncovered sherds when scraping the soil while opening up a trench. Scraping the layers by hand-held shovel produced more 'rabotage finds'. In some cases, for instance in test trenches, the finds were collected in stratification. By plotting the medieval sherds per trench, a good picture of the distribution of the finds arises. The 303 trenches, averaging 300m² in size, scattered over an area of about 16 hectares, were evenly distributed across the *enk*. It should be mentioned that in the northern part of the area about 2 hectares were disturbed in the second half of the 19th century. However, the test trenches and pits opened up in this part still provided a useful picture for the disturbed area as a whole.

If only the well-dated ceramics are considered, this spatial picture can even be analysed through time. The total number of sherds involved in this investigation is 1034. A selection of four clear-cut periods in terms of ceramics was made: the 9th and early 10th centuries with Badorf ware as its 'index fossil' (n=4), the later 10th, 11th and 12th centuries with Pingsdorf, Paffrath and *Kugeltopf* ceramics (n=211), the 13th and early 14th centuries with proto-stoneware and near-stoneware, predominantly from Siegburg (n=104), and the 14th and 15th centuries with especially Siegburg and Langerwehe stoneware. This last phase is supported by grey ware also known from Zutphen, especially from the 14th and 15th centuries, which disappeared after the first quarter of the 16th century (n=715). In the 13th-century phase, the *Kugeltopf* and the grey ware were deliberately left unconsidered because, although both products occur in that century, they cannot be distinguished from those of the earlier and the later phases. Sometimes the spatial distribution shows that these local products must be attributed to the 13th century.

The spatial distribution of potsherds shows two phenomena reflecting the history of cultivation and utilization of the area: 1. the presence of fields on the *enk* that were fertilized with domestic waste and manure; 2. the farmsteads themselves. The latter are identifiable by soil marks of buildings and related features such as waste pits, ditches, wells and fence posts. Three sites were identified showing soil marks of complete or partial structures: farmstead 't Loo on the site of the farm demolished in 2001, farmstead Berghege at the site of the farm demolished in 1971 and a site on the southeast edge of the *enk*, just north of 't Hummel. Farmstead 't Hummel remained outside the scope of the archaeological investigation because it was to be retained and incorporated into the new housing estate.
Another site is situated northeast of the *enk*, in a low-lying area; for the sake of convenience we shall call it Rouwbroek, after a farm situated more easterly, which without doubt derives its name from the low-lying area east of the Looërenk. In the course of a surface field survey and the subsequent excavation, this area produced a striking number of medieval sherds. Moreover, the

02 Location of the Looërenk on the military map of 1887.

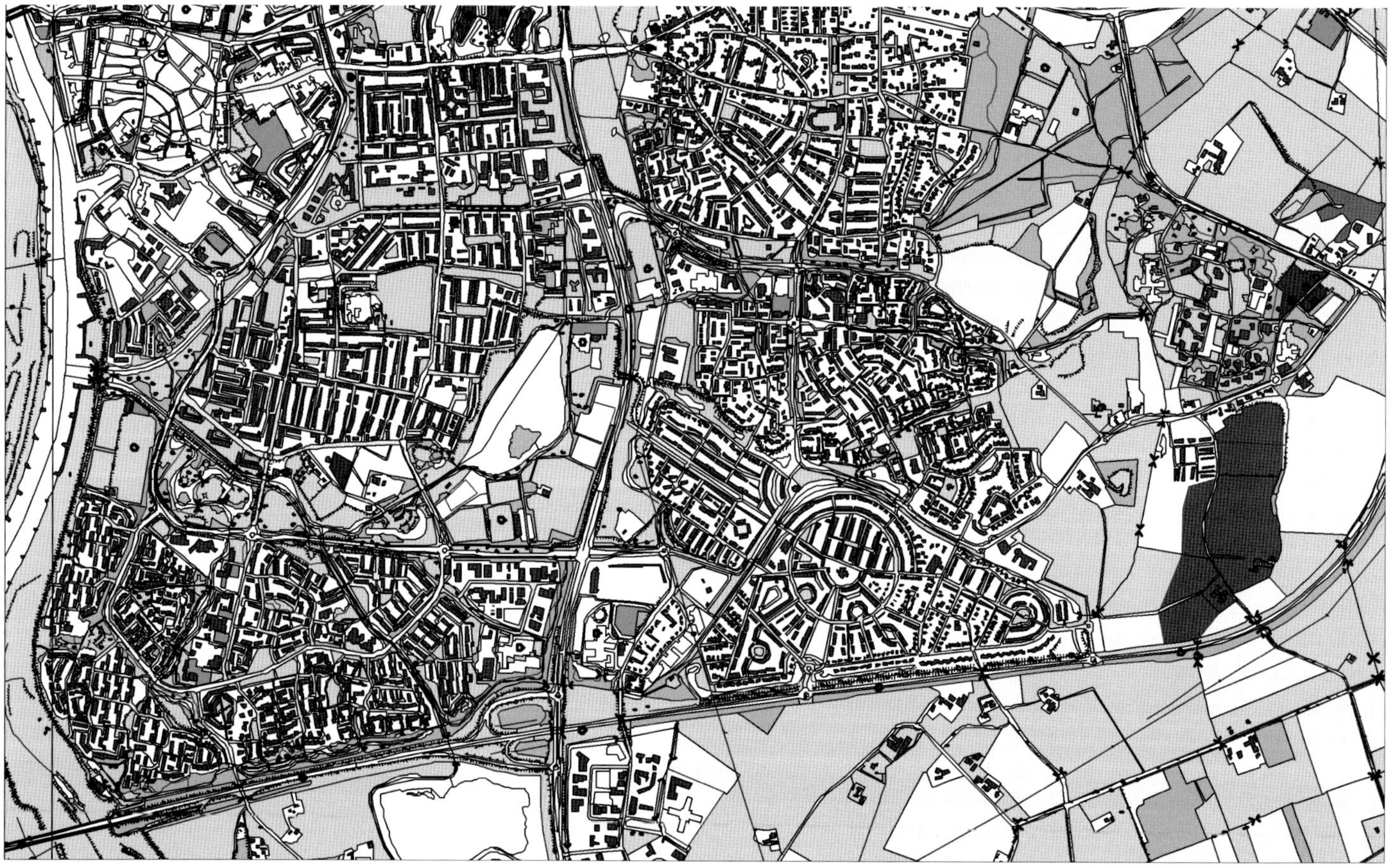

01 The investigated area of the Looërenk marked in dark grey.

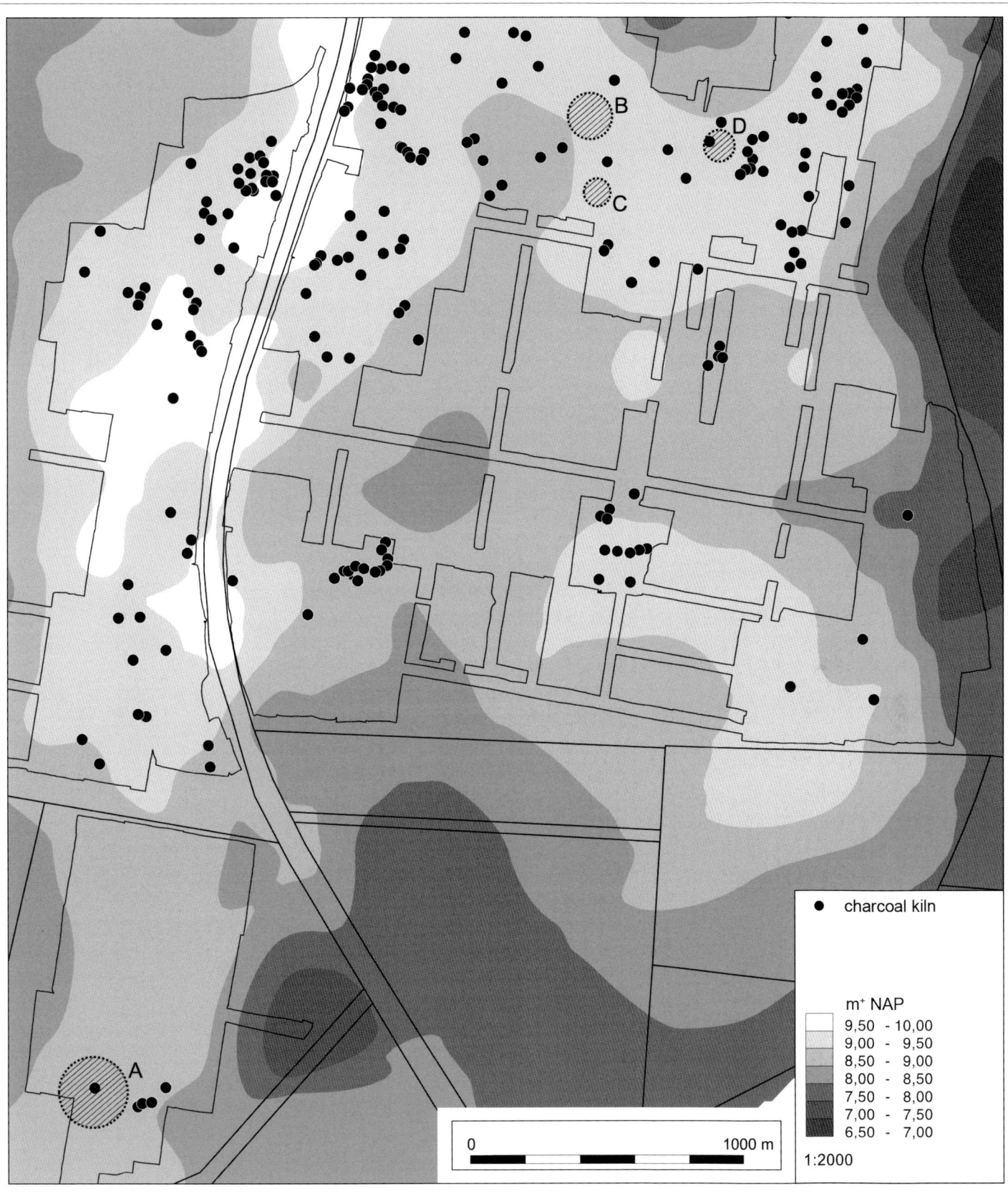

03 Distribution map of charcoal kilns on the southern part of the Looërenk. An estimated 350 charcoal kilns once burned here. (from Groenewoudt 2006, drawn by M. Kosian, RACM)

site rises slightly above the surrounding Rouwbroek area. Soil marks of a farmstead were completely lacking. Only a regular system of ditches, almost completely covering the area, oriented north-south and east-west, was uncovered. The meaning of these ditches is not clear. Are they late medieval? Or should they be attributed to a more recent period? Considering the number of recovered sherds, the possibility that this is the disturbed site of a dwelling cannot be ruled out.
During the Middle Ages the other parts of the Looërenk were used as fields.

The first phase (9th-10th century)

The earliest finds from the Middle Ages on the Looërenk date back to the Carolingian period. They comprise three Badorf sherds, one from the fill of a depression (late Badorf or early Pingsdorf pottery of the late 9th or early 10th century), one from the northern part of the *enk* (trench 252, standard pale yellow, chalky pottery) and one from a 15th-century ditch fill at farmstead 't Loo (pale yellow, chalky pottery, wall sherd with spout attachment). A fourth fragment, from Berghege, is too disputable to be used. The sherds found scattered across this area may well have been connected to the charcoal burning there in the 9th century when the area was still largely wooded with oak trees. These few sherds contrast sharply with the numerous finds on the *enk* from the 10th/11th century onwards, so that we cannot deduce human habitation from this evidence. Apart from the Carolingian charcoal kilns, a long, narrow ditch west of Berghege also provided a 9th-century dating (fig. 5).[3] The ditch was filled with large quantities of charcoal fragments (but not a single Carolingian sherd), which suggests that this ditch too must be linked to the production of charcoal. Possibly the ditch constituted a demarcation between the exploited forest (Looërenk) to the northeast and the settlement area of Leesten west of the ditch.

It is still a point of debate whether the cultivation of the area immediately followed the intensive charcoal production during the Carolingian era.[4] The oak wood, if not completely gone, would have been thinned out considerably after the charcoal-burners left. It is quite possible that from the nearby settlement, Leesten, the area was used for extensive cattle farming. It cannot be ruled out, however, that the area was under cultivation even from the 10th century on. After all, if the first fields were used by farmers from the Leesten settlement, which lies 750 to 1,500 metres southwest of the Looërenk, it is unlikely that domestic waste was deposited on these distant fields. Thus a possible first cultivation phase would probably elude our observation.

The first cultivated field area (10th-11th centuries)

The first period from which pottery was regularly found covers the late 10th and the 11th and 12th centuries. The 'index fossil' is Pingsdorf ware (fig. 6). Although Pingsdorf pottery already occurs in the late 9th and 10th centuries, this dating cannot be assigned to the first cultivation of the *enk*, as the early form of Pingsdorf ware can be distinguished very well from the later kind and this material has not turned up in the investigation.

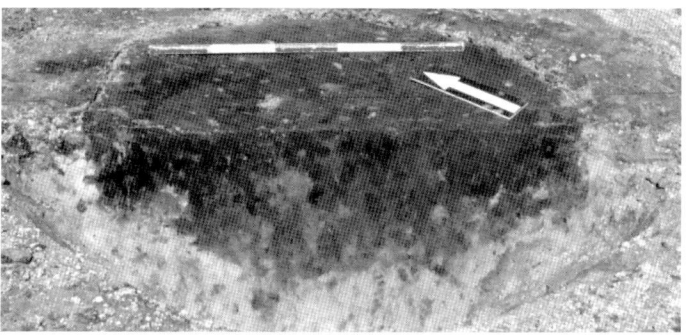

04 Three examples of sectioned charcoal pits. The pits had an average diameter of 1.20 metres and were originally 50 to 60 cms deep.

The first distinct concentration was found just west of farmstead 't Loo, on the narrow sand ridge connecting the plateau of the *enk* with the continuation of the ridge that accommodated the farmsteads Berghege and Meijerinck. The Pingsdorf and *Kugeltopf* pottery were mostly found in soil features, and to a lesser degree in the field's thin topsoil. The soil marks are too few in number to allow us to speak of a habitation. A ditch constitutes the only structural element in this part of the site. No soil features were found to the west, north or east. To the south, the area appears to have been dug over some decades ago for the purpose of levelling. The odds are that this was the site of an 11th- or 12th-century farmstead, peripheral evidence of which was found during the excavations. This hypothetical farm would have been situated between 't Loo and Berghege. This view is supported by a second concentration of finds of *Kugeltopf* and Pingsdorf sherds just west of Berghege (trenches 293, 296 and 297). These sherds are from the base of the upper layer of the cultivated field. Somewhat further southwest on the sand ridge, between Berghege and Meijerinck, some *Kugeltopf* sherds were collected from molehills as well. All in all, this evidence seems to indicate early habitation on the narrower part of the sand ridge of the Looërenk, taking into account that the supposed site of the earliest farm has probably disappeared as a result of levelling. The area to the southwest may have been used as an arable field. Whether the area north of Berghege had already been cultivated could not be said with certainty. The lack of Paffrath ware is conspicuous. In general, Paffrath pottery occurs in the 11th as well as in the 12th century, but in Zutphen the relative volume of Paffrath increases significantly during the 12th century, and subsequently decreases during the first half of the 13th century. The material from the areas west of 't Loo and Berghege appears mainly to be late 10th and 11th century. Subsequently the area seems to have been abandoned after the 11th (or 12th) century. It is only from the 15th century that any further material surfaces. This fact is no doubt related to the establishment of the farmsteads 't Loo (ca. 1460) and Berghege (between 1472 and 1494). Now a large part of the 15th-century sherds emerges from pits and ditches too, so that it remains unclear if the area was a cultivated field then. The lack of topsoil finds and the striking gap between 1200 and 1400 make a reasonable case for the finds and features originating from a nearby farmstead in the 11th/12th century and 't Loo and Berghege from the 15th century rather than from an earlier cultivated field. Apart from this, the sandy Pleistocene subsoil of the area is highly prone to drifting and hence probably less fertile than the firmer, loamy, wind-borne sand of the rest of the *enk*. Moreover, the higher part of the area is very small in size and on three sides plunges towards lower-lying, loamy and wetter soils.

Furthermore, the 1832 map of the cadastral register shows a noticeable difference in the pattern of land division between 't Loo and Berghege on the one hand, and the area north of these on the *enk*. The map shows a pattern of large plots around the farms, irregularly shaped with winding hedgerows, whereas the *enk* presents the regular east-west strip plots. The finds suggest that the hedgerows and field boundaries may date back to the earliest cultivation of the area. Groenewoudt even assumes that the pattern of land division and hedgerows are relics of an ancient forest fringe and a clearing in that woodland, which remained after the last prehistoric habitation

05 Part of the long Carolingian-period ditch west of the Berghege site.

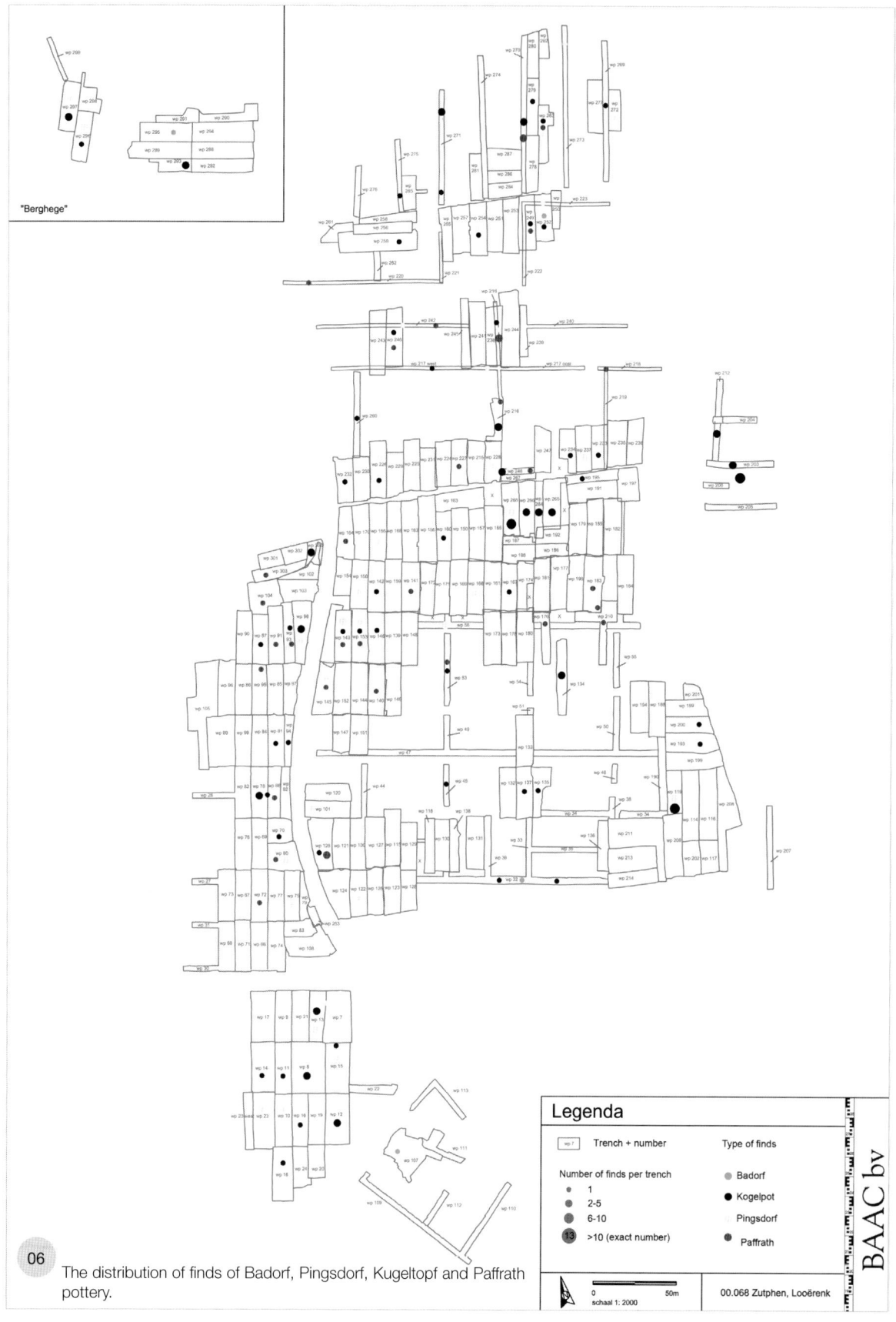

06 The distribution of finds of Badorf, Pingsdorf, Kugeltopf and Paffrath pottery.

disappeared around the beginning of the Christian era.[5] He suggests that the charcoal burning may have started here, near the woodland clearing; it next extended to the north.

Large-scale cultivation of the *enk* (11th-13th centuries)

The next concentration of sherds from the 11th and 12th centuries was found in a northeast- southwest-running zone ca. 500 metres long and ca. 100 metres wide on either side of the Looër Enkweg, at a distance of ca. 50 metres to the north of the area described above. In the middle of the *enk*, the zone is about 160 metres wide, and in the most northerly, tapering part, 11th–12th century material was found everywhere. This area corresponds with the high sandy ridge on the plateau of the *enk*, with a steep, eroded bank on the western side towards the valley of the Ooyerhoekse Laak. In contrast to the above-mentioned area, virtually all finds here were discovered right below and within the base of the topsoil ('plaggensoil') of the cultivated field. No medieval features younger than the 9th-century charcoal stacks were found here. Among these finds, Paffrath ware occurs very frequently, which suggests that the area was used as arable land, possibly in the 11th, but certainly in the 12th century. It was a substantial field system of ca. 70,000 sq m (7 hectares). On the eastern part of the plateau of the *enk*, scattered Paffrath and *Kugeltopf* sherds were also found, partly in the fill of depressions. There is a striking concentration of sherds in the former mesolithic pool (trenches 248, 264, 265, 266 and 268). The material is predominantly from the bottom sediments of the lake, which, in medieval times, must have been visible quite clearly as a deep depression in the field. The earliest fill, then, must be attributed to eroded matter from the adjoining parcels. The southeastern part of the *enk*, north of 't Hummel, is relatively empty. This included low-lying, wetter parts that would have been unsuitable for tillage. On the interjacent sandy surfaces, Paffrath and *Kugeltopf* sherds do occur in some places. These finds from the base of the topsoil may indicate that there was yet some arable land on the wetter part of the plateau.

The 13th and the early 14th centuries present a similar picture to that of the 11th and 12th centuries (fig. 7). The distribution of finds across the high ridge, and the large field system of the 11th and 12th centuries remain the same. The cultivated area seems to continue unaltered into the 14th century. People settled at two locations: the possibly disturbed site at Rouwbroek, just east of the *enk*, and marks of habitation on the south-east side of the '*enk*', north of 't Hummel. The Rouwbroek site appears to begin during the 13th century (earliest material: *Kugeltopf* and proto-stoneware) and continues into the 15th century. During this century the area appears to have been disturbed by the digging of a system of ditches. The second location on the southeast side of the *enk* also has its beginning in the 13th century, probably early in that century, judging by some Pingsdorf and *Kugeltopf* sherds and early proto-stoneware pottery. One or more building features uncovered in trench 119 can be assigned to the 13th century. Possibly this is when a system of ditches was created, running north-south across this part of the area, parallel to the contour lines of the sloping relief of the *enk* towards Rouwbroek. The earliest finds from the ditches date back to the 13th century (proto-stoneware). The system of ditches was dug out and shifted several times, and certainly survived into the 18th century. In fact, the extant ditch due east from here is a continuation of this system. The ditches probably kept the higher area to the west from eroding. Besides, the ditches constituted a clear demarcation line between the field system high up on the *enk* and the low-lying, marshy woodland of Rouwbroek.

Extension of the arable fields (14th-15th centuries)

During the 14th and 15th centuries, the distribution of the finds across the plateau of the *enk* remained more or less unaltered (fig. 8). At most, there seems to have been an extension of the cultivated area towards the eastern half of the *enk*, a zone running from along the south end of the fossil lake as far as the eastern slope of the *enk* near the site at Rouwbroek. The sparser distribution of finds in and between the depressions of the eastern part of the *enk* continues as well. Among the lower-lying (and wetter) parts of the plateau, there would have been scattered small fields, as was assumed for the previous periods. Pollen analysis of the contents of a probably 14th-century well in the southeast quarter of the area has shown that by then the *enk* must have been largely deforested.[6] The occurrence of hazel pollen indicates clumps of trees at most, but this could equally well have been deposited by a hedgerow on the edge of the *enk*, like the hedgerow of which a remnant still survives. For the 14th century there is clear evidence of arable farming on the *enk*, especially of rye. The same analysis showed that in the 14th century a dense alder thicket was still present in the adjacent Rouwbroek marshland. If the edge of Rouwbroek was inhabited from as early as ca. 1200, the area of the Rouwbroek itself had not yet been brought into cultivation. This habitation would have been geared to the utilization of the *enk*.

The depressions on the *enk* would have been filled in in phases between 1100 and the 15th century, as is indicated by soil analysis and the few sherds in the sections of the test trenches. A more precise dating cannot be given, as the test trenches

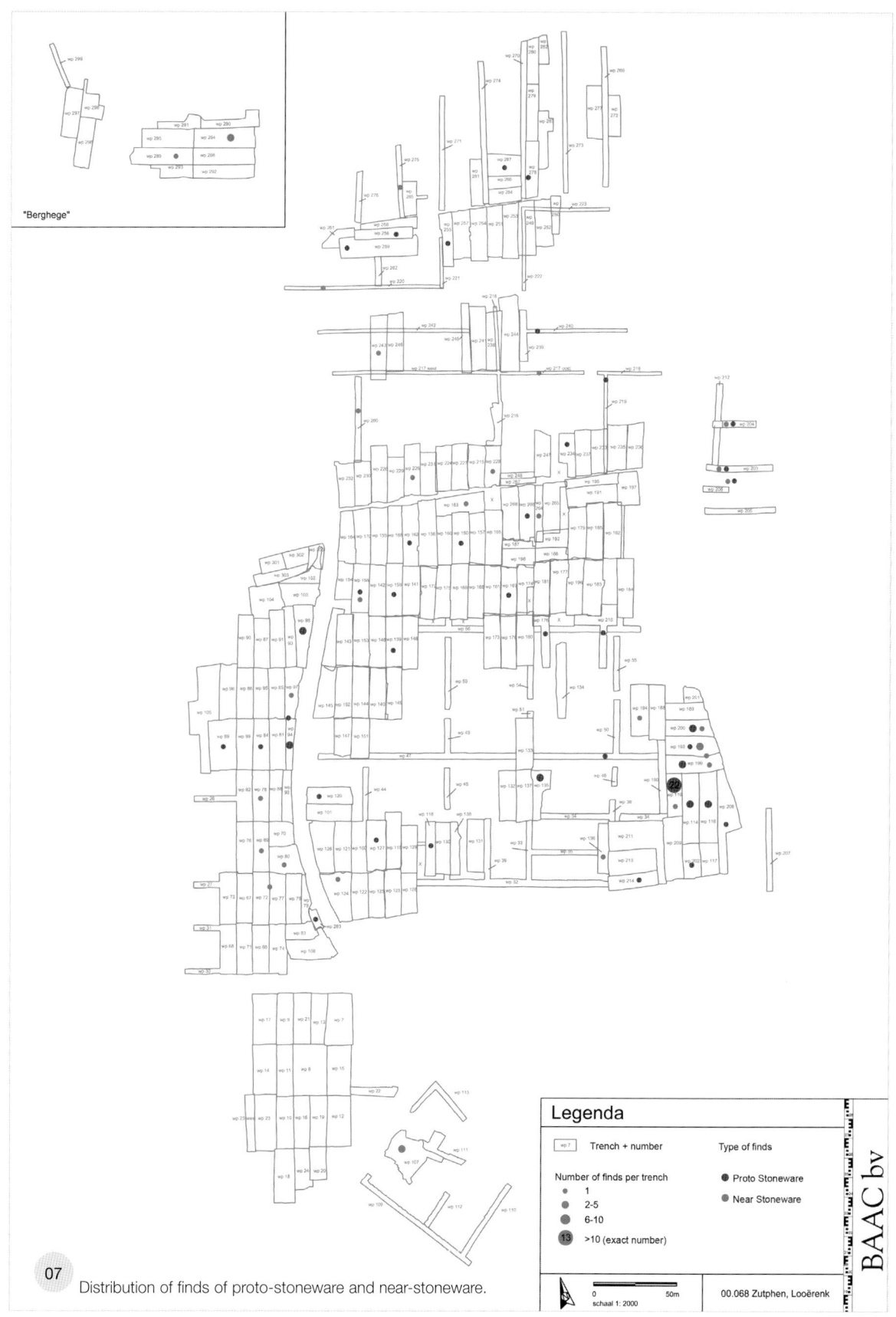

07 Distribution of finds of proto-stoneware and near-stoneware.

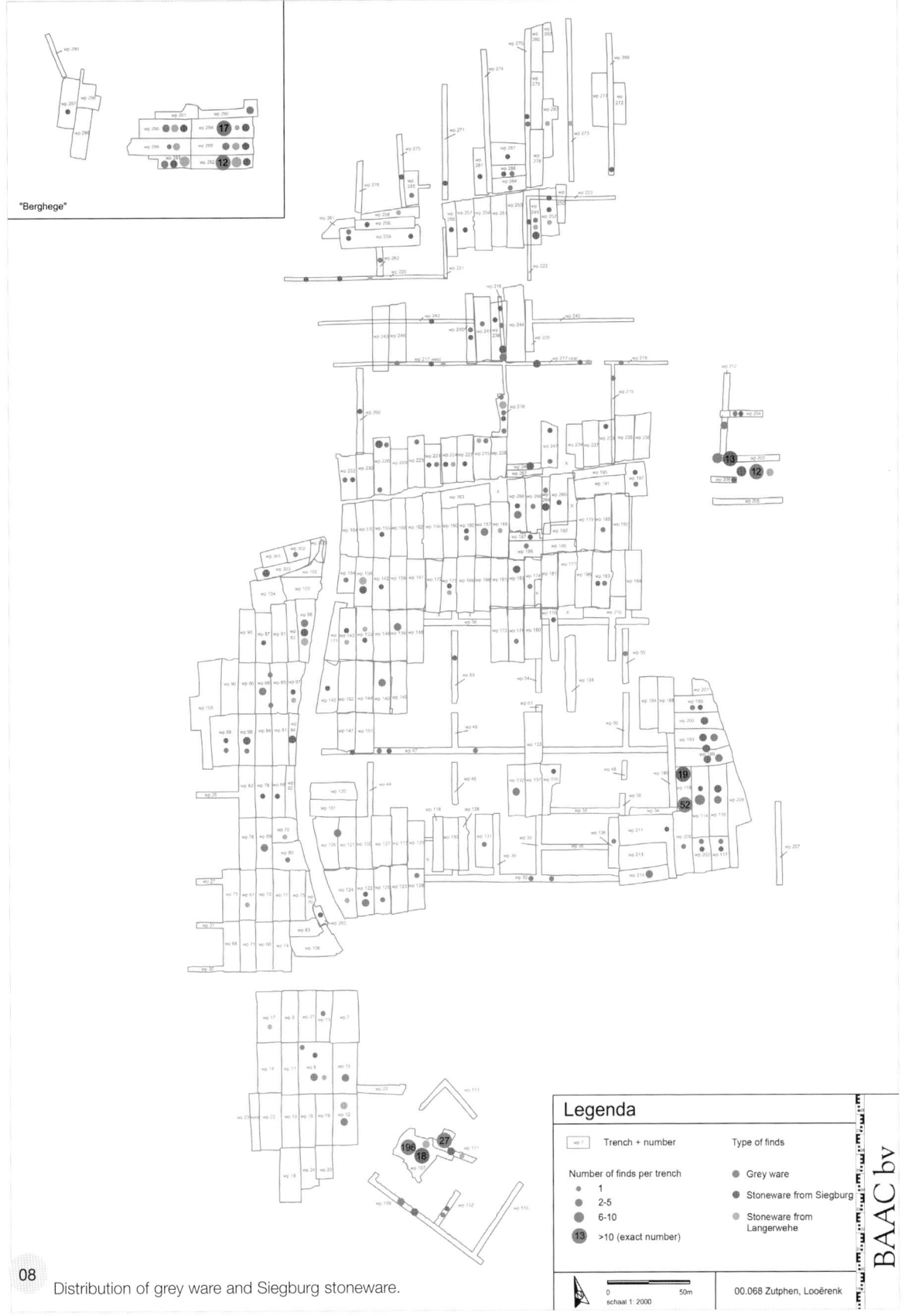

08 Distribution of grey ware and Siegburg stoneware.

did not produce much useful material. During the phase of the test trench investigation, material was collected from the sections and the various layers, but the finds are too few to allow definite conclusions. However, the report about the test trench investigation on the Looërenk does mention that the bottommost fill of the depressions corresponds to *plaggen* soil layer 1, which is dated to the 11th-12th centuries.[7] The finds from the earliest infilling of the small lake confirm this. The earliest deposits in the lake and the depressions are so thin that there is hardly a case for the fill being due to agriculture. On top of this there is a thick *plaggen* layer from the late Middle Ages (*plaggen* layer 1-2), which is remarkably lumpy in texture and a highly humic mixture, sandy (ferruginous sand, podzol) and clayey. The majority of the depressions were filled in this way. Is this the soil that was dug over in Rouwbroek in the late Middle Ages? The soil dug over would then be related to the preparation of the lower parts of the area for agriculture. The earliest finds from this layer point to the 15th century, a dating that corresponds to the earliest finds from the Rouwbroek site. As the purpose and dating of the ditches themselves are still unclear, this remains a hypothesis. The lumpy texture of this layer of the *plaggen* soil indicates that no arable farming took place then; this was introduced only in *plaggen* layer 2. The dating of the earliest use of this layer is as yet unclear. The 14th-century habitation is chiefly present in the southeastern quarter of the *enk* as a continuation of the 13th-century habitation. Trench 119 produced by far the most finds, also from the 14th century, so that we can assume that among the many postholes 14th-century structures will be present. Two wells in trench 116 also date from the 13th (dendro: 1242) and 14th centuries. The habitation at this site ended in the course of the 15th century. Although many postholes were found in this particular area, clear traces of farmhouses have not been demonstrated convincingly. It is highly likely that the supporting structure of such a main building would have been built on brick dies, no soil marks of which have been retrieved. The frequent occurrence of medieval brick in the relevant trenches (especially no. 119) may well indicate disturbed foundations of structures. The presence of an applied layer of loam in trench 119 also points to an occupation surface (floor) in a building.

Fundamental changes and new farmsteads in the 15th century

The most recent finds in the southeastern quarter of the *enk* are also the earliest finds of the habitation site of farmstead 't Loo (trenches 107, 109, 111 and 112). The lack of Langerwehe stoneware in the southeastern quarter of the *enk* is conspicuous. Although Langerwehe ware occurs as early as the 14th century, the ratio of Langerwehe stoneware to Siegburg stoneware increases significantly in the course of the 15th century. At the farmstead 't Loo, Langerwehe ware does occur. The earliest phase at this farmstead is represented by a substantial ditch running diagonally across the farmyard site. The ditch was filled in in the mid 15th century to allow the building of a new farm: 't Loo (trench 107).[8] The fact that when the farmhouse was first erected it incorporated a brick house front, reveals an urban influence. The earliest well, dendrochronologically dated to 1456 +/- 8 years, probably dates to the establishment of the farm at this spot. We must be dealing with a relocation of 't Loo, as this farmstead is already mentioned in the ducal tax accounts in 1304 and 1395.[9] In 1496, the farm 't Hummel ('t Hummeler) is first mentioned. Remarkably, while 't Loo is mentioned in all ducal land-tax accounts of 1463 up to 1496, 't Hummel is recorded only in 1494, even though the accounts for the other farms in Leesten and environs are fairly complete. In the accounts for 1494 't Hummel features as possibly belonging to 't Loo. The suggestion that 't Hummel belonged to 't Loo is supported by the fact that the two farms had the same owner in the accounts of 1649. The name 't Hummel(er) can etymologically be explained as *hummel* = hops, and *laar* is a woodland term associated with hop growing.[10] In fact, hop grows here naturally, as was already the case in the 14th century[11], and it still does.[12] The presence of hop in the pollen samples and in the environment does not necessarily mean that it was cultivated. In hop cultivation the female plant is selected and the pollen-producing male contaminant is eliminated. Yet it is an interesting fact that this farm was called after a hop-plant in the 15th century. The cultivation of hops is associated with the production of beer. In this very period, in 1435 to be precise, duke Arnold of Guelders granted the town of Zutphen the monopoly on brewing and selling beer in a large part of the duchy. In 1466, 23 Zutphen brewers, who had supplied casks of beer for a military campaign, are mentioned in a record. This record does not mention all known contemporary brewers, so the total number of brewers will have been larger, possibly some 40 to 50. The sudden boom in the production of beer in Zutphen must have had its repercussions on the surrounding countryside, where the ingredients, in particular hops, were grown. In this context it may be noted that in the well at 't Loo (dendro: 1456 +/- 8), containing a fill from the second half of the 15th century, no pollen from hops was found. This may be an indication for the elimination of the pollen-producing male component, undesirable in the growing of hops. An archaeological clue for the growing of hops could be a row of stake holes found north of 't Hummel. The configuration consists of stake marks, small in diameter, forming a regular pattern across dozens of square metres. The fill is not lumpy compared to other medieval features, which would mean that the stakes had been driven in and not set in dug holes.[13] Similar structures are known from the Rielerenk site at Deventer.[14]

With reference to the possible urban influence affecting the rural area it is interesting to mention that in the tax accounts for 1494 not only the farmers (tenants or freehold farmers) but also the landowners are given. Zutphen citizens owned more than half of all the mentioned farms at Leesten and other village territories around Zutphen. The farm 't Loo was owned by Hendrick Kreijnck, a very wealthy patrician and town councillor (he was an alderman for several years). He also owned the Leesten property of Overdijckinck, situated on the present Lansinkweg.[15] It is not (yet) known whether Hendrick Kreijnck was involved in the production of beer. In the tax accounts for 1649, garrison officer Biermans is named as the owner of 't Loo as well as 't Hummel. The owner's name is a curious but chance reference to the brewing of beer, and hence possibly to hop growing.

There was a general tendency for the town-dwellers, particularly the urban patriciate, to invest their capital in land. This process started as early as the 14th century, when the town's long-distance trade showed signs of decline. An ever smaller group of families remained involved in active trade. Many other families realized more favourable returns from the development of farmland and other regional (formerly regal) sources of reve-

09 The Looërenk in 1832, land use (the north is to the left).

nue, such as tolls, ferries and mills. The number of families that laid down the law in trade, ownership of property in town and country, and in urban and sovereign politics, decreased substantially from the 15th century onwards (oligarchization of society). After the abolition of the feudal domain system in the rural areas in the 12th and 13th centuries (increasing numbers of farmers leased land from secular and ecclesiastical institutions), we come across a far-reaching influence on the countryside from urban investors who employed a lease policy to determine actively what crops were grown. The success of Zutphen's beer production can only be explained in terms of the urban-rural relationship. It is tempting to suppose that the habitation site in the southeastern sector of the *enk* was the original farmstead 't Loo, which is mentioned in sources from 1304, and that this farm was abandoned in the mid 15th century. The original 't Loo was then split up into two new farms; (new) 't Loo and 't Hummel(er). This division and relocation might be related to the intensification of agriculture and hop growing for the purpose of the town's brewing industry. The influence from the urban owners on land use is quite distinct in this century. The brick facade of 't Loo reflects this influence.

The abandoned farmstead in the southeastern quarter of the *enk* bears the toponym 'Hummelstukken' (Hummel plots), so we may assume that traditionally it belonged to 't Hummel. In 1832 this was no longer the case: farmstead 't Hummel and the surrounding land were then owned by the Old and New Hospital at Zutphen, while the aristocrat G.J. de Leeuw van Coolwijk was the owner of farmstead 't Loo. Various other major landowners possessed Hummelstukken. The hedgerow, part of which still survives in the north, also ran across the former farmstead to the southeast of the *enk* (fig. 9). Anyway, the site of the supposed earliest medieval habitation southwest

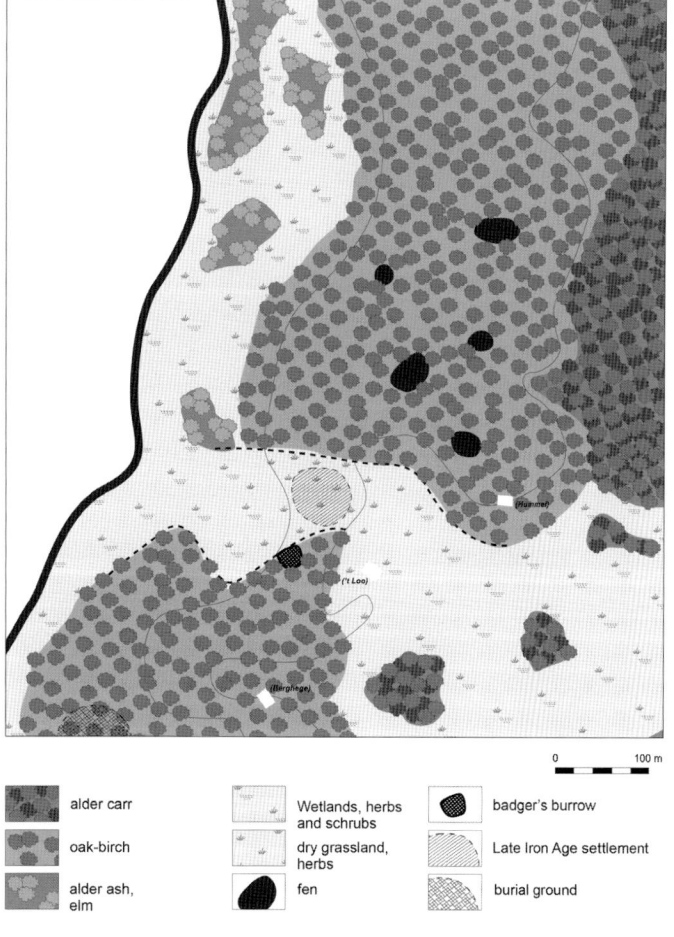

10 Schematic representation of the development of the Looërenk during the Middle Ages (from Groenewoudt 2006, drawing by M. Kosian, RACM)

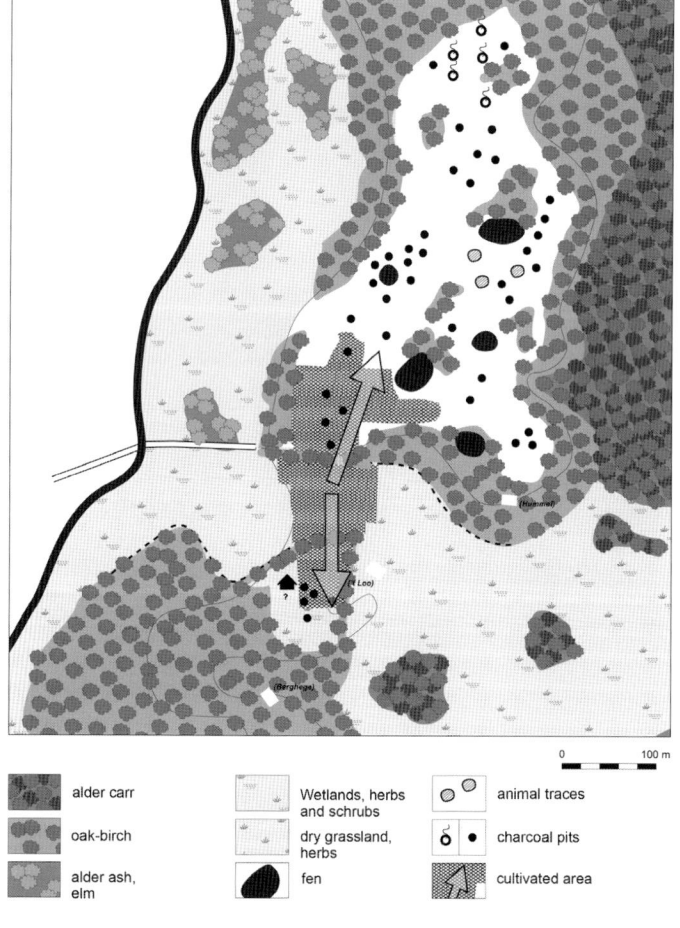

11 'Loo' woodland; Roman period - 8th century; Fig. 10b: Development in the 9th – 11th century.

of 't Loo (11th/12th century) in 1832 appears to belong not to this farm but to the farm Berghege to the southwest. In 1832 both were owned by Baron van Lamsweerde. Berghege and 't Loo may indeed have had a common origin. Berghege is not mentioned before 1494 and does not appear in the ducal tax accounts of 1463 and 1472. The excavations on the site demonstrate that the earliest pottery there consists of stoneware (Siegburg, Langerwehe and early Raeren) and grey ware that can be dated to the last quarter of the 15th century.[16]
The archaeological and historical evidence thus indicates that the farm was established between 1472 and 1494. Nothing is known about the first buildings, except that they were not brick-built. The farmhouse was not built in brick until 1817. The history of the medieval farmsteads on the Looërenk may then have evolved as follows: the earliest farm was established on the poor sandy ridge between (new) 't Loo and Berghege in the late 10th or 11th century. The first cultivated fields may have been in its immediate vicinity southwest of the farm. Between 1000 and 1200 seven hectares of land north of this farm were developed and brought into cultivation. About 1200 the first farm was abandoned and relocated to a site further northeast ('old' 't Loo). This farm stood on the eastern edge of the recently developed farmland. Possibly there was a second farm in the adjacent, low-lying area of Rouwbroek, somewhat further north. This site and 'old' 't Loo were in their turn abandoned around 1450, and relocated to 'new' 't Loo (ca. 1460). Between 1472 and 1494 two new farms were established: 't Hummel(er) and Berghege. The establishment of new farms coincided with the phase of farmland expansion after the lower-lying and wetter parts of the *enk* had been filled in. It is likely that hop growing for the brewing industry in the town played a part. By and large, the late medieval layout of the Looërenk and surrounding area remained intact into the late 20th century.

Conclusion: hypothetical phasing of medieval development on the Looërenk

The spatial analysis of systematically collected finds from the base of the upper layer of the arable field and the relevant features has proved to be a highly effective method for acquiring insight into the spatial development of the Looërenk. From the 11th century on, sufficient waste including sherds was spread over the land with the manure from deep litter layers to provide a convincing picture of the progress of development. Combined with documentary data, the archaeological evidence provided a detailed picture of the history of this development. Development may have started as early as the 10th century, but this hypothetical first phase failed to leave any recognizable material: little if any domestic waste reached these fields. Two great waves of development followed: the first in the 11th and 12th centuries (seven hectares) and the second in the 14th and 15th centuries (up to 12 hectares). In the second half of the 15th century new farms were established and fundamental agricultural reform took place, probably at the instigation of the urban landowners.

12 New farms in the 15th century

Notes
1. Groenewoudt *et al.* 1998.
2. Langeveld 2002.
3. GrN 28880: 1200+/- 35 BP: 779-883 cal AD (68,3%).
4. Groenewoudt 2006.
5. Groenewoudt 2006.
6. internal report archeobotany ROB 2003-1 by Otto Brinkkemper.

7. Langeveld 2002, 29, 30 and 33.
8. Bouwmeester, Fermin & Groothedde 2007, 5.4.2.
9. Ducal tax accounts (*hertogelijke thijnslijsten*) f 1395 (1304) in: Rijksarchief Arnhem. Archief van de graven en hertogen van Gelre, graven van Zutphen inv. 107), pond- en schildschattingen 1463-96 in: idem, inv. 697 (1463), inv. 1021 (1472), inv. 1022 (1494/96) and the 'Verpondingscohier 1646/49' in: Archief van de staten van het kwartier van Zutphen en hun gedeputeerden, inv. 293. Transcription by P.L.J. Dullaert.
10. Toponymical pilot study by J. ter Laak commissioned by the ROB. See also: Bouwmeester, Fermin en Groothedde 2007. Also: Verdam 1964.
11. Otto Brinkkemper: palynological survey of a 14th-century well in the southeast corner of the *enk*, internal report archeobotany ROB 2003-1.
12. Bert Maes, survey of the species in the hedgerow just north of this site. Internal report. Maes 2002.
13. See also section 7.6 in: Bouwmeester, Fermin en Groothedde 2007.
14. Bartels 2006.
15. Bouwmeester, Fermin & Groothedde 2007, 5.5.2.
16. Bouwmeester, Fermin & Groothedde 2007, 5.4.3.

References

Bartels, M.H. 2006: Hansebier aus Deventer. Die Räumliche Niederschlag einer Veränderung bei der Herstellung eines Handwerkliches Produkt. In: M. Gläser (rde.): *Lübecker Kolloquium zur Stadtarchäologie im Hanseruam 5: Das Handwerk* (Lübeck) 135-156.

Bouwmeester, H.M.P., H.A.C. Fermin en M. Groothedde (red.) 2007. Geschapen landschap. Tienduizend jaar bewoning en ontwikkeling van het cultuurlandschap op de Looërenk in Zutphen. Zutphen/Deventer/Den Bosch.

Brinkkemper, O. 2003: Pollen uit een 14^e-eeuwse waterput van Zutphen-Looërenk, *Intern Rapport Archeobotanie ROB 2003/1*, (Amersfoort).

Groenewoudt, B.J., Th. Spek, H.M. van der Velde, I. van Amen, J.H.C. Deeben & D.G. van Smeerdijk 1998: Raalte-Jonge Raan: de geschiedenis van een Sallandse bouwlandkamp, in: *Rapportage Archeologische Monumentenzorg* 58, (Amersfoort 1998).

Groenewoudt, B.J. 2006: Sporen van oud groen – Bomen en bos in het historische cultuurlandschap van Zutphen-Looërenk. In: O. Brinkkemper, J. Deeben, J. van Doesburg, D.P. Hallewas, E.M. Teunissen & A. D. Verlinde: Vakken in Vlakken. Archeologische kennis in lagen. *Nederlandse Archeologische Rapporten 32* (Amersfoort). 117-146.

Laak, J. ter 2003: *Toponiemen rond de Looërenk* (concept 21-03-2003, unpublished).

Langeveld, M. 2002: Landschappelijke context, in: H.M.P. Bouwmeester (red.), Prehistorie tussen de schapen - Archeologisch onderzoek Zutphen - Looërenk (Leesten-Oost), *BAAC rapport* 00.068, (Deventer), 25-38.

Maes, B. 2002: *Onderzoek naar autochtone bomen en struiken in de Graafschap met bijdrage: een houtwal bij de Looërenk*, unpublished report.

Verdam, J. 1964: Middelnederlandsch Handwoordenboek, ('s-Gravenhage).

Development phases of the Looërenk

Period	Description of the occupation
Roman Period:	probable regeneration of forest on the former Iron Age settlement site and fields, woodland possibly utilized by the existing settlement(s) of Leesten (and
9th century:	production of charcoal in the Loo wood from contemporary settlement(s) of Leesten (and Eme?), utilization by Frankish rulers in Zutphen and/or Counts of Hamaland?
10th-11th centuries:	first farmstead in the southwestern sector of the enk? Small arable field southwest of the enk.
11th century	development of the high ridge of the Looërenk: large open-field area of seven hectares (plaggen soil 1)
12th century	continued development, small fields on the eastern part of the enk (plaggen soil 1)
first half of 13th century	first farm abandoned, possibly relocated to new site in the southeastern sector of the enk ('old' 't Loo), and to Rouwbroek
shortly after 1242:	dendro-dating of earliest well near 'old' 't Loo
1304:	farms Ten Loe and (Clein) Graffel first mentioned (again in 1395)
14th century:	Looërenk largely deforested, extension of fields to the northeast, rye cultivation
mid 15th century:	occupation sites at Rouwbroek and old 't Loo in the southeastern sector abandoned. Infilling of depressions on the enk for expansion of farmland (plaggen soil 1-2), relocation of 'old' 't old Loo to a new site: 'new' 't Loo in 1456 (+/- 8 years)
Before 1456:	filling in of ditch under new farm 't Loo
1456 +/- 8:	earliest dendro date of a well at 't Loo, dating the establishment of the farm on this site
1463-1495:	mention of farms 't Loo, 't Hummel, Graffel and Berghege
1472-1494:	new farms 't Hummel and Berghege established. Possible hop cultivation for brewing industry at Zutphen
17th century (17A):	repair or rebuilding of farms (e.g. Meijerinck, Tjoeinck (de Keij) Wekenstroo and Overdijckink) after the Eighty Years' War
18th century, ca. 1775:	further brick construction at farm 't Loo (barn behind dwelling), brick well
1817:	brick farmhouse construction at Berghege
Ca. 1900:	rebuilding of farmhouse 't Loo
1971:	demolition of farm Berghege
1980:	fire at farmhouse 't Loo, followed by renovation
2001:	demolition of farm 't Loo
2004:	start of new housing estate

Columns in houses

Domestic architecture and the stone trade in late-medieval Flanders

Marie Christine Laleman

One of the achievements of urban archaeology under the inspiring leadership of Jan Thijssen is the investigation of the post-Roman urban development of Nijmegen. By means of full-scale excavations and more modest inspections, answers were sought to various questions, about changes in the spatial organization of medieval Nijmegen and the development of the site near the Valkhof, still very much linked to the Roman past, towards the centre of the 13th-century town, i.e. around the Grote Markt and the Sint-Stevenskerk. These developments also saw changes to the types of town houses. Whereas initially all construction was in timber, from the 13th century on some houses were partly or completely stone built. The stone construction material could be new or re-used Roman material. With these findings, Nijmegen joined the list of Northwest-European cities which have in recent years conducted research into medieval stone-built houses. Within this group, Nijmegen is one of the cities with a fairly modest, but no less important stock of stone houses, illustrating a type of medieval town different from the great trading centres with their opulent and huge merchants' houses such as Utrecht, Bruges and Ghent. As a tribute to the archaeological house research in Nijmegen, this contribution will highlight a neglected aspect of medieval domestic architecture in Ghent: the capitals that crowned the columns made of Tournai stone.

Medieval town houses

The numerous 13th-century houses in the centre of Ghent, which earned the city the title of 'Medieval Manhattan', bear witness to the standing and the power of the patricians of Ghent in the County of Flanders. The *Stenen* (singular: *Steen*), as these houses are referred to in late-medieval sources, reflect in stone the fortunes of several powerful families, whose wealth was based on the cloth industry, on long-distance trade and on various privileges (fig. 1). The investigations by the Department of Urban Archaeology of the City of Ghent,[1] supported by historical and scientific research, allow us to understand the *Stenen* of Ghent within their political, socio-economic and architectural-cultural contexts.[2] However, these houses above all constitute a stone-built environment where people dwelt, lived and worked. The Ghent method of house research, putting flesh on the bones of land-registry and fiscal data, imbues the material vestiges with life.[3] Of most of the over 230 investigated houses, the successive owners, users, occupants and their life histories can be traced in this way.[4] The largest houses are 25 to 30 m long, and generally 8 to 10 m wide (fig. 2). Often there were five floors. Many of the fronts facing the street had a tall screen façade with crenellations

01 The 12th-century town was the frame of reference for the tall, stone-built houses erected in the 12th and 13th centuries for the patrician elite of Ghent and known as *Stenen* (City of Ghent, Department of Urban Archaeology).

and corner turrets. The surrounding courtyard, sometimes enclosed, accommodated various outbuildings. Their structure and impressive height made the *Stenen* true status symbols (fig. 3). The builders distinctly opted for towering structures, despite there being sufficient space at the time to build a complex of lower buildings. The overall design and certain elements such as the crenellations were inspired by aristocratic and military architecture. And although defense was not their owners' primary concern, such a sturdy house would in times of war and rebellion provide welcome protection.

The ground-floor halls

The downstairs halls – in today's city sometimes referred to as undercroft or crypt – were originally ground-floor or basement rooms. These rooms usually received little daylight. In some houses there are niches (for lamps?) and occasionally a fireplace. Usually the first floor was the most representative, serving as the merchant-owner's reception halls. The low-ceilinged upper floors mainly served as warehouse space. It is quite likely that this also went for the ground floor, which was the best accessible from the street and the courtyard. There have been no indications so far that cloth or any other products were manufactured in these houses or their outbuildings, or that any part of the industrial process took place here, with the possible exception of the coordination of the production stages, the trading and selling.

In almost all of the houses still standing, the first hall was the one most easily investigated because through the centuries it had usually been subdivided into cellar spaces and thus remained structurally intact and visible *in situ*. Timber supports or stone columns subdivided the downstairs halls and supported timber-beam ceilings or stone vaulting.

02   A section of the inner city of Ghent, with the house plans of archaeologically identified *Stenen* (City of Ghent, Department of Urban Archaeology).

Tournai limestone

Of particular interest are the ground floors subdivided by columns of Tournai limestone. Over 90% of the materially investigated – stone built – medieval houses were in fact built of Tournai limestone.[5] This is a blue-grey limestone deposited in the carbonaceous era (Upper Tournaisian, Tn 3). This rock surfaces in the steep banks of the river Scheldt (or Escaut in French) upstream from Tournai, Hainaut. The principal quarries were located at Chercq, Vaulx, Calonne, Bruyelle, Allain and Antoing (fig. 4).

The limestone deposits were quarried from at least the turn of the Christian era, in open quarries. Archaeological research has shown that Tournai stone was exported on a quite significant scale, even in Roman times.[6] This exportation comprised building blocks and carved elements, as well as filler material for other industries. The earliest recorded applications of this stone in Ghent date from the Carolingian period. They relate to buildings for the important monasteries of Ganda and Blandinium, later known as St Bavo's and St Peter's abbeys. At the latter, also the burning of lime from Tournai limestone has been attested.[7]

Ghent did not have suitable building stone and therefore was obliged to import it. The river Scheldt, which directly connects Ghent with the Tournai region, without doubt facilitated its transportation. If one calculates the amount of Tournai limestone used in Ghent between 900 and 1300, the Ghent builders must have accounted for an important share of the quarrying industry's output. At any rate, builders in Ghent used more Tournai limestone over this period than they did in the vicinity of the quarrying centres.

Architectural applications and transportation

The house known as *Simon sRijkensteen* (fig. 5), situated in the Hof van Ryhove precinct, was closely studied in an attempt to estimate the volume of stone required for building an average-sized town house.[8] As a starting point were taken the dimensions of the house: a front wall 11.50 m wide, a rear wall 11 m wide, side walls 25 m long and 16 m high, the front and rear gables up to 23.50 m high, and all walls roughly 1 m thick. In the calculations, the current standard weight of 2791 kg per cu m was used as a reference, which without doubt is calculated for denser and far more regular masonry than was customary in the 12th and 13th centuries. To compensate, there probably is more waste nowadays, as a smaller proportion of the stone will be regarded as usable. The wall openings were not deducted in the volume calculation, as they probably would have barely affected the outcome, given the massiveness of the building as a whole. On the other hand, the volume of stone required for the stairways, columns, vaulting, floors and outbuildings as well as for making wall plaster and mortar, was not included in the calculation either. Allowing for these restrictions, the calculation came to a total requirement of 3471 tonnes of Tournai limestone for building a run-of-the-mill *Steen*. If we assume a

03 View of the courtyard façade of the house *De Grote Arend* (*Steen* S60), today one of the best preserved 13th-century houses, fronting onto the Hoogpoort (City of Ghent, Department of Urban Archaeology).

04 Location of the quarries of Tournai limestone, from where stone was transported to Ghent (City of Ghent, Department of Urban Archaeology).

load of 100 tonnes per shipload, which may well be too much for the wide and sluggish river Scheldt, then at least 35 shiploads of stone were needed to build the *Simon sRijkensteen*. With a more likely load of 65 tonnes per vessel, this would amount to 53 shiploads.

Apart from this quite average merchant's house, Tournai stone was needed also for building the abbeys, monasteries, churches and other places of worship, the Count's Castle and aristocratic residences, public buildings, city walls and towers, bridges, quaysides, roads and the many other stone-built private houses. Yet practically no written sources are known prior to the late Middle Ages about the importation of this amazing amount of building stone from the Tournai region.[9] This also explains why certain questions will have to remain unresolved. Did transportation indeed take place in barges? Or were the blocks of stone carried downstream on timber rafts, which were dismantled upon arrival in Ghent, as is thought to have happened in the case of Rhenish wine? Or were the building materials a return freight in exchange for Flemish cloth exported southward, while earlier Artesian grain and French wines were mentioned? Or did the trade in stone operate its own commercial circuit? Of the contemporary merchants' guild of Tournai, the Charité Saint-Christophe, we know that they were involved in both the local cloth industry and the production and trading of stone and lime.

Because none of the surviving toll tariffs, either those relating to Scheldt shipping or to road transport, mention anything on the stone trade, it has been suggested that the ships were owned by the abbeys and that the stone trade in general was in the hands of these monastic institutions, which operated free-trade systems. There are sources that corroborate the involvement of the abbeys, such as the procurement of stone for the St Peter's abbey in Carolingian times, or the Tournai abbeys of St Martin and St Nicholas, founded in 1092 and 1126 respectively, which exploited their own stone quarries. Yet there are also numerous records that clearly document the participation of other agents in quarrying, processing, trading and transportation. It is known that from the early 13th century on, the stone blocks that were not processed in the quarries, such as large grave slabs, were 'broken up' on the Scheldt quays to the south of the town.[10] This means that the stones were stacked on the quays and processed there before being transported to building sites at Tournai or destinations further afield. The site that later became known as *quay Taille-pierre* later developed into an entire district where stonemasons had their homes and workshops, but they also worked on the banks of the Scheldt and dumped their waste into the river. At the time of the town expansion of around 1300, in the course of which the parish of St Catherine was incorporated within the city boundaries, activities of this kind were banned. Such records give evidence that these stonemasons were not employed for specific building projects, but worked to supply the demand for Tournai stone in general — hence, that there was a proper market economy, in which the Charité Saint-Christophe played its part.

Master stonemasons

Did the creative impulse come solely from Tournai? The idea that only finished products were imported to Ghent has long been refuted by archaeology. Or did only the more highly finished products such as columns, corbels and capitals go to Ghent and was this transport comparable to what is known about the production and exportation of fonts and grave

05 View of the courtyard façade of the 13th-century *Simon sRijkensteen* (*Steen* S125), situated within the precinct of the later Hof van Ryhove and fronting onto the Onderstraat (City of Ghent, Department of Urban Archaeology).

slabs? Probably the system of quarrying, processing, trade and use at building sites was far more complex, with equally complex interactions in the exchange of raw materials, workers, skills and finished products between Ghent and Tournai. For instance, the presence of stonemasons' marks in the 13th-century St Nicholas Church[11] indicates the presence of a workshop at the site employing specialist stonemasons.

One of the best documented building projects, which can be followed through the city accounts of 1321-1324, relates to the now no longer extant *Gravenbrug* or Count's Bridge (at the site of the current *Vleeshuisbrug* or Meat Hall Bridge). Building activities started with the damming off of the river Leie (or Lys in French) and ended with the placing of a piece of sculpture on the completed bridge.[12] A considerable amount of Tournai stone was imported, largely as finished products. The accounts specify various shapes, including foundation stones, corbels, corner stones and foot stones. The materials were carried to the building site with wheelbarrows and sledges. The suppliers included one *Coning over de Leye* – possibly a master-mason's nickname – together with his valet both from Tournai, and others like Jan van Boekel, Jan de Brune, Coppin Blessard, Boidin de Puur, and Matheus de Mets. These names betray both a Flemish and a Picardian provenance. But stone was brought in also from the St John's Church (now St Bavo's Cathedral) and from the St James' Church. At the time, major building activities were taking place at both of these churches. So were these stones new or reused ones, left-overs or waste? This cannot be deduced from the archival sources. For the construction of the bridge use was also made of stone from the demolished house *In de Drake* and of two grave slabs from the St James' church. The sources relating to the building of the *Gravenbrug* also give evidence that local master-bricklayers conducted the construction work on site and that stonemasons from Antoing finished the outer facings. All this of course relates to the building of a bridge in the early 14th century, and the procedure cannot be simply extrapolated to any building site in any medieval period. Still, there are some prominent points: the collaboration of the local builders with stonemasons from Tournai, and the importation of stone from Tournai and other sources, including reuse. The use of recycled pieces, also for columns, had since long been documented archaeologically at various sites in Ghent, including the so-called *Huis van de Graaf* (Count's House) within the Count's Castle precinct, and in a house on the Hoogpoort (*Steen* S54). But also when not immediately visible, reuse may be involved. For example, it is quite likely that Tournai stone from a prior house was reused in the erection of the 13th-century *Simon sRijkensteen* (*Steen* S124) on the same site. And similar collaboration is also documented at other construction sites. Still in the early 14th century, the master bricklayer Andries den Quareelmakere and masterstonemason Coline van Antoenien (i.e. 'from Antoing' near Tournai) repeatedly worked together as supervisors on various building projects, including the construction of the Belfry and the earliest aldermen's halls (or Town Halls).

Chronological evidence

The use of Tournai limestone in itself offers no chronological clues, as this material was employed for architectural purposes from Roman times up to the 14th century and beyond. External dating evidence – such as archaeological findings in foundation trenches, reliable radiocarbon dating and dendrochronological data – being quite rare for medieval houses in Ghent, attempts were made to identify chronological clues in the way the Tournai stone had been worked.

In the earliest architectural applications in the Count's Castle and both abbeys, almost exclusively irregular rubblework is documented. Although all kinds of formats occur, there is an overwhelming predominance of small stone material. Often one also sees masonry in herringbone work (*opus reticulatum* and *opus spicatum*). When small, flat stones are used, such bonding offers better cohesion of the masonry than horizontally bonded rubblework. Also characteristic is the use of long, narrow stones in round arches over archways and doorways. This building technique in the Ghent region is currently tentatively regarded as characteristic of the 10th and 11th centuries, a period when building in stone was still reserved for the highest elite and any available stone material was used very economically.

Most urban houses show a different building technique. The entire shell was still largely built in rubblework. But the stone formats were significantly larger, at least in the visible facings. At the corners and around wall openings, we find mainly smooth-hewn, squared ashlars. Arches too were usually made from well-cut, approximately square blocks. This type of masonry is the most common in the medieval houses. In other buildings too it seems typical of the 12th-13th centuries in particular.

A third type of masonry used almost exclusively squared blocks (*opus quadratum*). The blocks all were regular in shape and had been smoothed on most sides. This allowed a very regular bond. In domestic architecture, this kind of masonry is fairly exceptional and it seems to be associated with the youngest generation of houses. This type mainly occurs in large, non-domestic buildings such as the St Nicholas Church (13th century) and the Belfry (14th century).

In examining the medieval houses we also investigated whether sculptured and moulded elements such as capitals, corbels, mullions, bases, abacuses, dripstones, keystones, vault ribs, and voussoirs with their various typologies might contribute to a more refined chronology of the medieval houses.[13]

Columns of Tournai stone

In an exceptional example (*Steen* S77 on the Veldstraat-Hoornstraat) the ground-floor hall was subdivided by columns with monolithic, octagonal shafts and stylized foliage capitals (fig. 6). Similar columns are found in the basement church or crypt of the St Bavo's Cathedral or its predecessor the St John's Church. There the transition from the shaft to the square abacus is formed by leaves with prominent veins. Firmin De Smidt dates this type of column to the second half of the 12th century.[14] The type was also recognized in the St Peter's Chapel in Bruges.[15]

Square stone piers, built in rubblework, from squared blocks or from a combination of these, and composite columns or piers as found in church and monastic architecture in Ghent, were not encountered in the private houses. There clearly the simple columns predominate (fig. 7). They mostly consist of a plinth, a base, a shaft comprising several drums, an astragal, a capital, and an abacus. Sometimes the base and plinth are absent, and the column rests upon a flagstone or stone slab. In the course of later alterations, the bottom section often disappeared from view below make-up layers and new, raised floors.

07 The ground-floor hall of a house on the Hoogpoort (*Steen* S47) is subdivided by four columns. After investigation and restoration, their bases once more disappeared beneath the raised floor (City of Ghent, Department of Urban Archaeology).

06 Stylized foliage capital (from *Steen* S77), presumably second half of the 12th century (City of Ghent, Department of Urban Archaeology).

08 Broad, stylized leaves with broken-off crockets crown the columns in *De Kleine Sikkel* on the Nederpolder (*Steen* S117), a *Steen* whose origins may well go back to the 12th century rather than the 13th (City of Ghent, Department of Urban Archaeology).

Capitals

The capital forms the transition from the round shaft to the square, polygonal or round abacus. Mostly the capitals were embellished with sculpture. All decorated capitals in the investigated houses display variants of floral motifs, particularly foliage. The highly stylized leaves on the monolithic columns are quite far removed from identifiable flora. Foliage and crocket capitals are the most numerous. In rare cases the capitals have a plain cup shape and are undecorated. This type only occurs with round abacuses and as a type appears to be younger than the foliage and crocket capitals.

In the study of the medieval houses in Ghent, various attempts were made to glean any chronological clues from the nature of the capitals. So far, this has failed to yield any concrete results, at best certain trends, which, however, are hard to pinpoint in time. So far no correspondence has been discovered between particular types of capital and types of base, abacus or ceiling (timber beams on supporting segmental arches or stone vaulting). A number of variants are explainable by the dimensions of the column (diameter, height) and its location in a hall with or without vaulting. Although most of the capitals in the medieval houses have a floral motif, and belong to the category of foliage and crocket capitals, a wide range of variation on this theme was documented. Any particular type rarely occurs in large numbers. Also, different variants may appear in a single hall. In many cases the distinction between foliage and crocket capitals is blurred. Among the documented examples there are some definite foliage capitals, with clear-cut representations of large, broad leaves or small, round ones. They may be stylized and in slight relief, as in *De Kleine Sikkel* on the Nederpolder (*Steen* S117). Or they may be executed, clearly by a very different hand (fig. 8), in high relief and less refined, as in a house on the Hoogpoort (*Steen* S54) (fig. 9). In foliage capitals where the emphasis is on the leaf tips, which initially curl up broadly

09 Example of a capital with foliage in more pronounced relief, in a house on the Hoogpoort (*Steen* S54) (City of Ghent, Department of Urban Archaeology).

10 Quite a few Tournai-stone capitals in Ghent show a transition from leaf to crocket motifs, as in a house on the Drabstraat (*Steen* S15) (City of Ghent, Department of Urban Archaeology).

and then become progressively pointed, we can note the development towards crocket capitals. Quite a few Ghent examples illustrate this transition from foliage to crocket capitals (fig. 10). Eventually, the progressively distinct crocket capital resulted. Not many examples of these were found in the halls of the houses (fig. 11). The very characteristic crocket capitals appear to be associated with younger houses. It seems that by the time the manufacture of virtually mass-produced crocket capitals took off, the heyday of the Ghent houses had already passed. That is to say, unless the Ghent burghers for some reason had no access to these capitals, because these capitals, at any rate initially, were the preserve of the great building projects of churches and abbeys. It is one of many aspects that require closer investigation. No detailed study of architectural sculpture, and of the columns and capitals of Tournai stone in particular, is available even for the monumental buildings such as the churches, and it is doubtful whether this is still possible nowadays. After all, all Ghent churches of Tournai stone have been thoroughly restored. Elements replaced in the course of restoration because parts were missing, or because they had become illegible or were considered aesthetically inferior, were replaced in the Neo-Gothic style. Thus the idealized, stereotypical model came to prevail, which – compared with the original as in the western naves of the 13th-century St Nicholas Church – is miles removed from the original design and tooling. The sad fact is that such technical details cannot always be studied on the original columns in the houses either. Apart from the raising of floors, which often obscure the foundation, base and lower part, the medieval halls usually were later subdivided and redecorated. Projecting crockets that got in the way were lopped off. Stone surfaces were chiseled smooth, or rehewn to produce a better attachment for fresh wall-plaster. Also there is the erosion of the flaky Tournai stone to contend with, which through time may have rendered the carved lines and the stonemasons' tool marks less distinct or indeed illegible.

Foliage capitals

An important group of capitals display broad leaves with often quite prominent veins (fig. 12). The leaf points sometimes end in outcurving tips which also support the corners of the overlying abacus. Per capital there are four or more broad leaves, which may be connected by a straight linear moulding, by a small leaf or by a frieze of many small leaves. Sometimes they are outlined against the background of a large, deep-lying leaf in between.

Foliage capitals were a very widespread phenomenon in medieval architecture. In certain architectural applications, as with the Cistercians where the call for simplicity did not allow the representation of human figures and historiated scenes, floral motifs were a very popular theme. One finds them both in stylized versions and in more realistic ones. In the case of the very naturalistic representations in stone one can tell where the masons found their inspiration. For instance, a study of Saint-Jean-des-Vignes at Soissons (Aisne, France)[16] established that the local vegetation had been translated into stone. However, the French white limestone was far more amenable to the carving of foliage than the harder and more refractive Tournai stone. In this type of stone the sculpture usually has little relief. The motifs seem closely bound to the cup shape of the capital. Motifs are more stylized than in other stone types, so there is less identifiable vegetation. It has been proposed that the large, broad leaves were inspired by those of cuckoopint (*Arum maculatum*). But in general, the natural vegetation, which of course had been the initial source of inspiration, had already been turned into an architectural convention. Yet this does not mean that its representation had become very stereotypical. The dozens of variants within this group attest to the stonemasons' imagination and skill. But the many variants of course are linked also to the very different dimensions and proportions of the stone supports.

11 The columns in the house Donkersteeg 2-4 (*Steen* S14) are capped by a crocket capital below a square abacus (City of Ghent, Department of Urban Archaeology).

12 The discovery in 1907 of the remains of a medieval house on the Kortedagsteeg (*Steen* S106) (City Archives of Ghent).

Rue Courte du Jour
Coin de la ruelle des Scieurs.
Cave de l'ancienne Petite Armée
Mai 1907.

Crocket capitals

In the crocket capitals, the foliage becomes more detached from the capital's cup shape. In the earliest crocket capitals, the shape of the crockets is still very closed and solid. The leaves beneath the corners of the abacus are usually rolled up on themselves (fig. 13). Fairly soon, the crocket capital grew to extend beyond the abacus, while its shape also changed. Gradually, the crockets opened out and evolved into playful, curly foliage. The crocket capitals found in the medieval houses almost all have the closed, curled-up crockets. Often the crocket ends had disappeared or become unrecognizable, having been lopped off during later alterations. Generally one crocket supported each corner of the abacus. The intervening space might be filled in with a leaf, with or without veins. As a type, the crocket capital evolved from the foliage capital. Crockets as sculptured architectural decorations were noted in the Île-de-France and Burgundy from the mid-12th century. The massive, rolled-up crockets were quite common there by the second quarter of the 13th century.[17] This capital type saw its heyday in the 13th century. The crockets multiplied and featured in many compositions, sometimes to excess. In the Scheldt style of architecture, influenced from Tournai, the crocket capital grew into an almost stereotypical design, to the extent that we might consider it to have been mass-produced.

Flanking columns

Apart from serving as supports in the lower halls, columns with capitals also occur with certain kinds of wall openings. The most common window type is the divided window with a mullion,[18] while the lintel and the sill are part of string courses which may or may not run across the entire façade (fig. 14). The relieving arches above the lintel are round, ogival or segmental. The voussoirs are mostly finished in a straight line and the tympanum is blind, sometimes recessed. The more elaborate mullions usually comprise a square plinth, a round, moulded base, a monolithic shaft and a foliage or crocket capital. In several houses, such as the *Korenstapelhuis* or Grain Warehouse on the Graslei (*Steen* S38) and the *Borluutsteen* (a private house built by the Borluut family) on the Grain Market or Korenmarkt (*Steen* S100), moulded bases or capitals with abacuses are absent, following a simplified design (fig. 15). Examples outside Ghent are found in, for instance, Tournai (e.g. on the *rue Barre Saint-Brice*), Bruges[19] and Damme. The

13 Example of an octagonal crocket capital beneath an octagonal abacus in a house on the Langemunt (*Steen* S111) (City of Ghent, Department of Urban Archaeology).

14 The front of the Grain Warehouse or *Korenstapelhuis* on the Graslei, a 13th-century town house (*Steen* S38) (City of Ghent, Department of Urban Archaeology).

divided window with a mullion was widespread in the medieval architecture of the Scheldt region, but is also found farther north, e.g. in The Hague and in Utrecht. In the 13th-century house *Fresenburg* on the Oude Gracht in Utrecht, it constituted a stone element in a brick-built structure.[20] Possibly the window type with a mullion was one of the architectural features that spread together with the building material. Examples outside Ghent are dated between the 12th and 14th centuries; those in Ghent are difficult to date closely, but in general seem to go back to the 13th century.

In the Ghent houses, the jambs usually have a smooth finish. Jambs with flanking columns, as known from Bruges[21] and Tournai, are only rarely seen in Ghent. A well-investigated example is an ogival opening in the side of a house on the Cataloniëstraat (*Steen* S12), of which both straight jambs take the form of three-quarter columns (fig. 16). They have a round, moulded base, an almost round shaft, an ornamented capital and an abacus. The observed traces indicate that the window also had a mullion, of similar design.

The divided windows with mullions were the basis for the development of the rectangular window with a cross mullion, as has since been familiar for centuries because of its execution in white sandy limestone. The fairly large window opening is

15 The less well-known vestiges include the traces of a divided window with a central mullion, as found in an investigated house on the Nodenaysteeg (*Steen* S120) (City of Ghent, Department of Urban Archaeology).

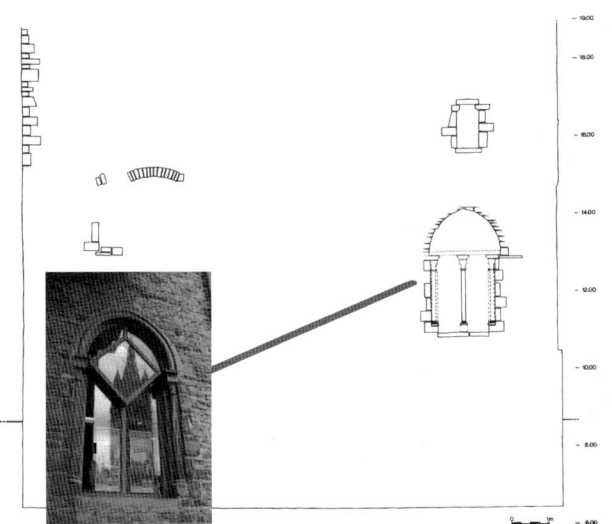

16 Ogival window flanked by colonnettes in the side wall of a house on the corner of what used to be the Kromsteeg and the Cataloniëstraat (City of Ghent, Department of Urban Archaeology).

17 Walled-up cross-window of Tournai stone with two superimposed mullions with capitals (*Steen* S60) (City of Ghent, Department of Urban Archaeology).

subdivided crosswise by a horizontal transom and two mullions, one above the other. This created four smaller window openings, which could be shut independently. The 13th-century house *De Grote Arend* on the Hoogpoort (*Steen* S60) shows one of the earliest examples (fig. 17). The cross windows are in the side walls of the residential body of the house, situated towards the rear, where among other things they lit the first floor. The two mullions each have a capital. Another, fully similar window was identified in the north façade of the house *De Inghel* (*Steen* S37) on the Graslei.[22] Written sources about the construction of three city gates in Bruges around 1400 mention three cross windows as *dornixsche* ('Tournai') windows.[23] Yet it is not clear whether this designation refers to this particular window type or just the material utilized. Other examples of cross windows in Tournai stone are known from Tournai and Sluis.

Conclusion

The study of stone-built medieval town houses allows many approaches. The most obvious is to investigate their relation to the development of the medieval town and to discover with what section of the population such houses were associated. Depending on the degree of conservation of this residential heritage, and certainly if, as in Ghent, dozens of these houses have survived at least in part, it is possible also to investigate their architecture: overall concept, building methods and material use, typology and detailed chronology. The analysis of capitals of Tournai stone in halls and wall openings is part of this endeavour. From the study itself as well as from this contribution it may be evident that as yet no clear-cut trends or chronologies have emerged from the fragmentarily preserved 'stone vestiges'. Whether such structural elements may be relevant to the study of non-ecclesiastical medieval architecture depends also on the findings of archaeological and architecture-historical research. May this contribution therefore serve as an encouragement to document any architectural feature of Tournai stone in great detail, and to allocate it a place in the broader contexts of distribution and dating.

Notes

1. Many thanks are due to all of the house owners and occupants and to all staff members of the Department of Urban Archaeology, who in the past three decades have investigated houses or contributed to this publication. Georges Antheunis, Eddy Raeymakers and Peter Steurbaut took excellent care of the illustrations.
2. In particular, see: Laleman & Raveschot 1991; Laleman 1992, 61-73; Laleman 1999, 143-153; Everaert, Laleman & Lievois 2009, 16-37.
3. Charles 1994; Charles *et al.* 2001.
4. See case studies by Laleman, Lievois & Raveschot 1986, 2-61; Boone, Laleman & Lievois 1990, 47-86; Everaert, Laleman & Lievois 1992, 5-8; Everaert *et al.* 1995, 119-176; Charles *et al.* 2003.
5. Laleman & Raveschot 1991, 133-139.
6. See, among others: Amand 1984, 209-219.
7. Laleman 1977-1979, 120-139.
8. Laleman 1992, 69-70.
9. See also: Nys 1993; Ghislain 1993, 115-208; Salamagne 1993, 366-369.
10. Nys 1993.
11. De Smidt 1974.
12. Laleman & Lievois 1987, 61-68.
13. See, among others: Laleman & Raveschot 1991, 153-159.
14. De Smidt 1962, 21 & 42.
15. Swimberghe 1987, 288-289.
16. Melki & Jagielski s.d.
17. Viollet-Le-Duc 1875, vol. 2, 528-532 & vol. 4, 400-418.
18. Laleman 1993, 20-34.
19. Esther 1989, 40-55.
20. Hoekstra & Klück 1990, 117.
21. Devliegher & Goossens 1980, 5-13.
22. Everaert 1995, 129-131.
23. Devliegher & Goossens 1980, 13-15; Devliegher 1988, 47-63.

References

Amand, M. 1984. *L'industrie, la taille et le commerce de la pierre dans le bassin du Tournaisis à l'époque romaine*, in: *Revue du Nord* (*Mélanges offerts à Ernst Will*). Lille. no. 260.

Boone, M., Laleman, M.C. & Lievois, D. 1990. *Van Simon sRijkensteen tot Hof van Ryhove. Van erfachtige lieden tot dienaren van de centrale Bourgondische staat*, in: *Handelingen der Maatschappij voor Geschiedenis en Oudheidkunde*. Gent. no. XLIV.

Charles, L., *et al.* 1994. *Huizenonderzoek in Gent. Een handleiding*. Gent.

Charles, L., *et al.* 2001. *Erf, huis en mens. Huizenonderzoek in Gent*. Gent.

Charles, L., *et al.* 2003. *De Berg van Barmhartigheid in Gent*. Gent.

Cnudde, V. *et al.* 2009. *Gent... Steengoed!*, (Academia press). Gent.

De Smidt, F. 1962. *De kathedraal te Gent. Archeologische studie*. Brussel.

De Smidt, F. 1974. *Enkele XIIIde-eeuwse steenhouwersmerken in de Sint-Niklaaskerk te Gent*. Brussel.

Devliegher, L. 1988. *De "nieuwe" 13de-eeuwse huisgevel, Grauwwerkersstraat 2-4, te Brugge*. in: *Academiae Analecta*. Brussel. vol. 49, no. 1.

Devliegher, L. & Goossens, M. 1980. *Vensters in West-Vlaanderen*. Tielt-Brussel.

Esther, J.P. 1989. *De cleene Buerse: het verhaal van Brugge's 'oudste' gevel*. in: *Monumenten en Landschappen*. Brussel. vol. 8, no. 4.

Everaert, G., Laleman, M.C. & Lievois, D. 1992. *Het huis met de houten achtergevel. Een nieuwe synthese*. in: *Stadsarcheologie. Bodem en monument in Gent*. Gent. vol. 16, no. 2.

Everaert, G., et al. 1995. *Het huis 'de Inghel' aan de Graslei te Gent*. in: *Handelingen der Maatschappij voor Geschiedenis en Oudheidkunde*. Gent. no. XLIX.

Ghislain, J.C. 1993. *La production funéraire en pierre de Tournai à l'époque romane. Des dalles funéraires sans décor aux oeuvres magistrales du 12e siècle*, in: *Les grands siècles de Tournai*, (Tournai - Art et Histoire, no. 7). Tournai.

Hoekstra, T.J. & Klück, B.J.M. 1990. *Utrecht. Archeologie en bouwhistorie in een bisschopsstad*. in: *Verborgen steden. Stadsarcheologie in Nederland*. Amsterdam.

Laleman, M.C. 1977-1979. *Het kalkovencomplex*, in: *De Sint-Pietersabdij. Historisch en archeologisch onderzoek*. Gent.

Laleman, M.C., Lievois, D. & Raveschot, P. 1986. *De top van de Zandberg. Archeologisch en bouwhistorisch onderzoek*. in: *Stadsarcheologie. Bodem en monument in Gent*, Gent. vol. 10, no. 2.

Laleman, M.C. & Lievois, D. 1987. *De Grasbrug*, in: *7 bruggen. Historiek & restauratie van zeven Gentse Leiebruggen*. Gent.

Laleman, M.C. & Raveschot, P. 1991 *Inleiding tot de studie van de woonhuizen in Gent. Periode 1100-1300. De kelders*. (Verhandelingen Koninklijke Vlaamse Academie voor Wetenschappen, Letteren en Schone Kunsten van België), Brussel.

Laleman, M.C. 1992, *De Gentse Stenen: getuigen van handel en laken, graan en bouwstenen*. in: *Rotterdam Papers* no. 7. Rotterdam.

Laleman, M.C. 1993. *De middeleeuwse vensters*. in: *Vensters. Zeeuwen techniek en esthetiek*. Gent.

Laleman, M.C. 1999. *Enkele aspecten van stedelijke ontwikkeling in Gent: percelen, huizen en bewoners*. in: *Rotterdam Papers* no. 10. Rotterdam.

Melki, F. & Jagielski, K. s.d. *Les herbes de Saint-Jean. Abbaye de Saint-Jean-des-Vignes à Soissons*, Soissons.

Nys, L. 1993. *La pierre de Tournai. Son exploitation et son usage aux XIIIème, XIVème et XVème siècles*, (Tournai - Art et Histoire, no. 8). Tournai.

Salamagne, A. 1993. *La fourniture et la mise en oeuvre de la pierre sur les chantiers du Hainaut médiéval du Cambrésis et du Douaisis (XIIe-XVIe siècles): état de la question et problématique*. in: *Actes du VIIIe Colloque International de Glyptographie d'Hoepertingen 1992*. Braine-le-Château.

Swimberghe, P. 1987. *"Sint-Katharina in de Krog" herontdekt*, in: *Handelingen van het Genootschap voor Geschiedenis* vol. 124, nos. 3-4. Brugge.

Viollet-le-Duc, E. 1875. *Dictionnaire raisonné de l'architecture française du XIe au XVIe siècle* vols 2 & 4. Paris.

Frankforter Potten

De import, de namaak en de invloed op het Nederlandse assortiment 1760-1940

Adri van der Meulen en Paul Smeele

In de loop van de 18e eeuw kreeg in Nederland de concentratie van pottenbakkerijen in vier centra zijn beslag: Friesland, Bergen op Zoom, Oosterhout en Gouda. Alle vier hadden ze een marktbereik tot ver buiten de eigen regio. Daarnaast was er van oudsher een omvangrijke import van aardewerk uit het Rijnland, vooral Frechen, en de Nederrijn. Die bestond hoofdzakelijk uit schotelgoed en werd als een aanvulling op de eigen productie beschouwd.

Toen er vanaf 1760 in toenemende mate aardewerk uit de omgeving van Frankfort naar Nederland werd verscheept werd daar met name door de pottenbakkers in Bergen op Zoom en Oosterhout heftig op gereageerd. Zij hadden zich gespecialiseerd in braad-, bak- en kookgerei en juist in dat segment bood het importaardewerk een alternatief assortiment dat aansloeg bij het publiek. Dat leidde ertoe dat de Frankforter potten al snel in ruime mate in Nederland werden nagemaakt en tot in de 20e eeuw deel uitmaakten van het aanbod aan gebruiksaardewerk.

Uit inventarissen van pottenbakkers en aardewerkhandelaren blijkt dat vanaf 1760 tot aan het eind van de 19e eeuw 'Frankforts aardewerk' een herkenbaar genre was. Toch stelt het ons, ondanks de nabijheid in de tijd, voor problemen. Hoe zag het importaardewerk er uit? Waar werd het gemaakt en hoe is het te onderscheiden van de Nederlandse namaak? Wie maakten het na en waar, en hoe komt het dat de imitaties door deskundigen uit de buurt van Frankfort nauwelijks als 'eigen' worden herkend? Ofwel: hoe Frankforts zijn de in Nederland gemaakte Frankforter potten?

Deze bijdrage geeft de stand van zaken weer van ons onderzoek naar deze materie, dat nog lang niet is afgerond. Onze kennis van het importaardewerk is nog steeds beperkt en heeft meer het karakter van veronderstellingen dan van conclusies. Krachtige steun vanuit de archeologie is nodig om verder te komen. Over de namaak is, door archiefonderzoek en door de beschikbaarheid van ovenafval van zes bedrijven, meer bekend.

Nagegaan wordt waar en door wie de namaak ter hand is genomen, en ook waar deze toe heeft geleid. Dat betreft niet alleen de blijvende introductie van nieuwe modellen, maar ook van nieuwe technologieën en nieuwe mogelijkheden op de arbeidsmarkt, waar vooral werkkrachten uit Duitsland gebruik van maakten. Zij hebben een centrale rol gespeeld bij de herintroductie van het pottenbakkersambacht in Gelderland en Overijssel in de eerste helft van de 19e eeuw.

Voorts zullen we proberen vast te stellen welke veranderingen het genre sinds de 18e eeuw heeft ondergaan doordat ook andere nieuwe modes in het assortiment werden geïncorporeerd.

Import en importheffing

De eerste berichten over Frankforter potten die we hebben gevonden dateren van 1759. In de Opregte Haarlemsche Courant van 26 juli adverteert schipper Hendrik Tetsch (ook wel Tets of Teets) dat hij op de Haarlemse kermis staat met 'allerhande soorten van Bovelands Frankforter aardewerk, waarin men kan stooven, braden en kooken zonder dat eenig vet daar ooyt kan doortrekken'. Ook het volgend jaar is hij present, nu met Frankforts en Keuls aardewerk.

Daarna wordt er jaarlijks geadverteerd; vaak zijn er twee schippers aanwezig, anoniem dan wel met name genoemd. Hendrik Tetsch is tot en met 1768 present, andere namen zijn Hendrik Paffrath, Peter Ket en de 'Keulse pottenvrouw'. Enkele keren wordt nadrukkelijk vermeld dat het om 'onvervalst' Frankforter aardewerk gaat, door de schippers zelf uit het land van herkomst gehaald. Dat zou er op kunnen wijzen dat al omstreeks 1762 met namaak rekening gehouden werd – of met import uit andere Duitse regio's. De namen Tetsch en Paffrath doen vermoeden dat het om Duitse schippers gaat.

De voorwerpen die genoemd worden zijn stoof- en braadpannen, tulband- en hazenpannen; ze zouden sterk zijn, geen vet

doorlaten en met weinig vuur kunnen worden gebruikt.
In 1768 houdt de jaarlijkse stroom advertenties in de Haarlemse Courant op, maar de verkoop gaat, ook in andere delen van het land, intussen gewoon door. Op de Leeuwarder kermis verschijnt vanaf 1767 een koopman met Frankforter aardewerk, in 1769 is dat Johannes Bynema, aardewerkhandelaar en schipper te Amsterdam, die later drie pottenbakkerijen in Dokkum zou verwerven.[1]

Juist omstreeks 1769 beginnen de pottenbakkersgilden te Bergen op Zoom en Oosterhout zich te roeren. Vanwege de geschiktheid van de West-Brabantse klei had men zich daar steeds meer toegelegd op het vervaardigen van bak-, braad- en kookgerei en de concurrentie van de Frankforter potten deed zich juist in dat marktsegment in alle hevigheid gelden. Hoe zij zich teweerstelden is door C.J.F. Slootmans beschreven aan de hand van het archief van het Bergen op Zoomse potmakersgilde.[2]

Als eerste verdedigingslinie stelde men zich ten doel om de import van het Frankforter goed te beperken door het heffen van aanzienlijke invoerrechten. Gepoogd werd om daarin ook de Goudse vakbroeders mee te krijgen, maar die waren in een slepend gevecht gewikkeld om de import van Fries aardewerk aan banden te leggen en kenden daaraan de hoogste prioriteit toe. Het Friese assortiment overlapte het Goudse veel meer dan het Brabantse, dat eerder als complementair dan concurrerend werd beschouwd. Op eigen kracht gingen de Brabanders verder met lobbyen; een invoerheffing was een zaak van de Staten-Generaal, en een positief besluit was alleen mogelijk wanneer alle gewesten het steunden.

Bij de voorbereiding van een en ander rees de vraag: wat zijn Frankforter potten nu eigenlijk en waar worden ze gemaakt? Het bleek niet eenvoudig daar een antwoord op te vinden. De schippers die het verkochten waren weinig mededeelzaam, en met name over de herkomst deden volstrekt tegenstrijdige verhalen de ronde - alleen dat ze niet in Frankfort zelf gemaakt werden was iedereen duidelijk. Door informanten in te schakelen die de streek goed kenden kwam men tenslotte tot een lijstje met plaatsen waar het aardewerk zou zijn geproduceerd. Vijf daarvan liggen dicht bij elkaar, iets ten zuiden van Frankfort en ten oosten van Darmstadt: Dieburg, Oberroden, Urberach, Münster en Eppertshausen. Voorts werden enige verder weg

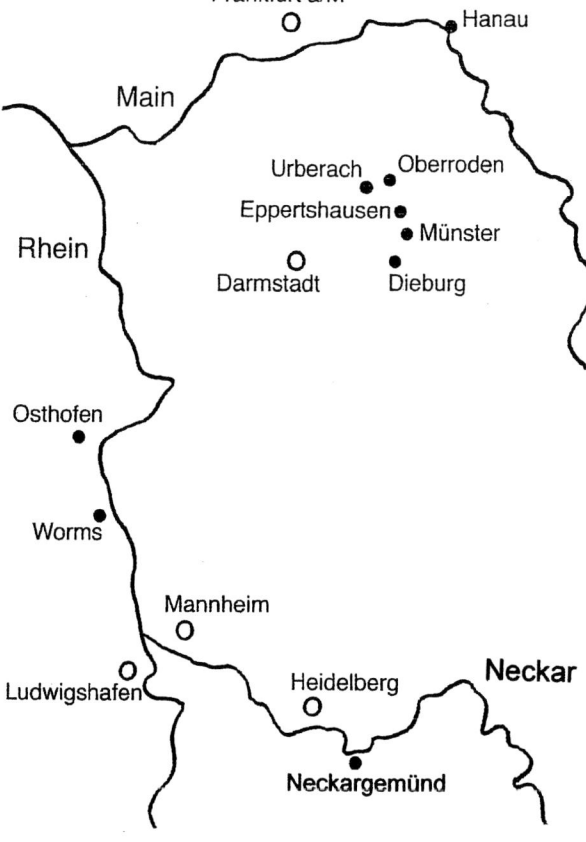

01 Herkomstgebied van de Frankforter potten (rechts) en plaatsen waar ze in Nederland zijn nagemaakt (links).

gelegen plaatsen genoemd: Osthofen en Worms aan de Rijn en Neckargemünd aan de Neckar (afb.1). Waarschijnlijk vormen de eerste vijf de kern van het productiegebied van de Frankforter potten.

Over de identiteit van de Frankforter potten zijn we in de eerste plaats geïnformeerd via de advertenties, waarbij steeds sprake is van kook- en braadpannen, hazenpannen, broederpannen en tulbanden. Een nauwkeuriger opgave ontlenen we aan een memorie uit 1771 van het Admiraliteitscollege, verantwoordelijk voor de douane, en opgesteld naar aanleiding van het verzoek om een speciale importheffing. Zo'n heffing was alleen mogelijk wanneer de te belasten artikelen duidelijk konden worden onderscheiden. De volgende lijst werd opgesteld:[3]

- Platte potten van binnen geglazuurd, van buiten ruw, met of zonder poten, rood of geel, in 9 grootten, variërend van 6 worp tot 3 in een worp;
- Sluitpannen met deksels met brede randen, gerekend als boven;
- Kannen, gerekend als boven;
- Schotelwerk en diepe kommen, met en zonder oren, rood of geel, in 9 grootten, variërend van 4 worp tot 4 in een worp;
- Per stuk worden verkocht vierkante braadpannen, hazenbakken, spitpannen, Poolse mutsen en taartpannen, broederpannetjes, bloempotten, deksels etc. Het stuk te rekenen 2 worp, ongeacht de grootte;
- Poppengoed, te belasten met 30 à 40 stuivers per 100 stuks.

Opvallend is dat er sprake is van pannen zonder en met poten, en een groot assortiment kannen en schotels - waar in de advertenties niet van wordt gerept. Van het bak- en braadgerei is niet altijd duidelijk hoe het eruit zag: Poolse muts, broederpannetje, spitpan.

Terug nu naar de pogingen om door middel van een importheffing de stroom aardewerk in te dammen. Het lobbywerk kostte veel tijd, maar uiteindelijk kreeg men alle gewesten mee en eind 1771 werd voor de tijd van twee jaar een draconische heffing op Frankforter aardewerk van kracht: zes stuivers per worp, dat is bijna evenveel als de normale verkoopwaarde. Daarnaast bestond al sinds 1725 de veel lagere heffing van acht cent per gulden op Nederrijns (Xantens) aardewerk en vijf cent per gulden op steengoed. Aangezien het Nederrijnse aardewerk, meest schotelgoed, en het steengoed als aanvullend op de Nederlandse keramiekproductie werden beschouwd wilde men de daarop gegeven invoerrechten beslist niet verhogen. Het is duidelijk met welke uitvoeringsproblemen men te maken zou krijgen: kunnen de douaniers Frankforts onderscheiden van Nederrijns aardewerk, en weten ze hoeveel een Frankfortse worp is, die weer afwijkt van de Friese, Brabantse, Goudse en Nederrijnse worp? Al gauw deden verhalen de ronde dat aan de grens de Frankfortse worp tot een veelvoud uitdijde en er op grote schaal met de herkomst werd gesjoemeld. Hoe succesvol deze dubieuze praktijken - in combinatie met smokkelhandel - waren blijkt uit het feit dat schippers ook na 1771 Frankforter aardewerk aanboden voor de oude prijs. Er werd zelfs beweerd dat de grensbeambten meewerkten aan de fraude, omdat anders de import zou eindigen en er helemaal geen accijns meer zou binnenkomen.

De heffing liep in 1773 af maar werd de nodige keren verlengd. Pogingen vanuit Brabant om de heffing per worp om te zetten in een heffing van een bepaald percentage van de waarde van de lading leden vooralsnog om onduidelijke redenen schipbreuk.[4] Wat is de achtergrond van deze stromen importaardewerk? Waar lag het initiatief: bij een plotseling toegenomen aanbod vanuit Duitsland of bij een snelle verandering van de vraag in Nederland? We houden het op het eerste. Het nieuwe aanbod van licht, goed hanteerbaar kookgerei met een vlakke bodem sloot goed aan bij de opkomst van kachels en fornuizen, maar deze verandering voltrok zich geleidelijk. Wij sluiten aan bij de verklaring van W. Loibl, destijds directeur van het Spessart-Museum in Lohr.[5] Door archiefonderzoek stelde hij vast dat aan het eind van de 18e eeuw het aantal pottenbakkerijen met name in Dieburg en Oberroden explosief steeg. Hij veronderstelde dat door politieke en bestuurlijke gezagsveranderingen in de regio de vanouds bestaande regulering van het aantal bedrijven een tijdlang niet meer heeft gefunctioneerd. De uitvoer zou hebben plaatsgevonden met schepen die als hoofdvracht eikenhout vervoerden, dat ongeschikt is om per vlot te worden getransporteerd. Wie de afnemers waren van het ontstane surplus in de aardewerkproductie was hem onbekend, maar de verhalen over de Nederlandse importen pasten goed in Loibls bevindingen. Nader archiefonderzoek ter plaatse zal nog veel met betrekking tot zowel de productie als de distributie moeten ophelderen. Of schippers-handelaren als Tetsch en Paffrath hun potten in het productiegebied afhaalden of niet verder kwamen dan een overslaghaven als Keulen is niet bekend.

Succesvolle namaak vóór 1800
Op jacht naar dukaten

Het succes van het Duitse importaardewerk vroeg uiteraard om een reactie. In 1777 was in Haarlem een speciale afdeling van de Hollandsche Maatschappij der Wetenschappen opgericht, met als doel het stimuleren van handel en nijverheid: de Oeconomische Tak.[6] Wat de aardewerknijverheid betreft vroegen twee problemen onmiddellijk om aandacht: het terreinverlies van de Delftse plateelbakkers die bedreigd werden door de toevloed van creamware uit Engeland en van de pottenbakkers die moesten concurreren met de aanvoer uit de omgeving van Frankfort. Fabrikanten werden opgeroepen en uitgedaagd om beide soorten na te maken via uitgeschreven prijsvragen waarmee dukaten en medailles te verdienen waren. In 1778 verscheen de eerste concept-versie van de prijsvraag voor de Frankforter potten. Deze dienden liefst van inlandse aarde te zijn gemaakt, met een flink aantal modellen tegen een zo laag mogelijke prijs.

Op deze prijsvraag hebben vier fabrikanten gereageerd die we achtereenvolgens zullen bespreken, omdat ze van groot belang geweest zijn voor de ontwikkeling van de Hollandse versie van de potten.

Het lijkt ons overigens onwaarschijnlijk dat zij de absolute pioniers geweest zijn. Tussen de eerste imports en de prijsvraag ligt een periode van bijna 20 jaar en er kunnen eerder, al dan niet geslaagde, experimenten zijn geweest. De Friese pottenbakkers Wopke Cnoop en Gerrit Middagten bijvoorbeeld, die in Bolsward vanaf 1765 experimenteerden met tuinpotterie en potten en vormen voor de suikerraffinaderijen adverteerden in de Leeuwarder Courant van 23 maart 1769 met artikelen uit het Frankforter repertoire: haaspannen, taartenpannen en bofferts, die allemaal het vuur zeer goed verdragen. Het is overigens denkbaar dat het hier om ingekochte handel gaat.[7]

Dankzij de prijsvraag van de Oeconomische Tak en de hiervan bewaarde documentatie en correspondentie krijgen we vanaf 1780 een goed zicht op de pogingen tot namaak.

Jan van der Aa te Delft

De eerste fabrikant die al in 1781 werd bekroond en 50 dukaten incasseerde was Jan van der Aa in Delft, die samen met de koopman Adam Holbeek in 1778 op de hoek van de Kolenvest en de Bastiaansvest een Frankforter pottenbakkerij had gesticht. Ze hadden in Delft het monopolie, dankzij een exclusief octrooi voor de periode van 15 jaar, later nog met vijf jaar verlengd.

In een brief van 23 mei 1785 rapporteert de fabrikant het volgende aan de Oeconomische Tak in Haarlem.

De pottenbakkerij bevindt zich in een zeer goede staat, hij werkt winter en zomer met acht knechten en zodra het aardewerk gebakken is wordt het verkocht. Hij hoopt dat de importheffing van 1771 gehandhaafd blijft en dat de commiezen niet al te veel laten passeren. Hij haalt nog steeds zelf, samen met zijn knecht, aarde uit de omgeving van Mainz, maar moet bij de grens steeds meer belasting betalen als compensatie voor de verminderde inkomsten van de Frankforter potten.

Al in een vroeg stadium had Van der Aa een meesterknecht uit het gebied van oorsprong laten overkomen. Franz Weeber, geboren in Oberroden, trouwde in 1781 in Delft en bleef het bedrijf en de familie Van der Aa tot aan zijn dood in 1829 trouw.

Jan van der Aa overleed in 1800, zijn vrouw, zoon Pieter (overleden in 1816), en diens vrouw Adriana van Houdt zetten de pottenbakkerij voort. Inmiddels waren de economische omstandigheden verslechterd en in 1820 werd in een bedrijvenenquête de toestand van de fabriek middelmatig genoemd, o.a. ten gevolge van de hoge belastingen op turf en Duitse aarde en de vele vreemde kooplieden die met hun buitenlandse waren de markt bederven. In die periode zijn er nog 5 werklieden actief. Het Nederlands Openlucht Museum in Arnhem is in bezit van een evenveeltjespan, voorzien van de initialen PvdA, die we, evenals een scherf van een kookpan met dezelfde letters, gevonden in Vlaardingen, aan het bedrijf toeschrijven. (afb.2) De pottenfabriek is nog door anderen tot omstreeks 1850 voortgezet. Mede door het octrooi zijn er in Delft geen andere initiatieven geweest.[8]

02 Evenveeltjespan, gemerkt PvdA, gemaakt door Pieter van der Aa te Delft. Nederlands Openluchtmuseum, Arnhem. d 31.

Teunis van Tellingen te Arnhem

In juni 1778 kreeg de Amsterdamse aardewerkkoopman Teunis van Tellingen toestemming van het Arnhemse gemeentebestuur om een pottenfabriek te bouwen aan de Klingelbeekseweg, buiten de Rijnpoort.

In eerste instantie wilde hij het steengoed gaan produceren dat hij tot dusver uit het Munsterland placht te betrekken. Van een half jaar later dateert het - toegestane - verzoek de potten te voorzien van het stadswapen. Een verzoek om het alleenrecht van de steengoedfabricage werd echter niet gehonoreerd.[9]
Van Tellingen & Comp. - er participeerden ook andere Amsterdamse kooplieden - voorzagen de fabriek al snel van een tweede pijler. Naast de productie van het al genoemde steengoed, de zogenaamde Munsterse of Moffenkruiken, ook wel Stadtlohnse kruiken, bronwaterkruikjes, witte en blauwe Keulse kannen en grote bruine voorraadpotten, ging de jonge onderneming zich toeleggen op de Frankforter potten. Al in 1780 wordt de Haarlemse Maatschappij benaderd; er is een aanzienlijke hoeveelheid steengoed verkocht en Haarlem stelt voor de fabriek ter aanmoediging hiervoor te belonen. Een jaar later wordt aan Van Tellingen de gouden medaille toegekend, en aan de opzichter van de fabriek, Jacob Beumer, de zilveren medaille. Ook de inzending van de Frankforter potten werd gehonoreerd, al moest Van Tellingen het uitgeloofde bedrag van 100 dukaten delen met Johannes Gibbon uit Gouda, waarover straks.

De Frankforter potten werden door de lokale afdelingen van de Maatschappij aan allerlei proeven onderworpen. In Leiden bijvoorbeeld werden huisvrouwen ingeschakeld en er werd daadwerkelijk in de pannen gestoofd. Vuurbestendigheid was een belangrijke eis en in het algemeen vielen de resultaten, anders dan bij de Engelse namaak, positief uit.

In het archief van de Oeconomische Tak bevindt zich een lijst met het assortiment uit deze eerste jaren van experimenten die waarschijnlijk afkomstig is van de Arnhemse fabriek; datum, plaats en afzender ontbreken.

Lijst van voorwerpen, omstreeks 1780 ter beoordeling gezonden naar de Oeconomische Tak te Haarlem, waarschijnlijk door Teunis van Tellingen:

- Een haasse Pan van ses worp
- Tulband van twee worp
- Dito anderhalf worp
- Een twee worps Pot
- Anderhalf worps dito
- Een worps Pot
- Een dito
- Een twijfelaars Pot van drie twee worp
- Een dito
- Half worps Pot
- Een dito
- Van drie in een worp
- Een dito
- Een dito
- Een dito geschildert
- Van vier in een worp
- Een dito
- Een dito
- Een dito geschildert
- Castrol van een half worp
- Een dito van drie in een worp
- Een dito van vier in een worp
- Een Broedertjes Pan van anderhalf worp
- Een Com van anderhalf worp
- Een dito van een worp
- Een dito twijfelaar van drie in twee worp
- Een dito van een half worp
- Een dito van drie in een worp
- Een Schotel van anderhalf worp
- Een dito van een worp
- Een dito twijfelaar van drie in twee worpen
- Een dito halfworps
- Een half worps Melkkan
- Een dito van drie in een worp
- Een dito van vier in een worp
- Neegen differente Formtjes

De Arnhemse fabriek was evenals de Delftse tot ongeveer 1800 zeer succesrijk. In 1804 en 1810 brengt Van Tellingen verslag uit aan Haarlem. In de goede beginjaren werkten er wel 27 mensen in de fabriek, in 1810 nog maar 13. Inmiddels hebben zich acht vergelijkbare fabrieken in de regio gevestigd, wat op zich niet zo'n probleem is, ware het niet dat er te veel invoer is van buitenlands aardewerk. Hieraan zou paal en perk gesteld moeten worden, mede omdat de belastingheffing op inkomende potten wordt ontdoken. De aarde voor de Frankforter potten betrekt hij uit het binnenland; met de Keulse en Munsterse kannen moest hij stoppen omdat goede grondstoffen vanuit Duitsland niet meer beschikbaar werden gesteld en ook omdat er te veel steengoed wordt ingevoerd.

In 1810 bericht hij over de introductie van een nieuw artikel, de namaak van Engels zwartgoed: keteltjes, trekpotten, melkkannetjes etc., waarmee hij in 1809 op de nijverheidstentoonstelling in Amsterdam had gestaan. De oorlog en de hiermee gepaard gaande schaarste werken in zijn voordeel. Ook de Frankforter potten maakt hij nog met succes; ze zijn mooi en kunnen goed tegen het vuur. Helaas blijft het buitenlandse goed maar binnenstromen en wordt er aan de grens massaal gerommeld. De strijd tegen importaardewerk loopt als een rode draad door zijn levensgeschiedenis.

Van Tellingen verkocht in 1812 de pottenbakkerij aan de koopman W.F. Dornseiffen en overleed in 1814 te Amsterdam, 88 jaar oud. Onder de nieuwe eigenaar ging het niet goed met de fabriek, die in 1815 in de Arnhemsche Courant tevergeefs te koop werd aangeboden met als omschrijving: 'Fabriek van Frankforther, Vriesch, Zwart en ander aardewerk'.

Pas in 1819 viel het doek, toen de eens zo succesvolle pottenbakkerij door Dornseiffen, die zich intussen in Utrecht gevestigd had als kaarsenmaker, aan kastelein Jan Grotenhuis werd verkocht. Deze transformeerde de gunstig gelegen panden tot een uitspanning.

We hebben indertijd in Arnhem uitgebreid onderzoek gedaan naar de pottenfabriek en de meeste werknemers opgespoord, waarvan we er een aantal in de volgende hoofdstukken zullen tegenkomen, omdat ze ook na de sluiting van de fabriek nog carrière hebben gemaakt.

Tot nu toe is één gemerkt stuk aardewerk ontdekt, een gehavende kookpot in het museum te Rijssen. (afb.3) Voorts is er een inventaris uit 1803, met een merkwaardige aanleiding. Evenals in Delft werkten in Arnhem vóór 1800 al enkele vakmensen uit het Duitse oorsprongsgebied, waaronder Frans en Christiaan Schlee of Slee. Frans Slee, geboren in 1770 in Oberroden, trouwde in 1802 in Arnhem met Anna Christina Hobergs. Niet lang daarna werd het echtpaar door enkele schuldeisers achtervolgd, wat resulteerde in het cederen van de boedel. Slee was op dat moment de pachter van de pottenfabriek van Van Tellingen, wat blijkt uit de vermelding van een 'pachtceduul'.[10] Uit de lijst van het in de pottenbakkerij aanwezige aardewerk blijkt dat het assortiment beperkt is en voornamelijk bestaat uit potten en schotels.

Aardewerk in de boedel van pottenbakker Frans Slee, pachter van de Arnhemse Frankforter pottenfabriek van Teunis van Tellingen op 3-12-1803:

- 131 stuks twijfelaarsschotels
- 219 stuks halve schotels
- 12 stuks worpse potten
- 35 stuks twijfelaarspotten
- 463 stuks halve potten
- 987 stuks drielingspotten
- 1697 stuks vierde potjes
- 624 stuks zesde potjes
- 28 stuks vuurtesten
- 197 stuks vuurpotten
- 25 stuks tulbandsvormen
- 17 stuks pofferspannetjes
- 1 stuks waterpot
- 5 stuks doorslagen
- 6 stuks kachelpijpen
- 46 stuks potjes
- 7 stuks deksels

Niet lang daarna stichtte Slee zelf een bedrijf in een aanvankelijk gehuurd en later gekocht pand. We belichten het vervolg van zijn carrière en die van zijn zoon in een volgend hoofdstuk.

Johannes Gibbon te Gouda

Anders dan Delft en Arnhem was Gouda in de 18e eeuw een belangrijk pottenbakkerscentrum met ongeveer 20 bedrijven, die een grote steun ondervonden van de honderden pijpenmakers die hun pijpen door de pottenbakkers lieten bakken. Johannes Gibbon, in Gouda de man die het eerst en het meest naar buiten treedt met Frankforter potten is dan ook geen buitenstaander maar een telg uit een pottenbakkersfamilie. Zijn ouders, François Gibbon en Maria Verveen leidden een

03 Kookpan waarvan de oren missen, gemerkt TvT, gemaakt door Teunis van Tellingen te Arnhem. Rijssens Museum.

bedrijf in de Peperstraat, dat later overging naar zoon Quirijn. Johannes verwierf in 1765 een andere pottenbakkerij, aan het Nonnenwater, alwaar hij zich ging toeleggen op de namaak van de Frankforter potten. Ook hij dingt op uitnodiging van de Haarlemse Maatschappij mee naar de uitgeloofde medailles en dukaten en wordt zelfs tweemaal bekroond. In 1781 moest hij de geldprijs delen met Arnhem, maar hij kreeg daarnaast wel de tweede gouden medaille omdat zijn fabrikaat voor driekwart uit inlandse Rijnaarde gemaakt was. In 1785 worden zijn potten nog eens geëxamineerd en hoewel enkele proefnemers aanvankelijk niet helemaal overtuigd waren omdat enkele potten waren gebarsten en nogal lomp bevonden, wordt hem nu het volle bedrag van 100 dukaten en de gouden medaille toegekend. De potten waren thans geheel uit inlandse aarde vervaardigd. Evenals Van Tellingen en Van der Aa heeft ook Gibbon de Oeconomische Tak inzage gegeven in zijn bedrijfsvoering en resultaten en wel in een brief van 13-6-1785. Hij bericht dat hij in 1782 een Frankforter knecht heeft ingehuurd teneinde beter aan de grote vraag van de winkeliers te kunnen voldoen. In 1784 heeft hij zijn pottenbakkerij uitgebreid met een nieuw werkhuis waarin hij zes schijven heeft laten plaatsen.

Tenslotte geeft hij een opgave van het aantal verkochte worpen aardewerk, dat zich in stijgende lijn beweegt. Voor 1784 is dat 5722 worp, naar onze mening een zeer bescheiden hoeveelheid. Hij beklaagt zich dat ook anderen zich in Gouda op de namaak toeleggen maar omdat ze onvoldoende verstand hebben van de vereiste aarde kunnen deze potten niet sterk zijn. Zijn eigen producten merkt hij terwille van de herkenbaarheid met de initialen IG. We hebben tot nu toe geen gemerkt voorwerp gevonden. In 1792 doet Gibbon een poging om in Gouda het alleenrecht te verwerven voor de productie van Frankforter potten. Hij vreest namaak en heeft veel geïnvesteerd; zijn jaarproductie ligt inmiddels op 30.000 worp. Overman en dekens van het gilde voelen hier echter niet voor omdat ook andere gildebroeders deze potten al 25 jaar (!) maken en dan geruïneerd zouden zijn. Concrete voorbeelden van collega's die in deze periode Gibbon hebben nagevolgd, dan wel gelijktijdig of eerder met de productie zijn begonnen zijn tot nu toe niet gevonden.[11]

Johannes Gibbon overleed in 1802 en zijn weduwe Leonora Groeneveld verkocht in 1804 het bedrijf aan dominee J.W. Bussingh, ten behoeve van diens zoon. Die deed in 1808, kort na het overlijden van Leonora, de pottenbakkerij over aan de zakenman A.H. van Wijn, die zich moeite gaf de enigszins in verval geraakte onderneming nieuw leven in te blazen. Hij nam in 1809 deel aan de tweede nationale nijverheidstentoonstelling in Amsterdam met een uitgebreid assortiment Frankforter aardewerk, waaraan ook tuinvazen en een vermiljoenpot waren toegevoegd.[12]

Inzending van A.H. van Wijn en Zoon te Gouda naar de nijverheidstentoonstelling te Amsterdam in 1809.
- Een Vermillioen Pot
- Een Tuyn Vaas waar in twee voet Stukken, op te staan benevens een dekzel en knop
- Een Haazepan met dekzel
- Twee Chocolade-Keetels
- Twee Groote Jacoba's Kannen
- Twee Kleyne dito
- Drie Zieke Potten met Deksel
- Een Tobaks Doos
- Een Fonteyn
- Twee Tulbanden met Deksels
- Een Sluytpan met vier hokken en Deksel
- Een dito met Twee hokken en Deksel
- Een sluytpan en Deksel
- Een ordinaire Pan met Deksel
- Een groote Schotel en Deksel
- Twee groote Melkkannen
- Een Vaasje met deksel en bakie
- Een groote Kom

Het jaar daarvoor had Quirijn Gibbon, de broer van Johannes, in Utrecht eveneens zijn Frankforter potten geëxposeerd. Beiden ontvingen een zilveren medaille.

Inzending van Quirijn Gibbon te Gouda naar de nijverheidstentoonstelling te Utrecht in 1808 Prijzen in guldens, stuivers en duiten.
- Prijse der Frankforter Potten de 100 Worp 25 Gulden.
- Een Haazepan en dekzel, 10 worp   2:10:-
- Een Pan, 1½ worp   -:7:8
- Een dito, een worp   -:5:-
- Een Twijfelaarspan, of de drie twee worp, met dito dito dekzel   -:7:-
- Een Sluytpan en dekzel te zamen twee worp   -:10:-
- Een Swarte Twijfelaarskan of de drie stuks twee worp   -:3:8
- Een dito van de drie een worp   -:1:12
- Twee bruyne Sous pannetjes   -:2:8
- Een worpse Schotel   -:5:-
- Een de twee een worp   -:2:8
- Een diepe Kom of Bak de drie twee worp   -:3:8
- Een Tulband en dekzel te zamen een worp   -:5:-
- Een Vierkante braadpan en dekzel 8 worp   2:-:-
- Een Tulband en dekzel te zamen twee worp   -:10:-
- Een Melon en dekzel te zamen een worp   -:5:-
- Een Kaakjes pan en dekzel te zamen 4 worp   1:-:-

Gouda zou zich de komende jaren ontwikkelen tot een belangrijk productiecentrum van Frankforter potten. In een volgend hoofdstuk worden de verschillende, al dan niet succersrijke, pogingen belicht en komt ook de laatste fase van de pottenbakkerij van Johannes Gibbon ter sprake

Jan Adriaanse Augustijn te Bergen op Zoom

De potmakers van Bergen op Zoom waren eeuwenlang belangrijke producenten van kwalitatief hoogstaand vuurbestendig kookgerei, melkteilen en ander aardewerk dat zijn weg vond naar grote delen van Nederland, met name ook naar de Noordelijke provincies. Juist zij ervoeren de Frankforter potten als een bedreiging en drongen als eersten bij de autoriteiten aan op tegenmaatregelen. In de tweede helft van de 18e eeuw waren er in Bergen op Zoom elf pottenbakkers die in gildeverband samenwerkten. Een van hen, Jan Adriaanse Augustijn, ging zich met toestemming van het gilde toeleggen op de namaak van Frankforter potten. Hij was eigenaar van potterij Croonenburgh, gelegen aan de Noordzijde van de Haven.
In 1787 stuurde Augustijn zijn proeven naar de Haarlemse Maatschappij ter beoordeling in het kader van de nog steeds lopende prijsvraag. Er waren aanvankelijk twijfels over het door hem toegepaste procédé, waarbij de gewone Bergse klei slechts voorzien werd van een laagje witte klei, een engobe. (afb.4) Andere aspecten, zoals de goede vuurbestendigheid en vooral de lage prijs van f.19,- per 100 worp pleitten weer in het voordeel van de fabrikant.
Augustijn hield de Maatschappij tot 1810 op de hoogte van zijn doen en laten en in 1803 luisterde hij in Haarlem het 25-jarig jubileumfeest op met een zending tuinvazen, waarop vooral zijn zoon Adriaan zich toelegde. De fabriek floreerde en er werden tal van nieuwe producten ontwikkeld, zoals de imitaties van het Engelse zwartgoed, eesttegels en vermiljoenpotten. De zwarte potwerken werden in 1808 op de Utrechtse tentoonstelling geëxposeerd, samen met een kleinere sortering Frankforter imitaties, zie afb.6.

Inzending van Jan Adriaanse Augustijn te Bergen op Zoom naar de nijverheidstentoonstelling te Utrecht in 1808.
In de zwarte couleur
- 2 Soup Terrines met Dexels en Schotels
- 1 Lampet Kan en Schotel
- 3 Fruyt Mantjes, doorgeslagen met Schotels
- 2 Tafel Tabaks Comfooren
- 2 dito dito Doosen
- 4 Quispedoren
- 2 Koffykannen
- 6 Lampet Kannen in zoort en grote
- 2 Nagtblakers
- 3 Jacobas Kannetjes in Zoort
- 1 Mostaard Potje
- 2 Tafel Sous Kommen
- 2 grote Theebussen
- 2 Zuyker Potten
- 2 Tafel Theestoofjes met Testjes
- 2 Zuyker Potjes met Dexels
- 1 Peper Bus
- 3 Kandelaars in zoort

05 Twee pannen met schenklip en lintoor; ovenafval Croonenburgh, Bergen op Zoom. h 12,8, d 20; h 10,9, d 20,2.

04 Twee steelpannen met witte engobe; ovenafval Croonenburgh, Bergen op Zoom. h 9, d 16; h 8,4, d 16.

- 3 Bloempotten en Schotels
- 2 Broeder-pannen
- 2 grote Comfoiren
- 1 doorslag
- 4 Kommen met 2 Ooren alias 2 Oorkommen
- 6 Theekopjes en Schoteltjes
- 1 Schotel met een Visplaat
- 1 Schotel
- 1 Assiet
- 2 Tafelborden
- 2 Boter Schoteltjes
- 3 Hande Waskommen
- 7 Theekommen in zoort
- 1 Schenkblad
- 2 Water of Nagt-potten
- 12 Thee- of Koffy Ketels met hun dexels in zoort
- 12 Trekpotten in zoort
- 2 Bierkannen
- 2 Bierpinten
- 6 Melk Kannen in zoort
- 3 Sous Kommen in zoort
- 2 Zout Vaatjes
- 2 Thee Busjes

De gecouleurde Sorteering
- 4 Tulbands Pannen in zoort
- 4 Engelse Bakken, of Kommen of Schotels in zoort
- 5 Vlakke Schotels in zoort (bruyne)
- 5 Bakken bruyne in zoort
- 5 Vlakke geele Schotels in zoort
- 5 Kommen dito in loort
- 5 Stoofpannen dito in zoort
- 4 Castrollen in zoort

Ook als handelsman moet hij vindingrijk zijn geweest. Blijkens de registers van patentschuldigen had hij niet alleen knechten voor zijn pottenfabriek in dienst, maar ook pottenkramers en -kraamsters, waaronder mensen uit het Westerwald, die met zijn waren op pad gingen.[13] Anders dan veel collega's, die steen en been klaagden over deze 'vreemde omlopers', maakte hij graag gebruik van hun diensten. Ze verkochten ook 'geleiwerk', tinglazuuraardewerk, dat Augustijn uit Friesland betrok, en wellicht ook uit Delft.

In de tuin van potterij Croonenburgh - het huis bestaat nog steeds - zijn de nodige misbaksels gevonden, die een beeld geven van de productie in deze periode. Voor een deel zijn het voorwerpen die ook bij het ovenafval van andere Frankforter pottenfabrieken opduiken, zoals pannen met een of twee lintoren of een steel en een zwarte bies (afb. 4 en 5), zwarte pannetjes en theegoed. (afb.6). Bijzonder zijn de kleine kannetjes met vlakke bodem en lintoor, van witbakkende klei, geel geglazuurd en voorzien van teksten die net niet te ontcijferen zijn. (afb.7) Ook de decors van de schotels (afb.8,9,10) wijken af van wat elders gevonden wordt en zijn verwant met die uit de regio Frankfort.

06 Zwartgoed van Croonenburgh, Bergen op Zoom: theepotten, deksel, pannetjes, schaal, wijwaterbakje?

07 Kannetjes met vlakke voet en lintoor en opschriften; ovenafval Croonenburgh, Bergen op Zoom.

08 Zwarte schaal met ringeloorversiering op de rand; ovenafval Croonenburgh, Bergen op Zoom. h 9,2, d 32,5.

09 Bruine schotel met ringeloorversiering; ovenafval Croonenburgh, Bergen op Zoom.

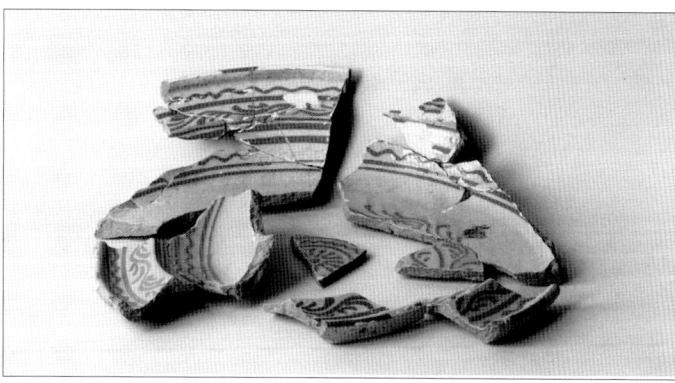

10 Schotel met gele engobe en versiering met bruine slib; ovenafval Croonenburgh, Bergen op Zoom.

Jan Augustijn overleed in 1830, zijn zoon en opvolger Adriaan al eerder, in 1827. De pottenbakkerij werd in 1829 tijdens een publieke verkoping verworven door de dochter van laatstgenoemde. Adriana Augustijn en haar echtgenoot Anthony Willekens zetten het bedrijf voort en toonden in 1830 op de nationale nijverheidstentoonstelling te Brussel een uitgebreid assortiment, wellicht als een eerbetoon aan de grootvader.

Inzending van Adriana Augustijn te Bergen op Zoom naar de nijverheidstentoonstelling te Brussel in 1830[14]:
- fopkan
- pan om haas te stoven
- peterseliepotten
- versierde bloempotten
- versierde tabakspotten
- tabakskomfoor
- kandelaars
- scheerbekkens
- breitobbetjes
- eetbakjes voor gevogelte
- chocolade- of punchketels
- koffiekannen
- theepotten
- Jacobakannetjes
- theestoofjes
- soepterrines
- melkkannen
- boterpannetjes
- peperbussen
- mosterdpotten
- zoutvaten
- tulbandvormen (van gemêleerde pot- en pijpaarde)
- rijstvormen
- broederpannen
- bruine en gele met pijpaarde beschilderde schotels
- zwarte diepe schotels
- ketels
- verschillende voorwerpen van pijpaarde

Een tabakspot uit onze verzameling, gedateerd 1827 en gemaakt voor C. Luisterburg de Jonge (afb.11), schrijven we toe aan de laatste fase van potterij Croonenburgh[15], die in 1837, na het overlijden van Willekens, werd verkocht en buiten bedrijf gesteld.

Conclusie

Uit bovenstaande beknopte bedrijfsgeschiedenissen en lijsten met assortimenten wordt duidelijk dat de Frankforter imitaties een tijdlang zeer succesrijk zijn geweest. Met name Van Tellingen, Gibbon en Augustijn hebben zich na 1800 niet beperkt tot deze Duitse imitaties maar zich ook toegelegd op ander producten: de namaak van het Engelse zwarte aardewerk, waarbij vooral Augustijn complete tafelserviezen ontwierp, aardewerk voor industriële doeleinden zoals eesttegels en vermiljoenpotten en in Arnhem ook Fries aardewerk - een ander succesartikel van die dagen.

Later gaat het minder goed. Enerzijds is dat te verklaren uit de economische neergang in de Franse tijd, anderzijds uit de toenemende concurrentie van bestaande en nieuwe bedrijven.

In het spoor van Van Tellingen: nieuwe pottenbakkerijen in Gelderland

Toen Teunis van Tellingen in 1778 in Arnhem zijn pottenfabriek stichtte had hij in de regio alleen concurrentie van het importaardewerk. Andere pottenbakkerijen waren er op dat moment niet maar dat zou in de 19e eeuw veranderen. In zekere zin werd in de provincie Gelderland een nieuwe markt geopend met deze producten naar buitenlands model en het idee van Van Tellingen vond navolging. Vooral pottenbakkers uit het Duitse grensgebied komen naar Nederland. Ze maken niet alleen de Frankforter imitaties maar ook Nederrijnse en het zwarte repertoire naar Engels voorbeeld. We zagen al dat de Arnhemse fabriek zich op dit laatste ging toeleggen en ook de anderen zullen alle genoemde soorten bijeenvoegen, soms, maar niet altijd, onder de vlag van een Frankforter aardewerkfabriek.

Arnhem

We volgen nu eerst de ontwikkelingen in Arnhem, waar in 1819 de pottenfabriek definitief werd gesloten. We introduceerden in het vorige hoofdstuk al Frans en Christiaan Slee[16], pottenbakkers uit Oberroden/Urberach, die even voor 1800 in Arnhem worden aangetroffen. Frans was in 1803 pachter van de pottenfabriek, maar ging twee jaar later aan de slag in een pand, gelegen aan de Nieuwe Kraan, dat eigendom was van Arend Goedhart. Hij werkte met ongeveer 5 knechts. In 1817 koopt hij de pottenbakkerij en verdere gebouwen van dochter Reynira Goedhart voor slechts achthonderd gulden. Het nieuwe bezit werd op naam gesteld van zijn twee minderjarige kinderen Frederik Wilhelm en Margaretha Elisabeth. Daarna verliezen we het gezin uit het oog, totdat we het terugvinden in Gouda, waar Frans en zijn zoon werk hebben gevonden als pottenbakkersknecht. Intussen was het Arnhemse bedrijf verhuurd aan de gebroeders Isselmann, die eerder ervaring hadden opgedaan in Wageningen, waarover straks.

Frans Slee diende in 1824 vanuit Gouda een verzoek in bij de Goeverneur van Holland om enige geldelijke ondersteuning in verband met door hem in 1813 te Arnhem geleden oorlogsschade. Een door Gouda verstrekt onderzoeksrapportje werpt enig licht op zijn levensloop. Slee werkte tussen 1817 en 1821 in Gouda als pottenbakkersknecht, maar was daartoe naderhand ten gevolge van lichaamsgebreken niet meer in staat. Hij voer nog enige tijd met een bootje rond om wat handel te drijven, maar in 1824 is hij afhankelijk van zijn zoon.[17] Frans Slee is in 1825 in Gouda overleden.

Zoon Frederik Wilhelm (meestal Willem Frederik genoemd) stichtte in diezelfde tijd in Gouda een Frankforter aardewerkfabriek aan de Oostzijde van de Kleiweg. Van augustus 1826 dateert zijn verzoek om de zogenaamde lange oven te verplaatsen omdat hij zijn bedrijf wil uitbreiden, zodat hij met drie knechten kan werken in plaats van met één.[18] In datzelfde jaar wordt de pottenfabriek aan de Nieuwe Kraan in Arnhem verkocht en door de nieuwe eigenaar verhuurd aan Jan Willem Stuber. Een volgende eigenaar liquideert echter in 1830 het bedrijf. Stuber vond een geldschieter met wiens hulp hij een klein bedrijf elders kon realiseren, maar omdat hij geen kans

11 Tabakspot met het opschrift "C. Luisterberg de Jonge Anno 1827', toegeschreven aan pottenbakkerij Croonenburgh, Bergen op Zoom. h 11,5, d 15.

zag aan zijn financiële verplichtingen te voldoen moest hij al in 1832 de nieuwe pottenbakkerij verlaten. Zowel Slee als Stuber vertrekt naar Utrecht - waarover straks.

Wageningen

In de statistieken van de gemeente Wageningen over de jaren 1812-1815 wordt melding gemaakt van twee pottenfabrieken, de ene opgericht vóór 1806, de andere van later datum, die samen 19.200 stuks aardewerk produceren uit 'potaarde voor zogenaamde Frankvoorder Potten'.[19] In de patentregisters van 1812 staan de eigenaren vermeld: Frederik Isselmann en Hendrik van Rennes. Laatstgenoemde was afkomstig uit Bennekom. Zijn bedrijf, dat omstreeks 1800 gesticht moet zijn, werd gedreven door de pottenbakkers Hendrik en Isaac Schoester, Wouter Beekman en zoon Willem van Rennes, die tevens 'tobakker' was, dus tabak verbouwde. Jan Frederik en zijn broer Bernard Hendrik Isselmann waren afkomstig uit Isselburg. Hun bedrijfsgebouwtje bevond zich bij de Buitenbleek, aan de Oude Beneden Arnhemseweg naar het Lexkesveer. Het werd in 1813 verworven, maar er was al eerder een oven geplaatst. Ze verkochten het in 1828 toen de broers al meer dan tien jaar in Arnhem verbleven. De pottenbakkerij van Van Rennes wordt in 1832 op een kadastrale kaart in wijk E bij de 'Vette Hen' gesitueerd, en is in 1845 opgeheven. In de laatste jaren werd ze bestuurd door Johannes Gerardus Deckers, een pottenbakker uit Kaldenkirchen.[20] Deze bescheiden bedrijven, waarvan tot dusver geen voorwerpen bekend zijn, waren de wegbereiders voor een opbloei van het pottenbakkersambacht na 1850. Dit valt echter buiten het bestek van deze studie.

Wehl

Een archiefbron van het Gelderse Wehl maakt in 1814 melding van een pottenbakkerij die drie jaar geleden is opgericht, met drie volwassenen en een hulpje werkt en drie draaischijven telt. Het laatste, een draaischijf per arbeider, wijst op een Frankforter pottenbakkerij. Tweederde van het gefabriceerd product, waarvan de waarde op 60 rijksdaalders per maand wordt geschat, gaat naar Holland, de rest gaat naar Kleef. Ook hier is de initiatiefnemer, Johan Friedrich Kastner, afkomstig uit Duitsland, en wel uit Kalkar. Kastner vertrekt in 1827 via Deventer naar Kampen en werkt daar omstreeks 1830 in de nieuwe fabriek van H.C. Schwartz. In Wehl werkt in die tijd de pottenbakker Gerardus Kaaken, afkomstig uit Issum, en van hem is er in 1835 een aanvraag voor een nieuwe pottenbakkerij, die wordt toegewezen.[21] In 1844 vertrekt Kaaken naar Nijmegen en wordt de pottenbakkerij gesloten.

Doesburg

In Doesburg, waar het pottenbakkersambacht in de 18e eeuw verloren was gegaan, vestigden zich na 1800 enkele nieuwe bedrijven. De eerste initiatiefnemer was in 1813 Gradus Stieber, afkomstig uit Bocholt.
Volgens een nijverheidsenquête uit 1816 telde zijn bedrijf drie werknemers en verkeerde het in vrij bloeiende staat. In 1825 verkoopt hij de pottenbakkerij aan Arend Coenraad Schunck, afkomstig uit Isselburg, die kort daarvoor ervaring in Arnhem had opgedaan in de pottenfabriek van de familie Slee. Hij is er in 1824 getrouwd. Schunck was een succesvol zakenman, die zeker in de eerste fase het Duitse imitatiegoed zal hebben vervaardigd. Later gaat hij, net als zoveel anderen, over op bloempotten, vazen en draineerbuizen.
Voor uitgebreider informatie over de pottenbakkers Schunck en de andere Doesburgse bedrijven van Theodoor Andree en Bernard Welling verwijzen we naar onze publicatie uit 1999.[22] Voor onze veronderstelling dat in Doesburg Frankforter aardewerk is gemaakt is alleen indirect bewijs: veel nieuwe eigenaren hebben hun opleiding voor een deel genoten in Frankforter aardewerkfabrieken in Arnhem en Gouda en zijn in dit klimaat opgegroeid.

Pottenbakkerijen in Doesburg 1813-1969
1. Buiten de Meipoort 1813-1905
    1813-1825 Gradus Stieber
    1825-1857 Arend Coenraad Schunck
    1857-1905 Johan H.C. Schunck
2. Ooipoortstraat 1820-1848
    1820-1844 Theodorus Andree
    1844-1848 Gerardus Johannes Andree
3. Kraakselaan I 1841-1969
    1841-1866 Bernard Welling
    1866-1885 Johan, Derk en Lodewijk Welling
    1885-1894 Derk Johan Welling en Zoon.
    1894-1937 Bernard A Welling en Zonen
    1937-1953 Johan B. en Bernard A Welling
    1953-1969 Jan F. Welling
4. Kraakselaan II 1861-1879
    1861-1879 Johan Valentin Schunck
5. Contrescarpe 1869-1871
    1869-1871 Albertus J. Taminiau

Zutphen

In 1835 werd in Zutphen door de drogist David Evekink beslag gelegd op huis en pottenbakkerij 'De Vredenberg' genaamd, 'gelegen aan de grote weg buiten de Hospitaalspoort'. De pottenbakker Josef Hasselman kon de hypotheek niet langer betalen, en werd na ruim 20 jaar op straat gezet. Hij overleed niet lang daarna en zijn vrouw Catharina Schouten ging verder als pottenkoopvrouw. Hasselman, geboren in Gennep, werkte voor hij naar Zutphen ging meer dan 10 jaar op de Arnhemse Frankforter pottenfabriek. In de leemte die ontstond door de gedwongen sluiting van zijn bedrijf werd in 1836 voorzien door Carolus Ludovicus Taminiau, die vroeger bij Hasselman gewerkt had en nu in Gouda ervaring opdeed. Hij richtte in Zutphen een nieuwe werkplaats in en breidde deze in 1844 uit. Het bedrijf, dat in de laatste jaren geleid werd door zoon Albertus bleef tot circa 1881 in bezit van de Taminiau's. Daarna is in Zutphen nog tot kort voor 1900 aardewerk geproduceerd door A.T. Derksen, die zijn oven in 1883 naar de Laarstraat verplaatste, en er tevens een handel in glas en aardewerk dreef.

Voor een Frankforter pottenfabriek is 1836 een laat stichtingsjaar. Dankzij de gelukkige omstandigheid dat van deze pottenbakkerij ovenafval bewaard en gepubliceerd is hebben we een indruk van het fabrikaat.[23] We herkennen de van buiten ongeglazuurde Frankforter pannen met een geschilderde zwarte bies (afb.12), het imitatie-Engelse zwarte theegoed (afb.13) en borden met eerder een Nederrijnse dan een Frankforter inslag. (afb.14) Kortom, een bedrijf dat alle gewilde soorten en modellen van die tijd leverde, en met succes opereerde. De materiaalvondst is uiterst welkom, omdat ze hopelijk ook representatief is voor al die fabrieken uit dezelfde periode waarvan geen aardewerk voorhanden is.

Neede en Apeldoorn

Met twee Gelderse bedrijven, die in de nadagen van de Frankforter pottenfabrieken zijn opgericht, besluiten we deze reeks.

In Neede werd in 1839 aan de bestaande steen- en pannenfabriek van notaris J.H.W. Ten Bokkel Huinink een pottenbakkerij toegevoegd, die onder leiding van Hendrik Peters tot 1859 heeft gewerkt. Peters (1809-1866), afkomstig uit Kaldenkirchen, kwam naar Neede via Weerselo, waar hij enkele jaren een fabriekje dreef van tegelkachels, zogenaamde porseleinen circuleerkachels. Ondanks een gunstig verslag in de Overijsselse Courant van 25-10-1836 was de onderneming

13 Zwartgoed; ovenafval Taminiau, Zutphen. Foto: Afd. Archeologie, Gemeente Zutphen.

12 Kookpannen met twee lintoren; ovenafval Taminiau, Zutphen. Foto: Afd. Archeologie, Gemeente Zutphen.

14 Bordjes in Nederrijnse trant; ovenafval Taminiau, Zutphen. Foto: Afd. Archeologie, Gemeente Zutphen.

geen lang leven beschoren. Peters trad in dienst van de notaris en heeft er vermoedelijk o.a. zwart aardewerk gemaakt, getuige de vondst van een zwarte pispot in de omgeving.[24] Peters vervolgde zijn loopbaan in Deventer, waar hij ook is overleden.
In Apeldoorn werkte vanaf 1840 Johan F.H. Andree, geboren in 1802 in Isselburg, in een nieuw gesticht bedrijf aan het Griftkanaal. Hij was een zoon van Jacobus Andree, pottenbakker in Vorden, een dorp dat we nog niet genoemd hebben, en waar Gradus Ventür (Issum 1748-Vorden 1813) omstreeks 1803 een pottenbakkerij was begonnen. Uit dit bedrijfje is een tabakspot bewaard, maar er zijn geen gegevens met betrekking tot de Frankforter potten.[25]
Van Johan Andree weten we dat hij evenals Taminiau geruime tijd in Gouda in het Frankforter-pottenmilieu heeft verkeerd, en voor hij zich in Apeldoorn vestigde in Putten heeft gewerkt. Pottenbakkerij Andree kreeg bekendheid in de 20e eeuw door het fraaie kunstaardewerk dat de inmiddels derde generatie er heeft vervaardigd. Van het vroegste aardewerk veronderstellen we dat het verwant is aan het Zutphense, en alle populaire Duitse imitaties omvat.

De nieuwe pottenbakkerijen in Overijssel
Rijssen en Winterswijk

Net als in Gelderland hebben pottenbakkers uit de Duitse grensgebieden in Overijssel een belangrijke bijdrage geleverd aan de wederopstanding van het ambacht. In de bedrijventelling van 1808 wordt in Overijssel geen enkele pottenbakkerij vermeld, maar dat verandert al in 1812 wanneer in Rijssen het eerste nieuwe bedrijf wordt gevestigd.
Eigenlijk hadden we deze geschiedenis in het Gelderse Winterswijk moeten laten beginnen. Twee kleine pottenbakkerijen, van de families Ribbink en Harmsen, maakten daar sinds onheuglijke tijden het lokale aardewerk, waaronder prachtige versierde schotels, verwant aan die uit Ochtrup. Bij Berend Harmsen trad even na 1800 Hendrik Mentink in dienst, afkomstig uit Rhede, net over de grens. Hij trouwde in 1806 met diens dochter en nam in 1809 een bijzonder initiatief: hij zond werk in naar de tweede nationale nijverheidstentoonstelling te Amsterdam. Zijn inzending bestond naast traditioneel Winterswijks materiaal uit Duitse imitaties: Frankforter, Neuss- en Bergs en Marburgs aardewerk. Vooral het Marburgs valt op, omdat we dat nog nergens hebben aangetroffen. Marburg was in die tijd bekend door zijn rode en zwarte, met opgelegde bloemen en andere motieven versierde koffiekannen en schotels. Met Neuss- en Bergs wordt waarschijnlijk Nederrijns aardewerk bedoeld.[26] Bergs slaat niet op Bergen op Zoom, maar vermoedelijk op Tönisberg.

Mentink en zijn schoonfamilie verhuisden naar Rijssen, waar op het adres Stege 244 het familiebedrijf tot aan het eind van de 19e eeuw heeft gefunctioneerd. Ook hier zal het assortiment zich in de loop van de tijd hebben aangepast aan de vraag, maar gezien de achtergrond van de stichter zullen er zeker in de eerste decennia Frankforter potten zijn gefabriceerd. Er hebben knechts uit Deurne en Ottersum gewerkt, en het bedrijf stond bekend om de goede kwaliteit van zijn product. Helaas kennen we dat niet; tot nu toe beschikken we alleen over de archiefgegevens. Wel zijn er bodemvondsten bekend, meest ovenafval van kort na 1800, van de pottenbakkerij van Ribbink in Winterswijk, en dat zal weing verschillen van dat van collega Harmsen. Tussen het versierde Winterswijkse schotelgoed (afb.15,16) ook hier van buiten ongeglazuurd Frankforter kookgerei, zwarte kookpotjes en theepotten. (afb.17)

15 Schotels met Ochtrupse invloeden; ovenafval Ribbink, Winterswijk

16 Schotels met Ochtrupse en Nederrijnse invloeden; ovenafval Ribbink, Winterswijk.

Kampen

In 1821 stichtte de van oorsprong Duitse koopman Hendrik Christiaan Schwartz in Kampen weer een pottenbakkerij, nadat in die stad enkele decennia daarvoor het laatste bedrijf was stilgelegd. Schwartz, zelf geen pottenbakker, voorzag zijn fabriek van twee pijlers: Duits en Fries aardewerk. Van de eerste productgroep hebben we veel minder sporen gevonden dan van de tweede. In 1830 werkt hier J.F. Kastner, de pottenbakker die omstreeks 1812 in Wehl een bedrijf was begonnen en zeker in de begintijd zullen er Frankforter potten zijn gemaakt. Later bestaat het personeel hoofdzakelijk uit Friezen, aangevuld met lokale werkkrachten. De fabriek van Schwartz, die na diens faillissement in 1835 door anderen is voortgezet tot omstreeks 1886, was een flink bedrijf met drie ovens en specialiseerde zich uiteindelijk in Fries aardewerk.[27]

Ommen

Ook in Ommen hebben enkele zakenlieden tussen 1840 en 1844 nog geprobeerd een nieuw gestichte aardewerkfabriek winstgevend te exploiteren. De Ommense kaarsenmaker Elias van Ravenshorst, Carel G. de Moen uit Leiden, en als laatste de Amsterdamse cargadoor J. Blikman Kikkert combineerden de fabriek, die in Stad Ommen gesitueerd was, met een steen-, tegel- en pannenbakkerij. De pottenfabriek specialiseerde zich in Venlo's, Frankforts en Fries aardewerk, zoals blijkt uit een personeelsadvertentie in de Leeuwarder Courant van 19-2-1841 waarin een handelaar gevraagd werd.[28] De nieuwe ondernemers traden naar buiten met hun fabrikaat en namen in 1840 en 1842 deel aan nijverheidstentoonstellingen in Zwolle en Deventer.[29] Vooral van de eerste deelname is een uitgebreide lijst van voorwerpen genoteerd in de catalogus waaruit blijkt dat ze rijk gesorteerd waren: het inmiddels vertrouwde zwarte aardewerk (Venlo's) in de vorm van koffie-, thee- en suikerpotten maar ook waskommen en pannen, vervolgens geel aardewerk, waaronder pannen en kommen, mogelijk uit de Frankforter traditie, 'Brabandsche' braadpannen en tenslotte Friese beslag- en melkpotten en komforen.

In 1842 meldt het Gemeenteverslag van Ommen dat de fabriek niet aan de verwachtingen voldoet, reden waarom de productie al snel is gestaakt. De initiatiefnemers hebben niet op tijd ingezien dat de exploitatie van een aardewerkfabriek een zaak is van lange adem, en geen object waarmee snelle winst gemaakt kan worden.

Deventer

Deventer ontwikkelde zich na 1850 tot een belangrijke aardewerkproducent, al is de stad zich hiervan nauwelijks bewust. Er waren in Deventer belangrijker industrieën, zoals de tapijtfabriek en de ijzergieterij, die de keramische activiteiten hebben overschaduwd. De terracottafabrieken van G.J. Hamer jr., Hamelberg en Co. en Grolleman en Nierdt boden werkgelegenheid aan tientallen pottenbakkers en er was gedurende 14 jaar een zogenaamde Keuls-aardewerkfabriek in werking, die een voor Nederland uniek product maakte. Tussen 1850 en 1872 had de Friese pottenbakker Douwe Draaisma er een gerenommeerd bedrijf, waarvan de producten veelvuldig op nationale en internationale tentoonstellingen zijn bekroond. Ten slotte maakten de Limburgse pottenbakkers Janssen er tot 1983 hun bloempotten.

Deventer is de kroon op het werk van de Duitse pottenbakkers, die, zoals we gezien hebben, belangrijke initiatiefnemers waren bij de stichting van nieuwe bedrijven in de provincies Gelderland en Overijssel in het begin van de 19e eeuw. Ook in Deventer was het een Isselburger, Johan Dieterich Berger, die in 1826 samen met de koopman G.J. Hamer sr. de eerste aanzet heeft gegeven. De aanvankelijk bescheiden pottenbakkerij, gevestigd in de Noordenbergstraat, werd tot 1857 bestuurd door mensen van net over de grens. Eerst Berger, totdat hij in 1832 door Hamer werd ontslagen, en vervolgens Willem Tangerink uit Süderwick en Jacobus Heutgens uit Kaldenkirchen. Laatstgenoemden vormden een onafscheidelijk duo en exposeerden twee keer hun koffie-, thee- en keukengoed op de nijverheidstentoonstellingen van Deventer (1842) en Kampen (1846).[30] Er is een bescheiden hoeveelheid ovenafval van het bedrijf gevonden, bestaande uit terracotta, wat scherven van Frankforter aardewerk en bloempotten. Onder leiding van G.J. Hamer jr. werd de pottenbakkerij naar de Zwolscheweg verplaatst en tot een moderne terracottafa-

17 Zwarte pannetjes, theepot en bakvorm; ovenafval Ribbink, Winterswijk.

briek getransformeerd met ornamenten voor de bouw, beelden en tuinvazen. Toch betekende dit geenszins het afscheid van het oude pottenbakkersrepertoire, al trad men daarmee minder naar buiten. Zo verhandelde de Delftse aardewerkkoopman Johannes Renaud in 1869 het 'Deventer zwart', een regelrechte voortzetting van de Engelse imitaties die aan het assortiment van de Frankforter pottenfabrieken waren toegevoegd.[31] We gaan er van uit dat deze en andere Frankforter producten in Deventer een belangrijk artikel zijn geweest. Na 1870 werden er nog Goudse pottenbakkers aangetrokken en dat er Frankforts werd gemaakt blijkt ook uit de advertentie die de Leeuwarder aardewerkfabrikant R.J. Dorama in de Deventer Courant van 18-6-1875 plaatste voor een 'Gouda's en Frankforts pottebakkersdraaier'.

De stad Utrecht, toevluchtsoord voor Arnhemse pottenbakkers

In Arnhem leerden we de pottenbakkersfamilies Slee, Hasselman en Stuber kennen. Frans Slee vertrok in 1817 naar Gouda, waar hij in 1825 is overleden. Zijn kinderen verkochten een jaar later de Arnhemse pottenfabriek aan de Nieuwe Kraan en bleven tot 1830 in Gouda werkzaam. Dochter Elisabeth was inmiddels getrouwd met Jacobus Hasselman, een zoon van Josef, die in Zutphen omstreeks 1812 een nieuw bedrijf had gesticht. Jan Willem Stuber huurde tussen 1825 en 1830 in Arnhem de toen nog in werking zijnde pottenbakkerij van de familie Slee maar moest zijn heil elders zoeken toen de fabriek andermaal verkocht en daarna ontmanteld werd. De weduwe van Frans Slee, Christine Hobergs, vroeg in 1830 in Arnhem vergunning voor de bouw van een nieuwe oven, vlak bij de voormalige pottenbakkerij. Haar voorstel werd echter van de hand gewezen en daarop zijn de families Slee en Hasselman, bestaande uit moeder Christine Hobergs, zoon Willem Slee en zijn Goudse echtgenote Catharina van Bovene, dochter Elisabeth en Jacobus Hasselman naar Utrecht vertrokken. De Stubers, die in 1832 op straat gezet werden door de verhuurder van de nieuwe werkplaats volgden niet lang daarna.
Deze drie families zullen tot aan het eind van de eeuw met hun eigen kleine bedrijven het ambacht aan de gang houden en doorgeven aan hun opvolgers. De Utrechtse wijk K, waarin ze werkten en woonden, ligt ten oosten van de Vaartse Rijn bij de Tolsteegpoort en omvat o.a. de Oosterkade, Rotsoord en de Helling. Het is een bedrijvig buurtje, met tal van kleine ambachtslieden en vooral ook het centrum van de Duitse pottenventers uit het Westerwald die daar hun uitvalsbasis hadden. Willem Slee, of eigenlijk aanvankelijk zijn moeder, want zij staat tot in haar overlijdensjaar 1834 als gepatenteerd pottenbakster te boek, was de eerste van het gezelschap die zich in 1831 zelfstandig vestigde en daartoe een deel van een steenoven benutte van de fabriek van de Wed. Rose op het Rotsoord.

Een bedrijvenenquête van 1838 bericht over Slee het volgende: 'Maakt vooral Frankforts aardewerk. Debiet f.3.000,-. Gedraaid op een wiel en vervaardigd van aarde welke gedeeltelijk in deze provincie wordt gegraven maar ook buiten 's lands wordt ingevoerd. Een lokaal waarin een oven. Personeel: 5 personen, groot en klein, loon van f.1,10 tot f.0,20 per dag. Het bedrijf is zeer winstgevend. Producten worden in het binnenland afgezet.[32] In 1838 blijkt ook zijn zwager Jacobus Hasselman over een eigen bedrijfje te beschikken, hoewel er geen aanvraag voor een oven in het archief van de provincie is gevonden.

Slee richt zich in 1842 wel met een verzoek tot Gedeputeerde Staten. Hij meldt dat hij de fabriek op Rotsoord moet verlaten en dat hij zich nu wil vestigen op de Helling met een oven die, uitgerust met een lange schoorsteen, geen brandgevaar zal opleveren.[33] Zijn werkplaats is sterk uitgebreid dankzij de vervaardiging van bloempotten 'naar Engels fatsoen' waarvan er vorig jaar meer dan 60.000 aan de bloemisten zijn geleverd. Provincie en gemeente gaan akkoord.

Het voert te ver om de Arnhemse pottenbakkers tot aan het eind te volgen. Uit het voorgaande wordt al duidelijk dat ook Slee in deze tijd zich op andere producten gaat toeleggen, met name bloempotten voor de bloemisterijen, schoorsteenpotten en rioolbuizen - en dat geldt ook voor de anderen. Willem F. Slee is in 1889 overleden en zijn drie zonen hebben het bedrijf nog een aantal jaren voortgezet. Omstreeks 1900 is het verkocht aan de gebroeders Hillebrand, die zich vooral in de buizen hebben gespecialiseerd.

De familie Hasselman was al eerder gestopt, mede door een aantal sterfgevallen. De Goudse pottenbakker A. Husselson heeft het bedrijf nog tot de Tweede Wereldoorlog in stand gehouden.

Jan Willem Stuber werkte vanaf 1842 als zelfstandig pottenbakker, aanvankelijk met vijf zonen. Na hun overlijden is de pottenbakkerij nog voortgezet door J. van de Ende uit Gouda. Niet alleen aan de zuidoostkant van de stad waren in de 19e eeuw pottenbakkerijen gevestigd. Al sedert de middeleeuwen was aan de noordwestkant het Lauwerecht een bekende pottenbakkersbuurt. In 1800 zijn er nog twee bedrijven over, van de families Martens en Van Blaricum. Het zijn traditionele bedrijven met een lange levensduur die tegelijk aardewerkhandel zijn en een marktkraam hebben bij de Bakkerbrug. Ze werkten met 6 à 9 knechten en hebben alle denkbare genres in productie gehad dan wel verhandeld. De pottenbakkerijen werden respectievelijk in 1845 en 1858 gesloten na het overlijden van de laatste fabrikanten.

In 1824 is er in deze buurt, op het Hogenoord door de aannemer en koopman Hendrik Verburg nog een derde bedrijf gesticht dat vanaf 1832 door de hovenier H. van Dam en zijn opvolgers meer dan 100 jaar in werking is gehouden. De laatste producten waren vooral buizen en bloempotten.

Ten slotte had Utrecht nog enkele dakpannen- en tegelfabrieken en aan de Amsterdamsestraatweg de befaamde Utrechtse Terracottafabriek die zich toelegde op porseleinen kachels en bouw- en tuinornamenten. Alles bijeengenomen is Utrecht, evenals Deventer, in de 19e eeuw een belangrijke keramiekproducent.

Intermezzo - vijf verspreide initiatieven

De boven beschreven ontwikkelingen in Gelderland, Overijssel en Utrecht vormen een samenhangend geheel, met als rode draad de komst van pottenbakkers uit het Duitse grensgebied, die onder de vlag van Frankforter aardewerkfabrieken in Oost-Nederland en in aansluiting hierop in de stad Utrecht het pottenbakkersambacht hebben verrijkt.

Alvorens de centrale rol van Gouda te belichten bespreken we vijf andere initiatieven, verspreid over het land, die enigszins op zichzelf lijken te staan. In bijna alle gevallen bleek er echter, via de werknemers, toch een verbinding gelegd te kunnen worden met de eerder genoemde vestigingsplaatsen. Het betreft hier pottenbakkers die kennelijk op zoek gegaan zijn naar financiers op nieuwe lokaties. Het succes was, met uitzondering van Alkmaar, zeer kortstondig.

Rotterdam

In de Rotterdamsche Courant van 1-10-1801 wordt geadverteerd 'dat de Frankfortsche Pottebakkerij, gestaan hebbende op de Korte Kaay verplaatst is op de Schie en met alle vlijt wordt voortgezet. Adres bij Van Hanswijk, op de Schie.' Zo'n onverwacht bericht vraagt om nader onderzoek, met het volgende resultaat.

Wilhelmus Petrus van Hanswijk kwam in 1795 met zijn gezin vanuit 's-Hertogenbosch naar Rotterdam en stortte zich daar in een aantal zakelijke avonturen waaronder een glashandel en een negotie in koffie, thee, tabak en snuif. In 1800 koopt hij van de smid Lodewijk Weijtze en de metselaar Ary Ketting de pottenbakkerij aan de Korte Kade te Kralingen. De verkopers hadden dit onroerend goed in 1796 gekocht van Neeltje Leeflang en er was toen al sprake van een pottenbakkerij. Wie de stichter geweest is hebben we niet kunnen achterhalen. Op 9-11-1802 staat Van Hanswijk wederom in de krant. Zijn boedel is insolvent verklaard en alles moet worden verkocht.[34] Uit zijn dossier blijkt de recente aankoop van het landhuis 'Ons Genoegen' aan de westzijde van de Schiekade en van een aangrenzende klederblekerij, 'De Lindeboom' genaamd die nu tot pottenbakkerij is ingericht. De koper moest een grote partij ongebakken potten en gereedschappen overnemen. Van Hanswijk had veel en grote schulden, waaronder een obligatie van f.40.000,- daterend van 1780, schuldbrieven met betrekking tot bovengenoemde panden, openstaande rekeningen van allerlei ambachtslieden voor de verbouwingen en arbeidsloon voor zijn pottenbakkers: Anthony Telafiel, Paulus Happel en Christiaan Meynard. Over laatstgenoemde hebben we geen nadere informatie; Happel vervolgde zijn loopbaan in Gouda. En Telafiel? Over de herkomst en identiteit van deze meesterknecht tasten we vooralsnog in het duister, evenals over zijn bezigheden in de vier volgende jaren. Op 19-12-1806 wordt een zekere Pieter van 't Hoff toestemming verleend om een Frankfortse pottenbakkerij in te richten in een voormalige branderij, 'Het lange Bos' genaamd aan de Baan, tussen de Binnenwegse en Schiedamse poorten.[35] Een maand later kopen Van 't Hoff en Telafiel dit pand samen voor f.6.000,- en transformeren het tot een pottenbakkerij. Ook deze Rotterdamse onderneming bleek tot mislukken gedoemd, waarschijnlijk door te hoge kosten van het onroerend goed en de verbouwing. In oktober 1808 wordt Telafiel via krantenadvertenties opgeroepen bij het gerecht te verschijnen. Er is beslag gelegd op de pottenfabriek door de timmerman en de metselaar die de verbouwing hebben uitgevoerd. Waarschijnlijk is Telafiel met de noorderzon vertrokken. Er volgen nog nieuwe oproepen en in maart 1810 vindt bij verstek de executoriale verkoop plaats.

Van Hanswijk en Telafiel zijn niet meer dan een voetnoot in de keramische geschiedenis. Hun wederwaardigheden tonen echter wel aan dat in het prille begin van de 19e eeuw een Frankforter pottenfabriek als een bron van inkomsten werd gezien door zakenlieden van het type Van Hanswijk en dat het effectueren hiervan toch minder eenvoudig was. Ten slotte attendeert deze toevallige ontdekking ons op de mogelijkheid dat er ook elders pogingen ondernomen zijn. Vóór 1824 werden vergunningen - als die al vereist waren - op lokaal niveau afgehandeld, waardoor ze gemakkelijk aan de aandacht kunnen ontsnappen.

Dordrecht

In de nijverheidsenquête van 1808 wordt het bestaan van een Frankforter pottenfabriek in Dordrecht gemeld.

In het Dordtse Gemeentearchief is het rekest gevonden van Johan Jac. Schenau met het verzoek om toestemming voor het oprichten van 'een fabriek van Bovenlandsch aardewerk of zogenaamde Pottenfabriek waarin alle soorten van Venlo's of Frankforter aardewerk gefabriceerd of gebakken werden zoude'.[36] De formulering is interessant vanwege de aanduiding 'Venlo's' voor het populaire zwartgoed dat in deze periode aan het Frankforts wordt toegevoegd. Schenau kreeg toestemming maar het tegelijk aangevraagde octrooi werd hem geweigerd. De fabriek stond aan de Riedijk, buitendijks bij het Melkpoortje. Ruim een jaar na de oprichting is er een vreselijke storm en extra hoog water. Verontruste buren doen verslag van wat er zich toen afspeelde bij de pottenbakkerij. De deuren van de fabriek stonden open. De oven verkeerde in hevige gloed en alles zag zwart van de rook. Er ontstond een oploop omdat er brand vermoed werd en de knechten, die boven op zolder om hulp riepen en bevreesd waren dat de oven zou springen door het binnenkomende water moesten worden gered. Het stadsbestuur werd door omwonenden verzocht om maatregelen te treffen, hetgeen resulteerde in strengere bouwtechnische eisen. Daarna is er van de pottenbakkerij niets meer vernomen, waarschijnlijk is ze niet lang daarna beëindigd. Schenau, die van beroep broodbakker was, bleef in de buurt wonen tot aan zijn overlijden in 1847. Hij moet, zoals dat ook elders gebeurde, benaderd zijn door een of meer werkzoekende pottenbakkers om als geldschieter en initiatiefnemer op te treden. In het Dordtse archief konden we het personeel niet achterhalen, maar we vermoeden dat het de drie knechten zijn die omstreeks 1809 in Gorcum zijn neergestreken. Van Michiel Groh, afkomstig uit Koblenz, is bekend dat hij zich in dat jaar vanuit Dordrecht heeft gevestigd. Hij moet eerder ook in Arnhem hebben gewerkt; zijn zoon Louis is daar in 1805 geboren. Hendricus Franciscus Miessens zou uit Maastricht komen en is in 1834 in Gouda overleden. Van de derde man, Simon Burghardus Reiss, ook uit Koblenz, hebben we geen verdere sporen. Hun aanwezigheid in Gorcum zou kunnen betekenen dat ook hier enkele jaren Frankforter potten zijn gemaakt in het bedrijf van Dirk van Herwaarden, dat tot 1815 heeft gewerkt.[37]

Pottenbakkerij Charlotteburg van F.A. Hubert te Austerlitz

François Antoine Hubert, omstreeks 1781 in de Elzas geboren, verzeilde tijdens de Franse bezetting van Nederland als legerofficier in Zeist. Hij trouwde met een Nederlandse vrouw, kocht een huis en heidegrond in Austerlitz en bleef er ook na het vertrek van de Fransen in 1813 wonen. Hij poogde enerzijds door bebossing, anderzijds door ontginning van de heide het gebied te ontwikkelen en werkgelegenheid te creëren voor de straatarme dorpsbewoners.
In 1828 stichtte hij met datzelfde doel een pottenbakkerij. Er werden enige geschoolde krachten aangetrokken: Gerardus Staats, eerder mede-eigenaar van een Frankforter aardewerkfabriek in Gouda, Pieter Jansen uit Venlo en de uit Kassel afkomstige Frederik Ditmar Dirks. Staats, die in de archieven als pottenbakker en bezembinder wordt vermeld, kreeg waarschijnlijk na enige tijd ruzie met Hubert en vertrok naar Utrecht, waar hij bij Slee werkzaam was.
In 1832, vier jaar na de oprichting, brandde de pottenbakkerij tot de grond toe af; de oorzaak was brandstichting. Openlijk, ook in kranten, werd Staats hiervan beschuldigd, maar tot een rechtszaak kwam het niet. Hubert, die toch al zwaar teleurgesteld was door de geringe waardering die de dorpsbewoners hadden voor zijn zegenrijke initiatieven, verkocht zijn bezittingen en werd kaarsenmaker aan de Overtoom in Nieuwer Amstel.
De achtergrond van de drie pottenbakkers doet vermoeden dat de producten van het bedrijf een hoog Frankfort-gehalte hebben - en dat blijkt ook zo te zijn. Dankzij opgravingen door een AWN-werkgroep is een grote hoeveelheid scherven geborgen, overwegend ovenafval.[38] Een deel ervan is voorzien van een ingestempeld merk met de initialen FAH. (afb.18) Tot het Frankforter assortiment horen grote aantallen kookpotten met een vlakke bodem en lintoor, ongeglazuurde buitenkant en vaak, maar niet altijd, een zwarte bies onder de rand. (afb.19) Voorts veel donkerbruin geglazuurde kannen met een vlakke bodem en lintoor, en soms aan de binnenkant een gele engobe. (afb.20) Veel schotelfragmenten doen door hun decoratie Rijnlands of Hessisch aan; een gemerkte scherf maakt het zeker dat ze hier gemaakt zijn, als onderdeel van het Frankforter repertoire.

18 Het merk F.A.H. van F.A. Hubert te Austerlitz

Daartoe behoren niet de vele bloempotten en de ronde kommetjes op standring en met geknepen oor en een ringeloorslinger op de rand. De laatste lijken aan het Friese assortiment ontleend en ze komen voor met en zonder engobe aan de binnenzijde. De Frankforter kookpotten hebben een iets lichtere scherf dan de Friese kommetjes; wellicht is pijpaarde door de klei gemengd, of een andere kleisoort gebruikt.

19 Kookpannen met schenklip en bandoor; ovenafval, Austerlitz.

20 Theepot en kannen; ovenafval, Austerlitz.

Alkmaar

In Alkmaar, waar in de 16e en 17e eeuw een bloeiende pottenbakkersnijverheid geweest moet zijn, is het ambacht vermoedelijk al heel lang verdwenen wanneer in 1832 en 1834 twee nieuwe bedrijven worden gesticht. Ze lagen in elkaars onmiddellijke nabijheid op het Zeglis en beide initiatiefnemers waren logementhouder.

Johannes Kehl krijgt op 12-7-1832 vergunning voor de bouw van een oven voor een Frankforter aardewerkfabriek. Zijn - bijna - buurman Dirk Kueter wordt in januari 1834 evenmin tegengewerkt. In zijn geval hoefden de buren niet te worden gehoord want Kueter was tevens eigenaar van de belendende percelen. In 1841 meldt zich een derde aanvrager: Johan Dieterich Berger, die in zijn woning aan de Schelphoek een pottenbakkersoven wil plaatsen.[39]

Berger ontmoetten we al in Deventer, waar hij samen met de koopman Gerrit Jan Hamer als eerste het pottenbakkersambacht weer deed herleven. Niettemin werd Berger in 1832 door zijn werkgever ontslagen, waarna we hem uit het oog verloren. Mogelijk heeft hij, voordat hij zelfstandig werd, bij Kehl of Kueter gewerkt.

De drie bedrijfjes hebben enkele tientallen jaren bestaan en er werkte een bont gezelschap pottenbakkers.

Frans Gibbon en Jan Pieter Hakmes, allebei uit Gouda, zijn er overleden, evenals Derk Jansen uit Arnhem, allemaal op betrekkelijk jonge leeftijd; Willem Stroeken uit Kaldenkirchen is er getrouwd. Naast deze vakmensen van elders waren er ook lokale werknemers.

Het is onduidelijk hoe lang de bedrijven precies hebben bestaan. De gemeenteverslagen geven onvolledige informatie. Kueter is al in 1843 overleden, maar zijn weduwe hertrouwde met Willem Pommer, een pottenbakker uit Westfalen. Toen laatstgenoemde als weduwnaar in 1859 hertrouwde bestond het bedrijf nog. Berger is in 1852 overleden, Kehl in 1858.

Op de plek waar Berger zijn bedrijf uitoefende, de Schelphoek, is enkele jaren geleden pottenbakkersafval gevonden, dat een indruk geeft van het Alkmaarse fabrikaat.[40] Frankforter kookpannen (afb.21), Goudse kannen (afb.22), speelgoedkomfoortjes, een chocoladeketel en bordjes in Rijnlandse trant, dit alles in overeenstemming met de 'allerhande soorten van aardewerken' waarmee Berger in de Alkmaarse Courant van 4-3-1842 adverteerde ter gelegenheid van de opening van zijn nieuwe pottenbakkerij, genaamd De Hoop. Zijn levensgeschiedenis illustreert dat een pottenbakker soms een lange weg te gaan heeft voor hij zijn doel: een eigen bedrijf, heeft bereikt. Vrijwel alle Duitse pottenbakkers, die meestal als jonge man naar Nederland zijn gekomen vanuit Kaldenkirchen of Isselburg zijn er op enig moment in geslaagd om hun ideaal te verwezenlijken. Enkelen van hen moesten echter na enige tijd hun bedrijf weer opgeven, zoals de genoemde Stroeken die in Haarlem aan het Spaarne een pottenbakkerij had gedreven.

Workum

Workum, aan het eind van de 18e eeuw de Friese stad met de meeste pottenbakkerijen, verloor na 1800 snel aan betekenis. Wel bedrijfssluitingen, maar geen nieuwe initiatieven, vandaar dat de poging van de boekdrukker Hessel Brandenburgh en de bakker Geert Roukema om in 1837 een Frankforter aardewerkfabriek te stichten een opvallende gebeurtenis is.

21 Kookpannen en zwarte pannetjes; ovenafval van Berger, Alkmaar.

22 Donkerbruine kannen met aan de binnenzijde gele engobe; ovenafval van Berger, Alkmaar. r: h 19,5.

Brandenburgh en Roukema bouwden hun zogenaamde lange oven, die slechts 14 à 16 uur gestookt hoefde te worden, in een pand in de Nonnenstraat. Ze spraken van 'Venloosch en Frankforter aardewerk', pretendeerden in Friesland de enigen te zijn en bevalen speciaal hun keukengoed aan 'in de vorm van Brabandsche pannen als in dien van het bekende Berger aardewerk, dat uitmuntend tegen het vuur bestand is'.[41] Deze chaotische typering roept nogal wat vragen op maar past wel in het soms onduidelijke assortiment in de nadagen van de Frankforter pottenfabrieken. Als meesterknecht is naar alle waarschijnlijkheid Jacob Draaisma aangetrokken. Deze was in 1837 uit Kampen teruggekeerd, waar hij jaren in het gecombineerde Duits-Friese bedrijf van Schwartz ervaring had opgedaan. De Workumer onderneming moet niet aan de verwachtingen van de initiatiefnemers hebben voldaan en werd enkele jaren na de oprichting gesloten. In 1840 was ze een van de gedupeerden in het faillissement van de Groninger aardewerkkoopman H. Zervaas. Een bewaarde rekening toont een leverantie van 2100 worp geel aardewerk, acht vaatjes en vier opgelegde ketels, in totaal voor bijna f.300,-.[42]

Gouda, het onbetwiste centrum

Van de vier bovenregionale pottenbakkerscentra reageerde alleen Gouda actief op de Frankforter potten. In Bergen op Zoom bleef Jan Augustijn de enige, terwijl van Oosterhout geen blijken van deelname zijn gevonden - al moet niets worden uitgesloten. Van Friesland is alleen de late stichting in Workum in 1837 bekend, maar die had geen blijvend succes. Dorama in Leeuwarden heeft Frankforts gemaakt, vermoedelijk op bescheiden schaal.

Wat Gouda betreft zagen we hoe Johannes Gibbon, de met medailles vereerde pottenbakker, bij zijn octrooiaanvraag door het gilde werd tegengewerkt omdat ook anderen zich op deze markt zouden hebben begeven. We vermoeden dat zelfs de meeste fabrikanten in die tijd zich mede toegelegd hebben op het nieuwe product, zonder zich hierin te specialiseren. Quirijn Gibbon, de jongere broer van Johannes, verwierf bijvoorbeeld in 1808 in Utrecht op de eerste nationale nijverheidstentoonstelling de zilveren medaille voor zijn Frankforter potten. Een andere aanwijzing is de officiële prijslijst van 1805, samengesteld door de commissarissen van het pottenbakkersgilde, waarin het 'Potwerk volgens Frankforts maakzel' genoteerd staat voor een prijs van f.27:10:- per 100 worp.[43] Ook in de boedelinventaris van Trijntje Braams, de weduwe van Jan van Bentum, die een pottenbakkerij aan de Raam dreef, worden in 1811 naast koppen en testen, loodwitpotten en schotels 1060 worp Frankforter pannen vermeld.[44]

Naast deze bedrijven, die een lange historie hebben, zijn er in Gouda nieuwe, zich Frankforter aardewerkfabriek noemende pottenbakkerijen opgericht met een wisselende levensduur. De befaamde pottenbakkerij van Johannes Gibbon is nog tot 1844 voortgezet door een reeks van nieuwe eigenaren met als laatste Jan van de Wepel, van huis uit scheepsmeter.

We noemen enkele andere pottenbakkerijen die een prominente rol in dit gebeuren hebben gespeeld. In 1820 werd door enkele zakenlieden op de Raam een nieuwe fabriek gesticht, die, twee verkopingen verder, in 1828 in handen kwam van Johannes Faessen, die er tot zijn overlijden in 1845 een succes van maakte.

Faessen, afkomstig uit Tegelen, dat beroemd was om zijn zwarte aardewerk, werkte in Gouda met 14 knechts en samen met zijn broer Lambertus, die vanuit Amsterdam opereerde, was hij ook koopman. In de uitgebreide boedelinventaris, opgemaakt na zijn overlijden, treffen we tal van voorwerpen uit het Frankforter repertoire: tulbandpannen met deksels, kaakjes-, hazen- en broedertjespannen en allerlei kookpannetjes en ketels.[45] Daarnaast ook het 'Hollandse' goed: komforen, testen, spaarvarkens, waterpotten, doofpotten, melktesten, duikerpotten en nog veel meer, waaruit blijkt dat Faessen van alle markten thuis was. Noch deze pottenbakkerij, noch die van Van de Wepel werd voortgezet en hiermee kwam een einde aan de twee grootste gespecialiseerde bedrijven.

Enkele kleinere ondernemingen waren al eerder gestopt. De zoon van de Arnhemse pottenbakker Frans Slee, die tussen 1825 en 1830 een Frankforter aardewerkfabriek aan het Lange Groenendaal had, verhuisde naar Utrecht en begon daar in 1831 opnieuw. Theodor Jansen, een pottenbakker uit Kaldenkirchen, die al vanaf 1817 in Gouda verbleef, beëindigde omstreeks 1841 zijn fabriek, gelegen aan de Turfsingel, waarvoor hij in 1827 toestemming had gekregen. De laatste officiële aanvraag, gevonden in het archief van Gedeputeerde Staten, die sedert 1824 deze vergunningen regelden, is van Adrianus Hornius en dateert van 1828.[46] Zijn bedrijf heeft overigens maar kort bestaan.

De economische bedrijvigheid rond de Frankforter potten bracht ook met zich mee dat tal van pottenbakkers, vooral afkomstig uit Oost-Nederland en de Duitse grensstreek, voor kortere of langere tijd in Gouda werk vonden. We noemden al Frans en Willem Frederik Slee, Carolus L. Taminiau en Johannes F. Andree.

Verder treffen we Christiaan Leutziewer uit Kellinghausen, die in 1809 bij Van Tellingen in Arnhem werkte, Leonard Glasmachers en Willem Stroeken uit Kaldenkirchen, Willem Berger uit Isselburg, Johan Welling uit Doesburg en vele anderen. Het centraal gelegen Gouda, met andere woorden, was een aantrekkelijke arbeidsmarkt en bovendien een goede leerschool voor pottenbakkers die we elders als zelfstandig ondernemer terugvinden. Het verdwijnen van de gespecialiseerde aardewerkfabrieken betekende overigens allerminst dat het aardewerk zelf uit de gratie was.

De ontvankelijkheid van Gouda voor het opnemen van de Frankforter potten in het eigen repertoire zodat het een onderdeel werd van de Goudse identiteit heeft te maken met de aparte positie van Gouda als pottenbakkerscentrum. Gouda had vanaf de 17e eeuw een vrij groot aantal pottenbakkers, die niet alleen aardewerk produceerden, maar ook in hun ovens de pijpen bakten die door de honderden Goudse pijpenmakers werden vervaardigd. Dit laatste was eigenlijk de basis van hun bestaan en de aardewerkproductie per bedrijf was dan ook veel geringer dan elders. De hoeveelheid was afhankelijk van de ruimte die er in de oven overbleef wanneer de aangeleverde potten met pijpen geplaatst waren.

De indruk bestaat dat het Goudse aardewerk niet zo'n duidelijke identiteit had als het Friese en Brabantse, en een kleiner assortiment. In inventarissen van pottenbakkers wordt vaak geel en groen aardewerk genoemd - wellicht een specialiteit, die te verklaren is uit de ruime aanwezigheid van pijpaarde in de stad. In de loop van de 19e eeuw deed zich in de pijpennijverheid een zekere concentratie en schaalvergroting voor, en enkele pijpenmakers kochten een of meer pottenbakkerijen op. Dat diende een dubbel doel: productdiversificatie, zodat schommelingen in de afzet van pijpen konden worden opgevangen, en zeggenschap over de benodigde ovencapaciteit, zonder van anderen afhankelijk te zijn.

Zo ontstonden enkele ondernemingen van een nieuw type, clusters van bedrijven waar pijpen, aardewerk, tegels en soms ook branchevreemde artikelen als textiel werden vervaardigd. De pottenbakkerijen hadden deel aan de schaalvergroting.

Van twee van deze bedrijven, Prince en Goedewaagen, hebben we inzicht in de voorraden aardewerk in de jaren 60 van de 19e eeuw. Daaruit blijkt dat die voor resp. 60 en 90% bestonden uit Frankforter aardewerk.[47] Helaas ontbreekt iedere specificatie.[48] Nieuwe aanknopingspunten zijn er in de 20e eeuw. Catalogi van de firma's Goedewaagen uit 1919 en Jonker uit 1936 tonen dat, wanneer we het aanbod vergelijken met de bodemvondsten van kort na 1800, het Frankforts nog springlevend is - al wordt die naam nergens meer genoemd. In het hoofdstuk over het aardewerk komen we daarop terug.

Het aardewerk nader beschouwd

Wanneer we archivalische berichten over import en namaak voegen bij de bodemvondsten ontstaat een conglomeraat van voorwerpen dat te enigertijd als 'Frankforter aardewerk' is benoemd. Ze hebben iets gemeen: ze komen voort uit een andere pottenbakkerstraditie dan de Nederlandse, soms door hun materiaalgebruik, soms door hun decoratie, altijd door hun vormgeving.

We onderscheiden een zevental groepen voorwerpen en in tabel 1 wordt weergegeven van welke rubrieken materiaal is aangetroffen in het ovenafval van zeven bedrijven die Frankforter aardewerk hebben nagemaakt.

Daaraan toegevoegd zijn enkele gemerkte stukken, met name van Arnhem en Delft, die elders gevonden zijn en met een * zijn aangemerkt.

a. Kookpannen

De kookpannen, van buiten ongeglazuurd met een geschilderde zwarte bies onder de rand en een of twee lintoren komen zo vaak voor en zijn zo gemakkelijk herkenbaar dat ze in hoge mate representatief zijn voor 'Frankforter potten'. Uit de afvalvondsten kennen we drie typen:
- met twee lintoren
- met een lintoor en een schenklip dwars op de tuit
- met een ronde steel en een schenklip dwars op de steel.

In de lijst met typen geïmporteerd Frankforter aardewerk die in 1771 door de Admiraliteit is opgesteld komen ze voor met en zonder poten. Hoe herkennen we de echte, geïmporteerde kookpannen? Onze zegslieden in de regio Frankfort zijn zeer resoluut: het type pan komt daar veel voor, zelfs met poten, maar als er sprake is van één oor staat de schenklip tegenover het oor en niet dwars erop. Dat type komt in de afvalvondsten niet voor en is in Nederland vrij zeldzaam; afb.23 toont drie voorbeelden waarvan één met poten. Ze wijken niet alleen af door de anders geplaatste schenklip maar ook door het oor, dat dicht bij de wand blijft, en het ontbreken van een rand aan de binnenzijde waar een deksel op kan rusten; wellicht zijn deze geïmporteerd.

Op afb.24 een pan met steel en een met één oor; beide hebben een dwarse schenklip en zijn geschikt voor het dragen van een deksel. Het oor van de rechter pan lijkt echter nog veel op dat van de pannen van de vorige afbeelding. Vroege namaak? Het type dat in de afvalvondsten voorkomt en tot in de 20e eeuw gangbaar is heeft een oor dat vanaf de rand eerst horizontaal loopt en dan naar beneden afbuigt, zoals op afb.25. De gebruikte klei is witbakkend of gemengd, later ook wel roodbakkend; de glazuur geel, bruingeel tot lichtrood.

In de genoemde catalogi van de Goudse aardewerkfabrikanten Jonker (1936) en Goedewaagen (1919) worden deze pannen nog vermeld onder de naam kaaspan. (afb.26,27) De grootste exemplaren met twee oren hebben een inhoud van meer dan 20 liter en zijn niet geschikt om in te koken; wellicht werden ze bij de kaasbereiding gebruikt, of als voorraadpot.

Al in de 19e eeuw zijn er varianten ontstaan met één oor en schenklip, binnen en buiten geglazuurd en voorzien van een deksel, van witbakkende of roodbakkende klei, met groene, donkerbruine of roodbruine glazuur. Goedewaagen vermeldt ze als 'dekselpannen'. (afb.28) Het type was zo populair dat het lange tijd ook in email is gemaakt. (afb.29)

b. Bak- en braadgerei

Bak- en braadgerei wordt bij inzendingen naar tentoonstellingen vaak genoemd en het moet de Nederlandse consument iets nieuws geboden hebben, naast het bestaande aanbod in aardewerk, koper en blik.

Vaak genoemd en tot in de 20e eeuw in Nederland in productie, o.m. door Goedewaagen, is de tulband, in een gipsen mal gemaakt, met een eigenaardig overhellend deksel dat van boven ongeglazuurd is en voorzien van zwarte geschilderde biezen en een ringvormige knop. (afb.30) Beweerd wordt dat op de deksel in de oven gloeiende kolen konden

	Bergen op Zoom	Deventer	Zutphen	Winterswijk	Alkmaar	Austerlitz	Arnhem	Delft
a. kookpannen	x	x	x	x	x	x	x*	x*
b. bakvormen	x			x				x*
c. borden en schotels	x		x	x	x	x		
d. kannen	x			x	x	x		
e. zwarte pannetjes	x		x	x	x			
f. zwart theegoed	x	x	x	x	x	x		x
g. overig zwart	x		x		x			

Tabel 1 – Ovenafval en gemerkte stukken naar rubriek
In de volgende paragrafen wordt de verscheidenheid aan voorwerpen nader uitgewerkt, waar mogelijk een vormontwikkeling daarin aangegeven en worden hypothesen geformuleerd met betrekking tot de herkomst. We refereren daarbij niet alleen aan de bovengenoemde afvalvondsten maar ook aan openbare verzamelingen, onze eigen collectie en vermeldingen in de archeologische literatuur.

23 Drie kookpannen met ongeglazuurde buitenzijde en zwarte bies, een lintoor dat dicht bij de wand blijft en een schenklip tegenover het oor. Mogelijk importwaar. h 9,4, d 17,4; h 13, d 13; h 8,2, d 14,5.

24 Twee kookpannen resp. met steel en lintoor, de schenklip dwars daarop; het oor lijkt op dat van afb.23. Waarschijnlijk in Nederland gemaakt. h 9,3, d 19; h 10,2, d 18,5.

25 Drie kookpannen met een lintoor dat eerst horizontaal loopt; het in Nederland gebruikelijke type. h 11,2, d 17,3; h 8, d 10,8; h 12,3, d 16,8.

26 Kaaspannen, zoals vermeld in de catalogus van Jonker uit 1936.

27 Kaaspannen met een en twee oren, en een variant zonder oren. h 18,5, d 28; h 14,2, d 20; h 19, d 27.

Dekselpannen.
Kleur: *lichtbruin.*

No. 4 hoogte tot rand ± 14 cM., inhoud ± 1³/₄ Lt.
" 5   "   "   " 13 "   "   " 1¹/₄ "
" 6   "   "   " 11 "   "   " ³/₄ "
" 8   "   "   " 9   "   "   " ¹/₂ "

Kartelpannetje zonder deksel.
Kleur: *donkerbruin.*

No. 6 hoogte ± 12 cM.. inhoud ± 1¹/₄ Liter.
" 8   "   " 11 "   "   " ³/₄ "
" 10   "   " 9 "   "   " ¹/₂ "

28 geheel geglazuurde pannen met schenklip en lintoor. Onder: het kartelpannetje, de moderne variant van het zwarte pannetje. Catalogus Goedewaagen, 1919.

29 Geheel geglazuurde pannen met lintoor en schenklip en een daarop geïnspireerde uitvoering in email. h 14,2, d 20; h 8, d 11,5; h 11,4, d 15; h 7,5, d 12,7.

30 Tulband met deksel. h 10, d 17; deksel d 31,3.

worden gelegd; wellicht zijn met 'vuurdeksels', die in een van de inventarissen genoemd worden, deze deksels bedoeld. Tulbandfragmenten zijn alleen in Bergen op Zoom gevonden; het model is gangbaar in de regio Frankfort.
Of vóór de komst van de Frankforter potten hier al tulbanden van dit type werden gemaakt is ons niet bekend. De Friese tulbanden komen uit een heel andere traditie: ze hebben geen deksels en zijn op de schijf gedraaid.
Hazenpannen komen regelmatig in één of enkele stuks voor in inventarissen en inzendingen naar tentoonstellingen. We kennen geen bodemvondsten en slechts één bewaard exemplaar. (afb.31) Ander bak- en braadgerei vinden we onder de namen broedertjespannen, zusterpannen, Poolse mutsen en spitpannen. Het is helaas niet duidelijk wat ermee bedoeld is. Wel vertrouwd zijn de poffertjes- en evenveeltjespannen die heel lang o.a. in Gouda gemaakt zijn, gevormd in een mal, al dan niet met poten, soms met oren, meestal met een ronde steel. Net als de tulbanden zijn ze gemaakt van witbakkende of gemengde klei. (afb.32) De gemerkte evenveeltjespan van Pieter van der Aa uit Delft doet door zijn decoratie vermoeden dat hier Frechens aardewerk de inspiratiebron is geweest(afb. 2).

c. Borden en schotels

In tal van afvalvondsten komen borden en schotels voor. Die van Winterswijk tonen invloeden uit Ochtrup, die uit Alkmaar, Zutphen en Austerlitz lijken vooral door Nederrijnse en Rijnlandse voorbeelden geïnspireerd.
Alleen de decors uit Bergen op Zoom zijn duidelijk verwant met wat er in die tijd in de regio Frankfort is gemaakt; dat

31 Hazenpan; Museum De Koperen Knop, Hardinxveld-Giessendam.

geldt ook voor de aan Bergen op Zoom toegeschreven tabakspot. (afb. 11)
Het is vooralsnog bijzonder moeilijk om in Nederland door Frankforter pottenbakkerijen gemaakt schotelgoed te onderscheiden van importgoed en van dat van Limburgse centra als Gennep.

d. Kannen

Traditionele Nederlandse kannen, waar ook gemaakt, hebben als regel een rond of geknepen oor en een standring. Daar kwam tegen het eind van de 18e eeuw verandering in; er ontstond een nieuw type, met een lintoor en vlakke voet. Het wordt in enkele afvalvondsten aangetroffen, maar in verschillende gedaanten. In Bergen op Zoom zijn het kleine gele kannetjes van witbakkende klei, van teksten en decoraties voorzien. In Winterswijk en Austerlitz zijn het forsere, donkerbruine, vrij grove kannen van roodbakkende klei met soms een gele engobe aan de binnenzijde. Het ziet er naar uit dat hieruit de bekende Goudse kan ontstaan is, waarvan de roodbruine, donkerbruine, gele, groene en zelfs blauwe versies in talloze maten tot na de Tweede Wereldoorlog gemaakt zijn. Of de regio Frankfort als herkomstgebied van dit nieuwe type beschouwd moet worden is de vraag; we kennen geen kan uit dat gebied die duidelijk model gestaan heeft, hoewel de lijst van de Admiraliteit uit 1771 kannen vermeldt. Andere, dichterbij gelegen Duitse centra kunnen een rol gespeeld hebben - en wellicht betreft het een Nederlandse vinding. (afb.33)
In dezelfde periode ontstaat ook een nieuw type po: niet meer met een geknepen of rond oor en een standring, maar met een lintoor en een vlakke voet. Hetzelfde geldt voor de zevenorenpot, een bijzondere verschijningsvorm van de po. Alleen in Friesland handhaaft de oorspronkelijke vorm zich lange tijd. Er zijn geen aanwijzingen dat er ooit Frankforter po's zijn geïmporteerd; wel zal dit nieuwe type, dat dominant werd in Nederland, in de Frankforter pottenbakkerijen zijn ontstaan.

e. Zwarte pannetjes

Een noviteit die door de Frankforter aardewerkfabrieken is geïntroduceerd is een donkerbruin of zwart geglazuurd pannetje met een vlakke bodem, een smal lintoor en dwars daarop een schenklip. Ook in schervenvondsten is dit pannetje direct herkenbaar door de eigenaardige ooraanzet, zie afb.34. In plaats van een oor hebben ze soms een lange, geribbelde steel. De pannetjes komen in vondstcomplexen vanaf het eind van de 18e eeuw vaak voor. In de regio Frankfort zijn ze volstrekt onbekend, dus waar komen ze dan wel vandaan? In de Duitse literatuur worden ze af en toe vermeld, zoals door Hackspiel en Segschneider.[49] We vermoeden daarom dat de zwarte pannetjes van Nederrijnse, of noordelijker oorsprong zijn.
In Nederland zijn ze lang gemaakt. In de catalogus van Goedewaagen komen ze voor als 'kartelpannetjes'; nog steeds donkerbruin, met smal lintoor en schenklip, en onder de rand de radstempelversiering waaraan ze hun naam ontlenen. (afb.28,35)

f. Theegoed

Elders hebben wij uiteengezet welke invloed er is uitgegaan van het Engelse, vooral in Staffordshire gemaakte zwarte aardewerk

32 Twee poffertjespannen en twee evenveeltjespannen. d 18,5; d 23; d 32,5; d 10,5.

33 Kan, po en zevenorenpot, alle drie met linto(o)r(en) en vlakke voet. h 15,5, d 21; h 26, d 16,5; h 14,5, d 22,5.

uit de 18e eeuw.⁵⁰ Het werd overal in Europa geïmporteerd en op tal van plaatsen nagemaakt, door faiencefabrieken en door pottenbakkers. Koffie- en theegoed was de kern van het assortiment. Na België en Duitsland werd ook in Nederland het zwartgoed nagemaakt, in Tegelen bijvoorbeeld, en door de Frankforter pottenbakkers. Dat gebeurde overigens pas na 1800, en niet in de beginperiode. Zowel Augustijn in Bergen op Zoom als Van Tellingen in Arnhem stortte zich hierop en op tal van plaatsen zijn theepotjes gevonden. Augustijn heeft getracht een door en door zwarte scherf te verkrijgen en zo het Engelse origineel te benaderen. Naarmate de tijd verstreek zijn er steeds meer roodbruin geglazuurde theepotten gemaakt. (afb.36)

g. Overig zwartgoed

Uit inzendingen naar tentoonstellingen zoals die van Augustijn uit 1808 blijkt dat er, naast het theegoed, een heel repertoire ontwikkeld werd van zwarte voorwerpen die soms op Engelse voorbeelden teruggrepen, zoals strooiers, terrines en sauskommen. Een typisch product van een Frankforter pottenbakker, dat noch met Frankfort, noch met Engeland iets te maken heeft en is ontsproten aan de creatieve geest van Augustijn of een van zijn collega's is het pijpenkomfoor van afb.34, voorzien van de geribbelde steel van de zwarte pannetjes. Augustijns inzending vermeldt een pijpenkomfoor, maar ook tal van zwarte voorwerpen die we tot dusver niet kennen.

Het repertoire van de Frankforter pottenbakkers overziende komen we tot enkele conclusies:
- Van het assortiment van de Frankforter pottenbakkers is slechts een deel geïnspireerd op uit de regio Frankfort afkomstige voorbeelden. Dat geldt voor de kookpannen en de tulbandsvormen, die tot na 1900 in meer of minder aangepaste vorm zijn nagemaakt. De invloed van het schotelgoed was kortstondiger; wellicht is de markt weer door Rijnlandse en Nederrijnse centra overgenomen. Onduidelijk is de betekenis van Frankfort voor de introductie van kannen met een vlakke voet en een lintoor.
- De regio Frankfort mag dan wel naamgever zijn van het genre, het is nauwelijks gelukt om voorwerpen aan te wijzen die daar gemaakt zijn en in Nederland ingevoerd. Alleen enkele kookpannen komen daar wellicht voor in aanmerking.
- De Frankforter aardewerkfabrieken hebben enkele modellen geïntroduceerd, geënt op voorbeelden uit verschillende windstreken, die tot het eind van de aardewerkproductie in Nederland populair zijn gebleven:
  - kookpannan, later kaaspannen en dekselpannen genoemd
  - tulbanden, poffertjes- en evenveeltjespannen
  - zwarte pannetjes, later kartelpannetjes genoemd
  - theepotjes
  - kannen met vlakke voet en schenklip.

Evaluatie van een marktverstoring - het effect van de Frankforter potten

Toen aan het eind van de jaren 60 van de 18e eeuw de import van aardewerk uit de omgeving van Frankfort omvangrijker werd moet deze in hoofdzaak hebben bestaan uit kookpannen,

34 Zwarte pannetjes met schenklip en smal bandoor of geribbelde steel en een pijpenkomfoor met geribbelde steel. h 7, d 11,5; h 6,3, d 9,7; h 7,7, d 12,7; h 4,6, d.7.

35 Twee kartelpannetjes, de moderne vorm van de zwarte pannetjes; onder de rand een radstempelversiering. h 10,5, d 13; h 8,7, d 12.

daarnaast uit bak- en braadgerei, schotelgoed en kannen. De pottenbakkers uit Bergen op Zoom en Oosterhout voorspelden in hun rekesten aan diverse overheden de ondergang van hun bedrijfstak tenzij door middel van een draconische belastingheffing aan dit marktbederf een einde zou worden gemaakt. De heffing kwam, was niet zo erg effectief, maar bleef tot na 1815 van kracht. Het is echter de vraag of de importstroom wel zo lang geduurd heeft. Veel archivalische sporen hebben we er, afgezien van de beginperiode, niet van kunnen vinden en ook archeologische sporen zijn schaars, al kan een nadere beschouwing van vondsten uit de periode 1760-1800 tot nieuwe inzichten leiden.

Het belangrijkste en duurzame effect van de import van Frankforter potten was de namaak ervan, en we zijn er van overtuigd dat veruit de meeste vondsten van Frankforter aardewerk imitaties betreffen die in Nederland zijn gemaakt. Onderzoek in de herkomstgebieden, niet alleen in de buurt van Frankfort, kan nadere informatie opleveren. Onder de Frankforter paraplu werden ook modellen van elders verzameld, die trouwens in de loop der tijd ook weer aanpassingen ondergingen.

De Oosterhoutse en Bergse pottenbakkers zijn niet ten onder gegaan. Wel hebben ze voorgoed een deel van hun markt voor kookgerei moeten prijsgeven. Het meest geprofiteerd hebben Gelderland en Overijssel, waar zich na 1800 weer pottenbakkers vestigden, en vooral Gouda.

Voor een aantal terreinen brengen we kort de effecten van de Frankforter potten in kaart: voor de consument, voor de producent en voor de arbeidsmarkt. We eindigen met enkele suggesties voor nader onderzoek.

Effecten voor de consument

In aanprijzingen van de geïmporteerde Frankforter potten wordt vooral het kookgerei genoemd en het wordt aanbevolen omdat het sterk is, niet barst, geen vet doorlaat en slechts

36 Diverse theepotten. h 19; h 11,5; h 19; h 10.

weinig vuur behoeft. De nadruk op sterkte was nodig, want deze pannen waren veel lichter en dunner dan de robuuste en loodzware Brabantse pannen, en dat zal aanvankelijk enig wantrouwen hebben gewekt. De gemakkelijke hanteerbaarheid moet een voordeel zijn geweest, terwijl de vlakke bodem bij uitstek geschikt was om te koken op een kachel of fornuis. Het kookgerei zal een moderne uitstraling hebben gehad. Of het goedkoper was dan het Brabantse is moeilijk na te gaan. We kennen wel de worpprijs, maar weten niet hoeveel potten van een bepaalde maat er in een worp gingen.

Wat het assortiment betreft is de conclusie dat de Frankforter pottenbakkers in Nederland een aantal modellen hebben geïntroduceerd die uiterst succesvol waren en tot het einde van de productie van gebruiksaardewerk populair zijn gebleven.

Effecten voor de producent

De gespecialiseerde Frankforter pottenbakkerijen werden indertijd wel aangeduid als 'oeconomische aardewerkfabrieken', en dat betekent dat ze, althans door sommige waarnemers, werden beschouwd als efficiënter en moderner dan de traditionele bedrijven. Dat 'oeconomische' karakter had betrekking op een aantal aspecten.

Enkele bedrijven introduceerden een in ons land - afgezien van Limburg - ongebruikelijk type oven, de lange oven. Dit is een liggende oven, waarbij de ruimte waarin het te bakken aardewerk geplaatst is zich niet boven maar achter het vuur bevindt. Ongetwijfeld hebben Duitse en Limburgse pottenbakkers hier de hand in gehad. Als voordeel van de lange oven werd genoemd: kortere stooktijd en mede daardoor een geringer brandstofgebruik. Door de kortere stooktijd, in Workum ging men uit van 14 tot 16 uur, hoefde er 's nachts niet te worden gestookt, waardoor er minder personeel nodig was en de overlast voor de omgeving beperkt bleef.

Een belangrijke besparing werd bereikt doordat de kookpannen, het hoofdproduct, een vlakke bodem hadden. Er was niet langer een specialist, de handelaar of hannever, nodig om een standring of poten aan te zetten; de draaier kon de stukken zelf afwerken. Het valt ook op dat er op het totale aantal werknemers meer schijven aanwezig zijn dan in een traditionele pottenbakkerij. Ook het ongeglazuurd laten van de buitenkant van de kookpotten heeft ongetwijfeld enige besparing opgeleverd. .
De lange ovens zijn na enkele decennia verdwenen, tegelijk met de gespecialiseerde bedrijven. Het is de vraag of ze de besparingen hebben opgeleverd die er van werden verwacht.

Al in een vroeg stadium was duidelijk dat, wilde men in Nederland de kwaliteit van het importaardewerk evenaren, als grondstof een andere kleisoort dan de gebruikelijke vereist was. Van der Aa haalde daarom klei uit Mainz en Augustijn gebruikte deels Bergse klei, maar niet de soort waar de pottenbakkers gewoonlijk mee werkten. Inzenders voor de prijsvragen van de Maatschappij werd gevraagd om uitsluitend Nederlandse aarde te gebruiken, waaraan Augustijn, Gibbon en Van Tellingen naar eigen zeggen uiteindelijk ook hebben voldaan. Anderen bleven een mengsel van Nederlandse en importklei gebruiken, de laatste bijvoorbeeld uit het Westerwald of Oost-Friesland. Hoe taai deze gewoonte was blijkt uit het feit dat tot in de 20e eeuw in Gouda kaaspannen, tulbanden en poffertjespannen werden gemaakt van een mengsel van rood- en witbakkende aarde.

Effecten voor de arbeidsmarkt

De opmars van de (namaak van de) Frankforter potten ging gelijk op met de intocht van Duitse pottenbakkers. Wat was oorzaak, wat gevolg?

De eerste initiatieven om Frankforter potten na te maken werden genomen door Nederlanders, die veelal de aardewerkbranche goed kenden. Enkelen haalden werknemers uit Oberroden en omgeving, zoals Teunis van Tellingen de gebroeders Slee en Jan van der Aa Franz Weber. Ook Johannes Gibbon meldt dat hij een Duitse knecht in dienst heeft genomen.

Groot zal het aantal 'echte' Frankforters niet geweest zijn, maar zij hebben in de pionierstijd een belangrijke rol gespeeld. Ze zijn waarschijnlijk door hun werkgevers actief geworven, mogelijk via schippers, en niet op de bonnefooi naar Nederland getrokken.

Iets later kwamen er grotere aantallen vaklieden de grens over, nu wel op goed geluk, of via bekenden die al eerder vertrokken. Enkelen kwamen uit het Westerwald via de handel in steengoed in Nederland terecht en vonden werk bij een pottenbakker. Anderen, zoals de bekende familie Andree, waren uit een van de Nederrijnse centra afkomstig. Opvallend is de rol die vrijwel onbekende pottenbakkerscentra als Isselburg en Kaldenkirchen - met het aangrenzende en veel bekendere Tegelen - bij de emigratie gespeeld hebben. Daarnaast zijn er nog enkele dorpen en stadjes, zoals Bocholt, van waaruit mensen naar Nederland trokken.

De migranten blijken twee kenmerken gemeen te hebben. In de eerste plaats zijn ze jong en ongehuwd. Ze trouwen met Nederlandse vrouwen en keren vrijwel nooit naar hun geboorteland terug. Ze passen zich in alle opzichten aan hun nieuwe vaderland aan.

Een tweede kenmerk is hun ambitie om een eigen bedrijf te hebben, en de meesten is dat na korte of lange tijd ook gelukt, zij het niet altijd blijvend. Dat betekent jaren lang als knecht werken en sparen, of een medefirmant annex geldschieter vinden die bereid is te investeren in een pottenbakkerij. De hoop op een positie als zelfstandig ondernemer zal zeker tot migratie van goede vaklieden hebben geleid.

Samenvattend: het ziet er naar uit dat de importeurs van Frankforter aardewerk en de eersten die het namaakten een markt hebben opengelegd voor dit nieuwe product, waardoor een vraag ontstond naar geschoolde pottenbakkers met een niet-Nederlandse achtergrond. Duitse pottenbakkers grepen die kans en hun ondernemingsgeest leidde ertoe dat in een aantal gebieden waar de pottenbakkersnijverheid in de loop van de 18e eeuw verloren was gegaan, met name in Oost-Nederland, nieuwe bedrijven zijn gevestigd. Halverwege de 19e eeuw konden de Nederlandse pottenbakkerscentra zelf in de vraag naar arbeidskrachten voorzien en hield de migratie op.

Suggesties voor nader onderzoek

Archiefonderzoek in de regio Frankfort, met name in Oberroden, Urberach, Dieburg en Eppertshausen, moet uitwijzen wat de achtergronden zijn geweest van de plotseling toegenomen export van aardewerk naar Nederland, hoe lang die duurde, via welke schakels die verliep en wat er precies werd uitgevoerd.

Evaluatie van aldaar reeds verricht archeologisch onderzoek kan een en ander ondersteunen.

Evaluatie van eerder verricht archeologisch onderzoek in het Duitse grensgebied kan uitsluitsel geven over andere invloeden op het in Nederland gemaakte Frankforter aardewerk.

In Nederland moet bij onderzoek naar vondstcomplexen uit de periode 1760-1850 - en bij hernieuwd onderzoek naar oudere vondsten - beter gelet worden op het Frankforter aardewerk, zodat het importaandeel kan worden geïdentificeerd en de verscheidenheid van het hier vervaardigde aandeel kan worden vastgesteld. Van de in inventarissen en inzendingen naar tentoonstellingen genoemde voorwerpen is immers nog maar een fractie bekend. Afvalvondsten van pottenbakkerijen verdienen daarbij bijzondere aandacht.

Verblijfplaats van de afgebeelde stukken

Nederlands Openluchtmuseum, Arnhem: 2.
Rijssens Museum, Rijssen: 3.
Regionaal Historisch Centrum, Bergen op Zoom: 4-10.
Adri van der Meulen en Paul Smeele, Rotterdam: 11, 23-25, 27, 29-36.
Afdeling Archeologie, Gemeente Zutphen: 12-14
Museum Freriks, Winterswijk: 15-17.
Archeologisch Depot Provincie Utrecht: 18-20.
Bureau Monumentenzorg- Archeologie Alkmaar: 21, 22.

'Frankfurt Pots', summary

Around 1750, Dutch households were supplied with their everyday crockery by four major pottery production centres. This concentration had evolved in the preceding century and had occurred mostly at the expense of potteries within the cities. The four centres, Friesland, Gouda, Bergen op Zoom and Oosterhout, together numbered a good 100 firms; apart from these there were a few dozen others, scattered around the country. Friesland and Gouda specialised in pottery for food preparation and serving and for holding live coals. In West-Brabant (Bergen-op-Zoom, Oosterhout) the emphasis lay on fireproof cooking pots and ovenware and implements for the dairy industry.

When around 1760 the country was suddenly flooded with large amounts of imported pottery from the Frankfurt region, panic arose among the Dutch potters, especially those in Brabant. The 'Frankfurt pots', largely modern kitchenware for cooking, frying and roasting, threatened their market position in particular. The attractions of Frankfurt ware were its favourable pricing, ease of handling due to its light weight, and its suitability for use on modern stoves because of the flat bases (figs 23-25). What would be the best strategy to head off this competition? The hefty import levy was dodged on such a massive scale as to be ineffective; but imitating the imported ware soon proved successful. The first initiatives along these lines were encouraged by the 'Oeconomic Branch' of the Hollandsche Maatschappij van Wetenschappen, established in Haarlem in 1777. To stimulate trade and industry, it would organise competitions, among others to imitate Frankfurt ware, offering rewards in the form of prize money and medals. Special Frankfurt-ware factories were founded in Arnhem, Delft, Bergen op Zoom and Gouda, and in these early days some workers were brought in from the Frankfurt region. This article starts by surveying the state of affairs regarding these new pottery firms and their many emulators across the country (fig. 1). It then presents lists of items that were produced, compiled from various archival sources. By no means all forms can be illustrated with surviving examples. The Frankfurt pots were a boon not only to the consumer. They were attractive to the producers as well, once the suitable raw materials could be obtained in the Netherlands or abroad. Flat-based kitchen ware could be finished by the thrower himself, so the skilled worker who attached the handles and feet could be dispensed with. Also experiments were made with a new kiln type, the horizontal kiln, which allowed a shorter firing and used less fuel.

Up to 1840, the Netherlands saw the establishment of specialised firms calling themselves 'Frankfurt potteries', which soon also took to making other imitations, such as 'black tea ware' after English examples, and Lower Rhineland platters. By no means all initiatives were successful; some failed to take off altogether, while others closed down after just a few years. Nonetheless, the new products profoundly and permanently influenced Dutch pottery production, particularly at Gouda. Here many new firms were started up to 1830, and when these disappeared, major producers such as Goedewaagen and Prince would pick up on their lines of production. They made large quantities of Frankfurt ware well into the 19th century, and even in their post-1900 catalogues the Frankfurt models are still quite recognisable, even though they are no longer called by this name and have undergone some adaptations (figs 26-30).

The new products meant an extension of the traditional range. They typically were externally unglazed cooking pots with one or two handles or a single stick handle, derived from models from the Frankfurt region, together with small black cooking pots modelled on Westphalian or Rhenish examples (fig. 34). Ring moulds, mini-pancake griddles and other baking moulds were borrowed from Frankfurt and Lower Rhenish forms, as were the platters (figs 2, 9, 10, 14, 16, 30). Roasting dishes and pots for cooking hares were somewhat less popular in the Dutch context. Important sources of evidence are the six assemblages of wasters from firms that produced Frankfurt-style ware.

A no less important effect of the popularity of Frankfurt pots was the revival of the potter's trade in the provinces of Gelderland and Overijssel, which in the course of the 18th century had been almost entirely lost.

From 1800 on, enterprising young potters left places such as Isselburg and Kaldenkirchen in Germany, to come and start up potteries in the Netherlands, often having previously worked in the Frankfurt workshops. The town of Deventer, for instance, owes its flourishing potteries in the latter half of the 19th century to their initiatives, and also in Wageningen and Utrecht these potters contributed significantly to local industry.

Research into this subject still is far from complete. Specifically, there is a dearth of evidence on the German side, about the production of this ware in its original provenance. What prompted the sudden spate of exports to the Netherlands, and how long did it last? Our knowledge about the ware itself too is still quite limited, particularly when it comes to the imported pots and their early Dutch imitations. Distinguishing the imports and the imitations still presents some difficulties. The great majority of the archaeological or otherwise preserved material appears to be imitation; imported pieces can be only tentatively identified (fig. 23). More research is needed also into sources of influence other than the Frankfurt region. Archaeology in particular is expected to provide further progress in this area, through new excavations as well as reconsideration of previously recovered material.

Noten

1. Leeuwarder Courant van 26-9-1767, 9-7-1768, 8, 12 en 14-7-1769.
2. Slootmans 1970, Hoofdstuk VI.
3. Slootmans 1970, 134.
4. Dat gebeurt pas decennia later; de Rotterdamsche Courant van 20-1-1810 meldt een besluit van Koning Lodewijk Napoleon van 29-12-1809 waarin de belasting op het Frankforter aardewerk wordt bepaald op 15% van de waarde. In 1815, dus na de Franse tijd, wordt het oude, veel hogere tarief van zes stuivers per worp weer ingevoerd, zie de Provinciale Groninger Courant van 20-1-1815.
5. Smeele 1995, 157-166.
6. De naam van de instelling is de nodige keren veranderd. Tussen 1777 en 1797 was het de Oeconomische Tak van de Hollandsche Maatschappij der Weetenschappen, daarna tot juni 1807 de Nationale Nederlandsche Huishoudelijke Maatschappij. De huidige naam is: Nederlandsche Maatschappij voor Nijverheid en Handel (NMNH), en zo worden de archieven ook aangeduid. Wij spreken gemakshalve van 'de Oeconomische Tak' of 'de Maatschappij'. Het archief van directie en hoofdbestuur over de periode 1777-1993 bevindt zich in het Rijksarchief in Noord-Holland te Haarlem. De archieven van de plaatselijke afdelingen, departementen genoemd, zijn soms in gemeentearchieven bewaard, waarvan dat van het departement Delft de belangrijkste bron is.
7. Van der Meulen en Smeele 2005. Leiden; hoofdstuk 2.
8. Van der Meulen en Smeele 2002, 2-31.
9. Gemeentearchief Arnhem, Oud Archief, inv.nr. 69.
10. GA Arnhem, Rechterlijke Archieven, inv.nr.603, omslag 16.
11. Streekarchief Midden Holland te Gouda, Oud Archief Gouda, inv.nr.219.
12. Van der Meulen en Smeele (2007), 2-17.
13. Gemeentearchief Bergen op Zoom, Stadsarchief inv.nrs. 2976 e:v. Tussen 1807 en 1810 telden we meer dan 25 namen.
14. Slootmans 1970, 206.
15. Daarvoor zijn twee redenen: de florale versiering lijkt op die op schotelfragmenten uit het afval van pottenbakkerij Croonenburgh, en de naam Luisterberg komt opvallend veel voor in Bergen op Zoom en omgeving.
6. Christiaan, waarschijnlijk de broer van Frans, is volgens de Arnhemsche Courant van 5-9-1818 ongelukkigerwijze van de Rijnbrug gevallen en verdronken.
7. Nationaal Archief, Provinciaal Bestuur Zuid-Holland 1814-1844, archiefnr. 3.02.20, Inv.nr.799, 30-3-1824.
8. Lange ovens of liggende ovens werden in Duitsland veel, maar in Nederland, afgezien van Limburg, zelden toegepast. De ruimte met het te bakken aardewerk ligt achter het vuur, en niet zoals bij de staande oven erboven.
19. Gemeentearchief Wageningen, Oud Archief inv.nr.92.

20. Van der Meulen en Smeele 2003, 78-89.
21. Gemeentearchief Wehl, Oud archief Wehl, inv.nr.36.
22. Van der Meulen en Smeele 1999.
23. Groothedde en Bartels 2000.
24. Schuitema 2001, 57. Zie voor Peters ook: Van der Meulen en Smeele 2003, 84.
25. Van der Meulen en Smeele 1999, 12.
26. Teller, Töpfer Traditionen; Zum Neusser Töpferhandwerk von 1750 bis 1870.
27. Van der Meulen en Smeele 2005, 203.
28. Een handelaar, in Gouda hannever genoemd, zet oren en voeten aan de gedraaide potten.
29. Catalogus van voortbrengselen van Overijsselsche nijverheid op de Tentoonstelling gehouden te Zwolle 1840; Idem, Deventer 1842.
30. Zie voor uitgebreider informatie over Deventer: Van der Meulen en Smeele 2003, 83 en 2000, 55.
31. Van der Meulen en Smeele 2002,12.
32. Kattewinkel 1952.
33. Utrechtse Archieven, Provinciaal Bestuur, toegang 79, inv.nr. 613, 4-10-1842 nr.16.
34. GA Rotterdam, Archief Ambachtsheerlijkheid Cool, inv.nr. 295, nr.108.
35. Gemeentearchief Rotterdam, Stadsarchief, inv.nr. 4988, f.182, 19-12-1806.
36. GA Dordrecht, Archief Bataafse Republiek, inv.nr.35, Notulen Raad 28-1-1807 nr.26 (aanvraag); inv.nr.79, Notulen Raad 7-3-1808 bijlage 46 (brand).
37. Van der Meulen en Smeele 2003.
38. Met dank aan Rutger Loenen van de Historische Werkgroep Austerlitz, die de resultaten van het archiefonderzoek van de werkgroep ter beschikking stelde, en Pieter van der Voorden van de AWN-werkgroep die de vondsten voor ons ontsloot. Een vondstbericht is opgenomen in: Cleij 1995.
39. Zie voor de vergunningen Rijksarchief Haarlem, Provinciaal Bestuur, inv.nr.4284 nr.60, 12-7-1832 (Kehl), inv.nr.4174, nr.25, 9-1-1834 (Kueter), inv.nr. 4221, nr.7, 18-11-1841 (Berger).
40. Van Benthem 2006.
41. Leeuwarder Courant 2-3-1838.
42. Van der Meulen en Smeele 2005, 154 e.v.
43. RAHM, Oud Archief Gouda, inv.nr.277, f.67, 6-9-1805.
44. RAHM, ONA Gouda, inv.nr.1183, akte 81, 26-6-1811.
45. RAHM, NNA Gouda inv.nr.75, akte 12, 19-1-1846.
46. Nationaal Archief, Provinciaal Bestuur Zuid-Holland 1814-1844, inv.nr. 916, 12-9-1826 (Slee), inv.nr. 942, 4-4-1827 (Jansen) en inv.nr. 995, 12-4-1828 (Hornius).
47. RAHM, Archief Goedewaagen, inv.nr. 119 en archief Prince.
48. Pijpenkabinet, Amsterdam.
49. Hackspiel 1993, Segschneider 2005. Hackspiel onderzocht huishoudelijk afval in de omgeving van Rheinberg aan de Nederrijn, Segschneider pottenbakkersafval uit Freren-Ostwie bij Lingen.
60. Van der Meulen en Smeele 2007, 2-17.

Literatuur

Benthem, A. van (2006). *Alkmaar Schelphoek*. Rapport 503, ADC Archeo Projecten. Amersfoort.

Cleij. Th. J. (1995), *Vondsten uit Zeist; 10 jaar archeologisch onderzoek geïnventariseerd*. Utrecht.

Groothedde, M. en M. Bartels (2000). Taminiau in Zutphen, archeologie, geschiedenis en producten van een 19de eeuwse pottenbakkerij. In: *Töpfer, Kramer, Pottenbakkers; Keramiek tussen IJssel en Berkel*. Borken. 173-221.

Hackspiel, W. (1993). *Der Scherbenkomplex von Haus Gelinde; Gebrauchsgeschirr des 18. und 19. Jahrhunderts*. Köln/Bonn.

Meulen, A. van der en P. Smeele (1999). *De IJsel, Doesburg 1841-1969; portret van een Gelderse pottenbakkerij*. Doesburg.

Meulen, A. van der en P. Smeele (2000). De opbloei van de aardewerknijverheid in Gelderland en Overijssel na 1800 en de rol van de Duitse immigranten. In: *Töpfer Kramer Pottenbakkers, keramiek tussen IJssel en Berkel*. Borken. 41-68.

Meulen, A. van der en P. Smeele (2002). Delftse pottenbakkers na 1675, van Pieter Vermeulen tot Johannes Renaud. In: *Vormen uit Vuur 179*, 2002/3, 2-31.

Meulen, A. van der en P. Smeele (2003a). Ver van huis; pottenbakkers uit Tegelen en Kaldenkirchen op zoek naar werk. In: *Sjerfkes; Nieuwe inzichten in het Nederrijns keramisch verleden van een aantal Noord- en Midden-Limburgse plaatsen*. Tegelen, 78-89.

Meulen, A. van der en P. Smeele (2003b). Gorcumse pottenbakkerijen en de oven van Arij van Dalem. In: *In Gorcum gebakken; aardewerk, kleipijpen, wandtegels*. Gorcum. 11-39.

Meulen, A. van der en P. Smeele (2005). *De pottenbakkers van Friesland 1750-1950, het ambacht, de mensen, het aardewerk*. Leiden.

Meulen, A. van der en P. Smeele (2007). De namaak bekroond; de keramiek ingezonden naar de eerste nationale nijverheidstentoonstellingen van 1808 en 1809. In: *Vormen uit Vuur 197; 2007/1*, 2-17.

Pause, C. e.a. (2004). *Teller, Töpfer Traditionen; Zum Neusser Töpferhandwerk von 1750 bis 1870*. Neuss.

Kattewinkel, R. (1952). *De industrie van de stad Utrecht*. Typoscript Utrechtse Archieven.

Schuitema G.A. (2001). Boven water gehaald; vondsten uit de gracht van havezate de Klamp. In: *Historische kring Neede* 2001.

Segschneider, E. H., (2005). *Pöttebackers Pottwerk; Leben und Wirken der Töpferfamilie Berndsen in Freren-Ostwie*, Emsland 1822 bis 1914. Sögel.

Slootmans, C.J.F. (1970). *Tussen hete vuren*, deel I. Tilburg.

Smeele, P. (1995). Die Regionalität der 'Frankfurter Töpfe' in: *Zur Regionalität der Keramik des Mittelalters und der Neuzeit; Denkmalpflege und Forschung in Westfalen 32*, Bonn, 157-166.

List of authors

Nico Arts (1954) studied Cultural Anthropology at Leiden University and Pre- and Protohistoric Archaeology at the University of Amsterdam. Since 1989 he has held the post of municipal archaeologist of Eindhoven; in the years 1992-2007 he was also municipal archaeologist of Helmond. He specialises in Stone-Age and late-medieval archaeology, and has published about these subjects in many books and periodicals. Since 2006 he has been involved part-time in the research programme 'Town and Countryside' of the Netherlands Organisation of Scientific Research, investigating the archaeological links between urban and rural life in the Late Middle Ages.

Michiel Bartels (1965) read Medieval Archaeology at the University of Amsterdam. In 1992 he entered the service of the ROB, where he mostly investigated the finds from medieval excavations. Between 1993 and 1996 his research focussed on the contents of rubbish pits and cesspits from Deventer, Dordrecht, Nijmegen and Tiel, which in 1999 resulted in his publication *Steden in Scherven*. From 1995 he was the project manager of the excavations of the early medieval settlement of Tiel. Between 1997 and 1999 he was involved as archaeological project manager in the railway construction of the Betuweroute. From 1999 until 2008 he was the municipal archaeologist of Deventer; since 2008 he has been the municipal archaeologist of Hoorn.

Peter Bitter (1953) graduated in Medieval Archaeology in 1984 at the University of Amsterdam, and in 2002 presented his PhD thesis on the archaeology and history of the Church of St. Lawrence in Alkmaar, entitled *Graven en Begraven. Archeologie en geschiedenis van de Grote Kerk van Alkmaar*. He worked for various institutions on several excavation projects until 1991. Since then he has held the post of municipal archaeologist in Alkmaar. A specialist in town archaeology, he is the author of a variety of publications on - amongst others - urban development, houses and ceramics.

Arnold Carmiggelt graduated in Cultural, Intellectual and Theoretical History (1987) and in Cultural Prehistory (1988) at the University of Groningen. Between 1990 and 2001 he conducted various investigations and for a range of Dutch archaeological organisations made presentations aimed at the public (publications, exhibitions). From 2001 he has worked with the Bureau Oudheidkundig Onderzoek of the City of Rotterdam; from 2009 he has headed this bureau. His publications mostly concern late- and post-medieval archaeology.

Hemmy Clevis (1953) in 1983 graduated in Medieval Archaeology at the University of Utrecht, and in 1990 presented his PhD thesis: *Nijmegen: Investigations into the Historical Topography and Development of the Lower Town between 1300 and 1500*. Between 1976 and 1987 he worked for the State Service for Archaeological Investigations (ROB). From 1988, he has been the municipal archaeologist of Zwolle. He publishes about town archaeology and late- and post-medieval archaeology, especially ceramics. He is one of the authors of the (also digital) Classification System for Late- and Post-Medieval Ceramics and Glass, the so-called 'Deventer System'. He runs two foundations to support colleagues with their publications on archaeology in the broadest sense.

Olaf Goubitz (1934-2007) worked for 25 years at the State Service for Archaeological Investigations (ROB). After his retirement in 1999, he started preparing a series of publications on leather finds. The first volume, *Stepping through Time: Archaeological Footwear from Prehistoric Times until 1800* appeared in 2001, to great acclaim, immediately becoming the standard work for medieval and post-medieval footwear, indispensable for archaeologists, re-enactment societies and fashion designers alike. This was followed in 2007 by *Purses in Pieces: Archaeological finds of late medieval and 16-th century leather purses, pouches, bags and cases in the Netherlands*. The third volume, about decorated leather knife sheaths, will appear in 2011. Olaf Goubitz wrote over a hundred articles about leather finds.

Michel Groothedde in 1991 graduated in Pre- and Protohistoric Archaeology at the University of Amsterdam. From 1992 he has worked as the municipal archaeologist of Zutphen. Between 1992 and 1999 he also held the part-time post of municipal archaeologist in Deventer. Since 2007 he has been an archaeological consultant to the city of Doesburg. In 1994, together with the then city archivist, he initiated the working group Building History Zutphen, of which he continues to be an active member. As a project manager he conducted large-scale excavations between 1990 and 2004, in the new 'VINEX' housing estates of Leesten near Zutphen. He has published extensively about the early urban development of Zutphen and Deventer from the Carolingian period onwards. His specialisms are early urban development and building history.

Piet Kleij graduated in Medieval Archaeology at the University of Amsterdam in 1987. From 1987 until 1990 he worked with the Underwater Archaeology department of the State Service for Archaeological Investigations (ROB); from 1990 to 1994 he was employed as the municipal archaeologist of Oosterhout (prov. Noord-Brabant) and as a field archaeologist for the Instituut voor Toegepast Historisch Onderzoek in Tilburg; from 1994 to 1996 as interim Provincial Archaeologist of Noord-Brabant for the ROB; from 1996 to 1998 as a material specialist and field archaeologist working on the Betuweroute railway-construction excavations; and from 1998 to 2000 as a pottery specialist for ADC Archeoprojecten in Amersfoort. Since 2000 he has been the municipal archaeologist of Zaanstad. He specialises in post-medieval ceramics.

Michael Klomp in 2000 graduated in Medieval Archaeology at the University of Amsterdam. But even from an early age (in 1987) he had been involved in archaeological research in Zwolle. Having worked for brief periods for the cities of Zwolle, Deventer and Nijmegen, he is now a *senior* archaeologist on the team of Zwolle's archaeological service. He has published extensively in the field of late-medieval archaeology. He specialises in late- and post-medieval material studies.

Marie Christine Laleman studied Art History and Archaeology at Ghent university. Her special fields of interest include medieval archaeology and building techniques. Since 1973, she has been committed to developing the Department of Urban Archaeology of the City of Ghent, of which she currently is the director. She has also coordinated interdisciplinary research and publication projects on subjects relating to the history of Ghent. She is a visiting professor at several universities, lecturing on urban and building archaeology.

Jasper Luijendijk (1981) is a student of Archaeology and Anthropology at Leiden University. In 2007 he worked as a trainee in the Medieval department of the National Museum of Antiquities in Leiden.

Adri van der Meulen and Paul Smeele studied Dutch and sociology, respectively, at the University of Utrecht, and formerly worked as a teacher at a polytechnic college and taught town and country planning at the Technical University of Delft. They collect Dutch domestic pottery and since 1986 have been researching the history of the Dutch pottery industry. Their publications in part have a regional or local focus, e.g. those about Friesland, Oosterhout, Groningen, Doesburg, Hazerswoude and Delft; and in part a thematic one: the identity of regional product ranges, potters' migrations, survival strategies, pottery trade and the competition among kinds of ceramics. They have also staged several exhibitions.

Marieke van Werven (1985) is a student of History at Leiden University and of Medieval Studies at Utrecht University. In 2007 she worked as a trainee in the Medieval department of the National Museum of Antiquities in Leiden.

Annemarieke Willemsen (1969) read Art History and Archaeology at the University of Nijmegen. Since 1999 she has worked at curator of the medieval department of the National Museum of Antiquities in Leiden. She wrote her PhD thesis on children's toys (1998), and books about Roman toys (2003) and the Vikings in the Netherlands (2004). In 2008 Brepols published her book *Back to the Schoolyard. The Daily Practice of Medieval and Renaissance Education*.